A Clinician's Guide to ADHD in Women

A Clinician's Guide to ADHD in Women provides readers with a toolbox of strategic therapeutic approaches for diagnosing, treating, and working with women with ADHD.

Clinicians are guided through an integrative approach to identifying and treating women with ADHD, including explorations of hormonal factors and psychiatric conditions that accompany ADHD in women. The psychotherapeutic approach outlined in this guide is pragmatic and solution-focused, including gender-sensitive approaches to treatment, medication, hormonal interventions, and psycho/social treatment. Case vignettes illustrate how an application of strategies, medication, social solutions, and care can facilitate and treat women with ADHD and co-occurring psychiatric conditions.

This book is an essential resource for clinicians and treatment providers who wish to transform the lives of women suffering with both diagnosed and undiagnosed ADHD.

Kathleen Nadeau, PhD, is an award-winning clinical psychologist, internationally recognized ADHD authority, and author of 15 books on ADHD.

Patricia Quinn, MD, is a developmental pediatrician and a prolific author and international lecturer on ADHD. She has been an ADHD specialist for over 50 years.

Michael Morse, MD, MPA, is Associate Professor and Director of the Complex ADHD Clinic at Georgetown University. At Alvord, Baker & Associates, he directs the ADHD and Anxiety Center.

"*A Clinician's Guide to ADHD in Women* is scientifically rigorous, well referenced, and directly usable in clinic. Nadeau, Quinn, and Morse distil three decades of research into a practical guide that updates current knowledge on ADHD in women. Clearly presented, the text integrates many aspects of female ADHD, while never losing sight of the patient in front of us. The book's clinical structure is especially useful. Chapters on diagnostic complexity and medical comorbidities offer clear assessment frameworks and differential considerations. Treatment pathways are extensively and holistically presented. The authors are also sensitive to diversity across culture and life stage, including explorations of ADHD and hormonal influences, masking, executive dysfunction, and emotional dysregulation. The writing is clear and explains complex subjects with nuance, free of medical jargon. This guide reframes ADHD in women as neither 'ADHD-lite' nor a niche topic, but a core competency. I will recommend it to trainees and colleagues across Europe and beyond and will refer to it in my own clinical and research practice."

Dora Wynchank, *MD, PhD, psychiatrist working in adult ADHD at PsyQ in the Hague, Netherlands, editor of the DIVA Foundation, and active contributor to the European Adult ADHD Network*

"If you treat girls and women with ADHD, then you need this book. And if you don't think you treat girls and women with ADHD, then you really need this book. It is filled with the kind of wisdom you only get from decades of practice and will make you a much better clinician."

Ari Tuckman, *PsyD, ADHD thought leader, author, and international presenter*

"This is a practical and insightful guide for clinicians to better understand and support women with ADHD that draws on decades of unparalleled expertise. Seasoned professionals and newcomers alike will find this an indispensable resource steeped in a well-crafted interweaving of research and clinical wisdom to improve their practice and, most importantly, to improve the lives of women with ADHD."

John Mitchell, *PhD, Associate Professor, Department of Psychiatry and Behavioral Sciences, Duke University, Durham, NC*

A Clinician's Guide to ADHD in Women

Diagnosis and Treatment

Kathleen Nadeau,
Patricia Quinn, and
Michael Morse

Routledge
Taylor & Francis Group
NEW YORK AND LONDON

Designed cover image: Getty Images

First published 2026
by Routledge
605 Third Avenue, New York, NY 10158

and by Routledge
4 Park Square, Milton Park, Abingdon, Oxon, OX14 4RN

Routledge is an imprint of the Taylor & Francis Group, an informa business

ISBN: 978-1-032-89322-8 (hbk)
ISBN: 978-1-032-88325-0 (pbk)
ISBN: 978-1-003-54212-4 (ebk)

DOI: 10.4324/9781003542124

Typeset in Bembo
by SPi Technologies India Pvt Ltd (Straive)

Contents

Foreword

We (Patricia Quinn, MD, and Kathleen Nadeau, PhD), have been focused on girls and women with ADHD for more than a generation. A baby girl born when we first started writing and lecturing about ADHD in girls and women would now be nearly 30 years old! The professional community has come a long, long way in its thinking and understanding of ADHD in girls and women since we shared the honor of receiving the CHADD "Hall of Fame Award" in 2000 for our groundbreaking work on girls and women with this condition. At that time, our goal was to raise awareness about and advocate for the many girls and women with ADHD who were still undiagnosed and misunderstood. Along with other pioneering psychotherapists including Sari Solden, MSW, and Ellen Littman, PhD, as well as researchers like Steven Hinshaw, PhD, we were beating the drum to raise awareness that ADHD was not primarily a disorder of males and that girls and women also experienced the challenges of living with ADHD, in much greater numbers than was previously understood. Over the past 25 or more years, clinical thinking has quite naturally evolved. It is now generally accepted that many girls and women have ADHD and that they continue to be underdiagnosed.

As awareness has grown, so too has the need for nuanced approaches that recognize the diversity of lived experiences among girls and women with ADHD. This journey of understanding has moved far beyond identifying symptoms or merely advocating for recognition; it now demands that we consider the interplay of intersecting identities, the subtle manifestations of ADHD that may be masked by social roles or expectations, and the evolving scientific landscape that shapes our perceptions. We have witnessed firsthand the impact of listening to women's stories and of appreciating the ways in which cultural context and individual variability often complicate the diagnostic picture. Increasingly, research and clinical practice point toward the necessity of adapting both our methods and our mindset—not only to ensure accurate diagnosis, but also to provide compassionate, effective care that affirms each woman's unique experience. This ongoing shift invites us to question inherited assumptions, support innovation in assessment and treatment, and advocate for the full inclusion of women's perspectives and needs within the broader field of ADHD.

Although more gender-sensitive diagnostic criteria for females were called for at a symposium held in the mid-1990s, these have yet to be developed. As is often the case in medicine, clinical observation and consensus are leading the way, with research to provide evidence following in their wake.

In this volume, we will review the research on women with ADHD that has been carried out since our earlier book, *Understanding Women with ADHD*, was published in 1999. However, we also take a much broader perspective on the experiences of women with ADHD today than we did then. Specifically, we examine how these experiences are deeply influenced by multiple factors inherent to being a woman. The impact of this complex condition that we call ADHD is influenced by the characteristics of women's brains and physiology, including hormonal fluctuations, as well as by their social connections and communication styles. It is also marked by the societal expectations placed upon females both while they are growing up and when they are adults.

In addition, perceptions around ADHD in general have evolved. Today it is widely recognized as a lifelong condition, whereas a generation ago it was mistakenly believed that most children diagnosed with it outgrew their symptoms by early adulthood. Although we still officially talk of ADHD as a categorical disorder—a condition that one either has or has not—there is a growing recognition that it should more accurately be thought of as a dimensional disorder. In other words, some are profoundly impacted by ADHD, while for others its effects may be more moderate. We are now recognizing that the degree of impact can wax and wane as we go through life stages and encounter different circumstances. There is talk among ADHD experts that other core symptoms should be recognized and included in the diagnostic criteria, such as emotional dysregulation and disordered sleep patterns.

Awareness is increasing that cultural, racial, religious, and ethnic factors affect ADHD. Although most diagnosed cases in the United States are among White individuals, this reflects greater familiarity and comfort with diagnosis rather than prevalence. More older women are also seeking ADHD diagnoses, sparking conversations about menopause, memory issues, Alzheimer's, and Parkinson's disease.

In this second book, we are aware that we are speaking about a new generation, one that has the benefit of much greater awareness of ADHD in women. With this in mind, we are highly motivated to explore and present this condition within the context of all the complex internal and external forces—social, cultural, and physiological—that impact the lived experiences of women with ADHD.

In this book, written nearly 30 years after its predecessor, we welcome the participation of Michael Morse, MD, MPA. Dr. Morse is Associate Professor and Director of the Complex ADHD Clinic at Georgetown University, and he directs the ADHD and Anxiety Center at Alvord, Baker & Associates. A child, adolescent, and adult psychiatrist, Dr. Morse specializes in the treatment of ADHD in women and girls, and is one of only a handful of males who have turned their clinical interest toward understanding and advocating for females with ADHD. We hope that Dr. Morse's participation will encourage other men to join the currently mostly female ranks of ADHD experts dedicated to understanding the distinct presentations and needs of females with ADHD. To further this goal, this guide aims to help medical and mental health professionals better understand, identify, and more effectively treat women with ADHD. We have come a long way.

Kathleen Nadeau, PhD
Patricia Quinn, MD

Acknowledgements

First, we want to recognize the many women we've worked with over the years, whose experiences have deepened our understanding of the complex and varied ways ADHD shapes women's lives. We are especially grateful to Frances Tye for her thoughtful and remarkably patient editing, helping bring clarity and coherence to our chapters. We also thank Arianna Cifone for her focused and diligent work completing the index under a tight deadline. And, of course, our sincere thanks to our editor, Alison Macfarlane—without all of their contributions, this book would not have come to fruition.

Kathleen Nadeau and Patricia Quinn

In addition to the appreciation extended by Dr. Nadeau and Dr. Quinn, I wish to add the following:

Thank you to my wife Miriam, for your wisdom and love.

Thank you to my mother Lonni, father Ken, and sister Meagan, for teaching me to pursue justice and equity.

Thank you to my children Lila (may your memory be a blessing), Yoni, Eliana, and Noa, for your light.

Thank you to my longtime mentors, Dr. Elizabeth Berger and Dr. James Griffith, whose rigorous thinking and compassionate stance I aspire to make my own.

Thank you to our sensitivity reader, Dr. Kimberly Sims, who taught us to look more carefully at our assumptions; remaining lapses are ours alone.

Thank you to Dr. Kathleen Nadeau and Dr. Patricia Quinn, who taught me much of what I know about ADHD, and to my patients, who taught me the rest.

Michael Morse

CHAPTER 1

The problem of underdiagnosis

INTRODUCTION

The public health consequences of the underdiagnosis of women are significant. Recent research suggests that on average, many women with ADHD have a shortened lifespan due to lifestyle issues associated with ADHD related to chronic stress, chronic sleep difficulties, disordered eating patterns, and inadequate exercise, all of which may be influenced by the anxiety and depression often experienced by women with ADHD.[1]

Yet, despite the significant consequences of undiagnosed or undertreated ADHD, the condition has become a meme, a cultural joke. And for women, ADHD has been especially trivialized. This attitude is reflected ironically in the title of one of the early books for women with ADHD, *You Mean I'm Not Lazy, Stupid or Crazy?!*[2] The book was written by two women with ADHD who had experienced the trivialization of their struggles. All joking aside about women being ditzy and disorganized, or flaky and forgetful, ADHD is a condition with serious consequences for women—in fact, with consequences more dire than those for men with ADHD.[3]

Women with untreated ADHD are at greater risk for significant anxiety and depression, are more likely to engage in self-harm and make suicide attempts, and are more likely to be psychiatrically hospitalized.[4] Feelings of low worth and social rejection by other girls may begin as early as elementary school.[5] Cigarette smoking, or vaping, starts as early as age 11 for some girls with ADHD, who may be simultaneously self-medicating with nicotine and seeking peer acceptance by developing this habit.[6] Teen pregnancies, dropping out of school, self-harm, suicide attempts, death by suicide, and psychiatric hospitalizations are greater risks for girls and women with ADHD compared to women without ADHD.[7,8] While men with ADHD

DOI: 10.4324/9781003542124-1

have higher rates of alcohol abuse overall, women with ADHD are more likely to abuse alcohol in an effort to address emotional dysregulation issues, especially when comorbid anxiety and depression are present. Women with ADHD are also at greater risk than male counterparts to develop eating disorders, experience intimate partner abuse, and struggle financially.

Women with ADHD are more likely to have children with ADHD, and may encounter increased stress related to household organization, relationship stability, and longstanding family patterns. These experiences may compound functional impairment and emotional distress.[9] Furthermore, research documents that mothers with ADHD often ignore their own needs while seeking help for their child(ren) because time and money are limited. As we have cautioned many women over the years, it's essential to "put on your own oxygen mask before assisting others." Raising a child with ADHD can be an intense, challenging, and relentless task, difficult enough for a mother without ADHD, and more so for a mother *with* ADHD who must cope with her own difficulties with consistency and emotional regulation.

In the event of divorce or separation, women with ADHD are most often the custodial parent, often raising one or more children with behavioral or developmental challenges.[10,11] Divorce may be an adaptive response to an untenable marriage, and single parenthood may be a deliberate and thoughtful choice. At the same time, single parenthood may reduce financial stability and childcare support—particularly for women whose education or earning capacity has been disrupted by untreated ADHD.[12]

For women of color, queer women—including trans women—and other women who experience marginalization, added stressors of discrimination can intersect with ADHD-related vulnerabilities in ways that intensify strain. For all these reasons, diagnosis and treatment of women with ADHD matters enormously, both for the women themselves and for their children. When they can bring more order and a sense of calm to themselves through diagnosis and treatment, women with ADHD can then begin to provide the support and structure that will help their children to thrive.

A POSITIVE TREND TOWARD SELF-ADVOCACY

Recently, increasing numbers of women with ADHD have become vocal self-advocates. There are countless stories shared between women of their failures to obtain a diagnosis, even when they felt quite sure that ADHD was at the core of their problems. What's more, there is an ever-increasing body of books written by women with ADHD *for* women with ADHD. Online, there is a large and growing cohort of women with ADHD reaching out to each other, supporting each other, and sharing their stories. It's time for all of us, medical and mental health professionals alike, to better understand the barriers to diagnosis experienced by women, their unique ADHD challenges, and their need for gender-specific treatment that addresses their overall quality of life rather than a narrow focus on ADHD symptoms as currently defined by the DSM-5.

WHY DO SO MANY WOMEN WITH ADHD REMAIN UNDIAGNOSED?

Multiple interwoven factors may interfere with the diagnosis of ADHD in women. First, the official diagnostic criteria for ADHD better describe men than women.[13] There have been calls for diagnostic criteria that are more gender sensitive since the mid-1990s,[14] yet there seems to have been little effort to undertake the research required to make such changes. Due to a combination of genetic and environmental influences, the expression of ADHD looks different in girls and women.[15,16] The characteristics of boys with ADHD, which are highly noticeable and more bothersome to adults, lead them to be referred for evaluation more often.

Girls tend to be diagnosed later in life due to their under-referral during childhood.[17] Because girls and women with ADHD often exhibit fewer overt symptoms, other diagnoses such as depression or anxiety are made in clinical settings before ADHD is considered.[18] It's important for us as primary care physicians, pediatricians, and psychotherapists to understand these very different patterns of ADHD presentation if we are going to address the chronic underdiagnosis of girls and women.[19] Women experience higher rates of certain comorbidities (see Chapters 3 and 7). Frequently, co-occurring anxiety and/or depression are identified as the primary disorder in women with ADHD while their ADHD is overlooked.[20] The lack of externalizing symptoms in some women with ADHD can make timely referral and diagnosis challenging.[21] Overall, there are multiple factors influencing the underdiagnosis of women with ADHD, including symptom presentation, comorbidities, and healthcare biases.

A brief history of ADHD and why current ADHD diagnostic criteria continue to miss the mark when it comes to women

Attention deficit hyperactivity disorder (ADHD) is the current name for the condition we are addressing in this book, despite a general agreement among ADHD experts that it is a misleading term given that attentional issues are only one of many factors that characterize people with ADHD.[22] ADHD has a lengthy history with a string of former names that reflect our evolving understanding of the condition, including Minimal Brain Dysfunction, Hyperkinesis, and Hyperactive Reaction of Childhood. In early years, it was considered the result of mild brain damage acquired after birth, as distinct from developmental disorders such as Down's syndrome.[23]

The initial focus was on children who were hyperactive, almost all of whom were boys. ADHD was conceived of as an "externalizing" condition, easily noted by and affecting the adults around them. These boys were hyperactive and additionally demonstrated a certain degree of immature motor development.[24] While there were always a few girls found in the mix, given the symptoms that were considered core elements it was thought to be an overwhelmingly male disorder of childhood. In earlier years, doctors mistakenly believed that it was largely outgrown by adolescence because by that time, hyperactivity had greatly reduced in most diagnosed children.[25]

In many ways, this condition received attention not so much due to the impact of ADHD upon boys but because their hyperactive and impulsive behavior bothered the adults around them.[26] Teachers were eager for such children to be treated so that they would not pose such classroom management challenges. Parents were eager for these boys to be treated so that they could calm down and be more manageable at home.

GIRLS WERE "BOTHERED" BUT NOT "BOTHERSOME," AT LEAST IN THE SCHOOL ENVIRONMENT

Girls with ADHD, for the most part, did not "bother" adults. Instead, they suffered internally, feeling anxious and having difficulty staying tuned in, keeping up with schoolwork, and fitting in with other girls.[27] Women diagnosed with ADHD in adulthood, still the most common path to diagnosis, tell us that as children they had felt "different" from other girls and didn't "fit in," but never understood why. Inattentive girls were seen as shy, anxious, awkward, or not very bright, while combined-type girls were seen as more bossy or instrusive, but it was never considered that they might have ADHD.

Girls were more likely to perform well academically, especially in the lower grades, because they were socialized to conform to the teacher's expectations and usually worked hard to comply.[28] One mother described her very bright, highly accomplished daughter with ADHD in the following way:

> The demands of masking at school were so high for her that she was extremely dysregulated at home, becoming physically and verbally aggressive with her younger sister. I convinced C's pediatrician to try her on a trial of stimulant medication. At home, C's behavior led to a diagnosis of Oppositional Defiant Disorder, very common among elementary school-aged children with ADHD. In great contrast, C's teachers and counselor questioned our decision to start a stimulant and described her as a "model student." Parent ratings on ADHD scales placed her in the "highly probable for ADHD" range, while teacher ratings placed her as "totally normal."

This discrepancy between school and home behavior is very common for girls with ADHD, who often work hard to conform and hide their struggles. "C" felt very anxious at school and reached out to her teachers for reassurance and support, leading them to see her as a model student.

Many of the women who seek diagnosis and treatment in adulthood report to healthcare providers that they were "good students" in early years. This misleads providers into believing that ADHD cannot be an appropriate diagnosis, since these women are not reporting school difficulties in their elementary school years, which providers assume to be necessary to identifying adult ADHD.

Women with ADHD are hiding in plain sight

Women with ADHD are "hiding in plain sight" because they are seeking help for the many medical and psychiatric conditions that are easier to recognize and that so often accompany ADHD in women. One such woman might be in your office seeking psychotherapy for depression or overwhelming anxiety. Maybe you are an addiction counselor treating her alcohol dependence. Or perhaps she has come to your center for eating disorders because she is trying to overcome years of bulimia. You might be her primary care physician, hearing complaints of fatigue and chronic pain, or a marriage counselor, to whom she is describing the constant conflict and criticism she experiences in her marriage. She rushes in late, sometimes forgets her appointments, and seems to be in a state of overwhelm. You are trained to focus on and treat the symptoms that she presents to you. Quite possibly, neither she nor you realize that these struggles are related to her undiagnosed ADHD.

If you've missed her ADHD, you are not alone. Most professionals miss ADHD in women because they expect ADHD to present as it does in young boys. Professionals are more familiar with kids' ADHD traits: for example, kids who fidget and pay little attention to their schoolwork, or kids who are spacey, daydreaming as they look out the window while the teacher is talking. Some of these children with ADHD are girls, but even in childhood they are usually overlooked. We are trained to be more aware of ADHD in boys. Studies show that even when girls show behavior in school identical to that of boys with ADHD, teachers are more likely to refer the boys for ADHD assessment.[29] As a result, by the time these girls become women, it's even more likely that their ADHD will be overlooked.

These childhood ADHD traits bear little resemblance to those of women with ADHD. So, it's not surprising that you, and countless other professionals, treat women for co-occurring conditions without ever suspecting ADHD. ADHD morphs, changes, and becomes ever more complex as a girl with ADHD leaves childhood, passes through puberty and adolescence, and becomes a woman.

At puberty, with the onset of their menstrual cycle, girls often begin demonstrating more ADHD symptoms.[30] Many girls who did well in elementary school, flying under the radar and working hard to escape the teacher's notice, start to feel the pressure at puberty, when fluctuating hormones intensify the mild anxiety, depression, and distractibility that they were able to manage in earlier years. As hormones fluctuate with the menstrual cycle, girls' difficulties focusing and concentrating increase along with their mood symptoms and anxiety. If a girl with ADHD is undiagnosed at this point in her development, she is likely to be diagnosed with anxiety and/or depression, while the professional making the diagnosis never suspects her underlying ADHD.

To become an ADHD specialist, we all must learn on the job. It is not the fault of medical or mental health professionals that they focus on co-occurring conditions while overlooking ADHD in the girls that they treat. Few, if any, healthcare and mental health professionals have received adequate training to understand how to diagnose ADHD with all its complexities and nuances. Child psychiatrists, even those trained in highly ranked child psychiatry fellowship programs, have typically never been taught about the significant differences between girls and boys with ADHD. And the training is no better for clinical psychologists and clinical social workers. Most medical and mental health providers are generalists, knowing about a wide range of psychiatric disorders without in-depth knowledge of ADHD. Our goal in this book is to fill that knowledge gap, with the hope that more training programs will bring this knowledge to students in these fields.

Adult ADHD is among the most common adult psychiatric disorders.[31] It would be scandalous if a mental health professional received no training in the treatment of anxiety, depression, or bipolar disorder. It is equally scandalous, and harmful, that so few of us are trained to recognize the nuances and complexities of ADHD in women and make a proper diagnosis. Without adequate understanding, professionals can only be helpful in a limited way that leaves women with ADHD at great risk—including risk of suicide attempts when an overwhelming life becomes impossible following a marital separation, a job loss, or a crisis with an ADHD child. Women with untreated ADHD are at greater risk of self-harm, psychiatric hospitalization, and raising children in dysfunctional, even violent homes. The significant risks of ADHD can be mitigated once it is accurately diagnosed, in combination with its multiple comorbidities, and adequately treated. The question is, what are these conditions, and when should we consider that ADHD is part of the clinical picture?

WHAT SHOULD WE LOOK FOR TO IDENTIFY WOMEN WITH ADHD?

Rather than turning to a quick self-report ADHD checklist that is more attuned to identifying men with ADHD, medical providers and psychotherapists should consider the possibility of ADHD in women who:

- Are mothers of children with ADHD.
- Appear emotionally dysregulated—easily hurt, easily angered, easily frustrated.
- Struggle with a low sense of self-efficacy and depressed mood—feeling that they are "not good at anything."
- Are bright, but dropped out of school and are underemployed.
- Are binge eaters who eat from boredom and can't seem to stop.
- Are highly accomplished but highly stressed, spending untold hours and constant effort on maintaining their level of functioning.
- Function well at work, while home is a disorderly disaster.
- Struggle with time management and time awareness, tending to run late and overcommit.
- Are highly forgetful about the details of daily life.
- Regularly misplace personal items.
- Live in a state of generalized anxiety and feelings of overwhelm as they struggle to manage their daily lives.

WHAT DO GIRLS WITH ADHD LOOK LIKE AFTER THEY GROW UP?

They struggle socially

We know that girls with ADHD struggle with social connections and peer acceptance as early as elementary school. Steven Hinshaw's seminal research[32] on social interactions between girls with and without ADHD found that most girls with ADHD experienced difficulties fitting in and finding acceptance by their non-ADHD female peers. He described that girls who were on the hyperactive/impulsive end of the ADHD continuum were socially rejected. Other girls found them to be loud, intrusive, bossy, opinionated, argumentative, and generally difficult. But girls who were quiet and inattentive experienced significant social difficulties as well. Rather than being rejected as difficult or unlikeable, they were simply left on the periphery of the social group. As Hinshaw described it, they were "socially neglected." These social issues don't go away. In fact, they tend to be magnified in middle and high school. Even those who didn't experience conflict with their female peers report that they "always felt different" but didn't understand what those differences were. While there are certainly women with ADHD who have strong friendships and good social skills, many have significant challenges in this area.

They are filled with self-doubt

Even those women who, to the outside observer, seem to function well, typically report that they live with self-doubt. They often express feeling like "an impostor," because while their life may look good on the outside, few observers understand how hard they try to mask their struggles and how much harder they must work to achieve what their non-ADHD peers achieve with significantly less effort and struggle.[33]

Self-doubt can also be the result of internalizing thousands of criticisms that they experienced during their growing-up years—criticism from parents, from teachers, and from peers. "I can't believe you forgot your jacket again!" "You're so messy!" "How many times do I have to remind you to …?"

They continue to struggle to live up to social norms and expectations

Girls with ADHD receive countless messages from their family, and from society in general, that girls are supposed to be pretty, well-groomed, polite, friendly, and agreeable to the adults around them. Girls internalize these messages at such an early age that those with ADHD are filled with anxiety in elementary school for fear that they will "get in trouble" or "make my teacher mad at me." They do everything they can to hide their struggles, and begin to develop pervasive feelings of anxiety.[34] By the time they reach adulthood, they have developed feelings of inadequacy and of not being successful at meeting the social norms for women. These are some of the most difficult aspects of being a woman with ADHD.[35]

For women, hyperactivity and impulsivity may still be there but are expressed differently in adulthood

They may still feel restless, many talk non-stop; some are easily bored and crave stimulation. But most have slowed down and may simply fidget when forced to sit in long, boring meetings. Impulsivity in childhood can result in loud, boisterous behavior and sometimes even in physical injury. During adolescence, impulsivity in girls can lead to experimentation with drugs, explosive arguments with parents, and ignoring rules and regulations at school. In adulthood, impulsivity in women may be reflected in saying things when upset that they later regret, making impulse purchases that can lead to living on the edge financially, interrupting others in conversation, and starting projects that they rarely complete.

As hyperactivity and impulsivity move a bit to the background, other things come to the forefront.

They struggle increasingly as adult life demands greater executive functioning skills—the skills we need to "get our act together"

A girl with ADHD has triumphed if she remembers her jacket, backpack, and house key. It's her parents who keep track of time, tell her when to leave, provide her meals, remind her of dental appointments, and make sure she takes her soccer cleats to school on practice days. But as these girls with ADHD leave home and enter adulthood, much more is expected. The people around them stop reminding, structuring, and supporting them. They are supposed to do "life" independently, yet many women with ADHD are ill-equipped to do so.

They are expected to be organized, to make plans and follow through on them, and to remember their schedules and fulfill multiple commitments as they navigate each day. Young women are expected to manage their money, pay bills, get a job and show up for work on time, and complete work tasks without reminders, while also managing their household, laundry, meals, and commitments to friends. All these skills fall into the general category of executive functioning (EF) skills.

And even as young women with ADHD struggle with the EF challenges of early adulthood, they haven't gotten to the phase when some of the heavy-duty adulting challenges begin—life partnership and/or parenthood. In fact, preliminary studies suggest that women with ADHD choose not to become parents more often than women in the general population.[36] Women with ADHD who were interviewed on their choice to remain "child-free" reported that they believed that the demands of parenthood would prove difficult if not impossible for them. They were already experiencing high levels of stress as they worked to manage their own lives as adults and couldn't imagine being successful in taking on responsibility for one or more children in addition.

In fact, because women partnered with men are often still expected to be the primary parent and responsible for most of the household labor while also holding down a full-time job, ADHD is *much* more difficult for mothers than for fathers.[37] Women with ADHD are more likely than men with ADHD to be divorced and more likely to become single parents raising children with ADHD; for some women this reflects chosen independence or improved well-being, while for others, particularly those without adequate financial or social support, it can intensify strain.[38]

ADHD IN WOMEN IS MORE COMPLICATED THAN MANY HEALTHCARE OR MENTAL HEALTH PROFESSIONALS MAY REALIZE

Co-occurring psychiatric disorders

By the time a woman with ADHD reaches adulthood, it's very likely that she will have one or more co-occurring psychiatric disorders—anxiety, depression, bipolar disorder, eating disorders, substance use disorders, borderline personality disorder, autism spectrum disorder, or learning disorders. Because mental health professionals have substantially more training in the diagnosis and treatment of these other conditions, ADHD may never be considered or may only rise to the surface after a significant time in treatment for one of the many comorbidities that can often mask a woman's underlying ADHD. You can find more information about these in our chapter on commonly co-occurring psychiatric conditions, Chapter 3.

Co-occurring medical problems

Living with the relentless high levels of stress that typically accompany ADHD can understandably lead to a variety of medical conditions including fibromyalgia, migraines, and type 2 diabetes. Other medical disorders that often accompany ADHD in women include polycystic ovarian syndrome, premenstrual dysphoric disorder, chronic fatigue syndrome, and sleep and eating disorders. We'll discuss all of these in detail in Chapter 7.

Untreated ADHD in women leads to serious risks

Suicide attempts and psychiatric hospitalization are troubling in their frequency among young women whose ADHD has gone unrecognized or has been inadequately treated.[39] Girls and young women who don't receive the support they need to understand and manage their ADHD symptoms are likely to struggle in many areas of their lives. Calling ADHD an "attention disorder" often leads to trivialization of a condition that often causes considerable suffering and distress that could have been mitigated with the right intervention.

Misunderstood and overlooked high-achieving women

Among the groups of women with ADHD least likely to receive the diagnosis are those with high levels of intelligence and those who are high achieving. Many professionals' concepts of ADHD derive from the stereotypical image of an academic underachiever. Many professional women seek a second opinion regarding ADHD diagnosis after being told by other providers, almost reflexively, "I can tell you right now that you can't possibly have ADHD, because you have a—[fill-in-the blank: medical degree, law degree, degree from a highly selective college or university]" or "because you hold a high position within an organization."

High-achieving women with ADHD become expert at masking their struggles, working long hours to achieve what others achieve in less time and investing great effort in appearing to be focused and organized. Many of these same women pay a high price for their success—living in a chaotic home environment, navigating difficult and unsatisfying relationships, being chronically sleep-deprived, and existing with a punishing level of anxiety, fearing they will not be able to keep up appearances.

ADHD IN WOMEN IS NOT "ADHD-LITE"

In the 1990s, we (Patricia and Kathleen) attended ADHD conferences at which we were invited to lecture on ADHD in girls and women. It was during these years, in the late 1990s, that we wrote our first books on girls and women with ADHD. Looking back, what was striking was the reception we received from male ADHD experts. We were teased for being "ADHD wannabes." ADHD in girls and women was viewed as a paler shade of ADHD—ADHD-lite. Men were the real deal. Even as adult ADHD diagnostic criteria are being developed, there is a persistent lack of focus on developing criteria that better describe women's experiences. Little research has focused on gender differences in ADHD and how to reflect these in diagnostic criteria. Because ADHD experts can only support diagnostic changes that are "evidence-based" findings, and because few are seeking that "evidence," we are caught in a circular argument. "Our hands are tied," we are told, in terms of creating more gender-sensitive diagnostic criteria, because there is so little research on gender differences in adult ADHD. But meanwhile, as is usually true in any medical field, clinical experience precedes research and prompts the research that can eventually document and support what has already been established in clinical practice.

Meanwhile, medical and mental health professionals are functioning in the real world where, despite inadequate research, we are faced with women in great need of diagnosis and treatment. ADHD is a very common condition among women, one that has significant negative consequences if adequate and informed treatment is not received.

Rather than having "ADHD-lite," women with ADHD face greater challenges than their male counterparts

We've learned a lot since the late 1990s. It's becoming clear that ADHD in women is not a milder version of the disorder; in fact, it is more challenging for women than for men. Let's examine why this is the case.

ADHD SOCIAL CHALLENGES HAMPER FRIENDSHIPS FOR WOMEN

Decades of research on how, in many instances, gender shapes social interactions demonstrates the depth, complexity, and importance of bonds between women. Strong social connections form the very backbone of the supports that allow women to lead healthy, satisfying lives. But ADHD gets in the way of building those essential relationships, with differing social relationship challenges reported by Stephen Hinshaw, Ph.D. at UC Berkeley, depending upon whether girls presented with the combined type or predominantly inattentive-type ADHD (see p. 8), with these same patterns persisting into adulthood.

Forming and maintaining friendships proves to be a major problem for many women with ADHD. The stress is twofold, and often of much greater significance than the social distress reported by men with ADHD. First, research suggests that women, on average, express a greater need for social acceptance and connectedness than men,[40,41] so feeling isolated and unsupported by other women is very painful. Second, many women with ADHD are particularly ill-suited to meeting the social expectations often placed on women. They may have difficulty showing up on time and remembering social commitments. During interactions, they may find it difficult to suppress their urges to interrupt in conversation ("I will forget what I wanted to say if I wait"), filter thoughts and reactions that might be considered rude or inappropriate, and curb their tendency to talk too much; they also struggle with following rapid-paced group conversations and becoming distracted, which can give the misimpression that they are not interested in what others are saying. The sadness expressed by women with ADHD due to their feelings of "never fitting in" to social groups is a major part of their lived experience.

LESS ACCEPTANCE OF ADHD IN WOMEN AND GIRLS WITHIN FAMILIES

Women and girls with ADHD not only experience rejection in the outside world, they also experience it within their families. Studies have shown that mothers react more negatively to the behaviors of daughters with ADHD than to those of sons.[42] ADHD symptoms such as impulsivity, emotional dysregulation, neglect of personal hygiene, trouble completing tasks and staying organized are inconsistent with societal expectations for girls. While some parents interpret ADHD behaviors in their sons as simply meaning that they are "all boy," a girl with ADHD is not fondly referred to as being "all girl." Girls often grow up, especially when raised by a mother who does not have ADHD, under a constant barrage of criticism for not being more agreeable, efficient, pleasant, well-groomed, and compliant. This lower acceptance of ADHD in girls in the family setting continues into adulthood. Art Robbins, a well-known authority on the impact of ADHD on couples, reported that he found husbands less tolerant of their wives' ADHD compared to wives' tolerance of ADHD in their husbands.[43]

WOMEN'S REACTIONS TO STRESS DIFFER FROM MEN'S

In contrast to the well-known "fight-or-flight" reaction to stress more typical of men, recent research suggests that women's response to stress is better described as "tend and befriend."[44] Women reach out to friends, family, and romantic partners for validation, and problem-solving in response to stress. Women with ADHD, who are less likely to have a well-developed social support network, are less able to find the supportive stress reduction that a strong social network can provide for many women.

INTERNALIZING TENDENCIES: WOMEN WITH ADHD BLAME THEMSELVES

Women with ADHD are more prone to internalize—blaming themselves for their struggles, leading to anxiety, depression, and complex trauma.[45] Twenty-five years ago, ADHD in women was dismissed as a less problematic version of ADHD. Then, research emerged that women with untreated ADHD are more likely to make suicide attempts and more likely to be psychiatrically hospitalized than their male counterparts.[46] Furthermore, ADHD in women often leads to complex post-traumatic stress disorder (C-PTSD), a more recently recognized condition that is the result of countless daily criticisms, rejections, and blame which elicit a significant and ongoing trauma response—"trauma by a thousand cuts." Women with ADHD are at significant psychiatric risk throughout their lifetimes.

THEIR BODIES PAY THE PRICE

Chronic stress inevitably impacts women's bodies. Over 25 years ago, Patricia Quinn and Kathleen Nadeau wrote about fibromyalgia in women with ADHD resulting from constant activation of the HPA axis (the body's main stress response system), but sadly, a generation later, fibromyalgia is only occasionally mentioned as a comorbid condition common among women with ADHD.[47]

Fibromyalgia is widely recognized as a "stress-related" disorder due to its frequent onset of its symptoms in the presence of stressful events, which can also lead to apparent exacerbation of existing symptoms. Fibromyalgia, leading to significant chronic pain, affects many more females than males, and recent studies have shown a high rate of ADHD in women diagnosed with fibromyalgia.[48]

Of additional concern is the fact that sleep disorders have been linked to *both* ADHD and fibromyalgia. Clearly there is a great need for awareness among pain and sleep specialists that there is a strong connection between these disorders and ADHD in females.[49]

IMPOSSIBLE ROLE EXPECTATIONS

Many women face impossible demands today. The majority of mothers in the United States are working while also raising children, tracking the schedules of all family members, organizing family events and celebrations, and managing their households. Even though there has been an ongoing shift in society's views of gender roles, the roles of wife and mother continue to be far more demanding than those of husband and father. A recent article from Pew Research notes that women have outpaced men in earning college degrees over the past 20 years. Today, 47% of US women ages 25–34 have a bachelor's degree, compared with 37% of men.[50] Despite this, women are still more likely to have responsibility for caring for a sick child and managing the household schedule.

While today 75% of mothers of school-age children are employed,[51] this huge social change has not been accompanied by affordable, available childcare. Both the cost and availability of good childcare place a huge burden on women who are working while raising children. Now, imagine that you are a woman with ADHD living under these expectations. It's easy to see why the word "overwhelmed" is the word most often used by women with ADHD to describe their lived experience. The very roles that women are traditionally "supposed to play" are roles for which many women with ADHD are particularly ill-suited.

MASKING

From an early age, girls with ADHD work hard to mask their struggles. Mothers of girls with ADHD often report that their daughters' teachers seem unaware of their difficulties, and certainly unaware of their daughters' ADHD. "She may talk a bit too much to her friends, but she tries to do her work." "She's quiet, a bit shy and rarely raises her hand in class." "She tries hard. I don't see any problems in school." Girls diagnosed with ADHD often report in therapy that they fear getting "in trouble" at school; they also describe feeling anxious about school and worrying that the teacher will reprimand or embarrass them. Some experience this anxiety to the point that they develop school-avoidance patterns. Many of these girls are quiet and compliant in class, only to be tearful, explosive, or angry once they are in the relative safety of home. Sadly, mothers are sometimes blamed for this discrepancy. "She's fine at school, so it must be a problem between her and her mother," the uninformed professional may conclude.

This pattern of "masking" ADHD in public starts early and continues into adulthood.[52] Women feel exhausted and ashamed. Women with ADHD who can function well at work may report that no one at work would guess that they had ADHD, but they take care never to invite friends or colleagues to their home to see behind the mask.

TREATMENT SHOULD FOCUS ON QUALITY OF LIFE, NOT ONLY ON SYMPTOM REDUCTION

In this opening chapter, we have focused on the significant risks associated with ADHD in women. The good news is that ADHD is a highly treatable disorder, and the earlier it is diagnosed, the better the outcome. In the chapters that follow, we will guide you through the risks of untreated or inadequately treated ADHD and introduce the treatment approaches that can mitigate those risks.

Ultimately, **your goal should be to improve the overall quality of life for the women that you treat, not to just treat "symptoms."** We need to help all women with ADHD understand that seeking treatment is important for their own well-being. For mothers, focusing on their own treatment needs will benefit everyone in their family. For far too long, we have asked women with ADHD, without diagnosis or treatment, to be the support system and provide the structure their children with ADHD so badly need—an almost impossible task when a mother has untreated ADHD herself! All women with ADHD—whether they are mothers, child-free, single, or partnered without children— need support to understand their needs, come out of the shadows, stop masking, to find "social support" and to build more satisfying, authentic lives.

Ultimately, everyone will have an opportunity to thrive if we can help women with ADHD to stop leading lives of relentless feelings of overwhelm and inadequacy, and if their partners and families join them in learning to create ADHD-friendly households.

SUMMARY

We will address all the issues we've introduced in this chapter in greater detail in later chapters, providing guidance that we as medical and mental health providers can use to diagnose, treat, and provide support for the women who come to us with a kaleidoscope of issues and challenges. Undiagnosed ADHD causes women to struggle with a confusing array of medical and mental health conditions. Furthermore, women with ADHD work hard to mask their struggles, making diagnosis an even greater challenge.

Our goal is to help clinicians to see behind the mask, avoid being led astray by co-occurring conditions, to recognize these women's complex struggles, and to identify the underlying ADHD that is so often at the core of these struggles.

In this chapter, we have introduced that:

- Common stereotypical views about ADHD that are held by the public as well as by healthcare and mental health providers cause ADHD to be missed or misdiagnosed in women.
- ADHD diagnostic criteria were initially developed to describe young boys, and therefore are poor at identifying girls and even less effective in identifying women.
- Women with ADHD often struggle with anxiety and depression, and their ADHD is often overlooked in favor of these diagnoses.
- Few medical or mental health professionals have received adequate training to understand the seriousness of the disorder and how to recognize and treat it.
- ADHD in women is not "ADHD-lite"—in fact, compared to men with ADHD, women are at greater risk of developing serious psychiatric disorders and encountering punishing life challenges including intimate partner abuse, single parenthood with limited support and resources, suicidal ideation, and suicide attempts.
- ADHD in women is a highly treatable condition when we provide them with treatment, self-understanding, coping tools, and support.

REFERENCES

1. O'Nions, E., El Baou, C., John, A., Lewer, D., Mandy, W., McKechnie, D. G. J., Petersen, I., & Stott, J. (2025). Life expectancy and years of life lost for adults with diagnosed ADHD in the UK: matched cohort study. *British Journal of Psychiatry: The Journal of Mental Science*, *226*(5), 261–268. https://doi.org/10.1192/bjp.2024.199
2. Kelly, K., & Ramundo, P. (2006). *You mean I'm not lazy, stupid or crazy?! The classic self-help book for adults with attention deficit disorder*. Simon and Schuster.
3. Skoglund, C., Sundström Poromaa, I., Leksell, D., Ekholm Selling, K., Cars, T., Giacobini, M., Young, S., & Kopp Kallner, H. (2024). Time after time: failure to identify and support females with ADHD—a Swedish population register study. *Journal of Child Psychology and Psychiatry, and Allied Disciplines*, *65*(6), 832–844. https://doi.org/10.1111/jcpp.13920
4. Young, S., Adamo, N., Ásgeirsdóttir, B. B., Branney, P., Beckett, M., Colley, W., Cubbin, S., Deeley, Q., Farrag, E., Gudjonsson, G., Hill, P., Hollingdale, J., Kilic, O., Lloyd, T., Mason, P., Paliokosta, E., Perecherla, S., Sedgwick, J., Skirrow, C. … Woodhouse, E. (2020). Females with ADHD: an expert consensus statement taking a lifespan approach providing guidance for the identification and treatment of attention-deficit/hyperactivity disorder in girls and women. *BMC Psychiatry*, *20*(1), 404. https://doi.org/10.1186/s12888-020-02707-9
5. Kok, F. M., Groen, Y., Fuermaier, A. B. M., & Tucha, O. (2016). Problematic peer functioning in girls with ADHD: a systematic literature review. *PLOS One*, *11*(11), e0165119. https://doi.org/10.1371/journal.pone.0165119
6. Rhodes, J., Pelham, W., Gnagy, E., Shiffman, S., Derefinko, K., & Molina, B. (2016). Cigarette smoking and ADHD: an examination of prognostically relevant smoking behaviors among adolescents and young adults. *Psychology of Addictive Behaviors*, *30*(5), 588–600. https://doi.org/10.1037/adb0000188
7. Hua, M. H., Huang, K. L., Hsu, J. W., Bai, Y. M., Su, T. P., Tsai, S. J., Li, C. T., Lin, W. C., Chen, T. J., & Chen, M. H. (2021). Early pregnancy risk among adolescents with ADHD: a nationwide longitudinal study. *Journal of Attention Disorders*, *25*(9), 1199–1206. https://doi.org/10.1177/1087054719900232
8. Trivedi, C., Nandakumar, A. L., Yousefzadehfard, Y., Goriparthi, T. S. K., Chaudhari, G., Vora, D., Mansuri, Z., & Jain, S. (2022). Suicide risk among adolescents with ADHD. *Journal of Nervous and Mental Disease*, *211*(3), 216–220. https://doi.org/10.1097/nmd.0000000000001587
9. Fuller-Thomson, E., Lewis, D. A., & Agbeyaka, S. K. (2016). Attention-deficit/hyperactivity disorder casts a long shadow: findings from a population-based study of adult women with self-reported ADHD. *Child Care Health and Development*, *42*(6), 918–927. https://doi.org/10.1111/cch.12380
10. Hayashi, W., Suzuki, H., Saga, N., Arai, G., Igarashi, R., Tokumasu, T., Ota, H., Yamada, H., Takashio, O., & Iwanami, A. (2019). Clinical characteristics of women with ADHD in Japan. *Neuropsychiatric Disease and Treatment*, *15*, 3367–3374. https://doi.org/10.2147/ndt.s232565
11. Gül, A., & Gül, H. (2018). ADHD partners, ADHD parents and ADHD children: relationship of ADHD symptoms in low socioeconomic status families from Turkey. *Journal of Mood Disorders*, 1. https://doi.org/10.5455/jmood.20180127072327
12. Holthe, M. E. G., & Langvik, E. (2017). The strives, struggles, and successes of women diagnosed with ADHD as adults. *Sage Open*, 7(1). https://doi.org/10.1177/2158244017701799
13. Vildalen, V., Brevik, E., Haavik, J., & Lundervold, A. (2016). Females with ADHD report more severe symptoms than males on the adult ADHD self-report scale.

Journal of Attention Disorders, 23(9), 959–967. https://doi.org/10.1177/1087054716659362
14. Le, A. (1996). Sex differences in ADHD: conference summary. *Journal of Abnormal Child Psychology, 24*(5), 555–569. https://doi.org/10.1007/bf01670100
15. Hasson, R., & Fine, J. (2012). Gender differences among children with ADHD on continuous performance tests. *Journal of Attention Disorders*, 16(3), 190–198. https://doi.org/10.1177/1087054711427398
16. Childress, A., Newcorn, J., & Cutler, A. (2019). Gender effects in the efficacy of racemic amphetamine sulfate in children with attention-deficit/hyperactivity disorder. *Advances in Therapy, 36*(6), 1370–1387. https://doi.org/10.1007/s12325-019-00942-5
17. McKechnie, D. G., O'Nions, E., Dunsmuir, S., & Petersen, I. (2023). Attention-deficit hyperactivity disorder diagnoses and prescriptions in UK primary care, 2000–2018: population-based cohort study. *BJPsych Open, 9*(4), e121.
18. Kopp, S., Asztély, K., Landberg, S., Waern, M., Bergman, S., & Gillberg, C. (2023). Girls with social and/or attention deficit re-examined in young adulthood: prospective study of diagnostic stability, daily life functioning and social situation. *Journal of Attention Disorders, 27*(8), 830–846. https://doi.org/10.1177/10870547231158751
19. Skogli, E. W., Teicher, M. H., Andersen, P. N., Hovik, K. T., & Øie, M. (2013). ADHD in girls and boys—gender differences in co-existing symptoms and executive function measures. *BMC Psychiatry, 13*(1), 298. https://doi.org/10.1186/1471-244X-13-298
20. Arout, C. A., Sofuoglu, M., Bastian, L. A., & Rosenheck, R. A. (2018). Gender differences in the prevalence of fibromyalgia and in concomitant medical and psychiatric disorders: a national Veterans Health Administration study. *Journal of Women's Health, 27*(8), 1035–1044.
21. Lau, T. W. I., Lim, C. G., Acharryya, S., Lim-Ashworth, N., Tan, Y. R., & Fung, S. S. D. (2021). Gender differences in externalizing and internalizing problems in Singaporean children and adolescents with attention-deficit/hyperactivity disorder. *Child and Adolescent Psychiatry and Mental Health, 15*(1), 3.
22. Asztély, K., Kopp, S., Gillberg, C., Waern, M., & Bergman, S. (2019). Chronic pain and health-related quality of life in women with autism and/or ADHD: a prospective longitudinal study. *Journal of Pain Research*, 2925–2932. https://doi.org/10.1177/10870547231158751
23. French, B., Nalbant, G., Wright, H., Sayal, K., Daley, D., Groom, M. J., Cassidy, S., & Hall, C. L. (2024). The impacts associated with having ADHD: an umbrella review. *Frontiers in Psychiatry, 15*. https://doi.org/10.3389/fpsyt.2024.1343314
24. Barkley, R. A., & Murphy, K. R. (1998). *Attention-deficit hyperactivity disorder: a clinical workbook*. The Guilford Press.
25. Athanasiadou, A., Buitelaar, J. K., Brovedani, P., Chorna, O., Fulceri, F., Guzzetta, A., & Scattoni, M. L. (2020). Early motor signs of attention-deficit hyperactivity disorder: a systematic review. *European Child & Adolescent Psychiatry, 29*(7), 903–916.
26. Kooij, J. J. S., Bejerot, S., Blackwell, A. D., Caci, H., Casas-Brugué, M., Carpentier, P. J., Edvinsson, D., Fayyad, J., Foeken, K., Fitzgerald, M., Gaillac, V., Ginsberg, Y., Henry, C., Krause, J., Lensing, M.B., Manor, I., Niederhofer, H., Nunes-Filipe, C., Ohlmeier, M. D., … Anderson, P. (2010). European consensus statement on diagnosis and treatment of adult ADHD: the European Network Adult ADHD. *BMC Psychiatry, 10*(1). https://doi.org/10.1186/1471-244x-10-67
27. Mowlem, F. D., Agnew-Blais, J., Taylor, E., & Asherson, P. (2019). Do different factors influence whether girls versus boys meet ADHD diagnostic criteria?

Sex differences among children with high ADHD symptoms. *Psychiatry Research, 272*, 765–773. https://doi.org/10.1016/j.psychres.2018.12.128

28. Kok, F. M., Groen, Y., Fuermaier, A. B. M., & Tucha, O. (2016). Problematic peer functioning in girls with ADHD: a systematic literature review. *PLOS One, 11*(11), e0165119. https://doi.org/10.1371/journal.pone.0165119
29. Quinn, P. O. (2005). Treating adolescent girls and women with ADHD: gender-specific issues. *Journal of Clinical Psychology, 61*(5), 579–587. 10.1002/JCLP.20121
30. Olsson, Å. (2022). Teachers' gendered perceptions of attention deficit hyperactivity disorder—a literature review. *European Journal of Special Needs Education, 38*(3), 303–316. https://doi.org/10.1080/08856257.2022.2076476
31. Eng, A. G., Phan, J. M., Shirtcliff, E. A., Eisenlohr-Moul, T. A., Goh, P. K., & Martel, M. M. (2023). Aging and pubertal development differentially predict symptoms of ADHD, depression, and impairment in children and adolescents: an eight-year longitudinal study. *Research on Child and Adolescent Psychopathology, 51*(6), 819–832.
32. Song, P., Zha, M., Yang, Q., Zhang, Y., Li, X., Rudan, I., & Global Health Epidemiology Reference Group (GHERG). (2021). The prevalence of adult attention-deficit hyperactivity disorder: a global systematic review and meta-analysis. *Journal of Global Health, 11*, 04009. https://doi.org/10.7189/jogh.11.04009
33. Hinshaw, S. P., Nguyen, P. T., O'Grady, S. M., & Rosenthal, E. A. (2022). Annual Research Review: attention-deficit/hyperactivity disorder in girls and women: underrepresentation, longitudinal processes, and key directions. *Journal of Child Psychology and Psychiatry, 63*(4), 484–496. https://doi.org/10.1111/jcpp.13480
34. Holthe, M. E. G., & Langvik, E. (2017). The strives, struggles, and successes of women diagnosed with ADHD as adults. *SAGE Open*, 7(1). https://doi.org/10.1177/2158244017701799
35. Caetano, S. C., Silva, C. M., & Vettore, M. V. (2013). Gender differences in the association of perceived social support and social network with self-rated health status among older adults: a population-based study in Brazil. *BMC Geriatrics, 13*(1), 122.
36. Fleck, C. (2025, May 12). The women saying no to motherhood. *ADDitude*. https://www.additudemag.com/childfree-by-choice-adhd-women-forgo-motherhood/
37. Kaufman, G., & Bair, M. (2021). Attitudes toward working mothers and work-oriented fathers in the US. *Journal of Family Issues, 42*(3), 650–670. https://doi.org/10.1177/0192513X20929069
38. Robin, A. L., & Payson, E. (2002). The impact of ADHD on marriage. *The ADHD Report, 10*(3), 9–14.
39. Dalsgaard, S., Østergaard, S. D., Leckman, J. F., Mortensen, P. B., & Pedersen, M. G. (2015). Mortality in children, adolescents, and adults with attention deficit hyperactivity disorder: a nationwide cohort study. *The Lancet, 385*(9983), 2190–2196.
40. Kok, F. M., Groen, Y., Fuermaier, A. B. M., & Tucha, O. (2016). Problematic peer functioning in girls with ADHD: a systematic literature review. *PLOS One, 11*(11), e0165119. https://doi.org/10.1371/journal.pone.0165119
41. Caetano, S. C., Silva, C. M., & Vettore, M. V. (2013). Gender differences in the association of perceived social support and social network with self-rated health status among older adults: a population-based study in Brazil. *BMC Geriatrics, 13*(1), 122.
42. Barkley, R. A., & Murphy, K. R. (1991). *Attention deficit hyperactivity disorder: a clinical workbook*. The Guilford Press.

43. Robin, A. L., & Payson, E. (2002). The impact of ADHD on marriage. *The ADHD Report, 10*(3), 9–14.
44. Taylor, S. E., Klein, L. C., Lewis, B. P., Gruenewald, T. L., Gurung, R. A., & Updegraff, J. A. (2000). Biobehavioral responses to stress in females: tend-and-befriend, not fight-or-flight. *Psychological Review, 107*(3), 411–429. https://doi.org/10.1037/0033-295X.107.3.411
45. Holthe, M. E. G., & Langvik, E. (2017). The strives, struggles, and successes of women diagnosed with ADHD as adults. *SAGE Open*, 7(1). https://doi.org/10.1177/2158244017701799
46. Di Salvo, G., Perotti, C., Filippo, L., Garrone, C., Rosso, G., & Maina, G. (2024). Assessing suicidality in adult ADHD patients: prevalence and related factors: suicidality in adult ADHD patients. *Annals of General Psychiatry, 23*(1), 42.
47. Arout, C. A., Sofuoglu, M., Bastian, L. A., & Rosenheck, R. A. (2018). Gender differences in the prevalence of fibromyalgia and in concomitant medical and psychiatric disorders: a national Veterans Health Administration study. *Journal of Women's Health, 27*(8), 1035–1044.
48. Battison, E., Brown, P., Holley, A. L., & Wilson, A. C. (2023). Associations between chronic pain and attention-deficit hyperactivity disorder (ADHD) in youth: a scoping review. *Children, 10*(1), 142. https://doi.org/10.3390/children10010142
49. Asztély, K., Kopp, S., Gillberg, C., Waern, M., & Bergman, S. (2019). Chronic pain and health-related quality of life in women with autism and/or ADHD: a prospective longitudinal study. *Journal of Pain Research, 12*, 2925–2932. https://doi.org/10.2147/jpr.s212422
50. Hurst, K. (2024, November 18). US women are outpacing men in college completion, including in every racial and ethnic group. *Pew Research Center*. https://www.pewresearch.org/short-reads/2024/11/18/us-women-are-outpacing-men-in-college-completion-including-in-every-major-racial-and-ethnic-group/
51. Kaufman, G. and Bair, M. (2020). Attitudes toward working mothers and work-oriented fathers in the US. *Journal of Family Issues, 42*(3), 650–670. https://doi.org/10.1177/0192513x20929069
52. Hinshaw, S. P., Nguyen, P. T., O'Grady, S. M., & Rosenthal, E. (2021). Annual research review: attention-deficit/hyperactivity disorder in girls and women: underrepresentation, longitudinal processes, and key directions. *Journal of Child Psychology and Psychiatry, 63*(4), 484–496.

CHAPTER 2

Diagnosis of ADHD in women

INTRODUCTION

How many adults have ADHD? Is the number increasing? How many women have ADHD? Is ADHD overdiagnosed?

These are all important questions, and their answers are sometimes unclear. The Centers for Disease Control and Prevention (CDC) estimates that the diagnosis of ADHD in adults is rising, and that as many as 6% of adults in the United States—roughly 15.5 million people—may have the condition.[1] The average age of diagnosis of adult ADHD is 28, but this number seems likely to change: at the time of writing adults over 50 years of age are increasingly being diagnosed, some for the first time. This increase over previous prevalence estimates of 4.4% is most likely the result of late diagnoses of ADHD being made in adults as awareness increases; most of these later diagnoses are of women.[2] Notably, while the diagnosis of ADHD remains at 3:1 boys vs. girls in children, the ratio in adults is nearing 1:1, with the diagnosis of ADHD in young adult women seeing the greatest increases in recent years.[3,4] This phenomenon can most likely be attributed to both an increase in awareness of the disorder in women and the ability of these women to self-refer to a professional for diagnosis and treatment. Along with this increase in ADHD diagnoses among women, there has been a significant rise in treatment rates.[5,6]

In 2020, the global prevalence of diagnosed persistent (childhood-diagnosed) adult ADHD was 2.58% and that of symptomatic adult ADHD was 6.76%, translating to 129.86 million and 366.33 million affected adults globally.[7] However, despite the fact that millions of women worldwide are

DOI: 10.4324/9781003542124-2

being diagnosed with ADHD, we have no idea about the true incidence of the condition in women. Even though more women are being diagnosed, few receive the comprehensive evaluation needed to delineate the full array of deficits that commonly appear in women, including cognitive impairments (memory and executive function), anxiety, and mood disorders that accompany the diagnosis. Even fewer receive a comprehensive treatment program to optimize day-to-day functioning and address the influence of fluctuating levels of circulating hormones, both monthly and over the lifespan. Designing a comprehensive treatment program is as important as establishing the diagnosis, and this issue will be discussed in depth in Chapter 4.

Prevalence differs depending on where you look

Studies have shown that the reported prevalence of ADHD among women varies widely depending on the population studied, with rates of ADHD being significantly higher in specific groups, such as women with eating disorders, obesity, mood disorders, and chronic pain. Women with self-reported ADHD exhibit higher rates of coexisting conditions, such as anxiety and depression, which complicates the clinical picture. These conditions are often treated first, while the ADHD goes undiagnosed,[8,9] highlighting the critical importance of diagnosis and treatment of women with ADHD. One national study (The Canadian Community Health Survey-Mental Health, 2012) compared women with ADHD and without ADHD and found strong evidence that women with ADHD were three times more likely to have insomnia, chronic pain, suicidal ideation, childhood sexual abuse and generalized anxiety disorder, and to report childhood sexual abuse. They were also twice as likely to be current smokers, to have substance use disorders and depressive disorders, to live in severe poverty, and to report childhood physical abuse. Even after adjustments for age, race, education, and income, women with ADHD had substantially higher odds of a wide range of problems.[10]

ADHD symptoms in women often differ from those in men. Research indicates that women and girls are more likely to have Predominantly Inattentive Presentation of ADHD, which can lead to a delay in diagnosis as these symptoms are less disruptive and may be less noticeable than the hyperactive behaviors more commonly observed in boys.[11,12,13] This discrepancy can lead to delayed and missed referrals for evaluation and treatment.

GETTING STARTED: SCALES USED FOR SCREENING FOR ADHD IN ADULTS

The choice of scale you use will depend on the specific needs of the assessment for ADHD (**screening versus diagnosis**), the availability of resources in your office, and your clinical expertise in diagnosing ADHD. A **comprehensive evaluation** involves a combination of **self-report scales**, **informant ratings**, **clinical interviews**, and, in some cases, **neurocognitive testing** to look at **cognitive** and **executive functioning** and arrive at a reliable ADHD diagnosis. The following are scales to assist you when considering a possible diagnosis of ADHD. Most are short, easy to complete, and score.

Adult ADHD Self-Report Scale (ASRS-v1.1): A validated screening tool to identify adults at risk for ADHD. Easy to administer and widely used.

Conners' Adult ADHD Rating Scales (CAARS): Assesses ADHD symptoms and has high sensitivity and specificity. Can be completed by patient, informants, or clinicians.

Wender Utah Rating Scale (WURS): Assesses retrospective symptoms of ADHD in childhood, which can aid in the diagnosis of adult ADHD. Relies on retrospective self-report, which may be subject to recall bias.

Brown Attention-Deficit Disorder Scales (Brown ADD Scales): Assesses a broad range of executive function difficulties associated with ADHD. Time-consuming.

ADHD Rating Scale-IV with Adult Prompts (ADHD-RS-IV): Based on DSM-IV-TR. May not capture full range of adult ADHD symptoms. Provides rating of severity. Requires clinician administration.

Barkley Adult Rating Scale IV: Assesses ADHD symptoms, domains of impairment, and symptoms during childhood. The BAARS-IV is linked to the DSM-IV criteria. Long version takes 5–7 minutes to complete, and the Quick Screen takes only 3–5 minutes.

The Adult Self-Report (ASR) and Adult Behavior Checklist (ABCL): Self-reports of functioning and problems (ASR). ACBL has norms for ages 18–35, 36–59, and 60 and above. Results are displayed on separate profiles for men and women.

WHAT IS THE DSM-5-TR? AND IS IT RELEVANT FOR DIAGNOSING WOMEN WITH ADHD?

The Diagnostic and Statistical Manual of Mental Disorders, fifth edition, text revision (DSM-5-TR) is a crucial reference in the field of psychiatric diagnostics, functioning as an updated version of the DSM-5, first published in 2013.[14] Released in March 2022, the DSM-5-TR incorporates new findings and updates that aim to enhance the diagnostic accuracy and consistency across various psychiatric conditions.[15] This revision has been informed by ongoing research and evolving clinical practices, offering a more nuanced understanding of mental health disorders and their cultural considerations.[16,17,18]

When using the DSM-5-TR to diagnose ADHD in women, effectiveness hinges on your understanding of gender differences in symptom presentation and on using a holistic approach to assessment that considers functional impairments and coexisting physical and mental health conditions. To diagnose ADHD in women, you must be vigilant in recognizing the different presentations in women and consider using comprehensive assessment tools that capture the breadth of symptoms beyond those specified in the DSM-5-TR. (We provide a more detailed discussion of the DSM-5 TR later in this chapter.)

The DSM diagnostic criteria for many mental health disorders have long been criticized for their gender bias. There is compelling evidence that this bias has hindered the accurate identification of ADHD in women and girls, and we believe that the increase in numbers of women currently being diagnosed represents at least a partial correction. However, to date, little attention has been paid to these concerns, despite their being raised before revisions of the manual.[19,20]

To be diagnosed with ADHD in adulthood according to DSM-5-TR, individuals must present with five or more symptoms of inattention and/or hyperactivity-impulsivity that have persisted for at least six months. These symptoms must also cause significant distress or interfere with functioning in areas like work, school, or social activities. Additional criteria for diagnosis and degree of severity are important for the diagnosis.[21] (Examples of the symptoms and criteria for diagnosis using DSM-5-TR are listed below.)

Inattention symptoms

- Lack of attention to detail: Making careless mistakes in work or daily activities.
- Difficulty sustaining attention: Struggling to focus during conversations, lectures, or lengthy reading.

- Difficulty listening: Appearing not to listen during conversations or when following instructions. Seeming to have one's mind elsewhere. Daydreaming.
- Difficulty organizing tasks: Struggling to manage work, deadlines, or belongings.
- Difficulty planning or prioritizing: Having trouble with organization, time management, and planning.
- Avoiding tasks requiring sustained mental effort: Disliking or avoiding tasks that require focused attention.
- Losing things: Frequently misplacing papers, keys, or other important items.
- Distractibility: Being easily distracted by unrelated thoughts or environmental stimuli.
- Forgetfulness: Forgetting daily tasks, appointments, or bills.

Hyperactivity/impulsivity symptoms

- Fidgeting or restlessness: Feeling restless, tapping fingers or feet, squirming in a chair, pacing, rocking, etc.
- Difficulty remaining seated: Struggling to stay in place when expected to, continually changing positions or standing up.
- Excessive restlessness: Feeling driven, on the go, or unable to sit still.
- Talking excessively: Talking more than usual, constantly interrupting, or blurting out answers before questions are finished.
- Difficulty waiting or taking turns: Having trouble waiting for their turn or difficulty taking turns in activities.
- Interrupting or intruding: Interrupting conversations, games, or other activities.

Additional criteria for diagnosis

- Symptom persistence: Symptoms must have been present for at least six months and to a degree that is inconsistent with the individual's developmental level.
- Impairment in functioning: Symptoms must significantly interfere with or reduce the quality of social, academic, or occupational functioning.
- Differential diagnosis: Symptoms should not be better explained by another mental disorder (like anxiety, depression, or a personality disorder).

- Early onset: It's important to note that while the DSM-5-TR requires symptoms to have been present before age 12 rather than 7, age of onset can be difficult to determine retrospectively in adults.
- Degree of severity: DSM-5-TR requests that the examiner specify the current degree of severity of the disorder, not just the number of symptoms. This helps quantify how much a person is impaired by their symptoms. It is not uncommon for a woman to have only a few symptoms but be severely impaired by those symptoms.
    - Mild: Few symptoms beyond those required to make the diagnosis, resulting in no more than minor impairments. Again, the degree of impairment is important. Treatment recommendations may depend on both the degree and area of impairment.
    - Moderate: Symptoms of functional impairment between mild and severe.
    - Severe: Many symptoms beyond those needed for diagnosis or several symptoms that are particularly severe, or symptoms that result in marked impairment in social or occupational functioning.

This degree-of-severity rating is extremely important but is often overlooked when diagnosing ADHD in women. Women may exhibit and/or report severe impairments in functioning that negatively impact their relationships, careers, and financial security, yet may still report fewer than five inattentive symptoms and only one or two hyperactive/impulsive symptoms.

CASE ILLUSTRATION: ISABELE

"I just lost my 5th job in a row! Please help me! I am desperate and don't know what to do or where to turn!!! What is wrong with me?" Isabele's email began.

Isabele is a 26-year-old who lives with her mom because of her precarious financial situation. She decided to seek treatment because of persistent sadness and fatigue, and after her intake you completed the ADHD evaluation you regularly give to new patients. When reflecting on her childhood, she did not report numerous symptoms or severe impairment. Isabele described herself as shy and somewhat daydreamy as a young girl. Her elementary school teachers frequently commented that she needed to start paying attention but did not recognize anything was wrong. As a teen, Isabele had some problems with organization, but her mom helped her stay on top of things, and she got what she referred to as "OK" grades. Looking back, Isabele feels her mother enabled her and helped too much, so she never learned organizational or time management skills. In high school, teachers frequently commented, "Isabele is a 'smart' girl, but not living up to her potential."

Over the 8 years since her graduation from high school, Isabele has held many jobs, but each was a poor fit and only lasted about 2 or 3 months before she quit or was fired. She worked as a nanny and enjoyed playing and having fun with the kids, but didn't consistently do the light housework chores her employer required and had trouble adhering to a regular schedule for the kids' meals, bedtime, and naps. She was a part-time receptionist in a doctor's office but frequently got distracted and made mistakes when scheduling appointments. During a brief stint as a driver for a grocery delivery service, she received complaints after confusing several orders and giving them to the wrong customers. Some jobs bored her; others required skills she found difficult to master. As a waitress, she would forget which tables had already placed orders and which had recently been seated, with her work performance getting worse the busier it got. Her last job was as an assistant in a hair salon where she was supposed to wash the brushes, sweep the floor, and do the laundry. The work was tedious and tiring, and she was eventually fired because the salon opened at 8:30 and Isabele always slept in and arrived 30 minutes late.

As she shared her story, she looked hopeless and dejected.

You diagnose Isabele with ADHD and depression. Her impairment was severe. She was placed on stimulant medication and an antidepressant and was referred to a psychotherapist and began Cognitive Behavioral Therapy (CBT). She responded very well to treatment. She also joined an adult ADHD group at the local CHADD chapter and learned more about ADHD.

One weekend, Isabele decided to join a yoga retreat that a friend was attending, and she loved it! When she returned home, she joined a class at a local yoga studio and began to practice mindfulness. With the benefit of medication, psychotherapy, mindfulness, and exercise, Isabele's focus was much better, and she was able to find and maintain employment for the first time. She eventually trained as a yoga teacher and began teaching yoga classes. One, two, then three classes a day. The movement and exercise that this work provided was a great match. She later discontinued her antidepressant and was discharged from her therapy. She'd never felt better! Eventually, she partnered with her friend to build a yoga studio and has never looked back. Isabele had found her niche, and her ADHD was no longer controlling her life.

The DSM-5-TR recognizes three presentations of ADHD: Predominantly inattentive, predominantly hyperactive-impulsive, and combined.

The DSM-5-TR outlines specific criteria for diagnosing ADHD, which include symptoms of inattention and/or hyperactivity/impulsivity, and remains the gold standard for diagnosing mental health conditions. DSM criteria from DSM-III through DSM-5 are all based on research predominantly involving young, male subjects, raising concerns about their applicability to women. Research indicates that women typically exhibit more inattentive symptoms and less overt hyperactivity compared to men, which can lead to underdiagnosis or misdiagnosis when relying strictly on DSM-5 criteria.

The prevalence of ADHD diagnoses in women may be underestimated due to the bias toward childhood male presentations of ADHD codified in earlier versions of the DSM, particularly the symptom of hyperactivity. However, prevalence rates for women have risen using DSM-5 criteria compared to DSM-IV (17.4% versus 15.8%).[22,23] In one study comparing DSM-IV to DSM-5 criteria, more adults were diagnosed using DSM-5, and **most of those were women**.

It has also been noted that for women to be diagnosed using these criteria, their symptoms and functional impairments need to be more severe. Functional impairment scales confirm that while women presenting for evaluation for ADHD report significant functional impairments, these may not always align with the DSM-5-TR's diagnostic framework due to differences in type and/or number (subclinical for diagnosis with four or three symptoms) of symptom presentations, e.g., inattentive versus combined presentation.[24,25]

> Women with ADHD may have fewer symptoms but experience greater impairment from those symptoms

In addition to ADHD symptoms manifesting differently in women, many women mask their ADHD symptoms and also develop coping strategies over time, making it harder to identify the disorder.[26] Unless you ask a woman with ADHD what is going on (self-report), you are unlikely to ascertain her symptoms and thus make the diagnosis. If they don't let you into their house, how will you know it's messy and disorganized? If they adopt perfectionistic tendencies, or stay up late every night to get everything done, how will you know they have problems with attention, distractibility, procrastination, planning, strategizing, short-term memory, time management, etc.? If you don't ask, how will you know about all the times they were unable to keep up, and something went very wrong?

Women diagnosed with Predominantly Inattentive Presentation of ADHD often have fewer total symptoms when compared to Combined Presentation ADHD. However, despite displaying fewer symptoms, women with ADHD often exhibit greater impairment than men with ADHD or women without ADHD. Women may also exhibit multiple symptoms from the inattentive and hyperactive/impulsive symptom lists combined and not reach the threshold for a clinical diagnosis of ADHD. These women, who present as subclinical for ADHD, may be just as impaired and respond just as well to treatment as women diagnosed with ADHD. On the other hand, subthreshold ADHD symptoms may sometimes be the result of other psychiatric conditions that cause problems with attention, requiring careful differential diagnosis.[27,28]

Of those women seeking treatment for late-onset ADHD, in most instances these women are likely to have ADHD; however, it's important to be aware that late-onset symptoms may also represent cognitive and memory deficits that are the result of declining estrogen levels, a coexisting condition, or the cognitive effects of substance use. Without careful assessment, false positive late-onset ADHD cases may occur. You should carefully assess impairment, psychiatric history, and substance use before diagnosing and treating potential late-onset cases of ADHD.

The delay in diagnosis for women is most likely exacerbated by the gender biases in the diagnostic criteria, which may not adequately capture the nuanced ways in which women experience their ADHD symptoms.[29,30] This pattern of late diagnosis may contribute to a higher prevalence of mental health issues among adult women with ADHD, as their ADHD goes untreated.[31] The implications of these findings are significant, suggesting that ADHD in women is often under-recognized and undertreated.[32]

USING THE DSM-5 OR DSM-5-TR CRITERIA AS PART OF YOUR COMPREHENSIVE ASSESSMENT FOR DIAGNOSING ADHD IN WOMEN

The use of the DSM-5 or DSM-5-TR for diagnosing attention-deficit/hyperactivity disorder (ADHD) in women presents both **advantages** and **challenges**. Understanding these aspects is crucial, as they can influence clinical practice and the overall experience of diagnosing women with ADHD.

The "pros" of using the DSM-5 TR diagnostic criteria include

- **Standardization of diagnostic criteria**: The DSM-5 or 5-TR provides a standardized framework for diagnosing ADHD, which helps ensure consistency in diagnosis across different practitioners and settings. The DSM-5-TR criteria include a revision that allows for a more nuanced understanding of ADHD, including traits that may manifest differently in women, such as inattentiveness and daydreaming[33] and emotional dysregulation rather than hyperactivity, and provides more gender-specific examples (hyper-talkativeness or feeling restless) of what has classically been understood as hyperactivity.[34] This TR (text revision) is intended to help clinicians identify ADHD symptoms more effectively in women, but it doesn't present the whole picture.[35]
- **Recognition of coexisting conditions**: The DSM-5 allows for a concurrent diagnosis of ADHD with other disorders, such as depression and anxiety, that disproportionately affect women.[36] This is particularly relevant given that many women may present with multiple coexisting conditions that complicate the clinical picture. For instance, research indicates that:

> **A significant proportion of women with a history of recurrent depression also exhibit symptoms of ADHD.[37,38]**
>
> Making this dual diagnosis in your patient is critical and can facilitate targeted treatment strategies.

- **Inclusion of gender-specific research in establishing the diagnosis**: The DSM-5-TR has been influenced by increased awareness of the gendered manifestations of ADHD. Several studies have shown that women with ADHD often face unique challenges, such as higher rates of psychiatric conditions and social hardships compared to men with ADHD.[39] As discussed in the previous chapter, women with ADHD often struggle with parenting tasks that require emotional regulation, organization, and problem-solving skills; and are likely to have children with ADHD, leaving them feeling perpetually behind and overwhelmed. They are more likely to have medical problems (Chapter 7) and mental health issues (Chapter 3). While executive dysfunction is considered in the DSM-5, emotional dysregulation and rejection sensitivity, both regularly seen in women, are not.

The "cons" of using the DSM-5 or DSM-5-TR diagnostic criteria include

- **Bias in diagnostic criteria**: Despite its advancements, the DSM-5-TR still relies on historically male-oriented symptoms, which can lead to underdiagnosis in women. Research suggests that providers may overlook ADHD symptoms in women due to diagnostic criteria that do not fully encompass the behavioral expressions typical of women and girls, such as hyperactivity being less visible or overshadowed by a woman's efforts to meet social expectations.[40] Consequently, this bias can perpetuate inequities and delay access to care for women.[41]
- **Limited awareness and training of practitioners**: Clinicians may not be adequately trained to recognize ADHD as it tends to present in women, leading to misdiagnosis or missed diagnoses. Studies show that women often present with less clear-cut and less observable symptoms.[42,43]

CLUES TO FINDING ADHD IN WOMEN

While the DSM-5-TR can be used to diagnose ADHD in women, its effectiveness hinges on your understanding of sex differences in symptom presentation and the utilization of a **holistic approach to assessment** that includes consideration of **functional impairments** and coexisting physical and mental health conditions. We must be vigilant in recognizing the different presentations of ADHD in women and consider comprehensive assessment tools that capture the breadth of symptoms beyond those specified in the DSM-5.[44] These discrepancies can be reduced through developing specific protocols generated to identify ADHD in women more effectively. There also remains a great need for the training of healthcare providers to place more emphasis on the gendered aspects of ADHD presentation.[45]

What should be Included in your assessment for ADHD in women?

1. *Patient interview*

   You may want to use a structured clinical interview as part of your comprehensive assessment for ADHD in women. Some examples can be found below.

   - **The Conners' Adult ADHD Diagnostic Interview for DSM-IV (CAADID)** is a validated semi-structured interview available for the accurate diagnostic assessment of ADHD in the adult population specifically based on the DSM-IV criteria.
   - **The DIVA (Diagnostic Interview for ADHD in Adults)** was released in 2019 and based on DSM-5 criteria. This version is available in several languages and includes updated examples of symptoms for adult ADHD compared to DSM-IV. It's important to note that while the DSM-5 is still widely used, a revised version, the DSM-5-TR, published in 2022, includes text revisions and updates to diagnostic criteria. The DSM-5-TR is considered the most current and accurate version of the DSM for diagnosing ADHD; however, we discuss both the DSM-5 and DSM-5-TR in this guide.
   - **The Diagnostic Interview for ADHD in Adults (DIVA-5)** emphasizes the necessity of chronicity and impairment assessment in determining the presence of ADHD, which can significantly clarify the diagnostic picture amid co-occurring conditions. This semi-structured interview allows for a thorough evaluation of the diagnostic criteria of DSM-5-TR for ADHD in adulthood. It has 100% concordance with DSM-5 diagnostic criteria when compared to the Conners' Adult ADHD Diagnostic Interview or CAADID, mentioned above, and shows good correlation with the WURS scale when assessing ADHD symptoms for inattention, hyperactivity/impulsivity, and total symptoms during childhood.

The DIVA-5 also deals with the impairment caused by ADHD symptoms in five areas of functioning (work and education; relationships and family life; social contacts; free time and hobbies; and self-confidence and self-image). Whenever possible, the adult is interviewed in the presence of the partner or close relative who is familiar with the patient's childhood, to allow for comparison of simultaneously collected collateral and retrospective information.[46]

The CAADID interview is based on the older DSM-IV, while the DIVA-5 is based on the DSM-5. The DIVA will shortly be updated to focus on the specific presentations in girls and women with the introduction of DIVA-5-R. (Personal communication)

- **The Self-Assessment Symptom Inventory for Women (SASI)** was developed by Drs. Quinn and Nadeau to be used as a structured interview in assessing potential ADHD in women. It is available as part of their book, *Understanding Women with ADHD*.[47] While the SASI has not been normed, it provides a valuable, clinical tool for use during a structured interview and allows the clinician and patient to delineate **problem areas** and establish **target symptoms** for treatment.

Your patient interview should also include a broader exploration of the following:

- **Symptoms related to co-occurring conditions**.
- **Developmental history**.
- **Medical history**.
- **Family history**: ADHD tends to run in families. First-degree relatives of people with ADHD are about nine times more likely to develop ADHD than the general population. Parents commonly become aware of their ADHD symptoms as their child is diagnosed.
- **Social and academic experiences**: many women with ADHD, particularly those with **high IQ** and **perfectionistic** or **obsessive/compulsive personality traits**, may have done well during their academic and professional careers. Women with ADHD may exhibit social issues, such as difficulty in making and/or keeping friends. If impulsivity is part of the picture, they may have had multiple partners, be divorced, or be single mothers raising multiple children, some of whom may also have ADHD.

2. *Interviews with significant others*
Collateral information from family members or significant others regarding the individual's history and symptomatology should be

obtained, if possible. This approach addresses the potential discrepancies in self-reported data and reinforces the identification of co-occurring conditions that could affect treatment.

Rating scales: Most of the standardized self-rating scales can also be used by significant others to report their observations. However, a lack of reports of ADHD symptoms by significant others should not be used to rule out an ADHD diagnosis. Remember, many symptoms are internalized and masked, and parental reports from a woman's childhood may not be accurate.

3. *Measurement of functional impairment*
   When evaluating functional impairments associated with ADHD, several standardized scales are used to assess the impact of the disorder on various life domains. These scales provide critical insights into how ADHD symptoms affect daily functioning and quality of life, aiding clinicians in treatment planning and outcome measurement. Below are some key functional impairment scales we can use in an ADHD assessment:

   - **The Weiss Functional Impairment Rating Scale (WFIRS)**: The Weiss Functional Impairment Rating Scale (WFIRS) is one of the most prominent tools specifically designed to assess ADHD-related functional impairment across various domains.[48] The WFIRS evaluates six clinically relevant domains typically affected by ADHD: family, work/school, self-concept, life skills, social activities, and risk-taking behaviors. This scale has demonstrated good psychometric properties, showing reliability and validity in both adult and pediatric populations.[49]
   - **The Barkley Functional Impairment Scale (BFIS)**: The Barkley Functional Impairment Scale (BFIS) is another important measure used to evaluate functional impairments in individuals with ADHD. This scale encompasses various domains including academic performance, social relationships, family interactions, and daily living skills. It provides a structured approach for assessing the degree of impairment across different environments and settings relevant to the individual's everyday life.

   Using these scales can enhance patient outcomes by:

   - Ensuring a thorough understanding of symptoms and degree of current **impairments**,
   - Helping set **treatment goals**, and
   - **Confirming** treatment results through a reduction of **target symptoms** and functional improvement.

4. *Assessment of executive function deficits*
   Anatomically, **executive functions** are associated with the **prefrontal cortex (PFC)**.[50] These executive functions have been found to be deficient in those with ADHD. The PFC has been referred to as the CEO of the brain and is responsible for the functions and difficulties listed below:

   - **Planning and organization**: Difficulty organizing tasks, setting goals, and following through with plans.
   - **Decision-making**: Impaired judgment, poor choices, and difficulty weighing consequences.
   - **Attention and focus**: Reduced attention span, difficulty concentrating, and easily distracted.
   - **Working memory**: Problems holding information in the mind for a short period of time. Trouble following directions.
   - **Emotional dysregulation**: Difficulty regulating emotions, leading to irritability, mood swings, or flat affect.
   - **Lack of motivation**: Reduced drive, initiative, and difficulty starting or completing tasks.
   - **Difficulty with multitasking**: Struggling to manage multiple tasks simultaneously.
   - **Difficulty with transitions**: Problems with stopping a task or activity once it has started and transitioning to another activity.

   Research has shown that a significant proportion of women with ADHD report high rates of **anxiety** (26%) and **executive dysfunction**.[51] This anxiety can magnify the impacts of executive dysfunction, affecting not only daily life but also educational and occupational outcomes. The presence of anxiety alongside executive dysfunction may make ADHD symptoms more apparent, facilitating diagnosis in adults.[52] It has been suggested that as many as 50% of individuals with ADHD may show impairments in executive functions.[53] This percentage only underscores the severity of the issue. While similarities exist in the prevalence of ADHD symptoms between genders, the presentation and impact of executive dysfunction often differs significantly, which may lead to underdiagnosis or misdiagnosis in women.[54]

   - **Function/attention scales (Brown EF/A Scales)**: This tool is designed to evaluate executive functioning in individuals, particularly those who have or are suspected of having ADHD. It assesses various aspects of executive function, including attention, memory, and impulse control, through multiple perspectives. It includes collateral information from family members or significant others regarding the individual's history and symptomatology. This approach addresses the potential discrepancies in self-reported data and reinforces the identification of co-occurring conditions that could affect treatment.

- **Delis Rating of Executive Functions, Adult (D–REF Adult)**: This scale makes it possible to quickly and easily administer, score, and report the frequency of the observed behaviors that identify executive function problems in adults. It was published in 2021 with an age range of 19 to 79:11 years. The scale takes 10–15 minutes to administer, which can be done online or using paper forms (available via download). Self-report and collateral report forms are also available.

5. *Behavioral observations*
   Direct observation of your patient's behavior as it relates to symptoms of ADHD and other disorders is critical. Is the patient restless and having difficulty remaining seated while waiting to be seen? Is she fidgety or hyper-talkative? Does she have pressured speech? Can she follow directions and respond appropriately to your questions? Or does she get "lost in the weeds" and just "wander" off topic most of the time? Do you have to keep redirecting the conversation? Does she present as sad or depressed? Is her affect appropriate for the content she is relating? Does she give good eye contact? Are her verbal interactions organized or "all over the place?" Is she ashamed? Discouraged? Overwhelmed?
6. *Physical exam/medical tests*
   A p**hysical examination** to identify deficits, including **hearing/vision screens** and other potential health conditions, is considered part of the assessment for ADHD. **Blood pressure** and **weight** baselines should be established. There is no medical test to determine whether someone has ADHD.

   Blood tests, however, may be necessary to rule out other conditions that might interfere with attention or complicate the diagnostic picture.

   Some physical conditions may present with symptoms resembling those of ADHD. For instance, conditions affecting thyroid function, iron deficiency, and other metabolic disorders can lead to cognitive symptoms that overlap with ADHD features. Utilizing blood tests to screen for systemic conditions like anemia, lead poisoning, and thyroid dysfunction is recommended when diagnosing ADHD.

   Research has suggested that specific blood parameters, such as folate, vitamin B12, zinc, and creatinine levels may correlate with

ADHD, as they are linked to dopamine regulation, and deficits in any one of these may affect symptoms and overall efficacy of treatment. Blood tests evaluating these physiological factors are critical for ensuring that conditions such as low estrogen, hypothyroidism, or vitamin deficiencies are not contributing to attention deficits observed in patients. Therefore, **blood tests** when assessing for ADHD in women might include: thyroid functioning (T3, T4, TSH levels); Hgb to assess for anemia; blood glucose and A1c levels to screen for diabetes; lead levels; hormone levels (FSH, LH, estrogen, and progesterone levels); and vitamin (particularly B12 and folate) and zinc levels to assess nutritional status.

7. *Exploration of lifestyle.* What foods does the patient usually eat? Does she exercise? How much? And what about sleep patterns/restless legs, etc.? A review of coexisting conditions shows that sleep disorders and endocrine issues are prevalent in adults prior to their ADHD diagnosis, emphasizing the importance of a holistic approach. Exploring these factors ensures that the evaluation of ADHD symptoms is comprehensive and not purely based on patient-reported measures or behavioral assessments alone.
8. *Hormonal considerations* (explored in depth in Chapter 8). In addition, it is critical to ascertain where a woman is in her **menstrual and life cycle**. Menstruating? Postpartum? Perimenopausal? Postmenopausal? Emerging research is exploring the usefulness of **biomarkers** in the diagnostic process for ADHD.[55]

Neuropsychological testing

To refer for testing or not to refer for testing? That is the question.

Neurocognitive/neuropsychological testing as part of an **ADHD evaluation** is neither necessary nor sufficient to make a diagnosis on its own. However, these tests can offer additional data to substantiate or question a diagnosis and inform treatment planning.[56,57] Neuropsychological testing is especially recommended when there is a suspicion of cognitive impairments affecting an individual's functional capabilities and when standard diagnostic criteria alone do not adequately explain the observed symptoms.[58] Such testing can provide insights into cognitive domains that are frequently impacted by ADHD, including attention, memory, and executive functions, which are not typically captured by self-reports or ADHD scales. About 50% of adults with ADHD have been classified as impaired across various cognitive domains using standardized assessments.[59]

Who can make the diagnosis of ADHD? How can I fit the care for women with ADHD into my busy practice?

Any qualified and licensed healthcare practitioner, mental health provider, primary care physician, neurologist, or pediatrician can make the diagnosis. There are several approaches that practitioners can take:

- In busy practices, many physicians have decided that they will screen for ADHD in all their patient population and refer for further evaluation when screening tools, or the patient's behavior or diagnosis, indicates the probability of ADHD.
- Other practices prefer to designate one or two clinicians who diagnose and treat patients who present with possible ADHD. These clinicians may receive additional training or attend various workshops to develop their skills in diagnosing ADHD in women.
- Still others prefer to treat their patients with ADHD themselves if it is a co-occurring condition that is interfering with the primary focus of their practice and/or reason for patient contact; e.g., at obesity, chronic pain, eating disorders, addiction, or geriatric clinics. As discussed in Chapter 7, there are several clues that can help identify these patients during routine clinical appointments.

Is there such a thing as adult-onset ADHD?

The concept of adult-onset ADHD is controversial, as ADHD is considered a **neurodevelopmental disorder** with symptoms that usually present from an early age (younger than 12). Yet it's possible to receive a diagnosis of ADHD later in life because symptoms became significantly more obvious in adulthood, and this is sometimes called **adult-onset ADHD**. While ADHD is usually diagnosed in childhood, some people may not experience symptoms that affect their functioning until they are adults. Women are often diagnosed with ADHD later in life by as many as 4 years compared to men. The debate continues regarding whether there is true adult-onset of ADHD, or if the symptoms of ADHD were subthreshold or were not recognized in childhood due to masking and high levels of support.

Factors that may contribute to adult-onset ADHD include:

- Increased life stressors.
- Higher demands on executive functions.
- Changes in brain structure or chemistry over time.

- Change in life situation.
- Loss of structure and support from others at home, work, and/or postsecondary education.
- The presence of other mental health conditions.

Symptoms of ADHD may improve as life situations change (e.g., obtaining the perfect job) or as a woman matures, but the structural brain differences that cause ADHD may remain. In other cases, symptoms may worsen, especially triggered by key life events, like retirement or after menopause.

Symptoms of ADHD may wax and wane over the lifespan depending on a woman's circumstances. For example, she may have been able to function well in high school with help from her parents and a tutor but fell apart when she had to navigate life on her own in college. A single woman living alone in a small apartment may be able to cope with only herself to take care of, but it may be another story when she has three children, a husband, a job, a house, and myriad relationships and responsibilities to navigate. As a single woman marries and has children, her world may shift from calm to chaos; or it may change regardless of marital status, because of a more demanding job, aging parents, or other factors that did not affect her in her youth. It's no wonder if she then develops depression, anxiety, or migraines. Her old coping skills aren't sufficient as her life demands ramp up.

IMPORTANCE OF RULING OUT OTHER DIAGNOSES

When diagnosing ADHD in adults, it is crucial to ensure that you rule out other possible diagnoses through clinical assessments. The recognition of potential coexisting conditions and their relationship with ADHD significantly influences the diagnostic process and subsequent treatment recommendations. Numerous studies highlight that ADHD commonly coexists with various psychiatric disorders, including mood disorders, anxiety disorders, and sleep disturbances, which may complicate the diagnosis. One study found that nearly 90% of adults diagnosed with ADHD also had at least one co-occurring psychiatric disorder.[60] Recognizing these overlaps is essential, as symptoms from coexisting conditions may mimic or exacerbate ADHD symptoms, leading to inaccurate diagnoses if not adequately assessed. Complex diagnostic cases will be discussed further in Chapter 3.

SUMMARY

In conclusion, integrating comprehensive clinical assessments into your diagnostic protocol for adult ADHD is vital to accurately identifying the disorder while ruling out potential confounding diagnoses. This strategy helps enhance diagnostic precision and effective treatment planning, ultimately improving outcomes for women with ADHD.

Viewing the diagnosis of ADHD through a gender-aware lens

We have explored the importance of viewing ADHD in women through a gender-aware lens. More specifically, we have shown that ADHD in women can present in multiple different ways:

- It may be masked, minimized, and overlooked during childhood.
- Symptoms wax and wane with female hormonal fluctuations.
- Symptoms increase as structure decreases (leaving home for college, for example) and as demands increase (marrying and having children).

CHAPTER SUMMARY

In this chapter, we have

- Counseled that DSM-5 TR diagnostic criteria need to be viewed with gender in mind and that just using a list of symptoms doesn't always capture women's experiences and impairments.
- Suggested ADHD scales and structured interviews that can aid in diagnosis.
- Provided comprehensive interview tools and self-rating scales and encouraged their use as part of the diagnostic process. However, it is important to note that these only help elicit the symptoms and don' t focus on the more important day-to-day functioning issues each woman with ADHD must face.
- Recommended rating the diagnosis as mild, moderate, or severe, and highlighted that only five symptoms are needed for the diagnosis in anyone over 17 years old, versus the six symptoms previously required to diagnose adults with ADHD.
- Discussed whether, and when, more in-depth neuropsychological testing may be warranted, especially in cases when a woman has learning or cognitive issues.

However, we also discussed why neuropsychological testing is **not** required for ADHD diagnosis and that neuropsychological testing **alone** can not make an accurate diagnosis of ADHD.

We recommend adopting a focus on a woman's lived experience of ADHD, and NOT merely on her symptoms, so that you can better recognize the greater mental health adversities and risks that going undiagnosed presents for women. If left untreated, ADHD can negatively impact a woman's quality of life in many areas, including employment, finances, relationships, and mental health. However, early intervention and treatment can help lessen the potential adverse consequences of untreated ADHD.

Women have been overlooked in the ADHD landscape for far too long. We need to acknowledge that the disorder exists in women in greater numbers than previously thought and that although symptoms may present differently in women, they are just as impairing; maybe more so, as they insidiously wreak havoc in a woman's life. While symptoms may be masked, there is no such thing as "ADHD-lite" in women!

REFERENCES

1. Staley, B. S. (2024). Attention-deficit/hyperactivity disorder diagnosis, treatment, and telehealth use in adults—National center for health statistics rapid surveys system, United States, October–November 2023. *MMWR. Morbidity and Mortality Weekly Report, 73*.
2. Kessler, R. C., Adler, L., Barkley, R., Biederman, J., Conners, C. K., Demler, O., Faraone, S. V., Greenhill, L. L., Howes, M. J., Secnik, K., Spencer, T., Ustun, T. B., Walters, E., & Zaslavsky, A. M. (2006). The prevalence and correlates of adult ADHD in the United States: results from the National Comorbidity Survey Replication. *The American Journal of Psychiatry, 163*(4), 716–723. https://doi.org/10.1176/ajp.2006.163.4.716
3. American Psychiatric Association. (2022). *Diagnostic and statistical manual of mental disorders* (5th ed., text rev.). https://doi.org/10.1176/appi.books.9780890425787
4. Skogli, E. W., Teicher, M. H., Andersen, P. N., Hovik, K. T., & Øie, M. (2013). ADHD in girls and boys—gender differences in co-existing symptoms and executive function measures. *BMC Psychiatry, 13*(1), 298. https://doi.org/10.1186/1471-244X-13-298
5. Fairman, K. A., Peckham, A. M., & Sclar, D. A. (2017). Diagnosis and treatment of ADHD in the United States: update by gender and race. *Journal of Attention Disorders, 24*(1), 10–19. https://doi.org/10.1177/1087054716688534 (Original work published in 2020).
6. London, A. S., & Landes, S. D. (2019). Cohort change in the prevalence of ADHD among US adults: evidence of a gender-specific historical period effect. *Journal of Attention Disorders, 25*(6), 771–782. https://doi.org/10.1177/1087054719855689 (Original work published 2021)
7. Song, P., Zha, M., Yang, Q., Zhang, Y., Li, X., Rudan, I., & Global Health Epidemiology Reference Group (GHERG) (2021). The prevalence of adult attention-deficit hyperactivity disorder: a global systematic review and meta-analysis. *Journal of Global Health, 11*, 04009. https://doi.org/10.7189/jogh.11.04009

8. Fuller-Thomson, E., Lewis, D., & Agbeyaka, S. (2016). Attention-deficit/hyperactivity disorder casts a long shadow: findings from a population-based study of adult women with self-reported ADHD. *Child: Care, Health and Development*, *42*(6), 918–927. https://doi.org/10.1111/cch.12380
9. Accardo, A. L., Pontes, N. M. H., & Pontes, M. C. F. (2024). Heightened anxiety and depression among autistic adolescents with ADHD: findings from the National Survey of Children's Health 2016–2019. *Journal of Autism and Developmental Disorders*, *54*(2), 563–576. https://doi.org/10.1007/s10803-022-05803-9
10. Fuller-Thomson, E., Lewis, D. A., & Agbeyaka, S. K. (2016). Attention-deficit/hyperactivity disorder casts a long shadow: findings from a population-based study of adult women with self-reported ADHD. *Child: Care, Health and Development*, *42*(6), 918–927. https://doi.org/10.1111/cch.12380
11. Martin, J., Taylor, M. J., Rydell, M., Riglin, L., Eyre, O., Lu, Y., Lundström, S., Larsson, H., Thapar, A., & Lichtenstein, P. (2018). Sex-specific manifestation of genetic risk for attention deficit hyperactivity disorder in the general population. *Journal of Child Psychology and Psychiatry, and Allied Disciplines*, *59*(8), 908–916. https://doi.org/10.1111/jcpp.12874
12. Hayashi, W., Suzuki, H., Saga, N., Arai, G., Igarashi, R., Tokumasu, T., Ota, H., Yamada, H., Takashio, O., & Iwanami, A. (2019). Clinical characteristics of women with ADHD in Japan. *Neuropsychiatric Disease and Treatment*, *15*, 3367–3374. https://doi.org/10.2147/NDT.S232565
13. Gilbert, M., Boecker, M., Reiss, F., Kaman, A., Erhart, M., Schlack, R., Westenhöfer, J., Döpfner, M., & Ravens-Sieberer, U. (2025). Gender and age differences in ADHD symptoms and co-occurring depression and anxiety symptoms among children and adolescents in the BELLA study. *Child Psychiatry and Human Development*, *56*(4), 1162–1172. https://doi.org/10.1007/s10578-023-01622-w
14. American Psychiatric Association. (2013). *Diagnostic and statistical manual of mental disorders (5th ed.)*. Arlington, VA: American Psychiatric Association.
15. American Psychiatric Association. (2022). *Diagnostic and statistical manual of mental disorders*.
16. Chakrabarty, A., Javadekar, A., & Chakrabarty, A. (2023). Diagnostic and statistical manual of mental disorders text revision—5th edition: What's changed from diagnostic and statistical manual of mental disorders—5th edition? A detailed review. *Annals of Indian Psychiatry*, 7(3), 283–287. https://doi.org/10.4103/aip.aip_152_22
17. First, M., Yousif, L., Clarke, D., Wang, P., Gogtay, N., & Appelbaum, P. (2022). DSM-5-TR: an overview of what's new and what's changed. *World Psychiatry*, *21*(2), 218–219. https://doi.org/10.1002/wps.20989
18. First, M., Clarke, D., Yousif, L., Eng, A., Gogtay, N., & Appelbaum, P. (2023). DSM-5-TR: rationale, process, and overview of changes. *Psychiatric Services*, *74*(8), 869–875. https://doi.org/10.1176/appi.ps.20220334
19. Vitola, E. S., Bau, C. H., Salum, G. A., Horta, B. L., Quevedo, L., Barros, F. C., Pinheiro, R. T., Kieling, C., Rohde, L. A., & Grevet, E. H. (2017). Exploring DSM-5 ADHD criteria beyond young adulthood: phenomenology, psychometric properties and prevalence in a large three-decade birth cohort. *Psychological Medicine*, *47*(4), 744–754. https://doi.org/10.1017/S0033291716002853
20. Kandeğer, A. (2025). Overlapping spectrum of impulsivity and compulsivity across psychiatric disorders: a narrative review on dimensional perspectives. *The Eurasian Journal of Medicine*, *57*(2), e24749. https://doi.org/10.5152/eurasianjmed.2025.24749
21. American Psychiatric Association. (2022). *Diagnostic and statistical manual of mental disorders* (5th ed., text rev.). https://doi.org/10.1176/appi.books.9780890425787
22. Adamis, D., Flynn, C., Wrigley, M., Gavin, B., & McNicholas, F. (2022). ADHD in adults: a systematic review and meta-analysis of prevalence studies in outpatient

psychiatric clinics. *Journal of Attention Disorders, 26*(12), 1523–1534. https://doi.org/10.1177/10870547221085503

23. Deberdt, W., Thome, J., Lebrec, J., Kraemer, S., Fregenal, I., Ramos-Quiroga, J. A., & Arif, M. (2015). Prevalence of ADHD in nonpsychotic adult psychiatric care (ADPSYC): a multinational cross-sectional study in Europe. *BMC Psychiatry, 15*, 242. https://doi.org/10.1186/s12888-015-0624-5
24. Adamis, D., Flynn, C., Wrigley, M., Gavin, B., & McNicholas, F. (2022). ADHD in adults: a systematic review and meta-analysis of prevalence studies in outpatient psychiatric clinics. *Journal of Attention Disorders, 26*(12), 1523–1534. https://doi.org/10.1177/10870547221085503
25. Vitola, E. S., Bau, C. H., Salum, G. A., Horta, B. L., Quevedo, L., Barros, F. C., Pinheiro, R. T., Kieling, C., Rohde, L. A., & Grevet, E. H. (2017). Exploring DSM-5 ADHD criteria beyond young adulthood: phenomenology, psychometric properties and prevalence in a large three-decade birth cohort. *Psychological Medicine, 47*(4), 744–754. https://doi.org/10.1017/S0033291716002853
26. Kandeğer, A. (2025). Overlapping spectrum of impulsivity and compulsivity across psychiatric disorders: a narrative review on dimensional perspectives. *The Eurasian Journal of Medicine, 57*(2), e24749. https://doi.org/10.5152/eurasianjmed.2025.24749
27. Schiavone, N., Virta, M., Leppämäki, S., Launes, J., Vanninen, R., Tuulio-Henriksson, A., Immonen, S., Järvinen, I., Lehto, E., Michelsson, K., & Hokkanen, L. (2019). ADHD and subthreshold symptoms in childhood and life outcomes at 40 years in a prospective birth-risk cohort. *Psychiatry Research, 281*, 112574. https://doi.org/10.1016/j.psychres.2019.112574
28. Sibley, M. H., Rohde, L. A., Swanson, J. M., Hechtman, L. T., Molina, B. S. G., Mitchell, J. T., Arnold, L. E., Caye, A., Kennedy, T. M., Roy, A., Stehli, A., & Multimodal Treatment Study of Children with ADHD (MTA) Cooperative Group (2018). Late-onset ADHD reconsidered comprehensive repeated assessments between ages 10 and 25. *The American Journal of Psychiatry, 175*(2), 140–149. https://doi.org/10.1176/appi.ajp.2017.17030298
29. Lynch, A., & Davison, K. (2024). Gendered expectations on the recognition of ADHD in young women and educational implications. *Irish Educational Studies, 43*(1), 61–81.
30. Morley, E., & Tyrrell, A. (2023). Exploring female students' experiences of ADHD and its impact on social, academic, and psychological functioning. *Journal of Attention Disorders, 27*(10), 1129–1155. https://doi.org/10.1177/10870547231168432
31. Skoglund, C., Sundström Poromaa, I., Leksell, D., Ekholm Selling, K., Cars, T., Giacobini, M., Young, S., & Kopp Kallner, H. (2024). Time after time: failure to identify and support females with ADHD—a Swedish population register study. *Journal of Child Psychology & Psychiatry, 65*, 832–844. https://doi.org/10.1111/jcpp.13920
32. Smith, Z. R. (2024). Inclusion and advocacy for women with ADHD: addressing inequities and challenging diagnostic bias on International Women's Day. *The Association for Child and Adolescent Mental Health Blog Series*. https://doi.org/10.13056/acamh.26609
33. Kandeğer, A., Güler, H. A., Özaltın, M. S., Bayırlı, Ö., Söylemez, H., Yıldız, E., & Semerci, B. (2025). Could maladaptive daydreaming delay ADHD diagnosis until adulthood? Clinical characteristics of adults with ADHD based on diagnosis age. *Journal of Attention Disorders, 29*(5), 387–396.
34. Magnante, A. T., Ord, A. S., Kuschel, S., & Shura, R. D. (2024). An evaluation of the relationship between objective and subjective measures of attention. *Psychology & Neuroscience, 17*(2), 104–121. https://doi.org/10.1037/pne0000333

35. Bottini, S., Polizzi, C., Vizgaitis, A., Ellenberg, S., & Krantweiss, A. (2019). When measures diverge: the intersection of psychometric instruments and clinical judgment in multimodal adult attention-deficit/hyperactivity disorder assessment. *Professional Psychology Research and Practice, 50*(6), 353–363. https://doi.org/10.1037/pro0000248
36. Hayashi, W., Suzuki, H., Saga, N., Arai, G., Igarashi, R., Tokumasu, T., Ota, H., Yamada, H., Takashio, O., & Iwanami, A. (2019). Clinical characteristics of women with ADHD in Japan. *Neuropsychiatric Disease and Treatment, 15*, 3367–3374. https://doi.org/10.2147/NDT.S232565
37. Powell, V., Martin, J., Thapar, A., Rice, F., & Anney, R. J. (2021). Investigating regions of shared genetic variation in attention deficit/hyperactivity disorder and major depressive disorder: GWAS meta-analysis. *Scientific Reports, 11*(1), 7353.
38. Powell, V., Agha, S. S., Jones, R. B., Eyre, O., Stephens, A., Weavers, B., Lennon, J., Allardyce, J., Potter, R., Smith, D., Thapar, A., & Rice, F. (2021). ADHD in adults with recurrent depression. *Journal of Affective Disorders, 295*, 1153–1160. https://doi.org/10.1016/j.jad.2021.09.010
39. Hayashi, W., Suzuki, H., Saga, N., Aral, G., Igarashi, R., Tokumasu, T., Ota, H., Yamada, H., Takashio, O. & Iwanami, A. (2019). Clinical characteristics of women with ADHD in Japan. *Neuropsychiatric Disease and Treatment, 15*, 3367–3374. https://doi.org/10.2147/NDT.S232565
40. Musullulu, H. (2025). Evaluating attention deficit and hyperactivity disorder (ADHD): a review of current methods and issues. *Frontiers of Psychology, 16*:1466088.
41. Smith, Z. R. (2024). Inclusion and advocacy for women with ADHD: addressing inequities and challenging diagnostic bias on International Women's Day. *The Association for Child and Adolescent Mental Health Blog Series*. https://doi.org/10.13056/acamh.26609
42. Skoglund, C., Sundström Poromaa, I., Leksell, D., Ekholm Selling, K., Cars, T., Giacobini, M., Young, S., & Kopp Kallner, H. (2024). Time after time: failure to identify and support females with ADHD - a Swedish population register study. *Journal of child psychology and psychiatry, and allied disciplines, 65*(6), 832–844. https://doi.org/10.1111/jcpp.13920
43. Powell, V., Agha, S. S., Jones, R. B., Eyre, O., Stephens, A., Weavers, B., Lennon, J., Allardyce, J., Potter, R., Smith, D., Thapar, A., & Rice, F. (2021). ADHD in adults with recurrent depression. *Journal of Affective Disorders, 295*, 1153–1160. https://doi.org/10.1016/j.jad.2021.09.010
44. Hayashi, W., Suzuki, H., Saga, N., Aral, G., Igarashi, R., Tokumasu, T., Ota, H., Yamada, H., Takashio, O. & Iwanami, A. (2019). Clinical characteristics of women with ADHD in Japan. *Neuropsychiatric Disease and Treatment, 15*, 3367–3374. https://doi.org/10.2147/NDT.S232565
45. Smith, Z.R. (2024). Inclusion and advocacy for women with ADHD: addressing inequities and challenging diagnostic bias on International Women's Day. *The Association for Child and Adolescent Mental Health Blog Series*. https://doi.org/10.13056/acamh.26609
46. Zamani, L., Shahrivar, Z., Alaghband-Rad, J., Sharifi, V., Davoodi, E., Ansari, S., Emari, F., Wynchank, D., Kooji, J. S., & Asherson, P. (2021). Reliability, criterion and concurrent validity of the Farsi translation of DIVA-5: a semi-structured diagnostic interview for adults with ADHD. *Journal of Attention Disorders, 25*(12), 1666–1675. https://doi.org/10.1177/1087054720930816
47. Quinn, P. O., & Nadeau, K. G. (2000). *Women's ADHD self-inventory*. Advantage Books.
48. Canu, W. H., Hartung, C. M., Stevens, A. E., & Lefler, E. K. (2020). Psychometric properties of the Weiss functional impairment rating scale: evidence for utility in

research, assessment, and treatment of ADHD in emerging adults. *Journal of Attention Disorders*, *24*(12), 1648–1660. https://doi.org/10.1177/1087054716661421

49. Sasser, T., Schoenfelder, E.N. & Stein, M.A. (2017). Targeting functional impairments in the treatment of children and adolescents with ADHD. *CNS Drugs*, *31*, 97–107. https://doi.org/10.1007/s40263-016-0400-1
50. Mesulam, M. (2002). The human frontal lobes: transcending the default mode through contingent encoding. In D. T. Stuss & R. T. Knight (Eds.), *Principles of frontal lobe function* (pp. 8–30). Oxford University Press. https://doi.org/10.1093/acprof:oso/9780195134971.003.0002
51. Hanssen, K. T., Brevik, E. J., Småstuen, M. C., & Stubberud, J. (2023). Improvement of anxiety in ADHD following goal-focused cognitive remediation: a randomized controlled trial. *Frontiers in Psychology*, *14*, 1212502.
52. Hutt Vater, C., DiSalvo, M., Ehrlich, A., Parker, H., O'Connor, H., Faraone, S. V., & Biederman, J. (2024). ADHD in adults: does age at diagnosis matter? *Journal of Attention Disorders*, *28*(5), 614–624. https://doi.org/10.1177/10870547231218450
53. Takahashi, N., Ono, T., Omori, Y., Iizumi, M., Kato, H., Kasuno, S., Persing, B. & Tsuchiya, K. J. (2024). Assessment of executive functions using a 3D-video game in children and adolescents with ADHD. *Frontiers in Psychiatry*, *15*: 1407703. https://doi.org/10.3389/fpsyt.2024.1407703
54. Zhu, Y., Liu, S., Zhang, F., Ren, Y., Zhang, T., Sun, J., Wang, X., Wang, L., & Yang, J. (2023) Response inhibition in children with different subtypes/presentations of attention deficit hyperactivity disorder: a near-infrared spectroscopy study. *Frontiers in Neuroscience*, 17, 1119289. https://doi.org/10.3389/fnins.2023.1119289
55. Chen, H., Yang, Y., Odisho, D., Wu, S., Yi, C., & Oliver, B. G. (2023). Can biomarkers be used to diagnose attention deficit hyperactivity disorder? *Frontiers in Psychiatry*, *14*, 1026616. https://doi.org/10.3389/fpsyt.2023.1026616
56. Fuermaier, A. B. M., Gontijo-Santos Lima, C., & Tucha, O. (2024). Impairment assessment in adult ADHD and related disorders: current opinions from clinic and research. *Journal of Attention Disorders*, *28*(12), 1529–1541. https://doi.org/10.1177/10870547241261598
57. Becke, M., Tucha, L., Butzbach, M., Aschenbrenner, S., Weisbrod, M., Tucha, O., & Fuermaier, A. B. M. (2023). Feigning adult ADHD on a comprehensive neuropsychological test battery: an analogue study. *International Journal of Environmental Research and Public Health*, *20*(5), 4070. https://doi.org/10.3390/ijerph20054070
58. Prentice, J. L., Schaeffer, M. J., Wall, A. K., & Callahan, B. L. (2021). A systematic review and comparison of neurocognitive features of late-life attention-deficit/hyperactivity disorder and dementia with Lewy bodies. *Journal of Geriatric Psychiatry and Neurology*, *34*(5), 466–481. https://doi.org/10.1177/0891988720944251
59. Fuermaier, A. B. M., Gontijo-Santos Lima, C., & Tucha, O. (2024). Impairment assessment in adult ADHD and related disorders: current opinions from clinic and research. *Journal of Attention Disorders*, *28*(12), 1529–1541. https://doi.org/10.1177/10870547241261598 (Original work published 2024)
60. Belirgan, S., Ersoy, M. A., & Topçu Ersoy, H. (2017). Prevalence of adult attention deficit hyperactivity disorder and comorbid axis-I disorders among first-time applied cases of a general psychiatry outpatient clinic and a private psychotherapy centre. *Psychiatry and Clinical Psychopharmacology*, *28*(1), 25–35. https://doi.org/10.1080/24750573.2017.1384194

CHAPTER 3

Diagnostic complexity

Co-occurring psychiatric conditions

INTRODUCTION

Co-occurring psychiatric conditions are the rule rather than the exception among adults with attention-deficit/hyperactivity disorder (ADHD), and even more so for women. Statistics vary widely regarding the frequency of these co-occurring conditions, but generally speaking, at least 95% of adults with ADHD have at least one co-occurring psychiatric condition. What's more, these commonly co-occurring conditions occur 1.5 to 10 times more often in adults with ADHD than adults without ADHD.[1] Women with ADHD experience an even greater burden, due in part to the harmful effects of late ADHD diagnosis combined with inequitable societal expectations of females[2] (also see Chapter 10). Hormonal factors, which are also central to the experience of women with ADHD and are often overlooked, are addressed in Chapter 8.

CASE ILLUSTRATION: REBECCA

Rebecca is a 39-year-old woman who works as an attorney and is married with twin preschool boys. Her initial presenting concerns included low mood, anxiety, difficulty falling asleep and waking up on time, and problems with concentration and procrastination. While her wife Tanya sought to be a helpful partner and parent, Tanya travels for work more weeks of the year than not, leaving the burden of childcare and household management to largely fall on Rebecca's shoulders.

DOI: 10.4324/9781003542124-3

A typical day starts with difficulty rising and "booting up" her brain and an "overwhelming and chaotic" rush to get her kids out the door and to school on time. She works at a prestigious law firm and is well regarded for her intellect, affability, and quick wit. Although she has always had difficulty keeping track of documents and starting work in time to complete it without a frenetic rush, her work product had historically been excellent. Since the birth of her twins, her work performance has been less consistent, and she has been unable to reliably meet her own high standards.

Her evenings are "almost as bad as the mornings," juggling work emails and corralling the kids to the dinner table and to bed. Post-bedtime efforts to manage parenting and household tasks further add to her overwhelm. When she drops the ball on these, she feels shame that compounds an underlying sense of sadness. She scrolls on her phone for "too long" before trying to fall asleep in an often unsuccessful effort to distract herself from racing and anxious thoughts.

Rebecca describes experiences of discrimination at work, such as when clients ignore her contributions and give junior male colleagues all the credit for winning cases. At church, she feels that members of the informal "mom networks" exclude her, judging her for being married to a woman. In general, there is no place in her life outside of home where she feels appreciated and accepted.

Rebecca reports that she was a good student who didn't need to try too hard. She acknowledged making simple mistakes and sometimes turning her schoolwork in late, but because she clearly understood the assigned material her teachers gave her a pass. She does recall being criticized for being "un-ladylike" because she was outspoken and liked competitive sports on the playground.

If Rebecca asked for your recommendations as to how she could feel better, you might recommend an antidepressant and/or therapy to target symptoms of depression and anxiety, and you might also offer sleep medication. In addition, you might encourage her to expand her support system, for example getting help to reduce her overload from household management and parenting responsibilities. You would discuss with her that discrimination was an important factor impacting her health and would support her efforts to combat its effects.

If you were *not knowledgeable* about female ADHD, you would lack an understanding of how Rebecca's ADHD might be a central element in her presentation that substantially explains the emergence and perpetuation of her other challenges. In the context of her academic successes and lack of behavioral problems in childhood, you might rule out ADHD. You might not realize that a bright, minimally disruptive girl with ADHD can slide by unnoticed by teachers. And you would then miss that ADHD must be addressed for Rebecca to achieve good mental health and overall well-being.

The purpose of this chapter is to help you look deeper when faced with a case that is not straightforward, and to think carefully about diagnostic complexity from multiple perspectives. ADHD, co-occurring conditions, and their interactions must be understood for treatment to be effective.

THE CHICKEN OR THE EGG, WHICH CONDITION CAME FIRST? USUALLY, ADHD

When a woman presents with multiple conditions, it can be helpful to determine which developed first. This applies to both psychiatric and nonpsychiatric conditions. For instance, when dehydration and headaches coexist, it is important to recognize dehydration as the primary issue, since treating it often resolves the headache. Similarly, a woman with social anxiety and depression might learn in therapy that her depression stems from chronic social anxiety that resulted in isolation, loneliness, and ultimately depression. In such a case, our treatment would focus on alleviating her anxiety and strategies to build relationships, which may alleviate her depression as well.

ADHD is a neurodevelopmental condition with symptoms usually emerging in early-to-mid childhood (keeping in mind that such symptoms may be present but overlooked). By contrast, most disorders that commonly co-occur with ADHD arise in later childhood, adolescence, or young adulthood (with autism as a prominent exception). Thus, when considering which condition came first, the answer is: ADHD probably did!

The prominent ADHD expert, Michael Jellinek, MD, has estimated that children with ADHD may receive 20,000 negative comments from their teachers by the age of 10.[3] Given the highly differing expectations of conscientiousness, social skillfulness, and rule-following placed on girls compared to boys, negative feedback from teachers (and peers, and family members!) may well be harsher for girls.[4]

ADHD behaviors in boys are sometimes commented upon with "boys will be boys," while girls' ADHD behaviors are decidedly not viewed as appropriate, or as to be expected for girls. Anxiety, depression, and other conditions can then emerge as a result of these repeated negative experiences. Girls with inattentive-type ADHD who are criticized for behavior adults see as careless, messy, or lazy may develop anxiety and obsessive perfectionism to defend against shame and embarrassment, while those with a more hyperactive/impulsive presentation, whose behaviors are often labeled inappropriate and unfeminine, may use angry outbursts to cloak deep sadness.[5,6] As Steve Hinshaw's extensive research on girls with ADHD has documented, few girls with ADHD find comfortable peer acceptance.[7] As Hinshaw describes it, hyperactive/impulsive girls are socially "rejected," while inattentive girls are socially "neglected" (i.e., left out and ignored).

In the following pages, we will introduce some of the most common co-occurring conditions and how to address them through an ADHD-informed lens.

ANXIETY AND ANXIETY-RELATED PERFECTIONISM

ADHD and anxiety co-occur in women via multiple pathways. One prominent pathway is the development of anxiety and anxiety-related problems in response to ADHD-associated mistakes in academic, work, and social contexts.[8,9]

As noted earlier, children with ADHD may receive 20,000 negative comments from their teachers alone by age 10. For many women with ADHD, these childhood experiences are compounded by continued negative feedback in adulthood. Studies of adult and late-diagnosed women document frequent experiences of stigma and social criticism related to their ADHD-associated difficulties. Gendered expectations of orderliness, emotion regulation, social skillfulness, and rule-following expand the distance between a woman's executive function capabilities and societal expectations, often engendering harsher feedback for mistakes than a male might receive under the same circumstances.[10]

In response to their ADHD challenges and the persistent criticism that these challenges generate, women often adopt rigid organizational systems, excessive checking routines, and intense self-monitoring in work and social situations. They worry and ruminate over what may seem to be a minor comment or misunderstanding with a female friend and cringe when they realize after the fact that they have sent an important work email that contained spelling errors. These women's over-preparation, hypervigilant self-monitoring, and people-pleasing behaviors initially serve as deliberate compensatory strategies to prevent errors or interpersonal missteps, masking underlying ADHD symptoms.[11] Over the course of time, however, such strategies can become maladaptive, escalating into clinical perfectionism.

ADHD and perfectionism: Key differences

Many women with ADHD develop highly ritualized coping mechanisms to counteract forgetfulness, inattention to detail, or time management issues, which may resemble perfectionism. However, unlike clinical perfectionism, where individuals use the same coping strategies in multiple areas of their lives, these rituals are developed to achieve positive outcomes in specific situations and are used only when necessary. In fact, many professional women with ADHD report that no one at work would ever suspect their ADHD due to these self-management routines. They report, however, that their behavior at home, where they are not under the watchful or judging eyes of colleagues, is a very different story. These women find their hyper-organization is burdensome and is a great relief to leave behind when they enter their front door. By contrast, a woman with clinical perfectionism (but not ADHD) is more likely to have rigid routines that pervade her life and high internal expectations for nearly all tasks—regardless of their importance.

Treatment response can also be informative. Stimulant medication treatment is likely to improve ADHD symptoms and subsequently allow for a softening of perfectionistic behaviors that emerge from ADHD. It is through a similar mechanism that ADHD treatment sometimes improves anxiety as well. However, if the fundamental issue is clinical perfectionism, it is unlikely that stimulants alone will be substantially helpful.[12]

Overlapping symptoms

ADHD and anxiety can also co-occur and share overlapping symptoms. These include concentration problems, sleep difficulties, mental and physical restlessness, emotion regulation challenges, and problems with task initiation/procrastination. Because these features can arise from either condition, distinguishing between them can be difficult, particularly when the onset and course of symptoms are unclear.

Symptom overlaps and distinctions: as illustrated by the Venn diagram in Figure 3.1, there is substantial overlap between the symptoms of ADHD and anxiety.

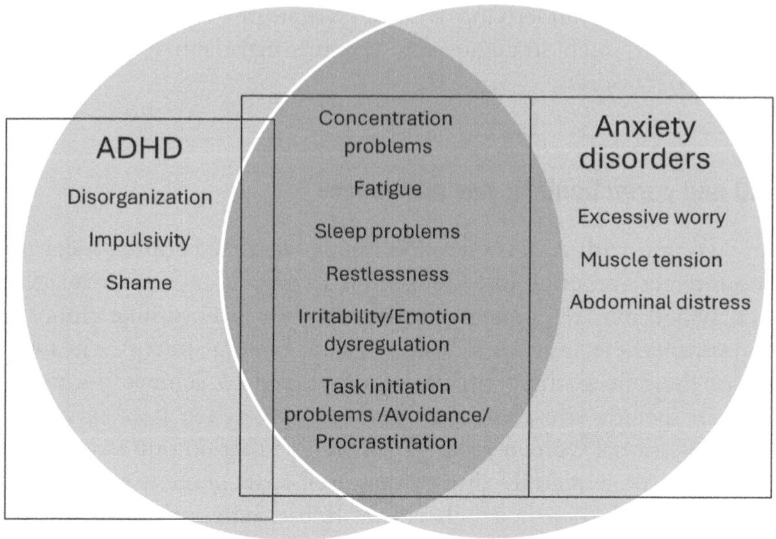

Figure 3.1 Symptom overlaps and distinctions

Created by Michael Morse

Among those symptoms that occur in both anxiety and ADHD, it is sometimes possible to identify the symptom as primarily growing out of either ADHD or anxiety because of its associated features.

For example, **difficulty concentrating** is a central feature of both ADHD and generalized anxiety. However, the phenomenology of concentration problems often differs between these conditions:

- In anxiety, the "worried mind" is preoccupied with anxious rumination and self-monitoring. Intrusive concerns (e.g., "Did I make a mistake?" or "What if I fail?") consume mental resources, undermining focus on the task at hand.
- In ADHD, internal distractibility or a "busy mind" is more prominent. The mind sometimes wanders productively, as its interweaving of ideas leads to creativity and innovation. At other times, internal distraction involves the mind darting from one mundane thing to another—not daydreaming or being creative—but just, "oh yes, I left my coffee cup in the bedroom; oh, I need to write 'milk' on the grocery list," or "Oh no, I forgot to email Emily last night."

Another overlapping symptom is **irritability** or a quickness to anger, which can emerge in both anxiety and ADHD. When irritability is part of an anxiety response, it often mobilizes the "fight" aspect of the classic fight-or-flight reaction—a stressed, over-aroused state wherein minor frustrations trigger disproportionate anger or panic. In contrast, irritability stemming from ADHD alone often involves poor impulse control and broader emotion regulation deficits, where anger flares in response to internal distress and external triggers that are not threats.[13,14]

PROCRASTINATION

Procrastination, difficulty initiating tasks, is a common self-regulation problem in which an individual opts for short-term emotional relief through avoidance, often at the expense of long-term goals and overall well-being.[15] When faced with unpleasant tasks—whether anxiety-provoking, boring, or otherwise undesirable—a woman typically experiences a negative emotional state. She can respond by confronting the task directly or by avoiding it. Avoidance offers immediate relief from negative emotions, but it often undermines future goal attainment, stress management, and well-being.[16,17] You may have treated anxious women who procrastinate and, as a result, come to associate procrastination with anxiety. In fact, however, both anxiety and ADHD are common causes of procrastination in women.

While task-initiation problems may stem from anxiety, ADHD, or both, the mechanisms differ. **In anxiety-driven procrastination, a woman is "pushed away" by distress**—fear of failure, not knowing how to begin, and feelings of overwhelm. Procrastination offers temporary relief from anticipated negative outcomes.[18] A woman may think: "I just can't stand to do it right now, I'll come back when I'm more in the mood," and then distract herself with other activities that aren't distressing. This cycle can become self-perpetuating, with avoidance confirming the individual's fears of inadequacy.

Executive functioning challenges can also play a strong role in task avoidance. When a task seems complicated and difficult to organize, putting off the task also delays feelings of overwhelm and confusion as she struggles to organize and prioritize elements of a complex task.

Low internal motivation is another ADHD factor leading to task avoidance. Tasks may be avoided not because they are anxiety-provoking but because people with ADHD find them unengaging. The task may seem too large or too tedious to accomplish after a long and fatiguing day. In ADHD, avoidance often reflects difficulty generating internal motivation for unstimulating tasks.

ADHD-related time distortion may also play a role in task avoidance. Russell Barkley[19] has described how people with ADHD often experience a distortion of time, underestimating how long tasks will take and putting off undesirable tasks because there is always "later." But there are other ways in which their sense of time is distorted; for example, they may become so immersed in a task that they have little awareness of the passage of time, and experience a feeling of "where did the time go?" after doing an engaging task. The "not-now" time frame represents a distant, abstract future in which there is "plenty of time," and which does not seem relevant enough to influence behavior in the "now." Some women with ADHD use the anxiety and adrenaline rush caused by a looming deadline to disrupt their avoidance and apathy. It's as if they are "treating" their ADHD with adrenaline to get the task done—whether it's completing a tax return, paying a bill, or getting that report done that is due in the morning.

For women with significant levels of impulsivity, there is another powerful factor preventing them from doing "what ought to be done." For them, boredom is not just unpleasant, it is actually painful, causing a stress response including elevated heart rate and cortisol levels.[20] Both executive function challenges leading to cognitive overwhelm (for complex tasks) and boredom are negative states that cause a woman with ADHD to avoid or delay initiating many of the tasks required to lead a functional life.[21,22]

CASE ILLUSTRATION: WHEN ADHD CAUSES PROCRASTINATION, WORRY ONLY ARISES WHEN THE NEGATIVE CONSEQUENCES ARE IMMINENT

Rebecca's case illustrates several points related to anxiety and procrastination. Her anxiety is rooted in specific, real concerns: she worries about missing work deadlines and being seen in a negative light when her kids are repeatedly late for school. You might attribute her perpetual worry to generalized anxiety alone, but a deeper understanding reveals that the frustrations and chaos she experiences each day due to her poor executive functioning skills are driving her anxiety. Rebecca does not simply feel anxious before a major deadline (as one might in "pure" anxiety); rather, she feels anxious because she has lost track of the deadline, failed to organize the work in advance, or procrastinated. In other words, her anxiety exists primarily in response to chaos created by ADHD.

Rarely able to meet all the various demands of each day, Rebecca lives in a state of nagging anxiety. And when the negative results of her task mismanagement and procrastination arrive, it triggers depression, low self-esteem and a pervasive feeling of shame. "What's wrong with me? Why can't I just get it together?" she repeatedly asks herself. Rebecca's anxiety cannot be adequately treated without also identifying and treating her ADHD, the underlying cause of her chronic distress.

DEPRESSION

Depression in women with ADHD often arises in response to ongoing demoralization. A feeling that no matter how hard they try, they are unable to succeed. Their chronic failures in managing the demands of daily life, their inability to control their emotional overreactions that arise from relentless stress, and the never-ending stressors in their lives take their toll. They develop feelings of hopelessness and a sense of being perpetually overburdened that over time moves beyond demoralization to depression—particularly when ADHD is undiagnosed or untreated.[23,24] Emotional dysregulation, a core feature of ADHD that is not yet officially recognized, is strongly associated with the severity of depression and may be the link between ADHD and depression.[25]

For many women, the absence of an ADHD diagnosis delays treatment causing their self-defeating coping strategies and negative image to become chronic. And when a woman in this state, with undiagnosed ADHD, finally seeks treatment, a clinician will typically focus on her depression while her underlying ADHD remains unaddressed. Understanding the role of ADHD in causing her depression is essential for effective treatment.

Of course, depression and ADHD can coexist, and both may need to be treated. When feelings of sadness, hopelessness, and loss of interest develop, depressive disorder not secondary to ADHD is present.

When trying to distinguish depression from ADHD-induced depression, it is helpful to remember that depression unrelated to ADHD is typically episodic, while depression associated with ADHD is more likely to be lifelong. We should always consider the possibility of ADHD in all women with depression, and especially in any woman with recurrent depressive episodes or treatment-resistant depression. Other clues that ADHD underlies a woman's depression include substantial problems with taking medication consistently and frequent late arrivals or missed clinic visits.

It's worth noting that there is evidence of a higher rate of Seasonal Affective Disorder among women with ADHD, which makes it important to inquire about recurring depression that is cyclical with the seasons.[26,27]

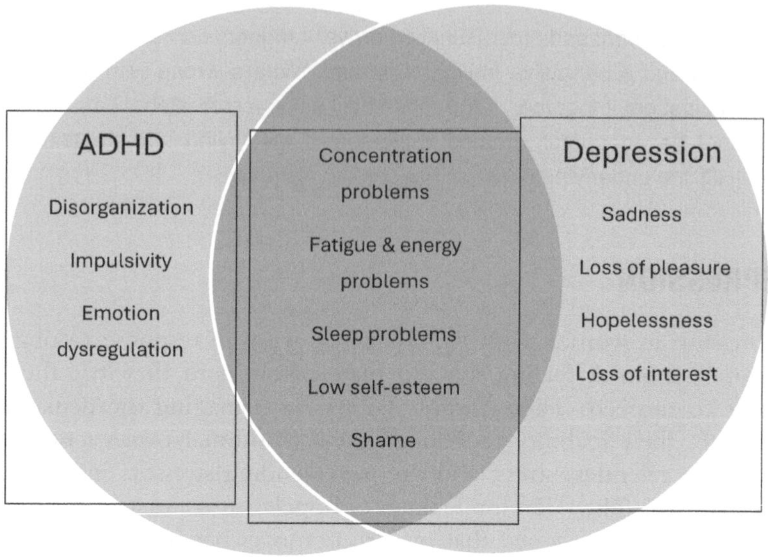

Figure 3.2 A simplified list of depression and ADHD symptoms

Created by Michael Morse

Figure 3.2 depicts a simplified list of depression and ADHD symptoms in a Venn diagram.

In this Venn diagram, we can see that we should expect co-occurrence (or comorbidity) between depression and ADHD—not only because of a causal pathway between ADHD and depression, but also because of symptom overlap.

Self-harm: Suicidal behavior and non-suicidal self-injury

Women with ADHD are more prone to non-suicidal self-injury (NSSI) and suicidal behavior compared to women without ADHD. One 10-year prospective study found that young women with childhood ADHD had a suicide attempt rate of 22%, compared to only 6% in women without childhood ADHD—nearly four times the rate. NSSI was also much more prevalent, with over 50% of women with combined-type ADHD reporting self-injury compared to 19% of women without ADHD. Risks were particularly concentrated in women with a combined presentation, reflecting the role of impulsivity in self-harm behaviors.[28] Importantly, NSSI is also related to histories of childhood trauma, negative parenting, and exposure to violence.[29,30]

NSSI often begins in early adolescence as an effort to regulate overwhelming emotions, engage in self-punishment, temporarily alleviate a crushing sense of powerlessness, and, in some cases, to communicate the intensity of suicidal feelings. Self-harm tends to be impulsive and carried out in secrecy, and is often influenced by the self-harm episodes of peers.[31] Wrist cutting is a predominant form of NSSI among adolescents and young adults. Clinicians treating adolescents or young adult women should look for signs that they are hiding their wrists, such as by always wearing long-sleeved shirts, even in warm or hot weather. Importantly, NSSI in teens strongly predicts later suicide attempts, which highlights the importance of early detection and treatment.[32]

Shame

Shame is not a psychiatric diagnosis, but it is a central experience for many women with ADHD. It often arises from the interaction between common ADHD challenges and gendered social expectations. While boys with ADHD may be excused as "just being boys," girls' ADHD behaviors receive no such tolerance, leading them to tend to develop an early and lasting negative self-image.[33]

By adulthood, women with ADHD may carry a long history of "always messing up," fractured relationships, and rarely feeling good about themselves or accepted by their peers. Because women often report that being socially accepted is central to maintaining a positive self-image, the experience of being left out of the social group or actively rejected by peers is painful, leading them to make intense efforts to mask their struggles through developing rigid routines and engaging in people-pleasing behaviors. Research shows that shame and depression are closely interconnected,[34] explaining why girls who experience shame associated with their ADHD so often become women with depression.

An ADHD diagnosis alone, even without treatment, can be a very healing experience, helping women move from a pervasive feeling of shame to an understanding that their struggles are not due to personal weakness, but to a brain difference that is not their fault and requires treatment. Shame can also be reduced through meeting and connecting with other women with ADHD. Group psychotherapy for women with ADHD can be a powerfully healing experience as it puts them, often for the first time, among other women with similar experiences who understand and accept them (see Chapter 9). Executive functioning coaching can also be a powerful intervention, giving women a greater sense of agency and control.[35,36]

CASE ILLUSTRATION

In Rebecca's case, her concentration problems worsened during postpartum sleep deprivation, which only made her challenges with focus and task completion even greater. She reports that she had postpartum depression and that she is not sure it has fully lifted. Her depressive symptoms made it even harder to manage her daily life, creating a vicious loop in which her low mood increased her ADHD symptoms, work underperformance, and shame, which all served to worsen her mood.

Insomnia

Insomnia can take numerous forms, including difficulty with falling asleep, difficulty returning to sleep after waking up, early morning awakenings, and delayed sleep phase. In women with ADHD, there are multiple contributors to insomnia. **Biologically**, women with ADHD are more likely to have a pattern of delayed melatonin secretion, leading their biological clock to signal sleepiness later than average and causing a "night owl" sleep pattern also known as "delayed sleep-phase syndrome."[37] This pattern leads to chronic sleep deprivation that only worsens their ADHD symptoms.

Disorganization and avoidance also play a role in disordered sleep patterns. Women with ADHD often lose track of time, have difficulty getting their children to bed on time, and, in addition, avoid going to bed on time themselves. This pattern of intentionally delayed bedtime has been dubbed "revenge bedtime procrastination" in the ADHD community and consists of a pattern of deliberately staying up to have time that is just for themselves after a long and frustrating day. Women report using this time for reading, streaming their favorite shows, online shopping, and engaging in social media as pastimes, despite knowing that it will result in fatigue the following day.[38] This pattern of bedtime delay reflects the low satisfaction many women experience during a typical day. They stay up to enjoy the only time of the day that feels relaxing or gratifying.

Emotional regulation challenges also drive insomnia. For women with undiagnosed or inadequately treated ADHD, the quiet of bedtime surfaces accumulated self-reproach over unresolved tasks and perceived failures.[39] Those women who are particularly anxiety-prone experience additional worry and rumination at this time.

An active Default Mode Network (DMN) also affects sleep. Although no known research exists regarding the intersection of ADHD, the DMN of the brain, and disordered sleep, we can extrapolate in ways that may be helpful to understanding this. One thing we do know is that, unlike their more "neurotypical" peers, in those with ADHD the DMN does not turn off when the Task-Mode Network is activated. For most people, once they engage in a task, the DMN disengages. However, in the case of those with ADHD, both networks are engaged and active simultaneously, which explains the internal distractions reported by so many with ADHD.

When women with ADHD report that their "busy mind won't turn off" at bedtime, it appears that these women are describing a very active DMN preventing their brain from shifting into the slow brain-wave patterns of impending sleep. It has been observed that the more the DMN is engaged, the less total sleep time that person has.[40] So, how do we turn down the DMN? We know that listening to a compelling narrative activates it. But what if we were to listen to a boring narrative? That seems to be just what the hugely popular podcast *Sleep with Me* is all about—it consists of a rambling, mildly engaging but pointless narrative that puts countless people to sleep on a nightly basis. Initial research suggests that suppressing the DMN activation in pre-sleep conditions weakens the connection between ruminative worry (or creative thinking) and complex cognitions in the prefrontal lobe, reducing problems in falling asleep.

When women come to you reporting presenting with chronic, treatment-resistant insomnia, especially when lifelong sleep challenges are evident, it's important to consider the presence of undiagnosed ADHD. Understanding the distinct patterns of insomnia typical among women with ADHD will allow you to identify and treat it.[41]

CASE ILLUSTRATION

Rebecca's sleep problems worsened after the birth of her twins, when hormonal disruption combined with the increased demands of caring for two children. Her ongoing sleep difficulties were fueled by executive functioning challenges. Her evenings felt overwhelming, and she was more emotionally reactive due to chronic fatigue and frustration. Difficulties preparing dinner and getting two children to sleep led to chronic feelings that her life was overwhelming and out of control. Her poor sleep then exacerbated her ADHD symptoms the following day, reinforcing the bidirectional relationship between ADHD and sleep problems.

COMPLEX POST-TRAUMATIC STRESS DISORDER AND POST-TRAUMATIC STRESS DISORDER

Complex post-traumatic stress disorder (C-PTSD) and post-traumatic stress disorder (PTSD) commonly co-occur with ADHD, especially among women. According to the DSM-5, PTSD develops following primary or secondary exposure to physical threat or violence, including sexual violence, and results in recurring intrusive memories that are triggered by reminders of the traumatic event. Women with PTSD can experience a wide variety of symptoms, including negative changes in thoughts and mood, accompanied by hyperarousal whenever a memory of the event is triggered.[42]

While PTSD can emerge after a single traumatic experience, C-PTSD typically develops in response to multiple, repetitive traumatic experiences that persist for an extended period of time, including sexual abuse, neglect, abusive criticism, or exposure to chronic family conflict and dysfunction. Most people who are diagnosed with C-PTSD have an extensive history of childhood trauma, and were often harmed by caregivers or other adults they trusted. When C-PTSD and ADHD co-occur, the emotionally abusive criticism and isolation girls with ADHD are often subjected to have often contributed to the development of C-PTSD. The cumulative effect of these co-occurring disorders can lead women to internalize many negative beliefs about themselves and have difficulty building trusting relationships.

For clinicians, it can be challenging to determine whether behavioral and emotional dysregulation stems from ADHD, C-PTSD, PTSD or a combination of all three. It's important to do a thorough trauma assessment on patients who have an ADHD diagnosis before formulating a treatment plan.[43,44]

When a diagnosis of C-PTSD or PTSD is indicated, patterns such as chronic disorganization, lifelong time-blindness, and academic underperformance may suggest co-occurring ADHD. Some researchers hypothesize that ADHD and PTSD-related inattention follow distinct patterns. In standard PTSD, attentional problems occur during periods of hypervigilance or intrusive thoughts triggered by a reminder of the trauma. In ADHD, attentional problems occur on a long-term basis due to mind-wandering, difficulty maintaining interest, or distractibility. While taking a careful developmental history and family history may help us to differentiate ADHD from trauma-related executive dysfunction, more research on the co-occurrence of ADHD and C-PTSD is needed.[45,46,47] Intergenerational ADHD and the traumatizing experiences of growing up with dysfunctional, emotionally dysregulated parents often occur together.

In women presenting with PTSD or C-PTSD, coexisting ADHD should be considered. Because of the highly genetic nature of ADHD, a detailed family history revealing ADHD-like patterns in siblings and parents offers a strong clue that ADHD could be part of the clinical picture.

CASE ILLUSTRATION: AUDHD—THE INTERSECTION OF ADHD AND AUTISM

Alice is a 25-year-old transgender woman working as a computer scientist at a startup developing AI tools for healthcare. She presented with concerns about depression and ADHD in the context of her self-identification as autistic. Her ADHD symptoms and autistic traits were not recognized in childhood: despite spending much of her time daydreaming, she performed adequately in most subjects and excelled in math and science. Early recognition of her ADHD was obscured by her high intellectual ability and her teachers' tendencies to refer only disruptive students for assessment of ADHD.

From an early age, Alice felt that there was something different about her gender, but it was not until college that she felt safe and could access medical care to medically affirm her gender as a woman. During every phase of her life, she has been marginalized, misgendered, and misunderstood. Even, and sometimes especially, in healthcare settings, she has encountered dismissive responses and pathologizing of her gender identity issues. In no context has she received a receptive caring response to her concerns related to autism and ADHD.

Alice's profile is characteristic of many AuDHD women, particularly those who are transgender. She reports intense mental exhaustion from living daily with the effects of her co-workers' prejudices. She effortfully masks her autistic traits and tries to manage her organizational and planning challenges with a slew of reminders, perfectionistic checking behaviors, and self-blame when she falls short. These efforts take their toll, reducing her ability to sustain a focus on her tasks, which amplifies both her ADHD and depression.

In some ways, Alice's experiences parallel those of Rebecca. Both experience the struggles of executive functioning while also experiencing the microaggressions of bias on the part of people around them. While Rebecca contends with the intersecting impacts of racism, sexism, and homophobia, Alice's challenges are shaped by transphobia and prejudice against her neurodivergence. For both women, unaddressed ADHD increases the toll of these experiences as they navigate environments marked by prejudice and misunderstanding. In such contexts, effective intervention must address the neurodevelopmental conditions themselves while also recognizing and mitigating the health impacts of chronic discrimination.

As clinicians, our understanding of autism in women has followed a delayed trajectory similar to that of ADHD in women (see Chapter 1). Our view of both conditions was formed through observation of mostly male children who displayed highly visible and disruptive behaviors. ADHD was long viewed as a disruptive behavior disorder, and while some girls fit this profile, most did not, leading to a strong male bias in diagnosis. A very similar pattern has shaped how we understand autism, termed autism spectrum disorder (ASD) in the DSM-5.[48] As boys' autistic behaviors tend to be more overt and therefore more easily recognized, while girls on the autism spectrum work hard to mask their symptoms in an attempt to avoid criticism and rejection.

Many girls were finally diagnosed with ADHD only after the recognition of inattention as a subtype of ADHD was included in 1980 in the DSM-III (American Psychiatric Association, 1980). In the world of autism, a similar shift took place in 2013 when Asperger's syndrome was eliminated as a diagnosis, incorporating neurodivergent individuals (then believed to be predominantly male) with low support needs into the broader spectrum of autism alongside those who require substantial assistance with communication and social interaction.

As we began to include men and boys who previously did not meet diagnostic criteria on the autism spectrum, we also began to recognize autism in women who worked hard to camouflage their symptoms. Societal pressures encourage autistic girls to mask their symptoms to better conform to gender expectations,[49] which, in turn, leads to fewer diagnoses of autistic women, a pattern that parallels the history of fewer diagnoses of ADHD in girls and women. Further studies of autistic women have found that women with low support needs tend to demonstrate more awareness of social cues than men and boys, which allows them to more successfully mask their autistic traits.[50] Women with co-occurring autism and ADHD are working hard to hide their struggles and, sadly, are paying a high price in the process.

Their efforts to conform to societal expectations and suppress their authentic behaviors often lead to increased anxiety and depression as they pretend to be "normal."[51,52] The constant monitoring of social cues, adjusting their behavior accordingly, leads to mental exhaustion, not to mention feelings of inadequacy and chronic internal stress.[53]

As a clinician seeking to understand and treat these interlocking conditions of autism, ADHD, anxiety, and depression, it is essential to conduct an in-depth clinical interview asking your female client about her internal experiences; not only about her anxiety and depression, which you may more easily discern, but also about her experiences of masking, pretending, and being on constant alert for missed social cues as she struggles to fit in.

Women with these two related diagnoses are now starting to advocate for themselves, calling their condition "AuDHD" and finding mutual support for being authentic rather than struggling to be otherwise. Online resources created by neurodivergent clinicians—such as Neurodivergent Insights by Megan Anne Neff—provide valuable learning opportunities for women and their clinicians (https://neurodivergentinsights.com).

It is also important to note that autistic traits are strongly correlated with gender identity diversity, with studies showing that up to 15% of people diagnosed with ASD are gender-nonconforming.[54] Other studies have shown a strong relationship between gender diversity and neurodivergent traits (measured as a spectrum by ADHD and autism rating scales).[55] Autistic, gender-nonconforming people are at an extremely elevated risk of suicidal thoughts and behavior relative to the general population, with studies showing a combined risk in this population relative to cisgender autistic and transgender nonautistic people.[56,57,58] Acceptance has been shown in many studies to reduce the health and suicide-related risks of transgender individuals.[59,60,61] While research has demonstrated that fluctuations in endogenous hormone levels influence ADHD symptoms in individuals assigned female at birth (see Chapter 8), more research is needed to understand how gender-affirming hormone therapy affects ADHD symptoms in transgender and gender-diverse individuals.

As clinicians, we are all learning together, to understand, support, and treat this heretofore-little-known group of women with AuDHD. They are leading the way through their self-advocacy, and in the process are teaching us, the clinical community, what we need to know to diagnose and treat them.

BIPOLAR DISORDER

Bipolar disorder is characterized by episodic disturbances in mood, alternating between mania or hypomania and depression, with periods of normal mood in-between. The subtypes differ in intensity: a diagnosis of Bipolar I involves at least one manic episode, while Bipolar II features at least one hypomanic (less severe) episode. Regardless of subtype, effective management must address both acute episodes and long-term maintenance to prevent recurrence.[62]

Co-occurring ADHD and bipolar disorder present unique challenges. Overlapping symptoms—talkativeness, hyperactivity, impulsivity, and emotional lability—can complicate diagnosis. If you are unfamiliar with adult ADHD, you may mistake a woman's baseline ADHD traits, including her chronic rapid speech and nonlinear thought patterns, for hypomania.[63]

ADHD is a neurodevelopmental condition with longstanding symptoms traceable to childhood. Symptoms wax and wane with environmental demands but persist over time. Bipolar disorder, by contrast, is episodic: distinct periods of mood elevation or irritability occur with excessive goal-directed activity, reduced need for sleep, and other features. These episodes remit and are followed by normal or depressed mood, though "mixed states" also occur. Accurate diagnosis requires distinguishing ADHD's chronic symptoms from bipolar disorder's episodic shifts.

One key distinction is **disorganized sleep vs. reduced *need* for sleep**. Women with ADHD may stay up late multiple nights in a row pursuing pleasurable activities, finishing work, or catching up on chores. They may also go to bed late chronically because of difficulty transitioning to a bedtime routine and insomnia. However, women with *only* ADHD feel tired when they don't sleep enough, and try to nap or "catch up" on the weekends. In mania or hypomania, however, people not only sleep less but also have a reduced need for sleep, a defining difference from ADHD-related sleep disruption.

Medication trials can clarify the picture. When treatment provokes irritability, marked goal-directed behavior, reduced need for sleep, and other hypomanic or manic symptoms, this suggests an underlying bipolar spectrum disorder rather than a simple adverse effect. Because ADHD medications can precipitate or worsen mania in untreated bipolar disorder, careful evaluation is essential before treatment. When bipolar disorder is present, guidelines recommend stabilizing mood with an antimanic agent prior to initiating ADHD pharmacotherapy.

BORDERLINE PERSONALITY DISORDER

Borderline personality disorder (BPD) typically onsets in adolescence and young adulthood, years after ADHD symptoms first emerge. The difficulties of living with ADHD, detailed already in this chapter, can contribute to the emergence of BPD. Both conditions are characterized by emotional dysregulation, behavioral impulsivity, interpersonal difficulties, and chronic shame,[64] and less experienced clinicians might prematurely conclude that they arise from a personality disorder when in fact their roots may require further evaluation for possible ADHD.

Emotion dysregulation and relationship difficulties are central in both combined-presentation ADHD and BPD, but they typically follow different patterns. In ADHD, emotion dysregulation can be triggered by frustration and shame related to executive dysfunction and interpersonal difficulties (see Chapter 9). In BPD, emotion dysregulation may emerge in response to perceived interpersonal slights or abandonment, with abrupt shifts in how others are perceived, alternating between idealization and devaluation. In a study of adults with ADHD, BPD, or both, emotional dysregulation was present across groups, and those with co-occurring ADHD and BPD experienced the highest severity.[65,66] Due to symptom overlap and high co-occurrence, accurate diagnosis requires attention to developmental history, symptom course, and contextual triggers.

SUBSTANCE USE DISORDERS AND ADHD

When evaluating a woman with a substance use disorder, it is important to carefully assess for ADHD. ADHD-related impulsivity can contribute to early experimentation with substances, difficulties delaying gratification, and the selection of peers with similar vulnerabilities. The drive to quickly relieve frustration, boredom, or negative emotions, combined with difficulty in fully appreciating long-term consequences, can accelerate the shift from occasional use to a substance use disorder.

Even when they recognize the harm, women with ADHD may struggle to initiate and sustain behavioral changes aimed at cutting down or stopping alcohol consumption. Once problematic use develops, they may also be less likely to accurately weigh the risks of continued use, further increasing vulnerability to addiction. Gender expectations that women remain organized, emotionally stable, and discreet in managing distress may intensify reliance on substances as a form of self-medication.[67,68]

About 20% of adults with substance use disorders have ADHD.[69] About 50% of adults with ADHD have a lifetime prevalence of a substance use disorder.[70]

ALCOHOL USE DISORDER

In our clinical experience, we have seen alcohol playing many roles in the lives of women with ADHD. It is consumed for pleasure, to slow racing or anxious thoughts before or during social activities, to ease emotional distress when alone, or to induce drowsiness at night—helping with sleep onset but worsening sleep quality later in the night. Because alcohol can seem useful in so many ways, women with ADHD may come to rely on one or more of these effects and gradually increase their consumption. Its accessibility and social acceptability further lower the threshold for regular use. Yet most of alcohol's short-term benefits fade with heavy or long-term use, while the risks of anxiety, depression, insomnia, and developing an alcohol use disorder steadily grow.[71]

CANNABIS USE DISORDER

Some of our female patients have shared their perception that cannabis is beneficial for them, calming their daytime overactive mind and facilitating sleep at night. This perception, further influenced by the "naturalness bias," may enhance the appeal of cannabis as a seemingly safer alternative to prescribed medications for ADHD, anxiety, and sleep problems.

In fact, even short-term **cannabis use can cause or worsen core ADHD symptoms** such as forgetfulness, distractibility, disorganization, and low motivation, and chronic use is associated with **IQ declines ranging from 2–8 IQ points** across multiple studies.[72,73,74] Use, including of high-potency THC products, is also linked to other serious psychiatric and safety risks such as the development of **psychotic disorders**.[75] Both cannabis use and ADHD independently elevate the risk of **deadly motor vehicle accidents**: adults with ADHD have an increased frequency of serious traffic crashes, and a recent study found cannabis users had a 55% higher risk of motor vehicle collision fatality and double the risk of injury compared to nonusers.[76] The combination of ADHD and cannabis use can be deadly.

Adolescents who use cannabis have elevated rates of **major depression, suicidal ideation, and suicide attempts** in adolescence and young adulthood,[77,78] and adults who use cannabis are at greater risk of **suicide ideation, suicide planning, and attempts**—with this association being even stronger in women than men.[79] Chronic use is also associated with **lower educational attainment, higher underemployment, and reduced income**.[80] These well-replicated findings underscore that cannabis use in people with ADHD can exacerbate the disorder's preexisting risks—including cognitive deficits, psychiatric destabilization, and life-course impairments—and thus should be a key clinical concern. While an ADHD clinical picture prior to cannabis use argues for underlying ADHD, once cannabis use becomes chronic it is impossible to fully distinguish between the deficits relating to cannabis use and those difficulties related to ADHD.

NICOTINE USE DISORDER

Women with ADHD are at an even greater risk than men with ADHD for nicotine dependence, and a leading explanation for this link is that nicotine use can be a woman's effort to self-medicate for inner tension and cognitive difficulties.[81,82] Women with ADHD tend to start smoking earlier than their male counterparts and may experience a heightened difficulty when attempting smoking cessation.[83] The immediate, temporary improvement in mood and focus makes smoking or vaping highly motivating, and ever more difficult to stop given that smoking cessation leads to an increase in ADHD symptoms.[84]

CASE ILLUSTRATION: FORMULATING REBECCA'S CASE

Rebecca is a 39-year-old attorney, married with twin preschool boys, who presents with low mood, anxiety, chronic sleep problems, and difficulties with concentration, procrastination, and follow-through. These challenges, emerging against a backdrop of lifelong but overlooked ADHD, have intensified since the birth of her children, as parenting and professional demands have grown. She faces discrimination based on race and sexual identity, which heightens vigilance, erodes confidence, and further taxes her executive functioning. Daily struggles with organization and task initiation fuel shame and worry, creating cycles of anxiety and depression that obscure ADHD's central role. Recognizing and treating ADHD as the core driver is essential, not only to alleviate her anxiety and depression but also to break these self-reinforcing cycles and promote her overall well-being.

REFERENCES

1. Bernardi, S., Faraone, S. V., Cortese, S., Kerridge, B. T., Pallanti, S., Wang, S., & Blanco, C. (2012). The lifetime impact of attention deficit hyperactivity disorder: results from the National Epidemiologic Survey on Alcohol and Related Conditions (NESARC). *Psychological Medicine, 42*(4), 875–887. https://doi.org/10.1017/S003329171100153X
2. Skoglund, C., Sundström Poromaa, I., Leksell, D., Ekholm Selling, K., Cars, T., Giacobini, M., Young, S., & Kopp Kallner, H. (2024). Time after time: failure to identify and support females with ADHD—a Swedish population register study. *Journal of Child Psychology and Psychiatry and Allied Disciplines, 65*(6), 832–844. https://doi.org/10.1111/jcpp.13920
3. Jellinek, M. S. (2010). Don't let ADHD crush children's self-esteem. *Clinical Psychiatry News, 38*(5), 12.
4. Kok, F. M., Groen, Y., Fuermaier, A. B. M., & Tucha, O. (2016). Problematic peer functioning in girls with ADHD: a systematic literature review. *PLOS One, 11*(11), e0165119. https://doi.org/10.1371/journal.pone.0165119
5. Brown, T. E. (2017). *Outside the box: rethinking ADD/ADHD in children and adults: a practical guide.* American Psychiatric Publishing.
6. Roberts, C., Sahakian, B. J., Chen, S., Sallie, S. N., Walker, C., White, S. R., Weber, J., Skandali, N., Robbins, T. W., & Murray, G. K. (2023). Impact and centrality of attention dysregulation on cognition, anxiety, and low mood in adolescents. *Scientific Reports, 13*(1), 9106. https://doi.org/10.1038/s41598-023-34399-y
7. Hinshaw, S. P., Owens, E. B., Zalecki, C., Huggins, S. P., Montenegro-Nevado, A. J., Schrodek, E., & Swanson, E. N. (2012). Prospective follow-up of girls with attention-deficit/hyperactivity disorder into early adulthood: continuing impairment includes elevated risk for suicide attempts and self-injury. *Journal of Consulting and Clinical Psychology, 80*(6), 1041–1051. https://doi.org/10.1037/a0029451
8. Brown, T. E. (2017). *Outside the box: rethinking ADD/ADHD in children and adults: a practical guide.* American Psychiatric Publishing.
9. Roberts, C., Sahakian, B. J., Chen, S., Sallie, S. N., Walker, C., White, S. R., Weber, J., Skandali, N., Robbins, T. W., & Murray, G. K. (2023). Impact and centrality of attention dysregulation on cognition, anxiety, and low mood in adolescents. *Scientific Reports, 13*(1), 9106. https://doi.org/10.1038/s41598-023-34399-y
10. Young, S., Adamo, N., Ásgeirsdóttir, B. B., Branney, P., Beckett, M., Colley, W., Cubbin, S., Deeley, Q., Farrag, E., Gudjonsson, G., Hill, P., Hollingdale, J., Kilic, O., Lloyd, T., Mason, P., Paliokosta, E., Perecherla, S., Sedgwick, J., Skirrow, C. … Woodhouse, E. (2020). Females with ADHD: an expert consensus statement taking a lifespan approach providing guidance for the identification and treatment of attention-deficit/hyperactivity disorder in girls and women. *BMC Psychiatry, 20*(1), 404. https://doi.org/10.1186/s12888-020-02707-9
11. Young, S., Adamo, N., Ásgeirsdóttir, B. B., Branney, P., Beckett, M., Colley, W., Cubbin, S., Deeley, Q., Farrag, E., Gudjonsson, G., Hill, P., Hollingdale, J., Kilic, O., Lloyd, T., Mason, P., Paliokosta, E., Perecherla, S., Sedgwick, J., Skirrow, C. … Woodhouse, E. (2020). Females with ADHD: an expert consensus statement taking a lifespan approach providing guidance for the identification and treatment of attention-deficit/hyperactivity disorder in girls and women. *BMC Psychiatry, 20*(1), 404. https://doi.org/10.1186/s12888-020-02707-9

12. Marraccini, M. E., Weyandt, L. L., Rossi, J. S., & Gudmundsdottir, B. G. (2016). Neurocognitive enhancement or impairment? A systematic meta-analysis of prescription stimulant effects on processing speed, decision-making, planning, and cognitive perseveration. *Experimental and Clinical Psychopharmacology, 24*(4), 269.
13. Shaw, P., Stringaris, A., Nigg, J., & Leibenluft, E. (2014). Emotion dysregulation in attention deficit hyperactivity disorder. *American Journal of Psychiatry, 171*(3), 276–293.
14. Abend, R. (2023). Understanding anxiety symptoms as aberrant defensive responding along the threat imminence continuum. *Neuroscience & Biobehavioral Reviews, 152*, Article 105305.
15. Sirois, F. M. (2022). *Procrastination: what it is, why it's a problem, and what you can do about it.* American Psychiatric Association.
16. Sirois, F. M. (2022). *Procrastination: what it is, why it's a problem, and what you can do about it.* American Psychiatric Association.
17. Simon, J. J., Walther, S., Fiebach, C. J., Friederich, H. C., Stippich, C., Weisbrod, M., & Kaiser, S. (2010). Neural reward processing is modulated by approach- and avoidance-related personality traits. *NeuroImage, 49*(2), 1868–1874. https://doi.org/10.1016/j.neuroimage.2009.09.016
18. Sirois, F. M. (2022). *Procrastination: what it is, why it's a problem, and what you can do about it.* American Psychiatric Association.
19. Barkley, R. A., & Murphy, K. R. (1998). *Attention-deficit hyperactivity disorder: a clinical workbook.* The Guilford Press.
20. Clay, J. M., Badariotti, J. I., Kozhushko, N., & Parker, M. O. (2024). HPA activity mediates the link between trait impulsivity and boredom. *Physiology & Behavior, 284*, 114637.
21. Leonardo, E. D., & Barrow, J. C. (2021). You're not alone: women and ADHD – Exploring procrastination and avoidance. *Journal of Attention Disorders, 25*(14), 2115–2117.
22. Sirois, F. M. (2022). *Procrastination: what it is, why it's a problem, and what you can do about it.* American Psychiatric Association.
23. Brown, T. E. (2017). *Outside the box: rethinking ADD/ADHD in children and adults: a practical guide.* American Psychiatric Publishing.
24. Roberts, C., Sahakian, B. J., Chen, S., Sallie, S. N., Walker, C., White, S. R., Weber, J., Skandali, N., Robbins, T. W., & Murray, G. K. (2023). Impact and centrality of attention dysregulation on cognition, anxiety, and low mood in adolescents. *Scientific Reports, 13*(1), 9106. https://doi.org/10.1038/s41598-023-34399-y
25. Welkie, J., Babinski, D. E., & Neely, K. A. (2021). Sex and emotion regulation difficulties contribute to depression in young adults with attention-deficit/hyperactivity disorder. *Psychological Reports, 124*(2), 596–610.
26. Szaniawska, M., & Kokoszka, A. (2025). Prevalence of ADHD among nonpsychotic patients of day-care centers and comparison of psychiatric comorbidities among persons with and without ADHD: a pilot study. *Journal of Clinical Medicine, 14*(4), 1153. https://doi.org/10.3390/jcm14041153
27. Yoshimasu, K., Barbaresi, W. J., Colligan, R. C., Voigt, R. G., Killian, J. M., Weaver, A. L., & Katusic, S. K. (2018). Adults with persistent ADHD: gender and psychiatric comorbidities—a population-based longitudinal study. *Journal of Attention Disorders, 22*(6), 535–546. https://doi.org/10.1177/1087054716676342
28. Hinshaw, S. P., Owens, E. B., Zalecki, C., Huggins, S. P., Montenegro-Nevado, A. J., Schrodek, E., & Swanson, E. N. (2012). Prospective follow-up of girls with

attention-deficit/hyperactivity disorder into early adulthood: continuing impairment includes elevated risk for suicide attempts and self-injury. *Journal of Consulting and Clinical Psychology, 80*(6), 1041–1051. https://doi.org/10.1037/a0029451
29. Meza, J. I., Owens, E. B., & Hinshaw, S. P. (2020). Childhood predictors and moderators of lifetime risk of self-harm in girls with and without attention-deficit/hyperactivity disorder. *Development and Psychopathology, 33*(4), 1351–1367.
30. Yu, P.-C., Chiang, Y.-H., Huang, S.-H., Chung, R.-J., Lin, I.-J., Wang, B.-L., Yu, C.-P., Chou, Y.-C., Sun, C.-A., Tang, S.-E., Huang, Y.-C., Chien, W.-C., & Chiang, C.-H. (2022). Adult abuse and poor prognosis in Taiwan, 2000–2015: a cohort study. *BMC Public Health, 22*, Article 2280.
31. Ahmad, S. I., & Hinshaw, S. P. (2024). A qualitative analysis of perspectives on self-directed violence in a prospective longitudinal study of young women with and without childhood ADHD. *Journal of Attention Disorders, 28*(9), 1255–1266.
32. Todzia-Kornas, A., Szczegielniak, A., & Gondek, T. M. (2024). Suicidality and nonsuicidal self-injury in females diagnosed with attention-deficit hyperactivity disorder: A narrative review. *Current Opinion in Psychiatry, 37*, 38–42.
33. Young, S., Adamo, N., Ásgeirsdóttir, B. B., Branney, P., Beckett, M., Colley, W., Cubbin, S., Deeley, Q., Farrag, E., Gudjonsson, G., Hill, P., Hollingdale, J., Kilic, O., Lloyd, T., Mason, P., Paliokosta, E., Perecherla, S., Sedgwick, J., Skirrow, C. ... Woodhouse, E. (2020). Females with ADHD: an expert consensus statement taking a lifespan approach providing guidance for the identification and treatment of attention-deficit/hyperactivity disorder in girls and women. *BMC Psychiatry, 20*(1), 404. https://doi.org/10.1186/s12888-020-02707-9
34. Kim, D., Kwon, H. J., Ha, M., Lim, M. H., & Kim, K. M. (2020). Network analysis for the symptom of depression with Children's Depression Inventory in a large sample of school-aged children. *Journal of Affective Disorders, 281*, 256–263.
35. Morgan, J. (2024). Exploring women's experiences of diagnosis of ADHD in adulthood: a qualitative study. *Advances in Mental Health, 22*(3), 575–589.
36. Attoe, D. E., & Climie, E. A. (2023). *Miss. Diagnosis: a systematic review of ADHD in adult women. Journal of Attention Disorders, 27*(7), 645–657.
37. Snitselaar, M. A., Smits, M. G., van der Heijden, K. B., & Spijker, J. (2017). Sleep and circadian rhythmicity in adult ADHD and the effect of stimulants: a review of the current literature. *Journal of Attention Disorders, 21*(1), 14–26.
38. Young, S., Adamo, N., Ásgeirsdóttir, B. B., Branney, P., Beckett, M., Colley, W., Cubbin, S., Deeley, Q., Farrag, E., Gudjonsson, G., Hill, P., Hollingdale, J., Kilic, O., Lloyd, T., Mason, P., Paliokosta, E., Perecherla, S., Sedgwick, J., Skirrow, C. ... Woodhouse, E. (2020). Females with ADHD: an expert consensus statement taking a lifespan approach providing guidance for the identification and treatment of attention-deficit/hyperactivity disorder in girls and women. *BMC Psychiatry, 20*(1), 404. https://doi.org/10.1186/s12888-020-02707-9
39. Quinn, P. O., & Madhoo, M. (2014). A review of attention-deficit/hyperactivity disorder in women and girls: Uncovering this hidden diagnosis. *Primary Care Companion for CNS Disorders, 16*(3), PCC-13r01596.
40. Killgore, W. D. S., Jankowski, S., Henderson-Arredondo, K., Lucas, D. A., Patel, S. I., Hildebrand, L. L., Huskey, A., & Dailey, N. S. (2023). Functional connectivity of the default mode network predicts subsequent polysomnographically measured sleep in people with symptoms of insomnia. *Neuroreport, 34*(14), 734–740. https://doi.org/10.1097/WNR.0000000000001949
41. Young, S., Adamo, N., Ásgeirsdóttir, B. B., Branney, P., Beckett, M., Colley, W., Cubbin, S., Deeley, Q., Farrag, E., Gudjonsson, G., Hill, P., Hollingdale, J., Kilic,

O., Lloyd, T., Mason, P., Paliokosta, E., Perecherla, S., Sedgwick, J., Skirrow, C. ... Woodhouse, E. (2020). Females with ADHD: an expert consensus statement taking a lifespan approach providing guidance for the identification and treatment of attention-deficit/hyperactivity disorder in girls and women. *BMC Psychiatry, 20*(1), 404. https://doi.org/10.1186/s12888-020-02707-9

42. American Psychiatric Association. (2022). *Diagnostic and statistical manual of mental disorders* (5th ed., text rev.; DSM-5-TR). American Psychiatric Publishing. https://doi.org/10.1176/appi.books.9780890425787
43. Bryant, R. A., Felmingham, K. L., Malhi, G., Andrew, E., & Korgaonkar, M. S. (2021). The distinctive neural circuitry of complex posttraumatic stress disorder during threat processing. *Psychological Medicine, 51*(7), 1121–1128.
44. Brown, T. E. (2017). *Outside the box: rethinking ADD/ADHD in children and adults: a practical guide*. American Psychiatric Publishing.
45. Bryant, R. A., Felmingham, K. L., Malhi, G., Andrew, E., & Korgaonkar, M. S. (2021). The distinctive neural circuitry of complex posttraumatic stress disorder during threat processing. *Psychological Medicine, 51*(7), 1121–1128.
46. Brown, T. E. (2017). *Outside the box: rethinking ADD/ADHD in children and adults: a practical guide*. American Psychiatric Publishing.
47. American Psychiatric Association. (2022). *Diagnostic and statistical manual of mental disorders* (5th ed., text rev.; DSM-5-TR). American Psychiatric Publishing. https://doi.org/10.1176/appi.books.9780890425787
48. American Psychiatric Association. (2022). *Diagnostic and statistical manual of mental disorders* (5th ed., text rev.; DSM-5-TR). American Psychiatric Publishing. https://doi.org/10.1176/appi.books.9780890425787
49. Schuck, R., Flores, R., & Fung, L. (2019). Brief report: sex/gender differences in symptomology and camouflaging in adults with autism spectrum disorder. *Journal of Autism and Developmental Disorders, 49*(6), 2597–2604. https://doi.org/10.1007/s10803-019-03998-y
50. Lai, M.-C., Lombardo, M. V., Pasco, G., Ruigrok, A. N. V., Wheelwright, S. J., Sadek, S. A., Chakrabarti, B., & Baron-Cohen, S. (2011). A behavioral comparison of male and female adults with high functioning autism spectrum conditions. *PLOS One, 6*(6), Article e20835. https://doi.org/10.1371/journal.pone.0020835
51. Cage, E., & Troxell-Whitman, Z. (2019). Understanding the reasons, contexts and costs of camouflaging for autistic adults. *Journal of Autism and Developmental Disorders, 49*(5), 1899–1911. https://doi.org/10.1007/s10803-018-03878-x
52. Bernardin, C., Lewis, T., Bell, D., & Kanne, S. (2021). Associations between social camouflaging and internalizing symptoms in autistic and non-autistic adolescents. *Autism, 25*(6), 1580–1591. https://doi.org/10.1177/1362361321997284
53. Bernardin, C., Lewis, T., Bell, D., & Kanne, S. (2021). Associations between social camouflaging and internalizing symptoms in autistic and non-autistic adolescents. *Autism, 25*(6), 1580–1591. https://doi.org/10.1177/1362361321997284
54. Kallitsounaki, A., & Williams, D. M. (2022). Autism spectrum disorder and gender dysphoria/incongruence: a systematic literature review and meta-analysis. *Journal of Autism and Developmental Disorders, 53*(8), 3103–3117. https://doi.org/10.1007/s10803-022-05517-y
55. Mo, K., Anagnostou, E., Lerch, J. P., Taylor, M. J., VanderLaan, D. P., Szatmari, P., Crosbie, J., Nicolson, R., Georgiadis, S., Kelley, E., Ayub, M., Brian, J., Lai, M-C., & Palmert, M. R. (2024). Gender diversity is correlated with dimensional neurodivergent traits but not categorical neurodevelopmental diagnoses in children. *Journal of Child Psychology and Psychiatry, 65*(9), 1223–1236.

56. Strauss, P., Cook, A., Watson, V., Winter, S., Whitehouse, A., Albrecht, N., Wright Toussaint, D., & Lin, A. (2021). Mental health difficulties among trans and gender diverse young people with an autism spectrum disorder (ASD): findings from Trans Pathways. *Journal of Psychiatric Research, 137*, 360–367.
57. Soto, E. F., Orantes, D., Russo, N., & Antshel, K. M. (2024). Autism and sexual and gender minority identity in college students: examination of self-reported rates, functional outcomes, and treatment engagement. *Autism, 28*(6), 1519–1539.
58. Strang, J. F., Anthony, L. G., Song, A., Lai, M.-C., Knauss, M., Sadikova, E., Graham, E., Zaks, Z., Wimms, H., Willing, L., Call, D., Mancilla, M., Shakin, S., Vilain, E., Kim, D.-Y., Maisashvili, T., Khawaja, A., & Kenworthy, L. (2023). In addition to stigma: cognitive and autism-related predictors of mental health in transgender adolescents. *Journal of Clinical Child and Adolescent Psychology, 52*(2), 212–229. https://doi.org/10.1080/15374416.2021.1916940
59. Strauss, P., Cook, A., Watson, V., Winter, S., Whitehouse, A., Albrecht, N., Wright Toussaint, D., & Lin, A. (2021). Mental health difficulties among trans and gender diverse young people with an autism spectrum disorder (ASD): findings from Trans Pathways. *Journal of Psychiatric Research, 137*, 360–367.
60. Soto, E. F., Orantes, D., Russo, N., & Antshel, K. M. (2024). Autism and sexual and gender minority identity in college students: examination of self-reported rates, functional outcomes, and treatment engagement. *Autism, 28*(6), 1519–1539.
61. Strang, J. F., Anthony, L. G., Song, A., Lai, M.-C., Knauss, M., Sadikova, E., Graham, E., Zaks, Z., Wimms, H., Willing, L., Call, D., Mancilla, M., Shakin, S., Vilain, E., Kim, D.-Y., Maisashvili, T., Khawaja, A., & Kenworthy, L. (2023). In addition to stigma: cognitive and autism-related predictors of mental health in transgender adolescents. *Journal of Clinical Child and Adolescent Psychology, 52*(2), 212–229. https://doi.org/10.1080/15374416.2021.1916940.
62. American Psychiatric Association. (2022). *Diagnostic and statistical manual of mental disorders* (5th ed., text rev.; DSM-5-TR). American Psychiatric Publishing. https://doi.org/10.1176/appi.books.9780890425787
63. Klassen, L. J., Katzman, M. A., & Chokka, P. (2010). Adult ADHD and its comorbidities, with a focus on bipolar disorder. *Journal of Affective Disorders, 124*(1–2), 1–8.
64. O'Grady, S. M., & Hinshaw, S. P. (2023). Developmental predictors of young adult borderline personality disorder: a prospective, longitudinal study of females with and without childhood ADHD. *BMC Psychiatry, 23*(1), 106.
65. American Psychiatric Association. (2022). *Diagnostic and statistical manual of mental disorders* (5th ed., text rev.; DSM-5-TR). American Psychiatric Publishing. https://doi.org/10.1176/appi.books.9780890425787
66. Rüfenacht, E., Euler, S., Götz, M. J., Schmeck, K., Walter, H., & Schäfer, I. (2019). Emotional dysregulation in adults with attention deficit hyperactivity disorder and borderline personality disorder—a transdiagnostic comparison using the DERS. *Borderline Personality Disorder and Emotion Dysregulation, 6*, 7.
67. Hartman, C. A., Larsson, H., Vos, M., Bellato, A., Libutzki, B., Solberg, B. S., Chen, Q., Du Rietz, E., Mostert, J. C., Kittel-Schneider, S., Cormand, B., Ribasés, M., Klungsøyr, K., Haavik, J., Dalsgaard, S., Cortese, S., Faraone, S. V., & Reif, A. (2023). Anxiety, mood, and substance use disorders in adult men and women with and without attention-deficit/hyperactivity disorder: a substantive and methodological overview. *Neuroscience and Biobehavioral Reviews, 151*, Article 105209.
68. Young, S., Adamo, N., Ásgeirsdóttir, B. B., Branney, P., Beckett, M., Colley, W., Cubbin, S., Deeley, Q., Farrag, E., Gudjonsson, G., Hill, P., Hollingdale, J., Kilic,

O., Lloyd, T., Mason, P., Paliokosta, E., Perecherla, S., Sedgwick, J., Skirrow, C. … Woodhouse, E. (2020). Females with ADHD: an expert consensus statement taking a lifespan approach providing guidance for the identification and treatment of attention-deficit/hyperactivity disorder in girls and women. *BMC Psychiatry, 20*(1), 404. https://doi.org/10.1186/s12888-020-02707-9

69. Rohner, H., Gaspar, N., Philipsen, A., & Schulze, M. (2023). Prevalence of attention deficit hyperactivity disorder (ADHD) among substance use disorder (SUD) populations: meta-analysis. *International Journal of Environmental Research and Public Health, 20*(2), 1275. https://doi.org/10.3390/ijerph20021275
70. Fuller-Thomson, E., Lewis, D. A., & Agbeyaka, S. (2022). Attention-deficit/hyperactivity disorder and alcohol and other substance use disorders in young adulthood: findings from a Canadian nationally representative survey. *Alcohol and Alcoholism, 57*(3), 385–395.
71. Fuller-Thomson, E., Lewis, D. A., & Agbeyaka, S. (2022). Attention-deficit/hyperactivity disorder and alcohol and other substance use disorders in young adulthood: findings from a Canadian nationally representative survey. *Alcohol and Alcoholism, 57*(3), 385–395.
72. Meier, M. H., Caspi, A., Ambler, A., Harrington, H., Houts, R., Keefe, R. S. E., McDonald, K., Ward, A., Poulton, R., & Moffitt, T. E. (2012). Persistent cannabis users show neuropsychological decline from childhood to midlife. *Proceedings of the National Academy of Sciences – PNAS, 109*(40), E2657–E2664. https://doi.org/10.1073/pnas.1206820109
73. Power, E., Sabherwal, S., Healy, C., O'Neill, A., Cotter, D., & Cannon, M. (2021). Intelligence quotient decline following frequent or dependent cannabis use in youth: a systematic review and meta-analysis of longitudinal studies. *Psychological Medicine, 51*(2), 194–200.
74. Meier, M. H., Caspi, A., Ambler, A., Harrington, H., Houts, R., Keefe, R. S. E., McDonald, K., Ward, A., Poulton, R., & Moffitt, T. E. (2012). Persistent cannabis users show neuropsychological decline from childhood to midlife. *Proceedings of the National Academy of Sciences – PNAS, 109*(40), E2657–E2664. https://doi.org/10.1073/pnas.1206820109
75. Di Forti, M., Morgan, C., Dazzan, P., Pariante, C., Mondelli, V., Marques, T. R., Handley, R., Luzi, S., Russo, M., Paparelli, A., Butt, A., Stilo, S. A., Wiffen, B., Powell, J., & Murray, R. M. (2009). High-potency cannabis and the risk of psychosis. *The British Journal of Psychiatry: The Journal of Mental Science, 195*(6), 488–491. https://doi.org/10.1192/bjp.bp.109.064220
76. Jin, A., Darzi, A. J., Dargham, A., Liddar, N., Bozorgi, S., Sohrevardi, S., Zhang, M., Torabiardakani, K., Couban, R. J., Khalili, M., Busse, W. J., & Sadeghirad, B. (2025). Cannabis consumption and motor vehicle collision: a systematic review and meta-analysis of observational studies. *International Journal of Drug Policy, 142*, 104832.
77. Agrawal, A., Nelson, E. C., Bucholz, K. K., Tillman, R., Grucza, R. A., Statham, D. J., Madden, P. A., Martin, N. G., Heath, A. C., & Lynskey, M. T. (2017). Major depressive disorder, suicidal thoughts and behaviours, and cannabis involvement in discordant twins: a retrospective cohort study. *The Lancet. Psychiatry, 4*(9), 706–714. https://doi.org/10.1016/S2215-0366(17)30280-8
78. Gobbi, G., Atkin, T., Zytynski, T., Wang, S., Askari, S., Boruff, J., Ware, M., Marmorstein, N., Cipriani, A., Dendukuri, N., & Mayo, N. (2019). Association of cannabis use in adolescence and risk of depression, anxiety, and suicidality in young adulthood: a systematic review and meta-analysis. *JAMA Psychiatry (Chicago, Ill.), 76*(4), 426–434. https://doi.org/10.1001/jamapsychiatry.2018.4500

79. Han, B., Compton, W. M., Einstein, E. B., & Volkow, N. D. (2021). Associations of suicidality trends with cannabis use as a function of sex and depression status. *JAMA Network Open*, *4*(6), e2113025.
80. Fergusson, D. M., & Boden, J. M. (2008). Cannabis use and later life outcomes. *Addiction*, *103*(6), 969–976.
81. Liebrenz, M., Frei, A., Fisher, C. E., Gamma, A., Buadze, A., & Eich, D. (2014). Adult attention-deficit/hyperactivity disorder and nicotine use: a qualitative study of patient perceptions. *BMC Psychiatry*, *14*(1), 141.
82. Elkins, I. J., Saunders, G. R., Malone, S. M., Keyes, M. A., Samek, D. R., McGue, M., & Iacono, W. G. (2018). Increased risk of smoking in female adolescents who had childhood ADHD. *American Journal of Psychiatry*, *175*(1), 63–70.
83. McClernon, F. J., Voorhees, E. E. V., English, J. S., Hallyburton, M., Holdaway, A., & Kollins, S. H. (2011). Smoking withdrawal symptoms are more severe among smokers with ADHD and independent of ADHD symptom change: results from a 12-day contingency-managed abstinence trial. *Nicotine & Tobacco Research*, *13*(9), 784–792. https://doi.org/10.1093/ntr/ntr073
84. Bidwell, L. C., Karoly, H. C., Hutchison, K. E., & Bryan, A. D. (2017). ADHD symptoms impact smoking outcomes and withdrawal in response to varenicline treatment for smoking cessation. *Drug and Alcohol Dependence*, *179*, 18–24. https://doi.org/10.1016/j.drugalcdep.2017.06.020

CHAPTER 4

Treating ADHD in women

A plan for success

ADHD: A HOPEFUL DIAGNOSIS

If a woman is fortunate enough to have her ADHD diagnosed (missed diagnosis or misdiagnosis are significant issues and occur all too often), her journey does not end there: it is just beginning. The diagnosis of ADHD opens the door to **treatment** and points the way toward reduction of symptoms, treatment of co-occurring conditions, and ultimately, improvements in functioning and overall **quality of life**. Therefore, ADHD should be viewed as a hopeful diagnosis! Medications are now available to treat ADHD, and have been shown to reduce symptoms and improve executive functioning in 90–96% of cases. Such results can usually be achieved by switching from one type of medication to another if the first one proves ineffective. Newer therapies (cognitive behavioral therapy, dialectical behavior therapy, and mindfulness training) are designed to help the patient rewrite scripts, increase their sense of self-efficacy and find practical solutions for day-to-day problems. Taking a holistic approach to well-being by encouraging exercise, adequate nutrition, and sleep, as well as addressing hormonal fluctuations that affect ADHD symptoms in women, will set the stage for improved day-to-day functioning and successful outcomes in most women with ADHD.

The next step after diagnosis is for the woman with ADHD and her clinician to work **together** to design an **individualized treatment plan** that addresses her unique needs. Here we reach the crux of the problem. How prepared are you to recommend appropriate treatment customized for women with ADHD? It appears not many clinicians are. In a recent survey of 11,000 adults with ADHD and caregivers of children with the condition conducted by ***ADDitude*** magazine from July to December

DOI: 10.4324/9781003542124-4

2023,[1] a lack of "access to treatment professionals with experience in ADHD" was listed as the **greatest impediment to effective treatment**. No matter what the focus of your formal training, it probably offered little if anything in the way of managing ADHD besides a couple of hours on symptoms and medication.

In this chapter, we will present both the **theory** and the **effectiveness** of targeted treatment recommendations. Together, the three of us have treated many thousands of patients with ADHD and other disorders, written over 30 books, and given hundreds of presentations and workshops in the United States and internationally. Drs. Nadeau and Quinn co-founded the National Center for Girls and Women with ADHD (initially the National Center for Gender Issues in ADHD) in 1999 to raise awareness, advocate for, and promote research on ADHD in women and girls. Our goal in this guide is to offer you practical how-to strategies for diagnosing and treating ADHD in women, while also outlining the latest research in particular areas.

When treating women and girls with ADHD, clinicians too often start with medication alone. In fact, workplace accommodations, diet, exercise, sleep, and other habits are essential, but they are rarely addressed.

> The primary recommendation for a woman with ADHD should be to simplify her life.

The primary recommendation for a woman with ADHD should be to simplify her life. While the task sounds simple, most women with ADHD find it extremely challenging! However, unless her ADHD symptoms, alongside any sleep problems or mood disorders, are treated first, she will likely be too exhausted, forgetful, or disorganized to make changes to her lifestyle. For this reason, it is advised that you address ADHD and target those symptoms to lay the groundwork for successful changes in other areas.

CASE ILLUSTRATION: SUZANNE

Suzanne was mother to five-year-old twin boys who had just been diagnosed with combined-presentation ADHD with significant hyperactivity and impulsivity and a two-year-old daughter (without ADHD so far). She presented for an evaluation for ADHD for herself after her twins were diagnosed. Feeling very distressed, she poured out her problems to her family physician. Her life always seemed to be one crisis after another.

She was overwhelmed, ate poorly, exercised sporadically, and got little sleep. She reported that she had always had difficulty in school keeping quiet and focused during class, and it seemed to her that she often said and did things without thinking she later regretted. This, she felt, had led to significant problems in many of her relationships. She continued to struggle with this pattern into adulthood and often felt very lonely as a result. Suzanne was an interior designer, but missing deadlines and multiple unfinished projects were an issue for her and threatened her career. She described her husband as "an easy-going guy, who always picked up the slack."

After a thorough evaluation, Suzanne's family physician diagnosed her with ADHD, combined presentation. She was prescribed medication and was referred to a therapist and an ADHD coach to work on making changes that would lighten her daily workload. At the start of her first visit to the therapist, she was very excited. She and her husband had just sold their house and were planning to buy an old farmhouse in rural Pennsylvania and completely restore it. She also thought that she might homeschool the boys! "Ahhhhhh," her therapist responded. "I thought you were here to simplify your life! Let's talk about this, shall we?"

The therapist saw that unless Suzanne began taking stimulants to address her impulsivity and other ADHD symptoms, she would make little progress in therapy and continue to feel stressed and overwhelmed.

What are the most frequent presenting complaints of women with ADHD?

- Feelings of inadequacy and overwhelm
- Emotional dysregulation
- Low self-worth
- Rejection sensitivity
- Relationship difficulties
- Challenges with managing work-related tasks
- Demands of parenting
- Household responsibilities—difficulties in maintaining organization
- Difficulty dealing with the societal expectations placed on women to be calm, attentive, and organized

As you can see, this list bears little resemblance to the DSM-5 TR list of ADHD symptoms. Significantly, many women report that ADHD has a profoundly negative impact on how they view themselves and how they relate to and are seen by others because they fail to live up to societal expectations regarding self-control, motherhood, and household management.

Designing an individualized treatment plan for each woman

ADHD in adult women often manifests more in lifestyle challenges and functional impairments than in overt behavioral problems, and treatment should reflect this. As part of the diagnostic process, be sure to use the comprehensive interview and rating scales presented in Chapter 2 to help you **identify** the specific issues facing your patient and **target** those issues for treatment.

List each treatment issue, then **link each issue to a specific treatment recommendation**. If you are also treating a woman with ADHD for other medical or psychiatric issues, you may need to **prioritize treatment** of her ADHD to ensure successful treatment in other areas. She will be able to better adhere to medication and treatment recommendations for her eating disorder, diabetes, fibromyalgia, or addiction if her ADHD is being effectively managed.

Next, address co-occurring conditions. If your patient presents with a severe mood disorder, severe anxiety, bipolar disorder, or suicidal ideations, and has ADHD, these conditions may need to be treated and stabilized first before you begin stimulant medication, as stimulants may destabilize these other conditions. (More about the treatment of complex diagnosis of ADHD and other psychiatric conditions can be found in Chapter 3.)

Encourage your patients to read more about ADHD and its treatment and seek out ADHD support groups or organizations either online or in person. To make sure they avoid the misinformation that is out there, it is important to have a few resources you can recommend to your newly diagnosed patients, such as books and online groups/podcasts.

TWELVE SPECIFIC TREATMENT RECOMMENDATIONS FOR ADHD IN WOMEN

Over the next several pages, we will discuss commonly recommended **treatments for women with ADHD**. Your patient may not need all 12, but you may be surprised at the results if you design a program that includes many of these recommendations.

> It's always important to reassess and ascertain how a specific recommendation worked for your patients and then adjust as necessary.

1. Prescribing medication for ADHD

Theory: The efficacy of stimulant medications for the treatment of ADHD is well documented, with many hundreds of studies over the years and with multiple decades of use. Thus, these medications have become the "gold standard" of pediatric and psychiatric practice guidelines as the primary pharmacological intervention for both children and adults diagnosed with ADHD. **Stimulant medications**, particularly methylphenidate (MPH) and amphetamines (AMP), have consistently shown significant efficacy in reducing core symptoms of ADHD, which include inattention, hyperactivity, and impulsivity.[2] Reviews conducted over the years confirm that medications used for the treatment of ADHD provide substantial improvements, with response rates varying between 60 and 90% depending on study population and the medication.[3,4,5]

In addition, medications used to treat ADHD have been shown to reduce morbidity and mortality associated with ADHD. In a Swedish nationwide cohort study, **lisdexamphetamine** and other amphetamine derivatives were associated with decreased risk of psychiatric hospitalization, nonpsychiatric hospitalization, and suicide attempts or death by suicide.[6] In another study, an 18.75% reduction in the overall risk of death was documented in the two years after diagnosis for those taking ADHD medication.[7]

MEDICATION EFFECTIVENESS IN WOMEN WITH ADHD VERSUS MEN WITH ADHD

As with most medical research, studies on the effectiveness of stimulants have been conducted with mostly male participants, which leads us to the next question. Are medications used to treat ADHD as effective in women as men? It is widely held that **stimulants** are as effective in women as in men with ADHD.

The **effectiveness of stimulants in women** can be influenced by unique female medical health considerations, including hormonal fluctuations. Research by Jong et al. highlights the changing efficacy of stimulant medications during different phases of the menstrual cycle, indicating that women may require dosage adjustments to maintain effectiveness.[8] (More about this in Chapter 9.)

The interplay between ADHD symptoms and associated mental health challenges may present another hurdle; women report higher levels of co-occurring conditions such as anxiety and depression, which may complicate treatment efficacy and adherence.[9] Changes in pharmacodynamics due to factors such as body composition and metabolism may also contribute to differences in treatment efficacy observed between genders, as discussed in the review by Rapoport and Groenman on sex and gender factors in ADHD treatment.[10]

THE PHARMACOLOGY OF COMMON MEDICATIONS TO TREAT ADHD

The **pharmacological action of stimulants**—primarily their ability to increase levels of dopamine, and to a lesser extent norepinephrine, at the neuronal synapse—underlies their effectiveness. Both MPH and amphetamines increase the availability of these neurotransmitters, which plays a crucial role in attention and behavior regulation.[11] However, it is essential to consider the tolerability of stimulants, as some patients report **side effects** such as insomnia, appetite suppression, and increased anxiety.[12,13] The discontinuation rates due to adverse effects suggest there is a need for careful monitoring and better communication about ways to prevent or reduce them. A trial period may sometimes be necessary to assess a medication's efficacy and duration of action, and combinations of medications with different attributes, side effects or duration of action may sometimes be necessary to optimize outcomes and compliance.[14]

Despite these potential challenges**, stimulant medications** remain the **first-line treatment** for ADHD and are critical in managing the disorder effectively. Recent research indicates that treatment with stimulants can also aid in addressing co-occurring conditions, such as substance use disorders, binge eating, and chronic pain (e.g., fibromyalgia) in patients with and without ADHD. However, in some of these studies, findings were mixed; further research is needed to clarify these relationships.[15,16] The use of stimulants in patients with ADHD and other medical conditions and their positive or negative impact will be discussed in depth in Chapter 7.

Non-stimulant medications have also been used to treat ADHD. Although their efficacy ratings are not quite as high as the stimulants, they do have unique characteristics that make them a preferred treatment in certain cases when stimulants don't work or when an alternate treatment is necessary. Pharmacologically, non-stimulants are more targeted on the norepinephrine transmitter systems. In some cases, non-stimulant medications may be used in combination with stimulant medications or other treatments to achieve optimal symptom management. These scenarios will be discussed in more depth along with the stimulants and other medications in Chapter 5.

> The goal of medication treatment is always to optimize symptom control and improve quality of life while minimizing side effects.

Practice: The goal of medication treatment is always to optimize symptom control and improve quality of life while minimizing side effects. ADHD affects a woman's life 24 hours a day, 7 days a week, and 365 days a year. It's important for you to choose a medication schedule that addresses this need for coverage by becoming familiar with long-acting preparations of stimulant and non-stimulant medications for treating ADHD. Twice-a-day dosing, multiple doses of a shorter-acting medication, or a combination of long-acting and short-acting formulations may be necessary to effectively and optimally address your patient's ADHD needs. While the efficacy of **stimulant medications** is well established, individual patient responses may vary significantly.

> Prepare your patients to understand that a trial of medication over several weeks may be necessary to find the **most effective preparation** and **dose** for them.

Preparing patients ahead of time prevents them from becoming discouraged, avoids needless contact with your office, and improves patient adherence. A brief weekly scheduled check-in virtually or by text or phone during the trial period to report on progress can also eliminate numerous calls and concerns. Dosage adjustment can also be made at that time. Several different medication changes may be necessary to achieve these goals, as there are numerous medications and formulations available at the present time. These pharmacologic choices will be discussed in Chapter 5. If a methylphenidate preparation is not effective, a switch to an amphetamine may be indicated, or vice versa. The use of **non-stimulants**, alone or in combination with stimulants, may also be necessary.

Trials should be conducted to **measure effectiveness**, both in terms of a decrease in target symptoms and improvement in overall functioning, while **monitoring side effects**. Discussing medication side effects and offering strategies for dealing with them in advance may be the best strategy for helping your patient cope during the trial period and is a more efficient use of your time. The most common **side effects** of stimulant medications are appetite decrease, insomnia, stomach aches, and headaches. Taking medication after eating a nutritious meal—rather than on an empty stomach or skipping meals—may eliminate stomach aches, and treating occasional headaches with a mild analgesic and/or a snack have also been found to be an effective treatments. Blood pressure, heart rate, and weight should be monitored during the trial period.

Women with ADHD should also be encouraged to monitor their symptoms and response to stimulant medication during their **menstrual cycles** for several months, as **hormonal fluctuations** can contribute to increased symptoms and decreased effectiveness of medication. It is important for clinicians to become familiar with the prevalence of this problem and to be prepared to adjust dosage of stimulants in response to reports of varying effectiveness throughout a woman's menstrual cycle. A recent study conducted in Denmark has confirmed the necessity and effectiveness of increasing the dose of **stimulant medication during the luteal phase** of the menstrual cycle when treating women with ADHD.[17] Many women with ADHD also report reduced medication effectiveness during times of decreasing estrogen, such as prior to menstruation, postpartum, and during perimenopause.

(See Chapter 5 for a more in-depth discussion of medications used to treat ADHD. See Chapter 8 for a more in-depth discussion of hormones.)

2. Adopting lifestyle changes: Simplify, simplify, simplify

Theory: Simplifying life is so important for a woman with ADHD that we have devoted an entire chapter to strategies for women to help them build a life more conducive to dealing successfully with their ADHD. Dr. Nadeau has also co-authored a book on the subject, ***ADD-Friendly Ways to Organize Your Life***.[18] Therefore, we will not discuss this topic in detail here. However, we would like to point out a couple of issues that might prove to be impediments to getting your female patient with ADHD to buy into this new way of dealing with her life. She has gotten this far in life with the help of certain strategies and adopted behaviors, some of which will not have served her well. She has most likely made some choices along the way that did not turn out like she had hoped. You are now asking her to look at these choices and simplify various areas of her life by making changes both big and small. Does she need to move? Change her job? Hire household help? Learn to say no to volunteering at her children's school? Declutter her closet and simplify her wardrobe?

The first step in simplifying her life is getting her to move away from elaborate rituals and give up her tendency to use **perfectionism** and/or **masking her** symptoms to conceal the challenges she faces every day. Instead of helping, these strategies are only adding hours to her day and increasing her feelings of **overwhelm and chaos**. Anything that is getting in the way of dealing with her ADHD and adds more stress to her life needs to go! The second step and perhaps an even more important hurdle to overcome is helping her to feel comfortable **"asking for help."**

Practice: To overcome the overwhelm and chaos and to make changes to simplify her life, a woman with ADHD will first need to be educated regarding the necessity and efficacy of such changes. To accomplish this enormous, yet necessary, lifestyle change, a woman with ADHD will need support.

- A **therapist** is almost always indicated to facilitate a change in mindset.
- An **ADHD coach** can work **with** her to arrive at practical solutions to everyday problems and to establish habits that will improve organization and executive functioning.
- A **professional organizer** can be invaluable in helping a woman with ADHD deal with handling clutter and organizing her home and office.
- A **cleaning service** can help women with access to more financial resources reduce the time spent on household labor. If hiring professional help is not in their budget, many women with ADHD who do the lion's share of the household labor could benefit from resisting unreasonable social pressure for perfect order and cleanliness and, whenever possible, seek support from friends, family, and/or other members of the household. (More information on this topic can be found in Chapter 10.)
- A **body double**: This is a concept developed by ADHD coaches and refers to someone (a friend, relative, or online body double) who provides a calm, consistent presence to a woman with ADHD as she tackles projects that would otherwise feel overwhelming. This technique has proven remarkably effective in helping people with ADHD stay on task and complete projects.

Keep in mind that most women cannot afford this team of professionals, and such professionals are not available in many places. Some of these services can be combined and offered by an experienced ADHD psychotherapist, eliminating the need for a coach. Support will be essential as these women work to make numerous significant changes in their lives. Free support may be available from friends and family, and from online support groups and organizations.

> To avoid overwhelm and discouragement, teach your patient that support from others will lighten her load!

3. Suggesting accommodations in the workplace

Theory: The symptoms associated with ADHD—such as inattention, impulsivity, and hyperactivity, alongside executive dysfunction—can manifest in various ways that hinder functioning in the workplace, affecting organization, time management, and interpersonal relationships. Employment levels, earning power, and productivity are often reduced in individuals with ADHD compared with those without ADHD.[19] Remember Isabele from Chapter 2, who had just lost her 5th job? These effects of ADHD symptoms make it important to implement specific accommodations tailored to a woman's needs in the workplace.

ADHD confers both strengths and limitations related to employment. Workers with ADHD can adapt and thrive in employment when the following three elements are in place:

- Right person–environment fit.
- Accommodations.
- Support.

While both men and women with ADHD experience challenges in the work environment, research has discovered several gendered differences in employment issues. A larger percentage of women with ADHD reported being unemployed, had far greater difficulty finding and keeping employment, and were significantly less integrated in the labor market than men of comparable age and education.[20] Other studies have emphasized the interpersonal aspects of workplace challenges for women, reporting that women are more distressed by perceived interpersonal problems at work, both with co-workers and supervisors. As is true for women with ADHD in all aspects of their lives, their ability (or inability) to get along with others has a substantial impact upon their life satisfaction.

You, as the primary care provider, can play an integral role in helping your female patients with ADHD function better at work by suggesting a career or job change, providing a list of helpful workplace accommodations, and/or referring to an ADHD coach, who can help a woman to improve organizational and task-completion skills. However, to request accommodations in the workplace, a woman must first disclose her ADHD diagnosis.

ACCOMMODATIONS AT WORK WITHOUT DISCLOSING HER ADHD

Dr. Nadeau, who has been a pioneer in helping people with ADHD find the right job fit and find ways to function better at work, often recommends "problem-solving" before deciding upon a formal disclosure of ADHD. Why? Because a supervisor receiving an ADHD disclosure may assume the worst and act accordingly. While accommodations are required by law, disclosure may lead to a supervisor assigning less interesting or less challenging tasks to a woman with ADHD, or assuming that she won't do a good job. In other cases, the supervisor may be on the lookout for errors and poor performance, placing her on a Performance Improvement Plan (PIP)—an intervention that can sometimes be a step toward building a case for dismissal. It is not enough for these accommodations to be in place—they must also enable the employee to fulfill all the job requirements. Instead of a formal disclosure, Dr. Nadeau has often found that it can be helpful to request solutions to specific problems, for example:

- I am finding it difficult to get my work done because my office-mate is often talking on the phone. Might it be possible to reassign me to a quieter workspace?
- Can we set up a weekly 15-minute check-in? That would be very helpful to me in prioritizing tasks and setting deadlines to get this project completed.

In other words, it can be most productive to approach ADHD challenges in a way that demonstrates motivation and constructive problem-solving.

THE DECISION TO DISCLOSE

In some cases, for example if a supervisor is not receptive to her constructive requests for ways to improve her workplace performance, then a formal disclosure of ADHD may be necessary, usually to HR and to her supervisor. For a list of common accommodations for ADHD, you or your patient can refer to the Job Accommodations Network (JAN), which can be found at https://askjan.org. JAN is the leading source of free, expert, and confidential guidance on workplace accommodations.

The **Americans with Disabilities Act, 1990 (ADA)**,[21] protects individuals with ADHD (and other disabilities) from discrimination in employment, education, public accommodations, and transportation. Today, in most workplaces, a woman with an ADHD diagnosis is more likely to be met with acceptance and helpful accommodations than in the past. However, requests for accommodations must be considered "reasonable," and not all employers can provide the same level of accommodations due to differences regarding tasks required and work environments.

Practice: What works? Accommodations might include:

- Establishing a quiet workspace.
- Flexible scheduling.
- Frequent breaks and/or movement.
- Task delegation.

Structured job roles with **clear expectations** can significantly reduce anxiety associated with ambiguity, fostering a better work environment and, thus, improve job performance.[22] **Regularly scheduled frequent check-ins** with supervisors or project heads can facilitate overcoming barriers early on, improve task completion, and contribute to improved performance overall. **Breaking tasks or projects into smaller units** with individual due dates for each step can assist in on-time task completion as well.

Providing access to resources that help women with ADHD develop **self-advocacy skills** or learn **coping strategies** can promote a sense of self-efficacy in the work environment. These skills can be more easily learned and developed by working with an **ADHD coach** or **therapist**.

4. Recommending exercise (for more information, see Chapter 11)

Theory: Exercise is important to maintain wellness for all women, but women with ADHD may especially see benefits to both their mental health and cognitive functioning from exercise. Physical exercise may serve as a valuable intervention, potentially improving cognitive functions and helping manage inattentive symptoms effectively. Incorporating exercise into a holistic treatment approach may foster better mental health outcomes, improve sleep, and enhance the overall quality of life for women affected by this disorder.[23]

Practice: Whether it's a structured aerobic exercise program or an increase in overall physical activity, exercise should be recommended as part of any treatment program for women with ADHD; but how can you increase a woman's likelihood of adherence to this advice? Here are some practical strategies to suggest when recommending exercise to your patient.

First, **connect** exercise to one or more desired outcomes—decreasing insomnia, improving mood or attentiveness, or decreasing restlessness or hyperactivity. **Choose** one or two outcomes and **measure** results at her next visit!

Second, **start slowly**, and build up. Don't suggest she go from **NO** exercise to running! Just suggest that she aim to increase physical activity each day by small increments.

Third, choose a **favored activity** (swimming or water walking) over a boring one (walking on a treadmill) as this will offer a greater chance of her succeeding.

Fourth, encourage her to **join a group** activity or **exercise with a friend** to help her stay motivated.

Fifth, **advise her on how to build exercise into her day**. For example, she could deliberately park 10–15 minutes away from her office to make walking part of her day. She could also walk up the stairs at work—or at home, if she lives in an apartment—instead of taking the elevator all the way to her floor.

And, lastly, suggest she write the activity into her **schedule**, not just wait for an opportunity for it to happen!

Eventually, once medication and other organization skills become established, exercise will get easier for her to remember. At that point, plans such as starting a structured program, joining a team or club, or having an exercise partner will have a better chance of success.

5. Improving diet and nutrition

Theory: Evidence for dietary/nutritional treatments of ADHD varies widely, but various studies do suggest that certain dietary approaches may positively influence ADHD symptoms, thereby improving overall quality of life for affected women. The study of the effects of good nutrition on more general cognitive functioning is in the process of developing into the field of "nutritional neuroscience," with university courses now on offer across the United States and the recent launch of the international online journal *Nutritional Neuroscience: An International Journal on Nutrition, Diet and Nervous System*.[24] Improving diet often leads to improved overall well-being.

One recent study examined the impact of the Dietary Approaches to Stop Hypertension **(DASH)** diet on ADHD symptoms. This randomized controlled trial highlighted the potential for structured dietary changes as an effective non-pharmacological intervention that ameliorates ADHD symptoms, suggesting a pathway for dietary management that may lead to additional health benefits.[25] While current studies have focused on improvement of ADHD in children, the positive results may also have implications for adult ADHD management, suggesting that this could serve as a supportive measure to mitigate women's symptoms.

Moreover, a systematic review indicated that various dietary practices, including certain **elimination diets** and the **Mediterranean diet**, have shown promise in managing ADHD symptoms. Specific elimination diets have demonstrated considerable effect in reducing symptoms by removing potential dietary triggers.[26] One study noted that increased dietary intake of omega-3s, particularly from fish, is related to improved cognitive function and reduced ADHD symptoms.[27] The potential benefits of **omega-3 fatty acids** are discussed in ADHD contexts under supplementation (see item 10 in this list, "Vitamins and Other Supplements").

Lastly, the microbiome's influence on ADHD is becoming an area of interest. An emerging study indicates that dietary interventions targeting the **microbiome** may enhance ADHD management, suggesting that the relationship between gut health and brain function could be relevant for women with ADHD.[28]

Practice: Evidence supporting the role of dietary modifications in managing ADHD symptoms among women points to a complex, yet positive, relationship. Interventions such as the **DASH diet, polyphenol-rich foods, and intake of omega-3 fatty acids (by supplementation or naturally in the diet)** seem to offer promising avenues to pursue for women with ADHD. As research progresses, these dietary changes could serve as vital components within a **comprehensive ADHD treatment** strategy.

In your practice, supporting overall good nutritional practices is important and women with ADHD may especially benefit from your attention to and recommendations for improvement in these areas. Recommending healthier dietary options could lessen symptom severity and improve your patient's overall well-being. While there is no causal link between ADHD and diet, an improved diet and adequate levels of certain nutrients are likely to lead to improved overall well-being and a small, but positive, effect on attention.

6. Getting enough sleep

Theory: Improving sleep for women with ADHD is a critical intervention area, given the increased prevalence of sleep disturbances in this population and the well-established link between poor sleep and reduced cognitive functioning. Women with ADHD often report insomnia and associated sleep issues at higher rates than their male counterparts, both of which can exacerbate ADHD symptoms and negatively impact their quality of life.[29,30] Adult women with ADHD reported significantly higher rates of **insomnia** compared with women without ADHD (43.9% vs 12.2%).[31]

Practice: One of the most effective methods of improving sleep in women with ADHD is to use behavioral sleep interventions. **Cognitive behavioral therapy for insomnia** (CBT-I) adjusted for ADHD has shown promise in enhancing sleep quality in women with ADHD. Such interventions focus on teaching **sleep hygiene, establishing consistent bedtime routines, and implementing relaxation techniques**. These interventions have been shown to produce meaningful reductions in sleep onset delay and night awakenings, along with decreased severity of ADHD symptoms.

Encouraging practices such as establishing and maintaining regular sleep/wake times, creating a conducive sleep environment (e.g., cool and dark), and minimizing screen time before bed (at least two hours prior to attempting sleep) are essential components that can significantly improve sleep. Addressing circadian rhythm disorders may alleviate some of the sleep issues faced by women with ADHD, as circadian misalignment is prevalent in this population (delayed sleep phase disorder is further discussed in Chapter 5 and Chapter 11).

Moderate to vigorous physical activity (PA) is particularly effective in establishing an improved sleep cycle. For women who cannot engage in vigorous exercise for whatever reason, incorporating increased physical activity into daily routines can be beneficial as well. **Exercise** has been linked both to improvements in sleep quality and to reductions in ADHD symptom severity, as higher levels of daytime activity are associated with shorter sleep latencies.

Medications that reduce ADHD symptoms can also improve sleep quality in women who report that they cannot shut off their brains and fall asleep. These women may be helped by having stimulant medication coverage lasting through the evening to assist them in addressing this symptom of ADHD. However, for some other women care must be taken as to how late their last dose of medication is taken, as some ADHD medications may have negative effects on sleep initiation; insomnia has been reported as one of the more common side effects of stimulants. Medications like **melatonin** have been utilized to manage sleep onset latency effectively, counteracting the delayed sleep phase syndrome often associated with ADHD.[32] It is crucial to monitor these outcomes closely, as the interplay between sleep medication and ADHD symptomatology can vary significantly across individuals.

7. Improving executive functions/organizational skills

Theory: Anxiety and executive dysfunction are closely associated with each other, and are seen in both adolescent and adult populations with ADHD. Research has shown that a significant proportion of women with ADHD report high rates of anxiety (26%) alongside executive dysfunction.[33] This anxiety can exacerbate ADHD-related executive dysfunction, affecting not only daily life but also educational and occupational outcomes. Furthermore, emotional dysregulation, frequently observed in women with ADHD, complicates the interplay between executive dysfunction and anxiety.[34,35]

Practice: As a result of these many intertwined factors holding her back, the **anxiety** seen in a woman with ADHD must first be addressed with **medication and therapy**. Additionally, organization and time-management skills, which seem to come naturally as part of the developmental process for those without ADHD, must be explicitly taught to women with ADHD. It is here that a referral to an **ADHD coach** and/or a **professional organizer** is invaluable.

HOW CAN AN ADHD COACH OR A PROFESSIONAL ORGANIZER HELP?

ADHD coaching can take place online or in person and helps the woman with ADHD address real-life issues using a **collaborative** approach. An effective coach will help a woman to develop organizational and planning solutions and also to **execute** these solutions, providing accountability to help her follow through on her intentions. A coach assists with time management, task completion, use of a calendar or planner, and establishing routines and schedules. A professional organizer may also need to step in for cases of extreme clutter or disorganization. Once order has been established, systems can be set up based on the woman's learning style to help keep things organized.

8. Prescribing therapy or counseling

Theory: Women with ADHD present with a multitude of challenges for which psychotherapy or counseling can be highly beneficial. The later in life the diagnosis is made, the greater the woman's need for therapeutic support. The following list of issues to focus on in psychotherapy is representative, but not even close to exhaustive.

- Learned helplessness
- Shame
- Low sense of self-worth
- Trauma/ PTSD
- Depression
- Intimate partner abuse
- Self-injury
- Anxiety
- Bipolar disorder
- Marital issues
- Divorce
- Parenting/family issues
- Body dysmorphia
- Eating disorders

Practice: As discussed earlier in this chapter, treatment of a woman with ADHD requires a comprehensive approach that attends to lifestyle factors. She will therefore need support and counseling to address all her issues and establish a lifestyle that ensures her happiness and success. A combination of medication and psychotherapy has been repeatedly found to be the most effective intervention.

COGNITIVE BEHAVIORAL THERAPY (CBT) AND DIALECTICAL BEHAVIOR THERAPY (DBT)

Theory: Evidence suggests that CBT can significantly reduce ADHD symptoms, even among those already receiving medication.[36] Studies indicate that combining psychotherapy with pharmacological treatment can lead to better outcomes for adult patients with ADHD.[37] Additionally, a meta-analytic review supports the efficacy of CBT in managing executive dysfunction and emotional dysregulation, both commonly found in adult women with ADHD.[38]

Similarly, DBT-informed therapy has shown effectiveness in managing emotional regulation issues related to ADHD. (We refer to "DBT-informed" therapy, an approach that uses many DBT intervention techniques, because formal DBT is much more intensive, requiring frequent individual and group psychotherapy sessions, and is typically used to treat borderline personality disorder, or BPD.) Research indicates that DBT can help mitigate impulsivity and emotional dysregulation, both of which are significant challenges for individuals with ADHD. Notably, studies have identified overlaps between the symptoms of ADHD and those addressed by DBT, such as difficulties in managing emotions and impulsivity.[39]

Practice: As discussed above and in Chapter 10, psychotherapy and counseling are recommended for females with ADHD. CBT and DBT are particularly important for addressing emotional dysregulation and enhancing overall functioning. These therapies reduce ADHD symptoms and foster skills that improve quality of life, and should be considered an essential part of comprehensive ADHD treatment in women.

9. Practicing mindfulness

Theory: Mindfulness is a practice that encourages focusing on the present moment. Patients learn different techniques to stay in the moment, such as deep breathing, meditation, and focusing on their thoughts, feelings, and bodily sensations. Learning to focus on the present helps the individual let go of what's happened in the past and avoid thoughts of what is going to happen. This helps reduce stress, negative self-talk, and anxiety.

Evidence supports the efficacy of these practices for women with ADHD, as the cognitive and emotional challenges associated with this condition can be particularly pronounced. Mindfulness has been shown to improve executive function and emotional regulation.[40,41] Further, in a feasibility study of mindfulness-based cognitive therapy, mindfulness was found to significantly reduce ADHD symptoms and improve executive functioning, self-compassion, and mental health.[42] Similarly, a meta-analysis by Cairncross and Miller in 2016 found that mindfulness-based therapies led to marked improvements in ADHD symptoms and enhanced awareness and control of mental processes, thus improving symptoms of disorganization and emotional dysregulation.[43]

Practice: Mindfulness should be considered as an adjunct to medication treatment for patients without optimal response or as a stand-alone treatment for patients who cannot tolerate or decline medication. It is simple, efficacious, and cost-effective.

Referring your patient to a counselor or therapist for **mindfulness-based cognitive therapy** (MBCT)[44] will provide her with an additional tool to manage her ADHD and can be extremely helpful in improving her overall mental health and quality of life. MBCT is a structured, group-based psychological intervention that integrates principles of CBT with mindfulness meditation practices. Mindfulness has also been found to be helpful for other conditions, including fibromyalgia, anxiety, stress, asthma, and insomnia and other sleep issues, to name just a few.

10. Vitamins and other supplements

Theory: While vitamins and minerals cannot replace traditional ADHD treatments, they can function as **adjunctive therapies** and potentially mitigate ADHD severity in cases of **nutritional deficiency**. Emerging research suggests that **micronutrients** may play a role in alleviating ADHD symptoms in adults.[45]

Cederberg et al. indicate that **vitamin D deficiency** could influence various conditions, including restless legs syndrome, and potentially affect ADHD symptoms.[46] Li et al. found that reduced serum concentration of **25-hydroxyvitamin D (25(OH)D) in children with ADHD** as compared with that in healthy children responded to supplementation as an adjunct therapy used to address symptoms of ADHD with comparatively few side effects.[47]

OMEGA-3 POLYUNSATURATED FATTY ACIDS (PUFAS)

A review by Agostoni et al. confirms that omega-3 fatty acids are important components of neuronal membranes and are integral for maintaining normal cognitive function.[48] Insufficiency of these fatty acids is thought to be associated with the increased prevalence and severity of symptoms characteristic of ADHD.[49]

While some meta-analyses report that **omega-3 supplementation** may contribute positively to cognitive function and behavior in ADHD populations, they also indicate a need for larger-scale, high-quality randomized controlled trials to draw definitive conclusions about its effectiveness.[50] While the supplementation may improve specific symptoms, such as impulsivity and emotional regulation, it should not be seen as a stand-alone treatment but rather as an adjunct to conventional interventions such as stimulant medications.

Practice: Addressing nutrient deficiencies should be done on an individual basis, as not all individuals with ADHD will have deficiencies. Screening for zinc and vitamin D levels at the beginning of an ADHD diagnosis might be beneficial, with treatment recommended if levels are deficient. Omega-3 supplementation may be more helpful for patients with lower baseline serum levels of omega-3, and EPA may be more effective than DHA for reducing inattentive ADHD symptoms and for treatment of depression. A dose-response curve has been noted, with EPA supplement levels of less than 500 mg daily showing no effect. A 1000-2000 mg dose of EPA, with the EPA:DHA ratio being equal or greater to 3:1, may be a more appropriate dose. In patients who already consume substantial omega-3s from their diet, it may be beneficial to consume an EPA-only product to shift the combined (diet + supplement) EPA:DHA ratio in the direction of 3:1. A 16-week trial is appropriate to assess for benefit.

MICRONUTRIENTS

ADHD specialists and researchers Julia Rucklidge, Ph.D., and Bonnie Kaplan, Ph.D., have intensively studied the impact of micronutrients on ADHD symptoms and take a markedly different approach from others in their research and recommended treatment. They believe that the modest gains shown in micronutrient supplementation is because studies only measure the impact of single micronutrients. As an analogy, it would be like studying the nutritional impact of carrots and then later the benefits of mushrooms. Instead, dietary recommendations are broad, involving a variety of foods offering different nutritional components. Likewise, Rucklidge and Kaplan have taken that approach to micronutrients and have found a positive response to a nutrient combination that they have developed to treat ADHD, for use as a supplementary treatment in combination with stimulant medications, or in place of stimulant medication for those who can't tolerate it or desire a non-medication treatment approach. For more information, consult *The Better Brain by* Bonnie Kaplan, Ph.D. and Julia Rucklidge, Ph.D.[51]

In conclusion, there is **no** overwhelming evidence to support the use of either vitamins, zinc, or omega-3 fatty acids as a **monotherapy** for the treatment of ADHD in adults. Although it is not definitively clear what percentage of individuals presenting with symptoms of ADHD have nutrient deficiencies, the existing literature suggests that a subgroup of those with ADHD are at risk of these, and that they may play a role in ADHD symptoms or response to medication.

11. Suggesting peer and support groups

Theory: A woman with ADHD often feels isolated and alone. She has struggled for years and has experienced rejection and failure. Even if she has managed some level of success, she will tell you, "Yes, but I always felt different," or "Yes, but it was harder for me," or "Yes, but I'm not as smart as others who … ." Self-acceptance is often a huge issue for women with ADHD! This issue is aptly captured in the title of Kate Kelly and Peggy Ramundo's book, ***You Mean I'm Not Lazy, Stupid or Crazy?!***[52]

Qualitative studies suggest that group settings can enhance self-acceptance and coping strategies among females with ADHD, thereby improving their relational dynamics.[53] Peer acceptance can lead to positive reinforcement, thus promoting emotional resilience in women with ADHD.

Support groups for women with ADHD play a vital role in providing emotional support and **validation**. Practical tips and coping strategies, which are particularly critical for these women due to the unique challenges they face compared to their male counterparts, are often provided in these settings. Members of such groups often report significant benefits, including enhanced self-esteem, a stronger sense of community, and gaining valuable insights into managing ADHD symptoms.[54] Women diagnosed with ADHD in adulthood often find that discussing their experiences in a safe environment reduces feelings of **stigma** and **isolation** while enabling them to see their struggles in a more supportive light.[55] This aspect of group participation is crucial, as it addresses societal stigma regarding ADHD, particularly in females, who may experience their symptoms being overlooked or misinterpreted. These groups are essential for building resilience and promoting a stronger sense of community among women navigating the complexities associated with ADHD.

Practice: As described elsewhere in this book, it is important for a woman with ADHD to connect with people she can relate to. Many women are unaware of how important this step is to gaining **self-acceptance** and life **satisfaction**. Your recommendations and encouragement will go a long way to encouraging your patients to seek out peer groups for support and friendship. There are also several online groups for women with ADHD.

12. Important additional treatment considerations for women with ADHD

Before we leave this chapter about treatment for women with ADHD, it would be remiss if we didn't shine a spotlight on two important treatments—in addition to ADHD medications—that need to be considered when working with women with ADHD. The first is **contraception** and the second is **hormone replacement therapy (HRT)** for women in peri/menopause who have significant memory or cognitive dysfunction and a worsening of ADHD symptoms.

As mentioned in several chapters of this book, the ADHD symptoms of impulsivity and executive dysfunction can impact women's sexual health. **Contraceptive counseling** is imperative for this group of women with ADHD. Keeping in mind the difficulties these women have in following through and remembering to take their medications, contraceptive methods should be convenient and longer term. In addition, since higher progesterone levels make symptoms of ADHD and depression worse, low-dose estrogen/progesterone combinations or estrogen therapies with intermittent progesterone periods about every three months are more ideal for women with ADHD. If progesterone is used alone, it should be at the lowest effective dose possible.

Women in **perimenopause** with increasing ADHD symptoms may benefit from estrogen given orally or by a patch, with progesterone given intermittently if they have a uterus. For women with ADHD in menopause, **HRT**, if begun early and not contraindicated for medical reasons (cardiovascular disease, hypertension, previous breast cancer, etc.), can be extremely helpful for them in dealing with their worsening ADHD and to support cognitive function during this phase of life. The goal of these **integrated treatment strategies** is to stabilize fluctuating or declining hormone levels, which can wreak havoc in the lives of women with ADHD by magnifying the symptoms of ADHD and/or reducing the effectiveness of stimulant medication.

ENDPOINT: AN INDIVIDUALIZED TREATMENT PROGRAM FOR WOMEN WITH ADHD

Intervention programs specifically tailored for women with ADHD are essential in helping them to overcome the overwhelm and manage their symptoms. Recently, specialized clinics have been opening to meet the needs of women with ADHD, like the new NovaVia Health clinic based in Arlington, Virginia, which also offers care to women with ADHD throughout the United States through telemedicine. For more information about this holistic, individualized approach to treatment, check out their website: https://www.novaviahealth.com/.

In this chapter, we have presented many recommendations for women with ADHD in addition to simply prescribing medication. While medication to treat ADHD is the cornerstone of treatment and other therapies may be futile without it, your commitment to your patient is not complete if medication is all that you recommend. Not every woman will need all these therapeutic interventions. Some recommendations will be more critical than others, depending on your patient's immediate stressors as she travels down the path toward better managing her ADHD.

Collaboratively designing a holistic, individualized treatment program is the goal. Remember, ADHD is a hopeful diagnosis, and you now hold the keys that can unlock the door to a successful future for your patient. We urge you to use them!

REFERENCES

1. Rogers, A. L., & Kear, N. C. (2024). 2024 scorecard on ADHD treatments. *ADDitude Magazine*. https://additu.de/spring-2024
2. Chang, Z., Ghirardi, L., Quinn, P. D., Asherson, P., D'Onofrio, B. M., & Larsson, H. (2019). Risks and benefits of Attention-Deficit/Hyperactivity Disorder medication on behavioral and neuropsychiatric outcomes: a qualitative review of pharmacoepidemiology studies using linked prescription databases. *Biological Psychiatry, 86*(5), 335–343. https://doi.org/10.1016/j.biopsych.2019.04.009
3. Cortese, S., Adamo, N., Del Giovane, C., Mohr-Jensen, C., Hayes, A. J., Carucci, S., Atkinson, L. Z., Tessari, L., Banaschewski, T., Coghill, D., Hollis, C., Simonoff, E., Zuddas, A., Barbui, C., Purgato, M., Steinhausen, H.-C., Shokraneh, F., Xia, J., & Cipriani, A. (2018). Comparative efficacy and tolerability of medications for attention-deficit hyperactivity disorder in children, adolescents, and adults: a systematic review and network meta-analysis. *The Lancet Psychiatry, 5*(9), 727–738. https://doi.org/10.1016/S2215-0366(18)30269-4
4. Cortese, S., Adamo, N., Del Giovane, C., Mohr-Jensen, C., Hayes, A. J., Carucci, S., Atkinson, L. Z., Tessari, L., Banaschewski, T., Coghill, D., Hollis, C., Simonoff, E., Zuddas, A., Barbui, C., Purgato, M., Steinhausen, H.-C., Shokraneh, F., Xia, J., & Cipriani, A. (2018). Comparative efficacy and tolerability of medications for attention-deficit hyperactivity disorder in children, adolescents, and adults: a systematic review and network meta-analysis. *The Lancet Psychiatry, 5*(9), 727–738. https://doi.org/10.1016/S2215-0366(18)30269-4
5. Spencer, T., Biederman, J., Wilens, T., Doyle, R., Surman, C., Prince, J., Mick, E., Aleardi, M., & Herzig, K. (2005). A large, double-blind, randomized clinical trial of methylphenidate in the treatment of adults with attention-deficit/hyperactivity disorder. *Biological Psychiatry, 57*(5), 456–463. https://doi.org/10.1016/j.biopsych.2004.11.043
6. Taipale, H., Bergström, J., Gèmes, K., Tanskanen, A., Ekselius, L., Mittendorfer-Rutz, E., & Helgesson, M. (2024). Attention-deficit/hyperactivity disorder medications and work disability and mental health outcomes. *JAMA Network Open*, 7(3), e242859. https://doi.org/10.1001/jamanetworkopen.2024.2859
7. Li, L., Zhu, N., Zhang, L., Kuja-Halkola, R., D'Onofrio, B. M., Brikell, I., Lichtenstein, P., Cortese, S., Larsson, H., & Chang, Z. (2024). ADHD pharmacotherapy and mortality in individuals with ADHD. *JAMA, 331*(10), 850–860. https://doi.org/10.1001/jama.2024.0851
8. De Jong, M. Wynchank, D. S. M. R., van Andel, E., Beekman, A. T. F., & Kooij, J. J. S. (2023). Female-specific pharmacotherapy in ADHD: premenstrual adjustment of psychostimulant dosage. *Frontiers in Psychiatry, 14*. https://doi.org/10.3389/fpsyt.2023.1306194
9. Rapoport, I. L., & Groenman, A. P. (2025). A review of sex and gender factors in stimulant treatment for ADHD: knowledge gaps and future directions. *Journal of Attention Disorders, 29*(8), 602–616. https://doi.org/10.1177/10870547251315601
10. Rapoport, I. L., & Groenman, A. P. (2025). A review of sex and gender factors in stimulant treatment for ADHD: knowledge gaps and future directions. *Journal of Attention Disorders, 29*(8), 602–616. https://doi.org/10.1177/10870547251315601
11. MacDonald, H. J., Kleppe, R., Szigetvari, P. D., & Haavik, J. (2024). The dopamine hypothesis for ADHD: an evaluation of evidence accumulated from human studies and animal models. *Frontiers in Psychiatry, 15*, 1492126. https://doi.org/10.3389/fpsyt.2024.1492126

12. Schein, J., Cloutier, M., Gauthier-Loiselle, M., Bungay, R., Guerin, A., & Childress, A. (2023). Symptoms associated with ADHD/treatment-related adverse side effects and their impact on quality of life and work productivity in adults with ADHD. *Current Medical Research and Opinion, 39*(1), 149–159. https://doi.org/10.1080/03007995.2022.2122228
13. Kok, F. M., Groen, Y., Fuermaier, A. B. M., & Tucha, O. (2020). The female side of pharmacotherapy for ADHD—a systematic literature review. *PLOS One, 15*(9), e0239257. https://doi.org/10.1371/journal.pone.0239257
14. Duric, N. S., Assmus, J., Gundersen, D., Duric Golos, A., & Elgen, I. B. (2017). Multimodal treatment in children and adolescents with attention-deficit/hyperactivity disorder: a 6-month follow-up. *Nordic Journal of Psychiatry, 71*(5), 386–394. https://doi.org/10.1080/08039488.2017.1305446
15. Manni, C., Cipollone, G., Pallucchini, A., Maremmani, A. G. I., Perugi, G., & Maremmani, I. (2019). Remarkable reduction of cocaine use in dual disorder (adult attention-deficit/hyperactivity disorder/cocaine use disorder) patients treated with medications for ADHD. *International Journal of Environmental Research and Public Health, 16*(20), 3911. https://doi.org/10.3390/ijerph16203911
16. Quinn, P. D., Chang, Z., Hur, K., Gibbons, R. D., Lahey, B. B., Rickert, M. E., Sjölander, A., Lichtenstein, P., Larsson, H., & D'Onofrio, B. M. (2017). ADHD medication and substance-related problems. *The American Journal of Psychiatry, 174*(9), 877–885. https://doi.org/10.1176/appi.ajp.2017.16060686
17. De Jong, M., Wynchank, D. S. M. R., van Andel, E., Beekman, A. T. F., & Kooij, J. J. S. (2023). Female-specific pharmacotherapy in ADHD: premenstrual adjustment of psychostimulant dosage. *Frontiers in Psychiatry, 14*. https://doi.org/10.3389/fpsyt.2023.1306194
18. Nadeau, K. G., & Kolberg, J. S. (2005). *ADD-friendly ways to organize your life* (2nd ed.). Routledge.
19. Sarkis, E. (2014). Addressing attention-deficit/hyperactivity disorder in the workplace. *Postgraduate Medicine, 126*(5), 25–30. https://doi.org/10.3810/pgm.2014.09.2797
20. Sarkis, E. (2014). Addressing attention-deficit/hyperactivity disorder in the workplace. *Postgraduate Medicine, 126*(5), 25–30. https://doi.org/10.3810/pgm.2014.09.2797
21. Americans With Disabilities Act of 1990, 42 U.S.C. § 12101 *et seq.* (1990). https://www.ada.gov/pubs/adastatute08.htm
22. Nagata, M., Nagata, T., Inoue, A., Mori, K., & Matsuda, S. (2019). Effect modification by attention deficit hyperactivity disorder (ADHD) symptoms on the association of psychosocial work environments with psychological distress and work engagement. *Frontiers in Psychiatry, 10*. https://doi.org/10.3389/fpsyt.2019.00166
23. Tucker, R., Williams, C., & Reed, P. (2025). Association of exercise and ADHD symptoms: analysis within an adult general population sample. *PLOS One, 20*(2), e0314508. https://doi.org/10.1371/journal.pone.0314508
24. Nutritional Neuroscience. (1998–present). Taylor & Francis. https://www.tandfonline.com/journals/ynns20
25. Khoshbakht, Y., Moghtaderi, F., Bidaki, R., Hosseinzadeh, M., & Salehi-Abargouei, A. (2021). The effect of dietary approaches to stop hypertension (DASH) diet on attention-deficit hyperactivity disorder (ADHD) symptoms: a randomized controlled clinical trial. *European Journal of Nutrition, 60*(7), 3647–3658. https://doi.org/10.1007/s00394-021-02527-x
26. Ríos-Hernández, A., Alda, J. A., Farran-Codina, A., Ferreira-García, E., & Izquierdo-Pulido, M. (2017). The Mediterranean diet and ADHD in children and adolescents. *Pediatrics, 139*(2), e20162027. https://doi.org/10.1542/peds.2016-2027

27. Fuentes-Albero, M., Martínez-Martínez, M. I., & Cauli, O. (2019). Omega-3 long-chain polyunsaturated fatty acids intake in children with attention deficit and hyperactivity disorder. *Brain Sciences*, *9*(5), 120. https://doi.org/10.3390/brainsci 9050120
28. Lawrence, K., Myrissa, K., Toribio-Mateas, M., & Stock, R. (2022). Trialing a microbiome-targeted dietary intervention in children with ADHD—the rationale and a non-randomised feasibility study. *Pilot and Feasibility Studies*, *8*, 108. https:// doi.org/10.1186/s40814-022-01058-4
29. Wajszilber, D., Santisteban, J. A., & Gruber, R. (2018). Sleep disorders in patients with ADHD: impact and management challenges. *Nature and Science of Sleep*, *10*, 453–480. https://doi.org/10.2147/nss.s163074
30. Ahlberg, R., Garcia-Argibay, M., Taylor, M. A., Lichtenstein, P., D'Onofrio, B. M., Butwicka, A., Larsson, H., & Rietz, E. D. (2023). Prevalence of sleep disorder diagnoses and sleep medication prescriptions in individuals with ADHD across the lifespan: a Swedish nationwide register-based study. *BMJ Mental Health*, *26*(1), e300809. https://doi.org/10.1136/bmjment-2023-300809
31. Fuller-Thomson, E., Lewis, D. A., & Agbeyaka, S. K. (2016). Attention-deficit/ hyperactivity disorder casts a long shadow: findings from a population-based study of adult women with self-reported ADHD. *Child: Care, Health and Development*, *42*(6), 918–927. https://doi.org/10.1111/cch.12380
32. Stein, M. A., Weiss, M. D., & Hlavaty, L. E. (2012). ADHD treatments, sleep, and sleep problems: complex associations. *Neurotherapeutics*, *9*(3), 509–517. https://doi. org/10.1007/s13311-012-0130-0
33. Hanssen, K. T., Brevik, E. J., Småstuen, M. C., & Stubberud, J. (2023). Improvement of anxiety in ADHD following goal-focused cognitive remediation: a randomized controlled trial. *Frontiers in Psychology*, *14*. https://doi.org/10.3389/ fpsyg.2023.1212502
34. Vater, C. H., DiSalvo, M., Ehrlich, A., Parker, H., O'Connor, H., Faraone, S. V., & Biederman, J. (2024). ADHD in adults: does age at diagnosis matter? *Journal of Attention Disorders*, *28*(5), 614–624. https://doi.org/10.1177/10870547231218450
35. Yang, H., Yang, Y., Wang, A., Yang, J., Yang, X., Zhou, J., & Luo, R. (2024). Brain functional networks and executive functions in children with attention-deficit/ hyperactivity disorder. *Research Square*. https://doi.org/10.21203/rs.3.rs-4278865/v1
36. Knouse, L. E., & Safren, S. A. (2010). Current status of cognitive behavioral therapy for adult attention-deficit hyperactivity disorder. *Psychiatric Clinics of North America*, *33*(3), 497–509. https://doi.org/10.1016/j.psc.2010.04.001
37. Emilsson, B., Gudjónsson, G. H., Sigurðsson, J. F., Baldursson, G., Einarsson, E., Ólafsdóttir, H., & Young, S. (2011). Cognitive behaviour therapy in medication-treated adults with ADHD and persistent symptoms: a randomized controlled trial. *BMC Psychiatry*, *11*(1), 116. https://doi.org/10.1186/1471-244X-11-116
38. López-Pinar, C., Martínez-Sanchis, S., Carbonell, E., Fenollar-Cortés, J., & Sánchez-Meca, J. (2018). Long-term efficacy of psychosocial treatments for adults with attention-deficit/hyperactivity disorder: a meta-analytic review. *Frontiers in Psychology*, *9*. https://doi.org/10.3389/fpsyg.2018.00638
39. Fleming, A. P., McMahon, R. J., Moran, L., Peterson, A. P., & Dreessen, A. (2014). Pilot randomized controlled trial of dialectical behavior therapy group skills training for ADHD among college students. *Journal of Attention Disorders*, *19*(3), 260–271. https://doi.org/10.1177/1087054714535951
40. Bigelow, H., Gottlieb, M. D., Ogrodnik, M., Graham, J. D., & Fenesi, B. (2021). The differential impact of acute exercise and mindfulness meditation on executive functioning and psycho-emotional well-being in children and youth with ADHD. *Frontiers in Psychology*, *12*, 660845. https://doi.org/10.3389/fpsyg.2021.660845

41. Mitchell, J. T., McIntyre, E. M., English, J. S., Dennis, M. F., Beckham, J. C., & Kollins, S. H. (2017). A pilot trial of mindfulness meditation training for ADHD in adulthood: Impact on core symptoms, executive functioning, and emotion dysregulation. *Journal of Attention Disorders, 21*(13), 1105–1120. https://doi.org/10.1177/1087054713513328
42. Janssen, L., Vries, A. M. D., Hepark, S., & Speckens, A. (2017). The feasibility, effectiveness, and process of change of mindfulness-based cognitive therapy for adults with ADHD: a mixed-method pilot study. *Journal of Attention Disorders, 24*(6), 928–942. https://doi.org/10.1177/1087054717727350
43. Cairncross, M., & Miller, C. J. (2016). The effectiveness of mindfulness-based therapies for ADHD: a meta-analytic review. *Journal of Attention Disorders, 24*(5), 627–643. https://doi.org/10.1177/1087054715625301
44. Aadil, M., Cosme, R., & Chernaik, J. (2017). Mindfulness-based cognitive behavioral therapy as an adjunct treatment of attention deficit hyperactivity disorder in young adults: a literature review. *Cureus.* https://doi.org/10.7759/cureus.1269
45. Rucklidge, J. J., Frampton, C. M., Gorman, B., & Boggis, A. (2014). Vitamin–mineral treatment of attention-deficit hyperactivity disorder in adults: double-blind randomised placebo-controlled trial. *British Journal of Psychiatry, 204*(4), 306–315. https://doi.org/10.1192/bjp.bp.113.132126
46. Cederberg, K. L. J., Silvestri, R., & Walters, A. S. (2023). Vitamin D and restless legs syndrome: a review of current literature. *Tremor and Other Hyperkinetic Movements, 13,* 12. https://doi.org/10.5334/tohm.741
47. Li, H., Yue, X., Wang, C., Feng, J., Wang, B., & Jia, F. (2020). Serum levels of vitamin A and vitamin D and their association with symptoms in children with attention deficit hyperactivity disorder. *Frontiers in Psychiatry, 11.* https://doi.org/10.3389/fpsyt.2020.599958
48. Agostoni, C., Nobile, M., Ciappolino, V., Delvecchio, G., Tesei, A., Turolo, S., & Brambilla, P. (2017). The role of omega-3 fatty acids in developmental psychopathology: a systematic review on early psychosis, autism, and ADHD. *International Journal of Molecular Sciences, 18*(12), 2608. https://doi.org/10.3390/ijms18122608
49. Bozzatello, P., De Rosa, M. L., Rocca, P., & Bellino, S. (2020). Effects of omega-3 fatty acids on main dimensions of psychopathology. *International Journal of Molecular Sciences, 21*(17), 6042. https://doi.org/10.3390/ijms21176042
50. Cooper, R. E., Tye, C., Kuntsi, J., Vassos, E., & Asherson, P. (2015). Omega-3 polyunsaturated fatty acid supplementation and cognition: a systematic review and meta-analysis. *Journal of Psychopharmacology (Oxford, England), 29*(7), 753–763. https://doi.org/10.1177/0269881115587958
51. Kaplan, B., & Rucklidge, J. (2021). *The better brain.* Harvest Books.
52. Kelly, K., & Ramundo, P. (2006). *You mean I'm not lazy, stupid or crazy?! The classic self-help book for adults with attention deficit disorder.* Simon & Schuster.
53. De Jong, M., Wynchank, D. S. M. R., Michielsen, M., Beekman, A. T., & Kooij, J. J. S. (2024). A female-specific treatment group for ADHD—description of the programme and qualitative analysis of first experiences. *Journal of Clinical Medicine, 13*(7), 2106. https://doi.org/10.3390/jcm13072106
54. Babinski, D. E., & Libsack, E. J. (2024). Adult diagnosis of ADHD in women: a mixed methods investigation. *Journal of Attention Disorders, 29*(3), 207–219. https://doi.org/10.1177/10870547241297897
55. Bradley, S., Parzych, I., Platts, J., & Powell, L. (2025). Understanding and harnessing differences in women with ADHD: a qualitative study. *Neurodiversity, 3,* 27546330251317199. https://doi.org/10.1177/27546330251317199

CHAPTER 5

Medications for the treatment of ADHD

INTRODUCTION

In this chapter, we will review several aspects of prescribing medications for ADHD. First, we look at what medication should do for the women we treat: (1) reduce symptoms, and (2) improve quality of life, assessed in terms of well-being goals. We will then address how the goals of medication have evolved, with current practice emphasizing daily coverage across most waking hours, in contrast to past assumptions that ADHD was only a problem of academic or workplace productivity. Next, we will explore differences between medications and when to switch or augment. And, finally, we will review the promises and pitfalls of integrative medicine and the natural-is-better bias, which can steer women away from evidence-based treatments.

What should the medication do? Target symptoms and well-being goals

If your framework for ADHD assessment were guided only by the DSM, you would focus narrowly on the inattentive and hyperactive/impulsive symptoms listed in the manual. Yet, as outlined in Chapters 1, 9, and 10, substantial research highlights emotion regulation difficulties as a third core domain of ADHD impairment. Importantly, evidence shows that ADHD medication can effectively address not only attentional and behavioral symptoms but also these emotion regulation challenges.[1] Therefore, a comprehensive, target-symptom-based treatment plan should include goals related to inattention, hyperactivity/impulsivity, and emotion regulation.

DOI: 10.4324/9781003542124-5

(See Chapter 2 for an in-depth discussion of how to formulate a comprehensive treatment plan.)

One limitation of a strictly target-symptom approach is that most women with ADHD are not seeking only the reduction or elimination of distressing symptoms. Rather, they aspire to lead full and flourishing lives. For this reason, clinicians should not stop at defining symptom-based targets but should also partner with women to articulate well-being goals that reflect their personal values and aspirations. A positive psychology approach, as exemplified by Martin Seligman's PERMA model, provides a helpful framework. The PERMA model, later expanded to include six domains under the acronym PERMA-H, positive emotion, engagement, relationships, meaning, accomplishment, and health, supplies a roadmap clinicians can follow to promote their clients' overall well-being.[2]

Applied to ADHD care, well-being goals are framed positively—for example, "to wake up feeling rested and relaxed," "to enjoy an entire movie," "to remain present while playing with my toddler," or "to find pleasure in a walk in the woods." These goals emphasize that wellness is not simply the absence of problems but the active presence of connection, fulfillment, and vitality. Framing ADHD treatment in terms of both symptom reduction and the cultivation of well-being provides an important complement to traditional pathology-focused models and aligns clinical care with women's own views on wellness.

When should the medication work?

If evaluated carefully, most women describe ADHD-related difficulties that extend across nearly every waking hour. These challenges often begin with booting up their brain in the morning, getting ready for work, perhaps shepherding children onto the school bus, sustaining focus and productivity through the workday, and then managing the "second shift" of household and perhaps caregiving responsibilities late into the evening. But for most women, the difficulties do not stop there: time-blindness, fluctuating levels of motivation, and inefficient routines all undermine a woman's ability to get into bed on time (see Chapters 3, 6, and 10). Once in bed, it can be difficult for her to quiet her mind sufficiently to initiate sleep. During the night, brief awakenings can transform into sustained insomnia, as intrusive thoughts or bursts of brainstorming crowd out the calm required to ease back into sleep. ADHD is a 24-hour condition, and effective treatment planning must account for this reality alongside a woman's target symptoms and well-being goals.

Medication and behavioral interventions are complementary

Some ADHD target symptoms and well-being goals may respond more effectively to behavioral strategies such as lifestyle modifications; others to modifications of home, work, and social environments; while still others are addressed more effectively with medication. Take the example of completing a large project: it requires breaking the work into medium-sized tasks and subtasks, prioritizing, delegating, and making sure not to be distracted by competing tasks or thoughts. Life satisfaction usually requires the development of interpersonal skills and establishing social networks that foster support and well-being.

Yet another barrier lies in the ADHD brain itself. The Default Mode Network (DMN), which engages at times of daydreaming and internal reflection, does not readily disengage when the Task Mode Network is active (see Chapter 10). Distracting thoughts remain constant companions during focused work periods, and especially when attempting to fall asleep at night. Medication is often essential to quiet this internal noise during daytime hours, enabling women with ADHD to focus fully on the task at hand. Neither medication nor behavioral interventions alone typically yield the strongest results.

OVERVIEW OF MEDICATION TREATMENTS

There is a broad consensus that stimulants, methylphenidate and amphetamines, are the most effective ADHD medications. They are also generally well tolerated, making them the first-line medications for ADHD. Research in adult populations has consistently shown a large effect size, in the range of 0.8–1.2. In adults, it appears that amphetamine-based stimulants are on average slightly more effective and slightly more likely to cause adverse effects than methylphenidate-based stimulants, but these differences are small, and starting medication treatment with either stimulant is appropriate. When one type of stimulant doesn't work or causes intolerable adverse effects, it is reasonable to switch to the other.[3]

Stimulant treatment has been associated with both mortality and morbidity benefits.[4] Potential adverse effects are (1) appetite suppression; (2) difficulty falling asleep, and (3) elevations in heart rate and blood pressure, all of which are typically manageable. Although stimulant treatment of ADHD generally leads to the improvement of co-occurring psychiatric conditions, less commonly, stimulants can cause increases in irritability, mood problems, and anxiety, and at very high doses, they may contribute to risk of psychosis. Methylphenidate treatment may present only a very small risk of worsening these psychiatric symptoms and conditions, with amphetamines being associated with greater risk. Stimulants are schedule II substances that can be misused; however, in our clinical experience, close monitoring of stimulant prescription use as part of a comprehensive treatment approach substantially minimizes the risk.[5,6,7]

Atomoxetine is a second-line medication for ADHD, with an effect size in the range of 0.6, and it is generally well tolerated. We also consider the alpha agonists clonidine and guanfacine to be second-line agents because of their unique potential role in targeting the evening and overnight hours, which a stimulant cannot do. Adverse effects can include orthostatic hypotension, rebound hypertension if the medication is abruptly stopped, and sedation, which can be beneficial for those that have difficulty falling asleep. Third-line medications include viloxazine and bupropion.[8,9] While there is some research to support the use of omega-3 fatty acids and broad micronutrients in the treatment of ADHD, their role in standard practice is not yet established.[10,11]

FIRST-LINE TREATMENT

For most adults, it makes sense to start with the most effective agents, the stimulants. Most stimulants have an onset of action within 30–90 minutes of ingestion and have a duration of action of 4–16 hours, depending on the formulation.[12]

Handedness (aka chirality)

Because small chemical differences between stimulant medications can meaningfully affect potency, duration, and clinical response, it is helpful to understand a basic concept in pharmacology known as molecular "handedness."[13] For many medications, including methylphenidate, left-handed molecules do very little. Some methylphenidate products are 50/50 mixtures of the right- and left-hand molecules, while others are right-hand only. For both methylphenidate products and amphetamines, the left-handed molecules are less effective. Given the numerous stimulant products on the market with varied compositions, release mechanisms, and other divergent properties, the simple generic names "methylphenidate" and "amphetamines" do not clearly differentiate one product from another. For this reason, we will provide both generic and brand names throughout the discussion.

Cardiac evaluation prior to stimulant prescription?

Although stimulants typically do not have major cardiac effects, they affect cardiac conduction, elevate heart rate, and elevate blood pressure. As such, a cardiac evaluation is appropriate prior to stimulant prescription under the following conditions:

1. age > 49
2. personal history of a cardiac problem, including but not limited to arrhythmia, tachycardia, and/or hypertension
3. family history in first- or second-degree relative of a congenital cardiac problem, heart problem in an adult prior to age 40, or event that may have resulted from an underlying cardiac problem such as drowning death or unexplained motor vehicle accident
4. significant gap in primary care (which increases risk that a cardiac problem has been missed due to lack of assessment)
5. any other relevant clinical concerns.

While some guidelines note that an EKG can be an adequate evaluation, there are important elements of cardiac pathology that cannot be identified without an echocardiogram or other cardiac tests. As such, there is no singular approach to cardiac evaluation or "clearance" for stimulant use in adults with risk factors. Rather, the depth of the evaluation should be personalized to the individual clinical situation, in consultation with the woman's primary care provider or cardiologist.[14,15,16]

Methylphenidate-based medications

If you or the women you treat have some concerns about stimulants, you are not alone: they have a reputation as strong medications, are controlled substances, and can be addictive when misused.[17] However, methylphenidate's safety profile is very well known. It has been prescribed in the United States since the 1950s and has been the subject of hundreds of studies since then. When prescribed and monitored properly to appropriate patients, the potential benefits are high and the risk of misuse is low.[18,19,20]

Methylphenidate's mechanisms of action include blocking reuptake of norepinephrine and dopamine at the neuronal synapse, which effectively increases their signaling efficiency. Primary sites of action include the circuits that include the frontal lobes (where it enhances executive functions including working memory, attention, and behavioral inhibition) and the striatum (where it improves reward processing and motor control). Research has supported its effectiveness for problems with attention, hyperactivity, behavioral impulsivity, and emotional impulsivity/regulation.[21,22]

IMMEDIATE-RELEASE METHYLPHENIDATE

Ritalin IR (methylphenidate IR) usually begins working within 30 minutes of ingestion when administered on an empty stomach. It reaches peak blood levels roughly 2 hours after ingestion and typically works for about 4 hours. Ritalin IR is usually initiated at 5 mg two to three times daily; each dose can be increased by 5 mg weekly as needed, to a maximum dose of 20 mg three times daily or 60 mg total dose. With this dosing regimen, 10–12 hours of coverage are achieved.[23]

The immediate-release (IR) formulation of methylphenidate (and of amphetamines) has several notable disadvantages:

- First, Ritalin IR requires multiple daily doses, which makes consistent adherence difficult.
- Second, its dosing results in multiple blood-level peaks and valleys over the course of the day, creating potential gaps in effectiveness, adverse effects associated with the peaks, and adverse effects from rapid shifts in blood levels. A steep drop-off after the last dose may trigger "rebound" symptoms—either a stronger return of ADHD symptoms or new issues such as fatigue or headaches.
- Third, Ritalin IR carries a higher risk of diversion and abuse. The rapid rise in blood levels increases the likelihood of euphoria compared to extended-release forms, and crushing and snorting IR stimulants can produce intense euphoria, greatly heightening abuse potential.[24,25,26] Extended-release products have been developed to address these disadvantages.

INTERMEDIATE-RELEASE METHYLPHENIDATE PRODUCTS (6–8 HOURS)

Ritalin LA (long acting) uses dual-bead technology, delivering 50% immediate release and 50% delayed release about four hours after ingestion. While clinical trials show 8 hours of efficacy, in practice many women only see about 6 hours of benefit. It is started at 10–20 mg every morning and increased by 10 mg weekly as needed, to a maximum of 60 mg every morning.[27]

Metadate CD also consists of immediate- and delayed-release beads, though in a different ratio: approximately 30% IR and 70% ER. The lower initial proportion of IR beads leads to a later and somewhat higher second peak compared to Ritalin LA. This may result in inferior coverage in the morning but better symptom control in the early afternoon. Metadate CD is dosed between 10 and 60 mg each morning and can be titrated weekly by 10–20 mg as tolerated.[28]

EXTENDED-RELEASE METHYLPHENIDATE PRODUCTS (UP TO 12 HOURS)

Concerta (osmotic release methylphenidate) is typically started at 18 mg each morning and can be increased weekly by 18 mg up to 72 mg. Its release occurs via an osmotic system in which water incrementally enters the tablet and pushes out the drug. Unlike other formulations, Concerta releases only 22% initially, with 78% released gradually, producing low early levels and a peak around 7 hours post-dose. In controlled studies, more than half of Concerta's overall drug absorption (systemic exposure) occurs after 7 hours, making it useful for patients needing peak coverage after lunch. While studies show 12 hours of efficacy, many patients report 8–12 hours.[29]

Focalin XR (dexmethylphenidate ER) has a dual-bead immediate/extended-release mechanism, is typically initiated at 10 mg every morning, and can be increased weekly by 5–10 mg up to Focalin XR 40 mg. Relative to Concerta, Focalin XR delivers a large percentage of methylphenidate by 8 hours (approximately 80% according to FDA data). Research comparing these medications indicates that Focalin XR provides superior benefits during the first 6 hours of the day, performs equivalently to Concerta between 7 and 9 hours, and is less effective than Concerta from 10–12 hours.[30] As such, Focalin XR may be an optimal option for patients who prefer strong coverage across the core workday but have less need for evening symptom control.[31]

VERY EXTENDED-RELEASE METHYLPHENIDATE PRODUCTS (12–16 HOURS)

Azstarys is a combination of dexmethylphenidate IR and serdexmethylphenidate, a prodrug (an inactive compound that is converted in the body to an active medication) that gradually releases dexmethylphenidate. Each capsule contains 30% of the immediate-release equivalent dose, which produces a small initial peak at 2 hours post-dose, and 70% as the prodrug extended release, which produces a second, larger peak about 8 hours post-dose. Azstarys is available in three dose strengths that can be titrated weekly from the starting dose of 5.2 mg IR/26.1 mg ER to 7.8 mg IR/39.2 mg ER, and then to 10.4 mg IR/52.3 mg ER.[32]

In our experience, many patients taking Azstarys experience benefit until bedtime, though this advantage may come at the cost of increased insomnia relative to shorter-acting medications. Its smooth release can lessen appetite suppression compared with agents that produce larger peaks and valleys. A notable limitation of Azstarys is its restricted dosing options: the lowest available dose is already 50% of the maximum, an unusual starting point for a stimulant. While patients transitioning from higher doses of other methylphenidate products may tolerate this, even the lowest Azstarys dose can be too aggressive for stimulant-naïve individuals.

Adhansia XR is composed of methylphenidate IR (20%) and multiple layers of methylphenidate ER (80%). It has two peaks, its first at about 1.5 hours, its second at about 12 hours, with an overall smooth release and clinical trial data showing effectiveness of 16 hours in adults. This makes it the methylphenidate product with the latest second peak and longest demonstrated duration of action on the market.[33] Adhansia may be particularly useful for women with evening responsibilities (e.g., night classes), but carries a heightened risk of insomnia. It is available in six doses from 25 to 85 mg, with initiation at the lowest dose and weekly titration upward. A slower titration may lessen insomnia-related intolerance.[34]

Jornay PM (delayed-release/extended-release methylphenidate) may be the most significant advance in stimulant delivery in the past two decades. It is the only stimulant taken at night that begins working in the morning, so patients wake with an effective level already in their system. This profile is achieved through three mechanisms: (1) a delayed-release coating that prevents release for about 8 hours, (2) pH-sensitive release favoring absorption in the large intestine, and (3) colonic absorption, which is slower and more prolonged than small-intestinal absorption. The latter ensures that more than half the dose is absorbed after the peak, producing a smooth rise in blood concentrations.[35,36]

In our experience, Jornay PM has been especially helpful to women of all ages by improving waking and cognitive "boot-up," thus allowing for an efficient morning. College students on academic probation, women facing job loss due to chronic lateness, and mothers burdened by the shame of repeatedly getting children to school late report that having medication active before waking transforms their mornings and the flow of the day. Retired women and those not in the workforce likewise note that waking medicated improves motivation to pursue a full and meaningful day even when parenting and work no longer compel them out of bed.

Jornay PM is available in five doses ranging from 20 to 100 mg. Since 60% of the dose is absorbed, a 100-mg nightly dose has an effect similar to Ritalin IR 20 mg three times daily or Concerta 54–72 mg every morning. In our experience, 20 mg rarely provides adequate benefit; starting at 40 mg nightly and titrating upward by 20 mg each week is often more efficient, with many achieving optimal control at 80–100 mg.

Unlike standard ER stimulants, where higher doses yield only modestly longer coverage, Jornay PM's release and absorption profile allows higher doses to significantly extend duration. Low-to-medium doses may cover mornings and the school or workday, while higher doses often sustain benefits into the afternoon and evening. Clinicians can thus extend symptom control through dose adjustments alone, often without the need for supplemental IR stimulants.[37,38]

OTHER METHYLPHENIDATE PRODUCTS

There are also other methylphenidate products on the market. They are unlikely to be superior to the options listed above for most patients. However, given that each has its own unique release mechanism, some patients may tolerate one of these other products or may find its duration of action to be superior to that of the medications detailed above. A quick reference to the medication's pharmacokinetics can be helpful in personalizing treatment.

Amphetamine-based medications

Amphetamines have been prescribed for ADHD for nearly a century. Like methylphenidate, they act on the prefrontal cortex, striatum, and connected circuits governing attention and impulse control, blocking norepinephrine and dopamine reuptake to enhance signaling. Amphetamines also exert a unique second action: they recycle these neurotransmitters from within the receiving neuron back into the synapse. This mechanism may help explain why some studies show that amphetamines are slightly more effective than methylphenidate in adults, but also higher risks for common (irritability) and rare (psychosis) adverse effects. In clinical practice, they can represent a slightly higher-risk, higher-reward option for some women. Yet this is not universally true; for example, a woman struggling with early-morning functioning may derive greater benefit and less risk from Jornay PM than from an amphetamine.

IMMEDIATE-RELEASE AMPHETAMINE PRODUCTS (4–6 HOURS)

Adderall IR is the most widely used IR amphetamine formulation. It contains four distinct amphetamine compounds in a 3:1 ratio of dextroamphetamine to levoamphetamine—meaning it is composed of 75% dextroamphetamine and 25% levoamphetamine by weight. The duration of action of Adderall IR is 4–5 hours, and when dosed twice daily it produces benefits for 8–10 hours. It is typically initiated at 5–10 mg once or twice daily, with titration in 5–10 mg increments every 4 to 7 days. The FDA-approved maximum dose is 40 mg/day in divided doses, allowing for higher doses according to clinical judgment.[39]

Like all immediate-release stimulants, Adderall IR has several disadvantages, including greater variability in blood levels, reduced adherence due to more frequent dosing, and a higher risk of rebound symptoms as medication levels fall. Adderall IR also appears to carry a higher misuse potential than Ritalin IR, due to its more noticeable reinforcing effects in some individuals.[40]

Dexedrine IR (dextroamphetamine sulfate immediate release) contains only the right-handed molecule. On a mg/mg basis, Adderall IR is roughly 25% less potent than Dexedrine IR, meaning that 5 mg Adderall IR has similar potency to 4 mg of Dexedrine IR. In clinical use, Dexedrine IR plays roughly the same role as Adderall IR and they tend to be dosed equivalently. It is typically initiated at 5 mg once or twice daily and titrated in 5 mg increments every 4 to 7 days. The FDA-approved maximum dose is 40 mg daily in two divided doses, although some guidelines and experts allow for higher doses in rare cases.[41,42,43]

EXTENDED-RELEASE AMPHETAMINE PRODUCTS (8–16 HOURS)

Adderall XR is a mixed amphetamine formulation that contains the same four amphetamine compounds as Adderall IR in a 3:1 ratio of dextroamphetamine to levoamphetamine. The formulation uses a dual-bead delivery system in which 50% of the beads are immediate release, producing an initial peak within 30 to 60 minutes, and the remaining 50% are delayed-release, dissolving approximately four hours later to generate a second peak. The duration of action is approximately 8–10 hours. Adderall XR is typically initiated at 10–20 mg once daily in the morning, with titrations of 5–10 mg per week as needed. The FDA-approved maximum dose is 20 mg daily, but in clinical practice 40–60 mg per day is sometimes superior to lower dosing.[44,45,46]

Vyvanse (lisdexamfetamine) is an inactive prodrug consisting of dextroamphetamine bound to the amino acid lysine. After entering the bloodstream, the bond is cleaved to release active dextroamphetamine. This release mechanism contributes to a smooth rise and fall of blood levels and precludes easy abuse: unlike other amphetamines, Vyvanse cannot be activated via insufflation or injection, and the smooth release on oral ingestion makes it less acutely reinforcing. Vyvanse is often preferred by patients who are sensitive to the more abrupt onset and offset of other stimulants. However, some patients report that the gentle onset is actually *too* slow, as they are trying to get their day started. For these patients, combining both Vyvanse and a low dose of Adderall IR in the morning can address problems with slow onset. Vyvanse can be initiated at 20–30 mg every morning and titrated weekly in increments of 10–20 mg, up to a maximum dose of 70 mg per day.[47]

Mydayis is a very extended-release formulation that has the same ratio of amphetamine compounds as Adderall XR. The key difference is that while Adderall XR has a double-bead system, Mydayis uses a triple-bead system that enables a longer duration of action: it provides up to 16 hours of coverage in trials, with about 14 hours more typical in practice. Mydayis offers once-daily coverage into the late evening, but its prolonged action also increases risks of insomnia and appetite suppression later in the day. The usual starting dose in adults is 12.5 mg once each morning, titrated by 12.5 mg weekly as needed, to a maximum of 50 mg/day.[48]

There are other amphetamine formulations on the market that are not covered here. While these agents are not typically first-choice treatments, some may offer advantages in niche clinical scenarios or for patients who have failed to respond to more commonly prescribed agents.

SECOND-LINE MEDICATIONS

Atomoxetine (Strattera), a selective norepinephrine reuptake inhibitor, is the most extensively studied nonstimulant for adult ADHD. Unlike stimulants, it does not typically promote alertness. It provides 24-hour coverage, and benefits take several weeks to emerge. Adults typically start at 40 mg daily, increasing to 80 mg after 3–7 days, and then two weeks later to a maximum dose of 100 mg daily. Atomoxetine is 50–60% as effective as stimulants. Side effects include fatigue, insomnia, dry mouth, headache, and gastrointestinal discomfort, though serious adverse effects are rare. Since it is not habit-forming, it is not a controlled substance.[49] Overall, atomoxetine is the best-supported nonstimulant for adult ADHD and the preferred second-line option when stimulants are ineffective, poorly tolerated, or declined.[50]

Alpha agonists

Clinical research on the use of alpha agonists (clonidine and guanfacine) in adults with ADHD is limited. They were initially used as blood pressure medications and then later identified as highly effective treatments for children with ADHD; however, research on their effectiveness in adults has not kept up.

Guanfacine ER (Intuniv): The two studies that have evaluated guanfacine ER in adults (in addition to dozens of studies in youth) demonstrate a moderate level of effectiveness that is comparable to other nonstimulants. It is started at 1 mg nightly, with dose increases of 1 mg every 3–7 days to minimize the risk of somnolence, hypotension, and bradycardia. Extrapolating from the pediatric literature, the most effective dose is likely to be in the upper end of the dose range, which was 0.15 mg/kg per pediatric trials. In adult clinical trials, the mean final dose was approximately 5–6 mg daily. Guanfacine ER should be taken at the same time each day, typically in the evening, due to its sedating properties.[51,52]

GUANFACINE IR AND CLONIDINE IR TO TARGET NIGHTTIME ADHD "RACING MIND"

As discussed elsewhere (Chapters 3 and 12), the shift from wakefulness to sleep in ADHD hinges on a sequence of evening steps ending in a deliberate "lights-out" decision—often despite a racing mind. Research on this transition in women with ADHD is limited, and data on alpha agonists to promote sleep in ADHD are sparse. Therefore, the guidance below reflects our clinical experience.

In addition to their modest ADHD benefits, clonidine and guanfacine are often sedating, with IR formulations more sedating than ER formulations. Taken about an hour before bedtime, an IR dose can reliably promote sleepiness, and women usually do not develop full tolerance. When used consistently, this sedation makes stimulating activities less appealing and going to bed more attractive.

Alpha agonists may also ease the "racing mind." Many women delay bedtime not only due to logistics, but also because persistent, urgent thoughts sustain arousal that prevents sleep onset. These medications seem to reduce the intensity of such thoughts, allowing the mind to quiet and sleep to come more readily. In this way, an evening IR dose can act as a commitment device: a choice made when motivation is stronger (an hour before bedtime) increases the chance of disengaging from stimulating activities later, when motivation wanes, and settling into sleep on time.

Since clonidine IR is more sedating than guanfacine IR and has a shorter half-life (approximately 6–10 hours versus 10–17 hours for guanfacine IR), it may be more effective in the evening without causing excessive morning sedation. Clonidine IR can be started at 0.1 mg in the evening and titrated by 0.1 mg weekly to a target dose of 0.2–0.4 mg at bedtime. Guanfacine IR can be initiated at 0.5–1 mg nightly and titrated weekly. A target dose of 2 mg at bedtime is reasonable, though some patients may benefit from slightly higher doses depending on tolerability and therapeutic response.[53,54]

THIRD-LINE MEDICATIONS

Viloxazine ER (Qelbree)

Viloxazine ER (Qelbree), a serotonin–norepinephrine modulating agent, was approved by the FDA in 2022 for adult ADHD. The standard titration begins at 200 mg daily, with weekly increases of 200 mg as tolerated, up to 600 mg. In the only randomized controlled trial (n = 374), viloxazine ER produced symptom improvement within two weeks, with effect sizes slightly smaller than atomoxetine.[55] Common adverse effects include insomnia, fatigue, nausea, and appetite suppression. Although the safety profile is generally favorable, evidence is limited to this single short-term study, with no head-to-head comparisons or functional outcome data. By contrast, atomoxetine is supported by more than 15 RCTs and bupropion by at least six. Clinicians should balance viloxazine ER's modest efficacy and tolerability against its limited evidence base and the absence of replication studies.[56]

Bupropion (Wellbutrin)

Bupropion (Wellbutrin), an antidepressant with dopaminergic and noradrenergic effects, has been evaluated in six RCTs and two meta-analyses for adult ADHD. Bupropion XL is typically initiated at 150 mg daily and titrated weekly in 150 mg increments up to 450 mg. Across studies, its effectiveness is similar to atomoxetine. It is generally well tolerated, though it carries an increased seizure risk in vulnerable populations. The evidence base, while more extensive than that of viloxazine ER, is of lower quality, with most trials small, short (6–10 weeks), and methodologically limited. No studies assess long-term safety or functional outcomes, and bupropion has not been compared directly with viloxazine ER or atomoxetine. Although not FDA-approved for ADHD, it may be appropriate for women who have not benefited from other ADHD treatments and who have co-occurring depression.

Broad-spectrum micronutrient supplements

Broad-spectrum micronutrient supplements have been shown to be moderately effective in ADHD, with multiple randomized controlled trials (RCTs) in children and one in adults showing improvements in clinician-rated symptoms and overall functioning. The most common brand studied has been Hardy's Daily Essential Nutrients. In the pediatric studies, effect sizes are typically in the medium range ($d \approx 0.5$), similar to atomoxetine. Benefits extend beyond core ADHD symptoms to include enhanced emotional regulation, mood stability, and reduced aggression, with some sustained improvements observed at one year follow-up. Across both pediatric and adult trials, micronutrients have been well tolerated with no serious adverse effects, supporting their potential as an alternative treatment strategy. There is no evidence for their adjunctive use in combination with a stimulant, but the risks of such a combination are likely low. While preliminarily promising, the research on micronutrients remains much more limited than the data available for stimulants and atomoxetine, and larger, more definitive trials would be required before micronutrients could be considered a first- or second-line intervention in adults.[57,58,59,60]

Omega-3 fatty acids

Research on omega-3 fatty acids for ADHD has mostly been conducted in children. Several trials and meta-analyses indicate that omega-3 supplements rich in EPA (≥1 g/day) given over long durations (≥16 weeks) can modestly reduce ADHD symptoms. A 2011 meta-analysis of 10 RCTs (699 children) showed a small but significant improvement in overall ADHD ratings, with higher EPA doses correlating with greater efficacy. A more recent meta-analysis failed to replicate the finding that EPA dose matters, but demonstrated that treatment with omega-3s for at least 16 weeks is the definitive factor in effectiveness. At higher doses, there is concern for bleeding risk. Almost all of this research is on the use of omega-3s as monotherapy; there is no evidence that it augments stimulant treatment of ADHD. Given the uncertainty of the research, we offer omega-3s as an option to women who have not benefited, or who have not benefited adequately, from more evidence-based options.[61,62]

STIMULANT USE DURING PREGNANCY AND BREASTFEEDING

As more women of childbearing age are being treated for ADHD, the question of the continued use of psychostimulants during pregnancy and lactation has arisen. The question is complex and is still being studied. Despite the lack of a definitive response, more women with ADHD are deciding to stay on medication during pregnancy, as both patients and clinicians recognize that stopping treatment can have consequences. For women with moderate-to-severe ADHD, stopping medication may compromise safety, strain relationships, affect work, and worsen depression or anxiety. The small but real risks of fetal or infant exposure must be weighed against the often greater risks of leaving maternal ADHD untreated. Shared decision-making, behavioral supports, and medication when needed are essential.[63]

In pregnancy, stimulants are the best-studied medications. Methylphenidate and amphetamines have not shown a consistent increase in birth defects. Some studies suggest slightly higher risks of preeclampsia, preterm birth, or newborn adjustment problems, but results are mixed and the overall risk is low. If medication is required, the safest path is to continue the agent that works, at the lowest effective dose, and avoid sudden discontinuation. Nonstimulants such as bupropion or atomoxetine may be considered in some cases, though data are more limited. What is clear is that untreated ADHD carries its own dangers—greater risk of accidents (such as car accidents), poor prenatal self-care, medication errors, and worsening mood and anxiety symptoms. These maternal risks can affect both fetal growth and pregnancy outcomes.[64]

During breastfeeding, methylphenidate exposure in infants is very low: less than 1% of the mother's dose, and infant blood levels are usually undetectable. Amphetamine levels in breast milk are considerably higher, and guidelines usually favor methylphenidate in breastfeeding, with some recommending against amphetamines.[65] Infants should be watched for irritability, sleep problems, feeding issues, and weight changes. Data on nonstimulants are limited and less reassuring, so caution is advised.[66]

In practice, methylphenidate and amphetamines remain the most reassuring options in pregnancy and lactation. Nonstimulants can be considered when appropriate, but they require close monitoring. A comprehensive management plan should document symptom severity and risks, include nonmedication supports, use of the lowest effective dose, and a structured monitoring plan for both mother and infant. Plans should be revisited as pregnancy progresses and reviewed again after birth, when daily executive-function demands surge along with increased sleep deprivation. Coordinated care across obstetrics, pediatrics, and mental health, with documented shared decisions and monitoring, supports clinical safety and well-being for both mother and infant.[67]

INTEGRATIVE MEDICINE IN TREATING ADHD

CASE ILLUSTRATION: JANIE

Janie is a 22-year-old woman who presented seeking ADHD treatment. Her mother believes in the power of natural supplements to address ADHD, and for the last four years Janie had been taking about 25 vitamin and mineral pills daily. Janie wasn't sure that they were helping and was interested in trying prescription medication for the first time, but she stopped medical treatment and all supplements a few months after initial presentation, reporting "burnout" from all the years of failed trials.

Evidence-based, nonpharmacologic ADHD treatments can and should be integrated with more standard medical approaches. We have devoted an entire chapter to the importance of lifestyle changes in treating ADHD because they improve treatment outcomes (Chapter 12). However, the use of *nonevidence-based* complementary and/or alternative (CAM) treatments carries numerous risks that are not always recognized.

Stimulant medications have often been misrepresented with false and alarming claims—for instance, the charge that their use is the equivalent of prescribing "speed" to children, implying addiction and destruction, despite decades of evidence for their safety and efficacy. In fact, research shows that stimulant treatment may reduce the risk of later substance-use disorders and support healthier lifestyles, including better diet, improved sleep, and more exercise.[68,69,70]

In contrast to the inflated risks of stimulants, some women will tell you that they will only consider "natural" treatments because natural treatments are best. Most of us have this intuition, which is termed the natural-is-better bias or naturalness bias.[71] But it is not hard to find counterexamples. We can point out that arsenic, lead, and botulinum toxin, poisonous when ingested, are natural. "Natural" is not always good.

The naturalness bias can lead individuals to prefer CAM treatments, which in turn may undermine adherence to evidence-based care. Research indicates that people with ADHD who use CAM are less likely to adhere to prescribed medication.[72] Similarly, CAM use has been linked to delayed initiation of cancer treatment[73] and to reduced treatment adherence in chronic illnesses such as diabetes and HIV.[74,75] Additional cancer research is even more alarming: in one study, patients who began with alternative treatments had five times higher mortality over a half-decade compared to those who had initiated evidence-based therapy.[76] Parallel findings showed the use of any nonevidence-based CAM alongside at least one evidence-based treatment was associated with a doubling of cancer mortality—apparently reflecting unwillingness to fully follow evidence-based recommendations.[77]

You might be tempted to say "but ADHD isn't cancer," and you are right. However, ADHD *is* a condition associated with *dying nearly 10 years younger.*[78] It is therefore essential that you assess for the substitution of evidence-based treatments with untested or ineffective CAM treatments. Ultimately, however, your patient is in the driver's seat. Your role is to gently encourage and educate her and suggest that she might benefit from attending ADHD support groups and hearing from other women about their treatment results.

SUMMARY

ADHD medications play a central role in reducing symptoms and enhancing daily functioning for women across the lifespan. Stimulants remain the most effective medication treatment for ADHD, with some of the nonstimulants as second-line options, while a few emerging treatments should be considered as well. Evidence highlights the importance of tailoring treatment to target symptoms, well-being goals, and the 24-hour challenges of ADHD, while evaluating safety during pregnancy, breastfeeding, and increased cardiovascular risk in your patients. Integrating behavioral strategies with pharmacotherapy strengthens outcomes, whereas overreliance on unproven "natural" remedies risks delaying effective care. Shared decision-making, individualized dosing, and vigilant monitoring ensure that treatment aligns with women's goals for improved health, resilience, and overall quality of life.

REFERENCES

1. Surman, C. B., & Walsh, D. M. (2022). Do treatments for adult ADHD improve emotional behavior? A systematic review and analysis. *Journal of Attention Disorders, 26*(14), 1822–1832.
2. Young, J. A., Serwint, J. R., Crampton, R. E., & Mahan, J. D. (2025). Sustaining and training for resilience, engagement and meaning (STREAM): Program model, rationale and early implementation. *BMC Medical Education, 25*(1), 720.
3. Cortese, S., Adamo, N., Del Giovane, C., Mohr-Jensen, C., Hayes, A. J., Carucci, S., Atkinson, L. Z., Tessari, L., Banaschewski, T., Coghill, D., Hollis, C., Simonoff, E., Zuddas, A., Barbui, C., Purgato, M., Steinhausen, H-C., Shokraneh, F., Xia, J., & Cipriani, A. (2018). Comparative efficacy and tolerability of medications for attention-deficit hyperactivity disorder in children, adolescents, and adults: a systematic review and network meta-analysis. *The Lancet Psychiatry, 5*(9), 727–738. https://doi.org/10.1016/S2215-0366(18)30269-4
4. Li, L., Zhu, N., Zhang, L., Kuja-Halkola, R., D'Onofrio, B. M., Brikell, I., Lichtenstein, P., Cortese, S., Larsson, H., & Chang, Z. (2024). ADHD pharmacotherapy and mortality in individuals with ADHD. *JAMA, 331*(10), 850–860. https://doi.org/10.1001/jama.2024.0851
5. Oliva, H. N. P., Prudente, T. P., Mayerson, T. F., Mignosa, M. M., Oliva, I. O., Potenza, M. N., Jegede, O. O., & Angarita, G. A. (2025). Safety of stimulants across patient populations: a meta-analysis. *JAMA Network Open, 8*(5), e259492.
6. Cortese, S., Adamo, N., Del Giovane, C., Mohr-Jensen, C., Hayes, A. J., Carucci, S., Atkinson, L. Z., Tessari, L., Banaschewski, T., Coghill, D., Hollis, C., Simonoff, E., Zuddas, A., Barbui, C., Purgato, M., Steinhausen, H-C., Shokraneh, F., Xia, J., & Cipriani, A. (2018). Comparative efficacy and tolerability of medications for attention-deficit hyperactivity disorder in children, adolescents, and adults: a systematic review and network meta-analysis. *The Lancet Psychiatry, 5*(9), 727–738. https://doi.org/10.1016/S2215-0366(18)30269-4
7. Han, B., Jones, C. M., Volkow, N. D., Rikard, S. M., Dowell, D., Einstein, E. B., Guy, G. P., Tomoyasu, N., Ko, J., Baldwin, G., Olsen, Y., & Compton, W. M. (2025). Prescription stimulant use, misuse, and use disorder among US adults aged 18 to 64 years. *JAMA Psychiatry, 82*(6), 572–581. https://doi.org/10.1001/jamapsychiatry.2025.0054
8. Cortese, S., Adamo, N., Del Giovane, C., Mohr-Jensen, C., Hayes, A. J., Carucci, S., Atkinson, L. Z., Tessari, L., Banaschewski, T., Coghill, D., Hollis, C., Simonoff, E., Zuddas, A., Barbui, C., Purgato, M., Steinhausen, H-C., Shokraneh, F., Xia, J., & Cipriani, A. (2018). Comparative efficacy and tolerability of medications for attention-deficit hyperactivity disorder in children, adolescents, and adults: a systematic review and network meta-analysis. *The Lancet Psychiatry, 5*(9), 727–738. https://doi.org/10.1016/S2215-0366(18)30269-4

9. Cortese, S. (2020). Pharmacologic treatment of attention deficit–hyperactivity disorder. *New England Journal of Medicine*, 383(11), 1050–1056.
10. Rucklidge, J. J., Bruton, A., Welsh, A., Ast, H., & Johnstone, J. M. (2025). Annual research review: micronutrients and their role in the treatment of paediatric mental illness. *Journal of Child Psychology and Psychiatry*, *66*(4), 477–497.
11. Liu, T. H., Wu, J. Y., Huang, P. Y., Lai, C. C., Chang, J. P. C., Lin, C. H., & Su, K. P. (2023). Omega-3 polyunsaturated fatty acids for core symptoms of attention-deficit/hyperactivity disorder: a meta-analysis of randomized controlled trials. *The Journal of Clinical Psychiatry*, *84*(5), 48752.
12. Childress, A. C. (2021). Novel formulations of ADHD medications: stimulant selection and management. *Focus*, *19*(1), 31–38.
13. Childress, A. C., Komolova, M., & Sallee, F. R. (2019). An update on the pharmacokinetic considerations in the treatment of ADHD with long-acting methylphenidate and amphetamine formulations. *Expert Opinion on Drug Metabolism & Toxicology*, *15*(11), 937–974.
14. Cortese, S. (2020). Pharmacologic treatment of attention deficit–hyperactivity disorder. *New England Journal of Medicine*, *383*(11), 1050–1056.
15. Wolraich, M. L., Hagan Jr, J. F., Allan, C., Chan, E., Davison, D., Earls, M., Evans, S. W., Flinn, S. K., Froehlich, T., Frost, J., Holbrook, J. R., Lehmann, C. U., Lessin, H. R., Okechukwu, K., Pierce, K. L., Winner, J. D., Zurhellen, W., & Subcommittee on Children and Adolescents with Attention-Deficit/Hyperactive Disorder. (2019). Clinical practice guideline for the diagnosis, evaluation, and treatment of attention-deficit/hyperactivity disorder in children and adolescents. *Pediatrics*, *144*(4), e20192528.
16. Tadrous, M., Shakeri, A., Chu, C., Watt, J., Mamdani, M. M., Juurlink, D. N., & Gomes, T. (2021). Assessment of stimulant use and cardiovascular event risks among older adults. *JAMA Network Open*, *4*(10), e2130795.
17. Han, B., Jones, C. M., Volkow, N. D., Rikard, S. M., Dowell, D., Einstein, E. B., Guy, G. P., Tomoyasu, N., Ko, J., Baldwin, G., Olsen, Y., & Compton, W. M. (2025). Prescription stimulant use, misuse, and use disorder among US adults aged 18 to 64 years. *JAMA Psychiatry*, *82*(6), 572–581. https://doi.org/10.1001/jamapsychiatry.2025.0054
18. Han, B., Jones, C. M., Volkow, N. D., Rikard, S. M., Dowell, D., Einstein, E. B., Guy, G. P., Tomoyasu, N., Ko, J., Baldwin, G., Olsen, Y., & Compton, W. M. (2025). Prescription stimulant use, misuse, and use disorder among US adults aged 18 to 64 years. *JAMA Psychiatry*, *82*(6), 572–581. https://doi.org/10.1001/jamapsychiatry.2025.0054
19. Taipale, H., Bergström, J., Gèmes, K., Tanskanen, A., Ekselius, L., Mittendorfer-Rutz, E., & Helgesson, M. (2024). Attention-deficit/hyperactivity disorder medications and work disability and mental health outcomes. *JAMA Network Open*, 7(3), e242859. https://doi.org/10.1001/jamanetworkopen.2024.2859
20. Deckler, E., & Coffey, B. M. (2024). Treatment of attention-deficit/hyperactivity disorder in adults. In A. F. Schatzberg & C. B. Nemeroff (Eds.), *The American Psychiatric Association Publishing textbook of psychopharmacology* (6th ed., 1195–1217). American Psychiatric Association Publishing.
21. Deckler, E., & Coffey, B. M. (2024). Treatment of attention-deficit/hyperactivity disorder in adults. In A. F. Schatzberg & C. B. Nemeroff (Eds.), *The American Psychiatric Association Publishing textbook of psychopharmacology* (6th ed., 1195–1217). American Psychiatric Association Publishing.

22. Faraone, S. V. (2018). The pharmacology of amphetamine and methylphenidate: relevance to the neurobiology of attention-deficit/hyperactivity disorder and other psychiatric comorbidities. *Neuroscience & Biobehavioral Reviews, 87*, 255–270.
23. Novartis Pharmaceuticals Corporation. (2023a). *Ritalin (methylphenidate hydrochloride) [Prescribing information]*. Novartis Pharmaceuticals Corporation. https://www.novartis.com
24. Greenhill, L. L., Pliszka, S., Dulcan, M. K., Bernet, W., Arnold, V., Beitchman, J., Benson, R. S., Bukstein, O., Kinlan, J., McClellan, J., Rue, D., Shaw, J. A., Stock, S., & American Academy of Child and Adolescent Psychiatry (2002). Practice parameter for the use of stimulant medications in the treatment of children, adolescents, and adults. *Journal of the American Academy of Child and Adolescent Psychiatry, 41*(2 Suppl), 26S–49S. https://doi.org/10.1097/00004583-200202001-00003
25. Volkow, N. D., & Swanson, J. M. (2003). Variables that affect the clinical use and abuse of methylphenidate in the treatment of ADHD. *American Journal of Psychiatry, 160*(11), 1909–1918.
26. Novartis Pharmaceuticals Corporation. (2023a). *Ritalin (methylphenidate hydrochloride) tablets [Prescribing information]*. Author.
27. Novartis Pharmaceuticals Corporation. (2023b). *Ritalin LA (methylphenidate hydrochloride extended-release capsules) [Prescribing information]*. Author.
28. UCB, Inc. (2017). *Metadate CD (methylphenidate hydrochloride extended-release capsules) [Prescribing information]*. Author.
29. Janssen Pharmaceuticals, Inc. (2023). *Concerta (methylphenidate hydrochloride extended-release tablets) [Prescribing information]*. Author.
30. Coghill, D., Banaschewski, T., Zuddas, A., Pelaz, A., Gagliano, A., & Doepfner, M. (2013). Long-acting methylphenidate formulations in the treatment of attention-deficit/hyperactivity disorder: a systematic review of head-to-head studies. *BMC Psychiatry, 13*(1), 237.
31. Novartis Pharmaceuticals Corporation. (2017). *Focalin XR (dexmethylphenidate hydrochloride extended-release capsules) [Prescribing information]*. Author.
32. Corium, Inc. (2021). *Azstarys (serdexmethylphenidate and dexmethylphenidate capsules) [Prescribing information]*. Author.
33. Childress, A. C., Komolova, M., & Sallee, F. R. (2019). An update on the pharmacokinetic considerations in the treatment of ADHD with long-acting methylphenidate and amphetamine formulations. *Expert Opinion on Drug Metabolism & Toxicology, 15*(11), 937–974.
34. Purdue Pharma L.P. (2019). *Adhansia XR (methylphenidate hydrochloride extended-release capsules) [Prescribing information]*. Author.
35. Childress, A. C., Komolova, M., & Sallee, F. R. (2019). An update on the pharmacokinetic considerations in the treatment of ADHD with long-acting methylphenidate and amphetamine formulations. *Expert Opinion on Drug Metabolism & Toxicology, 15*(11), 937–974.
36. Ironshore Pharmaceuticals Inc. (2023). *Jornay PM (methylphenidate hydrochloride extended-release capsules) [Prescribing information]*. Author.
37. Childress, A. C., Komolova, M., & Sallee, F. R. (2019). An update on the pharmacokinetic considerations in the treatment of ADHD with long-acting methylphenidate and amphetamine formulations. *Expert Opinion on Drug Metabolism & Toxicology, 15*(11), 937–974.
38. Ironshore Pharmaceuticals Inc. (2023). *Jornay PM (methylphenidate hydrochloride extended-release capsules) [Prescribing information]*. Author.
39. Teva Pharmaceuticals USA, Inc. (2017). *Adderall (dextroamphetamine/amphetamine tablets) [Prescribing information]*. Author.

40. Han, B., Jones, C. M., Volkow, N. D., Rikard, S. M., Dowell, D., Einstein, E. B., Guy, G. P., Tomoyasu, N., Ko, J., Baldwin, G., Olsen, Y., & Compton, W. M. (2025). Prescription stimulant use, misuse, and use disorder among US adults aged 18 to 64 years. *JAMA Psychiatry, 82*(6), 572–581. https://doi.org/10.1001/jamapsychiatry.2025.0054
41. Aiken, C., & Quiñones-Laracuente, K. (2023, August 7). Stimulant dosing limits. *The Carlat Psychiatry Report.* https://www.thecarlatreport.com/articles/4464-stimulant-dosing-limits
42. Olagunju, A. E., & Ghoddusi, F. (2024). Attention-deficit/hyperactivity disorder in adults. *American Family Physician, 110*(2), 157–166.
43. Teva Pharmaceuticals USA, Inc. (2017). *Adderall (dextroamphetamine/amphetamine tablets) [Prescribing information].* Author.
44. Aiken, C., & Quiñones-Laracuente, K. (2023, August 7). Stimulant dosing limits. *The Carlat Psychiatry Report.* https://www.thecarlatreport.com/articles/4464-stimulant-dosing-limits
45. Olagunju, A. E., & Ghoddusi, F. (2024). Attention-deficit/hyperactivity disorder in adults. *American Family Physician, 110*(2), 157–166.
46. Shire US Inc. (2013). *Adderall XR (mixed salts of a single-entity amphetamine product extended-release capsules) [Prescribing information].* Author.
47. Takeda Pharmaceuticals America, Inc. (2023). *Vyvanse (lisdexamfetamine dimesylate capsules and chewable tablets) [Prescribing information].* Author.
48. Takeda Pharmaceuticals America, Inc. (2023). *Mydayis (mixed salts of a single-entity amphetamine product extended-release capsules) [Prescribing information].* Author.
49. Radonjić, N. V., Bellato, A., Khoury, N. M., Cortese, S., & Faraone, S. V. (2023). Nonstimulant medications for attention-deficit/hyperactivity disorder (ADHD) in adults: systematic review and meta-analysis. *CNS Drugs, 37*(5), 381–397.
50. Eli Lilly & Company. (2022). *Strattera (atomoxetine hydrochloride capsules) [Prescribing information].* Author.
51. Radonjić, N. V., Bellato, A., Khoury, N. M., Cortese, S., & Faraone, S. V. (2023). Nonstimulant medications for attention-deficit/hyperactivity disorder (ADHD) in adults: systematic review and meta-analysis. *CNS Drugs, 37*(5), 381–397.
52. US Food and Drug Administration. (2025a, January 22). *Highlights of prescribing information: Intuniv® (guanfacine) extended-release tablets [Package insert].* DailyMed. https://dailymed.nlm.nih.gov/dailymed/lookup.cfm?setid=fae2df3c-2298-a3e1-e053-6294a90aeac4
53. Promius Pharma, LLC. (2013). *Tenex (guanfacine hydrochloride tablets) [Prescribing information].* Author.
54. Boehringer Ingelheim Pharmaceuticals, Inc. (2009). *Catapres (clonidine hydrochloride tablets) [Prescribing information].* Author.
55. Nasser, A., Hull, J. T., Chaturvedi, S. A., Liranso, T., Odebo, O., Kosheleff, A. R., Fry, N., Cutler, A. J., Rubin, J., Schwabe, S., & Childress, A. (2022). A phase III, randomized, double-blind, placebo-controlled trial assessing the efficacy and safety of viloxazine extended-release capsules in adults with Attention-Deficit/Hyperactivity Disorder. *CNS Drugs, 36*(8), 897–915. https://doi.org/10.1007/s40263-022-00938-w
56. US Food and Drug Administration. (2025, August 15). *Qelbree (viloxazine hydrochloride) capsules [Prescribing information].* DailyMed. https://dailymed.nlm.nih.gov/dailymed/drugInfo.cfm?setid=aedf408d-0f84-418d-9416-7c39ddb0d29a
57. Rucklidge, J. J., Eggleston, M. J. F., Johnstone, J. M., Darling, K., & Frampton, C. M. (2018). Vitamin-mineral treatment improves aggression and emotional regulation in children with ADHD: a fully blinded, randomized, placebo-controlled trial. *Journal of Child Psychology and Psychiatry, 59*(3), 232–246.

58. Johnstone, J. M., Hatsu, I., Tost, G., Srikanth, P., Eiterman, L. P., Bruton, A. M., Ast, H. K., Robinette, L. M., Stern, M. M., Millington, E. G., Gracious, B. L., Hughes, A. J., Leung, B. M. Y., & Arnold, L. E. (2022). Micronutrients for attention-deficit/hyperactivity disorder in youths: a placebo-controlled randomized clinical trial. *Journal of the American Academy of Child and Adolescent Psychiatry*, *61*(5), 647–661. https://doi.org/10.1016/j.jaac.2021.07.005
59. Rucklidge, J. J., Frampton, C. M., Gorman, B., & Boggis, A. (2014). Vitamin–mineral treatment of attention-deficit hyperactivity disorder in adults: double-blind randomised placebo-controlled trial. *British Journal of Psychiatry*, *204*(4), 306–315. https://doi.org/10.1192/bjp.bp.113.132126
60. Rucklidge, J. J., Bruton, A., Welsh, A., Ast, H., & Johnstone, J. M. (2025). Annual research review: micronutrients and their role in the treatment of paediatric mental illness. *Journal of Child Psychology and Psychiatry*, *66*(4), 477–497.
61. Bloch, M. H., & Qawasmi, A. (2011). Omega-3 fatty acid supplementation for the treatment of children with attention-deficit/hyperactivity disorder symptomatology: systematic review and meta-analysis. *Journal of the American Academy of Child & Adolescent Psychiatry*, *50*(10), 991–1000.
62. Liu, T. H., Wu, J. Y., Huang, P. Y., Lai, C. C., Chang, J. P. C., Lin, C. H., & Su, K. P. (2023). Omega-3 polyunsaturated fatty acids for core symptoms of attention-deficit/hyperactivity disorder: a meta-analysis of randomized controlled trials. *The Journal of Clinical Psychiatry*, *84*(5), 48752.
63. Scoten, O., Tabi, K., Paquette, V., Carrion, P., Ryan, D., Radonjic, N. V., Whitham, E. A., & Hippman, C. (2024). Attention-deficit/hyperactivity disorder in pregnancy and the postpartum period. *American Journal of Obstetrics and Gynecology*, *231*(1), 19–35. https://doi.org/10.1016/j.ajog.2024.02.297
64. Scoten, O., Tabi, K., Paquette, V., Carrion, P., Ryan, D., Radonjic, N. V., Whitham, E. A., & Hippman, C. (2024). Attention-deficit/hyperactivity disorder in pregnancy and the postpartum period. *American Journal of Obstetrics and Gynecology*, *231*(1), 19–35. https://doi.org/10.1016/j.ajog.2024.02.297
65. Association of Women's Health, Obstetric and Neonatal Nurses. (2023). Breastfeeding recommendations for people who use substances: AWHONN practice brief number 16. *Journal of Obstetric, Gynecologic & Neonatal Nursing*, *52*(1), e1–e4. https://doi.org/10.1016/j.jogn.2022.12.001
66. Scoten, O., Tabi, K., Paquette, V., Carrion, P., Ryan, D., Radonjic, N. V., Whitham, E. A., & Hippman, C. (2024). Attention-deficit/hyperactivity disorder in pregnancy and the postpartum period. *American Journal of Obstetrics and Gynecology*, *231*(1), 19–35. https://doi.org/10.1016/j.ajog.2024.02.297
67. Scoten, O., Tabi, K., Paquette, V., Carrion, P., Ryan, D., Radonjic, N. V., Whitham, E. A., & Hippman, C. (2024). Attention-deficit/hyperactivity disorder in pregnancy and the postpartum period. *American Journal of Obstetrics and Gynecology*, *231*(1), 19–35. https://doi.org/10.1016/j.ajog.2024.02.297
68. Mian, A., Jansen, P. W., Nguyen, A. N., Bowling, A., Renders, C. M., & Voortman, T. (2019). Children's attention-deficit/hyperactivity disorder symptoms predict lower diet quality but not vice versa: results from bidirectional analyses in a population-based cohort. *The Journal of Nutrition*, *149*(4), 642–648. https://doi.org/10.1093/jn/nxy273
69. Chang, Z., Lichtenstein, P., Halldner, L., D'Onofrio, B., Serlachius, E., Fazel, S., Långström, N., & Larsson, H. (2014). Stimulant ADHD medication and risk for substance abuse. *Journal of Child Psychology and Psychiatry, and Allied Disciplines*, *55*(8), 878–885. https://doi.org/10.1111/jcpp.12164

70. Brevik, E. J., Lundervold, A. J., Halmøy, A., Posserud, M. B., Instanes, J. T., Bjorvatn, B., & Haavik, J. (2017). Prevalence and clinical correlates of insomnia in adults with attention-deficit hyperactivity disorder. *Acta Psychiatrica Scandinavica, 136*(2), 220–227. https://doi.org/10.1111/acps.12756
71. Rozin, P., Fischler, C., & Shields-Argelès, C. (2004). Preference for natural: instrumental and ideational/moral motivations, and the contrast between foods and medicines. *Appetite, 43*(2),147–154.
72. Wang, C., Li, K., Seo, D. C., & Gaylord, S. (2020). Use of complementary and alternative medicine in children with ADHD: Results from the 2012 and 2017 National Health Interview Survey. *Complementary Therapies in Medicine, 49*, 102352.
73. Malik, I. A., & Gopalan, S. (2003). Use of CAM results in delay in seeking medical advice for breast cancer. *European Journal of Epidemiology, 18*(8), 817–822.
74. Alfian, S., Sukandar, H., Arisanti, N., & Abdulah, R. (2016). Complementary and alternative medicine use decreases adherence to prescribed medication in diabetes patients. *Annals of Tropical Medicine and Public Health, 9*(3).
75. Ekwunife, O. I., Oreh, C., & Ubaka, C. M. (2012). Concurrent use of complementary and alternative medicine with antiretroviral therapy reduces adherence to HIV medications. *The International Journal of Pharmacy Practice, 20*(5), 340–343. https://doi.org/10.1111/j.2042-7174.2012.00204.x
76. Johnson, S. B., Park, H. S., Gross, C. P., & Yu, J. B. (2018a). Use of alternative medicine for cancer and its impact on survival. *JNCI: Journal of the National Cancer Institute, 110*(1), 121–124.
77. Johnson, S. B., Park, H. S., Gross, C. P., & Yu, J. B. (2018b). Complementary medicine, refusal of conventional cancer therapy, and survival among patients with curable cancers. *JAMA Oncology, 4*(10), 1375–1381.
78. O'Nions, E., El Baou, C., John, A., Lewer, D., Mandy, W., McKechnie, D. G. J., Petersen, I., & Stott, J. (2025). Life expectancy and years of life lost for adults with diagnosed ADHD in the UK: matched cohort study. *British Journal of Psychiatry, 226*(5), 261–268. https://doi.org/10.1192/bjp.2024.199

CHAPTER 6

Medication treatment for co-occurring psychiatric conditions

INTRODUCTION

As we covered in Chapter 3, up to 95% of people with ADHD meet the criteria for at least one co-occurring psychiatric condition, and many are diagnosed with two or more. These co-occurring conditions are associated with distress, interpersonal and occupational difficulties, and reduced quality of life. Women with ADHD experience an even greater burden of co-occurring conditions than men, due in part to the accumulated secondary harms of late ADHD diagnosis and to inequitable societal expectations of girls and women.

This chapter addresses medication management of several common psychiatric conditions co-occurring with ADHD. The following four principles of treatment guide medication selection for women with ADHD and co-occurring conditions: (1) treatment is never medication-only; (2) address the most serious condition first; (3) treat ADHD first if it is causing the other conditions; (4) use the most effective medication for each condition.

Women with co-occurring conditions do best with a nuanced and individualized treatment approach that frequently combines medications, psychotherapy, and lifestyle modification for optimal outcomes. **Treatment is never optimized with a medication-only strategy**. Medication doesn't work as well if a woman's brain isn't rested and nourished, if her body is entirely sedentary, or if her spirit is worn down by chronic loneliness. Whether you are a therapist, partner, friend, or a prescribing clinician, it is essential that you review Chapters 4 and 9–11 for recommendations on nonmedication aspects of the treatment plan.

DOI: 10.4324/9781003542124-6

You need to **first address acute and destabilizing co-occurring conditions** such as *severe* depression, *severe* anxiety, or self-harm. You need to complete a risk assessment and formulate a plan for these conditions. However, ADHD is sometimes driving the co-occurring condition—for example, in a woman whose severe anxiety primarily results from missed deadlines. In this case, you should **treat ADHD first if it is causing the other condition**, because adequate treatment of ADHD will bring about resolution or at least substantial improvement in both conditions. Treating ADHD first would also improve treatment-plan adherence, overall cognitive function, and the real-time use of psychological coping skills to manage the co-occurring condition. Note that when co-occurring conditions have evolved beyond their ADHD origins and become self-sustaining, they require separate treatment strategies.[1]

You should typically **use the most effective medication for each condition**. While it might be attractive to try a depression medication that is somewhat helpful for ADHD, or an ADHD medication that has mild anti-anxiety activity, the promise of this superficially efficient approach is often too good to be true. We have treated thousands of women whose recovery was limited by these one-medication-fits-all approaches, when in fact there are no medications that are first-line for both ADHD and its most common co-occurring conditions. If ADHD is dominant and the other conditions are mild, treat ADHD first and see if the other conditions melt away. And if a co-occurring condition is burdensome, treat it with a first-line agent that gives the woman you are treating the best chance of remission.

In this chapter, we will summarize Rebecca's case from Chapter 3 and explore treatment options for her co-occurring conditions. In addition, we will review the treatment of a few other conditions that are not present in her case. The treatment options for each condition summarized below are not an exhaustive list of all effective treatments. Rather, they include a few of the typically preferred options chosen for discussion based on effectiveness and tolerability.

CASE ILLUSTRATION: CASE DISCUSSION AND TREATMENT FORMULATION

Rebecca is a 39-year-old attorney and mother of two young boys whose presenting problems included escalating anxiety, depressed mood, concentration and procrastination issues, and insomnia. These symptoms manifest in the context of lifelong, yet partially masked, executive function deficits consistent with ADHD. Her intelligence, wit, and perseverance were strengths that generally allowed her to compensate/mask until the birth of her twin preschoolers.

Depression

Rebecca's case is challenging to formulate, in part because of the breadth of her symptom profile and the presence of multiple potential diagnoses. Symptoms such as low mood, insomnia, concentration problems, shame and guilt, and low self-concept can all reasonably be viewed as evidence of a **depressive episode**. The racist and homophobic behavior she encounters must be judged on ethical grounds as immoral behavior, and, in addition, it puts her at increased risk of poor mental health, including depression.

Pharmacotherapy for depression

If Rebecca reports that her most prominent symptoms are low mood, anhedonia, depressive rumination, and insomnia, it may be sensible to prioritize pharmacotherapy for depression. Since anxiety is also burdensome, she should be treated with an antidepressant that is also first line for anxiety: a selective serotonin reuptake inhibitor (SSRI) or a serotonin-norepinephrine reuptake inhibitor (SNRI).

Selective serotonin reuptake inhibitors (SSRIs): Many women with ADHD and depression also have co-occurring anxiety. Starting a serotonin-based antidepressant effective for both conditions is optimal. SSRIs are generally preferred, with no strong evidence that one is superior. When choosing an SSRI, review predictors of response and safety, including prior trials and drug–drug interactions. If adherence is a concern, select an antidepressant with a long half-life to reduce the risk of discontinuation symptoms when doses are missed.

The most prominent adverse effects of SSRIs are sexual side effects, which affect more than half of patients and remit spontaneously in only about a third of cases.[2] SSRIs may also cause modest weight gain and transient headaches or abdominal distress. In our experience, most women starting SSRIs for depression or anxiety find the benefits outweigh these risks. For patients unwilling to tolerate sexual side effects, other agents may be preferable.[3,4,5]

Fluoxetine has a half-life of 2–4 days, and its active metabolite norfluoxetine lasts about a week. It is usually started at 10–20 mg daily and can be titrated to 60 mg daily. Missing a single dose rarely causes adverse effects, discontinuation symptoms, or loss of benefit, making fluoxetine one of the most ADHD-friendly antidepressants. While SSRIs generally lack significant interactions with stimulants, fluoxetine carries higher risk of interactions with nonpsychiatric medications and with the ADHD medications atomoxetine and bupropion. Thus, it may be best for women who are unlikely to take interacting medications but who are prone to missing doses.[6]

Sertraline and escitalopram have fewer drug–drug interactions than fluoxetine and are similarly effective. Both have half-lives of about one day, so missed doses may be inconsequential for some women but cause discontinuation symptoms for others. Sertraline is initiated at 25–50 mg daily and titrated up to 200 mg daily; escitalopram starts at 5–10 mg daily and may be titrated to 20 mg daily. Sertraline appears somewhat more likely to cause gastrointestinal side effects. For women with reliable adherence or when interaction risk is a concern, either sertraline or escitalopram may be good options.[7,8]

Serotonin-norepinephrine reuptake inhibitors (SNRIs), like SSRIs, are effective for depression and anxiety but are less preferred for women with ADHD. They raise heart rate and blood pressure, adding risk when combined with stimulants, and more often cause discontinuation syndromes due to short half-lives and norepinephrine withdrawal effects such as autonomic hyperarousal.[9] Missing a single dose can trigger dizziness, nausea, "brain zaps," neurological pains, and dysphoria. SNRIs share most of the same adverse effects as SSRIs. For women with good adherence who are not on stimulants, SNRIs may be a reasonable option, but overall they are often not ADHD-friendly medications.[10]

Bupropion is a norepinephrine-dopamine reuptake inhibitor (NDRI) effective for depression, comparable to SSRIs and SNRIs. It is often considered an "energizing" antidepressant, and is particularly helpful for low motivation, psychomotor slowing, and cognitive problems in depression. Bupropion XL starts at 150 mg daily and can be titrated up to 450 mg daily. Benefits over SSRIs include fewer discontinuation symptoms and reduced sexual side effects; in some cases, it can improve SSRI-induced sexual dysfunction. Adverse effects include insomnia, appetite suppression, and elevated seizure risk, especially in bulimia, traumatic brain injury, or alcohol withdrawal. Unlike SSRIs and SNRIs, bupropion is not effective for co-occurring anxiety, an important consideration since many women with ADHD and depression also experience anxiety.[11]

Vortioxetine is a novel antidepressant with multiple effects on the serotonin system. It is comparable to SSRIs in treating depression and, with a half-life of 2–3 days, is somewhat forgiving of a missed dose—making it relatively ADHD-friendly. The typical starting dose is 5–10 mg daily, titrated up to 20 mg daily. It is generally well tolerated, with low rates of sexual side effects; when nausea occurs, it is usually mild and short-lived. Its main limitation is inconsistent benefit for anxiety, so like bupropion, it may be most appropriate for depression without significant co-occurring anxiety.[12]

Ketamine: Intravenous ketamine is a rapidly acting and highly effective treatment for severe, treatment-resistant depression. It can reduce symptoms within 1–4 hours of the first infusion, with a medium-to-large effect size (0.6–0.9) at 24 hours—greater than the average benefit of SSRIs or SNRIs, which appears after 2–6 weeks. Because the effect of a single infusion fades within a week, ketamine is usually given as a six-dose induction (two to three doses weekly for two to three weeks) to sustain benefits for a month or more. In addition to treating depression, ketamine can reduce suicidal thinking within hours.[13]

Bright light therapy

Bright light therapy (BLT, light therapy, phototherapy) is a therapy in which patients are exposed to a light with a strength of 10,000 lux for 30 minutes every morning, and is an effective treatment for depression. It has been shown to work for both nonseasonal Major Depressive Disorder (MDD) and seasonal MDD (Seasonal Affective Disorder). BLT works as a monotherapy for depression and can be combined with an antidepressant. BLT appears to work synergistically when combined, accelerating treatment response; such use is associated with greater effectiveness than antidepressant treatment alone.[14,15,16] BLT use is supported by prominent reviews and practice guidelines for depression.[17,18]

INTERVENTIONAL PSYCHIATRIC TREATMENT OF DEPRESSION

Transcranial magnetic stimulation (TMS) is a noninvasive brain stimulation technique that is highly effective for depression. It involves applying repetitive magnetic pulses to modulate neural circuit activity using a device placed against the scalp. The initial approach to TMS involved 30-minute sessions delivered 4–5 times weekly over a 4–6-week course, totaling 20–30 sessions. More recent approaches allow for shorter treatment sessions (3 minutes) and numerous daily sessions so that the whole treatment can be given within a week. Effect sizes have ranged from 0.6 to 0.8 or greater, making it, like ketamine, a more effective short-term treatment than standard medications. Common side effects include mild scalp discomfort or headaches.[19,20,21]

Self-harm: Suicidal behavior and nonsuicidal self-injury

The most effective and evidence-based psychotherapeutic treatment for self-harm is dialectical behavior therapy (DBT, see Chapter 10). Medications also have an important role. Stimulant treatment for ADHD is associated with lower risk of suicide attempts across age groups and in patients with depression or substance use disorder. Nonstimulants, in contrast, do not consistently show this benefit.[22,23] Direct evidence on nonsuicidal self-injury (NSSI) remains limited; however, in females with ADHD, impulsivity is strongly linked with NSSI, suggesting that effective ADHD pharmacotherapy may indirectly reduce NSSI risk by improving impulse control.[24]

ANXIETY AND ANXIETY-RELATED PROBLEMS: PROCRASTINATION AND PERFECTIONISM

CASE ILLUSTRATION

Rebecca's ADHD and anxiety overlap in multiple domains. For example, procrastination emerges from a combination of executive dysfunction and anxious avoidance. If Rebecca reports that her most prominent symptoms include some combination of persistent and intense worry, muscle tension, a sense of restlessness, and concern for social judgment, it is appropriate to prioritize pharmacotherapy for anxiety. Breaking a cycle of anxious avoidance has the potential to increase her work and home productivity, pushing back on the negative cycles.

SSRIs and SNRIs: As reviewed above, SSRIs and SNRIs are effective treatments for anxiety. The principles of depression and anxiety treatment are similar, but anxiety may require a higher dose of medication than depression to have an optimal result.[25]

Pregabalin reduces anxiety by decreasing excitatory neurotransmitter release through its binding to calcium channels. It is usually dosed at 150–600 mg daily in 2–3 divided doses. For generalized anxiety disorder, pregabalin is as effective as or more effective than SSRIs and SNRIs, with generally fewer side effects. Adverse effects include dizziness, dry mouth, psychomotor impairment, and sedation, which may worsen ADHD symptoms if persistent. Guidelines differ on misuse risk: some classify pregabalin as low risk and first-line, while others consider it moderate risk and second line. In the United States, where it is not approved for generalized anxiety, guidelines typically place it as second-line. Since it is not approved for generalized anxiety in the United States, nonspecialists may choose to be cautious about its prescription.[26,27,28]

Silexan is an orally administered lavender essential oil with comparable effectiveness to SSRIs for generalized anxiety disorder. The usual dose is 80 mg daily, although 160 mg may be slightly more effective. Silexan is generally well tolerated, with side effects limited to mild gastrointestinal upset and burping with a lavender aftertaste. It does not cause sedation, dependence, withdrawal, or sexual dysfunction, and clinically relevant interactions are not expected.[29] This safety profile is more favorable than SSRIs and far better than benzodiazepines. Real-world data on more than 67,000 adults show that extended use was also well tolerated.[30] For women with ADHD, Silexan may be attractive given its once-daily dosing, benign side-effect profile, minimal interactions, and lack of cognitive dulling.

When procrastination arises from anxiety, it can be targeted with the medications noted above combined with CBT. Perfectionism is typically treated with therapy, not medication (see Chapter 10).

INSOMNIA

Treatment of insomnia in ADHD should address both the insomnia itself and the underlying executive dysfunction, emotion regulation issues, and "busy mind" phenomena that contribute to it. Cognitive behavioral therapy for insomnia (CBT-I) and other behavioral interventions are first-line treatments (see Chapter 9). When CBT-I is declined or insufficient, pharmacologic options are considered second-line. A full review of medications for insomnia is beyond the scope of this chapter.[31] Instead, we will highlight an ADHD-specific approach.

Alpha agonists

As discussed in Chapter 5, alpha agonists are well-supported treatments for pediatric ADHD. In adults, extended-release guanfacine (guanfacine ER) shows modest benefits for core ADHD symptoms, but research on the sleep-promoting effects of alpha agonists is limited. This gap is notable given that sedation is a common effect of alpha agonists, making them particularly suitable for evening use.

Clinical experience suggests evening dosing of alpha agonists aids sleep in several ways:

1. **Sedation and overcoming behavioral inertia**: Sedation from immediate-release alpha agonists reduces the appeal of stimulating evening activities. As sedation increases, the discomfort of resisting sleep outweighs the enjoyment of screens or other stimulation, facilitating a woman's transition to bed.
2. **Reduction in racing thoughts**: Many women with ADHD struggle to fall asleep due to an overabundance of thoughts, even in the absence of anxiety. Alpha agonists appear to lessen the intensity and urgency of these thoughts, lowering arousal and easing sleep onset.
3. **Commitment device**: Taking a sedating agent an hour before bedtime can serve as a commitment device. Women decide on sleep when motivation is higher (one hour before bedtime), increasing the likelihood that they will follow through on the intention.

Choice of agent and dosing

Clonidine IR is more sedating than guanfacine IR and has a shorter half-life (6–10 hours), making it useful for initiating sleep without causing excessive morning grogginess. Typical dosing begins at 0.1 mg nightly, titrated weekly by 0.1 mg to a target of 0.2–0.4 mg nightly.

Guanfacine IR, with a longer half-life (10–17 hours), may be preferable for women who struggle with both sleep onset and maintenance. It is usually started at 0.5–1 mg nightly and titrated weekly to 2 mg nightly.

Taking either medication about an hour before the desired bedtime and allowing for at least 8 hours of sleep reduces the risk of morning sedation. Careful patient selection is important, as adverse effects include hypotension, orthostatic hypotension, and rebound hypertension if stopped abruptly.[32] Note that these recommendations are based largely on clinical experience at doses comparable to those studied in pediatric ADHD, as robust adult trial data remain limited.

CASE ILLUSTRATION

Rebecca's sleep difficulties reflect common ADHD-related executive function challenges. Evenings feel overwhelming, with problems sequencing tasks, managing time, and regulating emotions. To cope, she uses devices to quiet her mind; unfortunately, this approach worsens her sleep deficit, aggravates ADHD symptoms the next day, and reinforces the ADHD–insomnia cycle. Our first-line choice for Rebecca would be clonidine IR, provided she can take it at least 8 hours before waking. We recommend setting one alarm to remind her to take the dose and another 30 minutes later as a prompt to transition to bed. Her wife Tanya should help reinforce this routine by checking in each evening, even when traveling, to support consistent adherence and timely use of clonidine IR.

(For more discussion of approaches to improve sleep in those with ADHD, see Chapter 12.)

COMPLEX POST-TRAUMATIC STRESS DISORDER AND POST-TRAUMATIC STRESS DISORDER

The most effective treatments for adult PTSD are trauma-focused psychotherapies (see Chapter 9). Pharmacotherapy is generally considered second-line or adjunctive, reserved for situations in which psychotherapy is unavailable, declined, or insufficient. Selective serotonin reuptake inhibitors (SSRIs), specifically sertraline and fluoxetine, are beneficial and dosed in roughly the same range as for major depressive disorders (sertraline: 50–200 mg/day; fluoxetine: 20–60 mg/day).[33]

Evidence to guide pharmacologic management of ADHD in the presence of PTSD is limited because most randomized controlled trials exclude patients with significant co-occurring conditions including PTSD.[34] Clinical experience suggests that, while rapid stimulant titration may exacerbate anxiety or hypervigilance in some women, slow titration of smooth, extended-release stimulants is generally well tolerated.

AUTISM AND ADHD, OR AUDHD

Many autistic people find the notion of treatment for autism to be offensive, like treatment for other identity markers such as being Jewish or Black.

When it has been studied, medication treatment does not impact core autistic features.[35] Many autistic self-advocates agree that treating co-occurring challenges is an appropriate goal. In AuDHD, ADHD medication often improves attention, organization, and therapy engagement, with similar benefits and side-effect profiles to those of women who are not autistic.[36] In the absence of adult-specific guidelines, we rely on pediatric recommendations and clinical experience, using cautious titration to minimize adverse effects.[37] Also note that affirmation is central to the treatment of autistic transgender women. Acceptance has been shown in many studies to reduce health and suicide-related risks of transgender individuals.[38,39,40]

BIPOLAR DISORDER AND ADHD

General treatment of Bipolar I, Bipolar II, and bipolar-spectrum conditions

Bipolar disorder is characterized by recurring mood episodes of mania, hypomania, and depression, with intervals of normal mood. Mania involves a sustained period of abnormally elevated, expansive, or irritable mood, often with increased energy, reduced need for sleep, and impaired judgment. Bipolar I requires at least one manic episode, while Bipolar II features hypomania—less severe but still impairing. Some women experience clinically significant symptoms without meeting full criteria; this is described as bipolar-spectrum condition.[41,42]

Treatment of mood episodes typically requires mood stabilization with a second-generation antipsychotic, a mood stabilizer, or both, and women with severe mania may require hospitalization as well.[43,44] Adequate sleep is critical (as reduced sleep can trigger a manic episode), but ADHD-related behavioral challenges and delayed sleep phase can complicate this goal. Because bipolar disorder is lifelong and relapsing, effective management must address both acute episodes and long-term maintenance. Combining evidence-based psychotherapies with medication provides superior outcomes, and lifestyle modification further supports recovery (see Chapter 10).[45]

Managing ADHD in the context of bipolar disorder

When ADHD co-occurs with bipolar disorder, treatment sequencing is critical. Mood stabilization must precede ADHD pharmacotherapy, as stimulants or other ADHD agents can precipitate or worsen mania when mood instability is present.[46,47] ADHD medication should be initiated only when the patient is (1) stabilized on an appropriate bipolar regimen and (2) you have helped maximize the likelihood of adherence to the bipolar disorder treatment plan, ideally with support from a family member, friend, or other accountability partner.

For women with bipolar disorder, stimulants remain first-line treatments for ADHD. Evidence suggests that methylphenidate treatment in stabilized bipolar disorder may reduce the risk of recurrent mania,[48] aligning with broader findings that effective ADHD treatment can improve management of co-occurring conditions. Nonetheless, it is essential to closely monitor for early signs of mood destabilization, such as irritability, heightened goal-directed activity, euphoric mood, or reduced need for sleep, since stimulant treatment has the potential to be destabilizing.[49,50]

Nonstimulants, while generally less effective, may carry a lower mania risk in patients whose adherence to their bipolar disorder regimen is not optimal. They can also serve as adjuncts—for example, an evening alpha-2 agonist to address ADHD-associated insomnia. Choice of stimulant, nonstimulant, or combination therapy should be guided by individual risk: long-term stable patients with significant ADHD impairment may benefit from carefully monitored stimulants or combination therapy, while women with hard-to-stabilize bipolar disorder may do better with nonstimulants or delayed stimulant initiation.[51]

In summary, treating co-occurring ADHD and bipolar disorder requires care: stabilize mood first, address ADHD pharmacologically with careful monitoring, and maximize benefits of psychotherapy and lifestyle interventions. Note: too much "caution" about ADHD pharmacotherapy can actually backfire, leaving patients without tools to maintain habits that support bipolar stability.[52,53]

BORDERLINE PERSONALITY DISORDER

The most well-supported treatment for borderline personality disorder (BPD) is dialectical behavior therapy (DBT; see Chapter 9). At present, there are no medications approved by the FDA specifically for BPD. Instead, pharmacotherapy is generally used in an adjunctive and symptom-focused way, often aimed at managing particular difficulties such as mood instability, impulsivity, or anxiety, or directed toward co-occurring psychiatric conditions.[54] Importantly, in individuals who have both ADHD and BPD, treatment with ADHD medications appears to offer broader benefits. Research suggests that such treatment can lower the likelihood of psychiatric rehospitalization, reduce overall hospitalization rates, and even decrease risk of premature death.[55,56]

SUBSTANCE USE DISORDERS

On a population level, treatment of ADHD with medication is associated with a reduced risk of substance misuse.[57,58] However, in women with a substance use disorder, research shows mixed results regarding the impact of ADHD treatment on their substance use.[59] While a detailed review of these inconsistent results is beyond the scope of this chapter, we share below available evidence and our clinical experience working with women with ADHD and substance use and detail psychotherapeutic approaches in Chapter 10.

Alcohol use disorder

Treatment for alcohol use disorder (AUD) should at the minimum include brief evidence-based interventions grounded in motivational interviewing and related approaches (see Chapter 10). Pharmacotherapy should also be considered.

First-line medications for AUD in women with ADHD are those that facilitate adherence—medications that are dosed daily or less frequently. **Naltrexone** (oral 50 mg daily or intramuscular 380 mg monthly) supports abstinence and harm reduction, decreasing heavy drinking. Monthly IM naltrexone can be a valuable option for women who struggle with adherence and cannot access a reliable accountability partner. Common adverse effects include sedation, insomnia, and gastrointestinal symptoms.[60]

Disulfiram (250 mg daily), by contrast, is highly effective when a reliable accountability partner is available to supervise medication intake and a woman is willing to take the medication when reminded. Disulfiram is an aversive agent with a unique mechanism: it is biologically inactive in the absence of alcohol but causes flushing, nausea, tachycardia, and hypotension when alcohol is consumed. Thus, it acts as a psychological deterrent, with its effect dependent on a woman's knowledge that drinking will result in a severe reaction. Because of disulfiram's psychological mechanism, the appropriate approach to research its effectiveness is an open-label trial in which patients are aware that they have taken disulfiram. Such trials show a large effect size (approximately 0.8)—a greater level of effectiveness than other pharmacologic treatments for AUD. It is typically dosed 250 mg daily. Approximately 8% of patients experience moderate to severe drowsiness, but severe adverse effects are rare.[61,62]

Cannabis use disorder and cannabis use

Unfortunately, no medications have shown consistent benefit for cannabis use disorder. In our experience treating women who have been motivated enough to seek treatment for ADHD, psychoeducation regarding the negative impact of cannabis on the brain and its executive function capacities is a highly effective initial intervention. We emphasize the risks of cannabis use that we highlighted in Chapter 3, and most women choose to reduce their use, with some stopping entirely. It is our practice to treat ADHD assertively in patients with cannabis use and cannabis use disorders, including with stimulants where clinically appropriate.

Nicotine use disorder

For women with nicotine use disorder and ADHD, it may work best to stabilize the ADHD first.[63] Subsequent to ADHD treatment, pharmacotherapy with varenicline, nicotine replacement therapy, or bupropion are evidence-based options.[64] We recommend always combining behavioral interventions with medication. Nicotine use often starts early in girls with ADHD. Many have speculated that its use serves as an attempt at self-medication, as nicotine is a powerful stimulant that can have similar effects to those of the psychostimulant medication prescribed for ADHD.[65]

CONCLUSION

Medication treatment of co-occurring psychiatric conditions in women with ADHD requires a structured and individualized approach. This chapter emphasized four guiding principles: treatment is never medication-only, acute and destabilizing conditions must be addressed first, ADHD treatment should be prioritized when it is driving other conditions, and the most effective medication should be selected for each disorder. Applying these principles ensures that treatment sequencing, adherence, and functional outcomes are optimized. By combining pharmacotherapy with psychotherapy and lifestyle interventions, clinicians can better support women in achieving stability and recovery across multiple domains of mental health.

REFERENCES

1. Canadian ADHD Resource Alliance. (2020). *Canadian ADHD practice guidelines* (Version 4.1). https://adhdlearn.caddra.ca/wp-content/uploads/2022/08/Canadian-ADHD-Practice-Guidelines-4.1-January-6-2021.pdf
2. Montejo, Á. L., Calama, J., Rico-Villademoros, F., Montejo, L., González-García, N., Pérez, J., Sánchez, C., de la Iglesia, J., Montejo, L., Franco, M., Prieto, N., Chacón, F., Martín-Carrasco, M., & Arango, C. (2019). A real-world study on antidepressant-associated sexual dysfunction in 2144 outpatients: The SALSEX I study. *Archives of Sexual Behavior, 48*(3), 923–933. https://doi.org/10.1007/s10508-018-1365-6
3. Aboujaoude, E., Rosenbaum, J., Ionescu, D., & Koran, L. (2025). Fluoxetine and fluvoxamine. In *The American Psychiatric Association publishing textbook of psychopharmacology*. https://doi.org/10.1176/appi.books.9781615375523.as12
4. Howlett, J., & Schatzberg, A. (2025). Sertraline and paroxetine. In *The American Psychiatric Association publishing textbook of psychopharmacology*. https://doi.org/10.1176/appi.books.9781615375523.as13
5. Shelton, R. (2025). Citalopram and escitalopram. In *The American Psychiatric Association publishing textbook of psychopharmacology*. https://doi.org/10.1176/appi.books.9781615375523.as14
6. Aboujaoude, E., Rosenbaum, J., Ionescu, D., & Koran, L. (2025). Fluoxetine and fluvoxamine. In *The American Psychiatric Association publishing textbook of psychopharmacology*. https://doi.org/10.1176/appi.books.9781615375523.as12
7. Howlett, J., & Schatzberg, A. (2025). Sertraline and paroxetine. In *The American Psychiatric Association publishing textbook of psychopharmacology*. https://doi.org/10.1176/appi.books.9781615375523.as13
8. Shelton, R. (2025). Citalopram and escitalopram. In *The American Psychiatric Association publishing textbook of psychopharmacology*. https://doi.org/10.1176/appi.books.9781615375523.as14
9. Kalfas, M., Tsapekos, D., Butler, M., McCutcheon, R. A., Pillinger, T., Strawbridge, R., Bhat, B. B., Haddad, P. M., Cowen, P. J., Howes, O. D., Joyce, D. W., Nutt, D. J., Baldwin, D. S., Pariante, C. M., Lewis, G., Young, A. H., Lewis, G., Hayes, J. F., & Jauhar, S. (2025). *Incidence and nature of antidepressant discontinuation symptoms: A systematic review and meta-analysis. JAMA Psychiatry*. Advance online publication. https://doi.org/10.1001/jamapsychiatry.2025.1362
10. Thase, M. (2025). Venlafaxine and desvenlafaxine. In *The American Psychiatric Association publishing textbook of psychopharmacology*. https://doi.org/10.1176/appi.books.9781615375523.as19
11. Stevenson, K., Hamilton, D., & Clayton, A. (2025). Bupropion. In *The American Psychiatric Association publishing textbook of psychopharmacology*. https://doi.org/10.1176/appi.books.9781615375523.as18
12. Desfossés, C.Y., & Blier, P. (2025). Vortioxetine. In *The American Psychiatric Association publishing textbook of psychopharmacology*. https://doi.org/10.1176/appi.books.9781615375523.as16
13. Dean, R. L., Hurducas, C., Hawton, K., Spyridi, S., Cowen, P. J., Hollingsworth, S., Marquardt, T., Barnes, A., Smith, R., McShane, R., Turner, E. H., & Cipriani, A. (2021). Ketamine and other glutamate receptor modulators for depression in adults with unipolar major depressive disorder. *Cochrane Database of Systematic Reviews, 2021*(9), CD011612. https://doi.org/10.1002/14651858.CD011612
14. Geoffroy, P. A., Schroder, C. M., Reynaud, E., &, Bourgin, P. (2019). Efficacy of light therapy versus antidepressant drugs, and of the combination versus monotherapy, in major depressive episodes: a systematic review and meta-analysis. *Sleep Medicine Reviews, 48*, 101213.

15. Lam, R. W., Levitt, A. J., Levitan, R. D., Michalak, E. E., Cheung, A. H., Morehouse, R., Ramasubbu, R., Yatham, L. N., & Tam, E. M. (2016). Efficacy of bright light treatment, fluoxetine, and the combination in patients with nonseasonal major depressive disorder: A randomized clinical trial. *JAMA Psychiatry*, *73*(1), 56–63. https://doi.org/10.1001/jamapsychiatry.2015.2235
16. Özdemir, P. G., Boysan, M., Smolensky, M. H., Selvi, Y., Aydin, A., & Yilmaz, E. (2015). Comparison of venlafaxine alone versus venlafaxine plus bright light therapy combination for severe major depressive disorder. *The Journal of Clinical Psychiatry*, *76*(5), e645–e654. https://doi.org/10.4088/JCP.14m09376
17. Geoffroy, P. A., Schroder, C. M., Reynaud, E., &, Bourgin, P. (2019). Efficacy of light therapy versus antidepressant drugs, and of the combination versus monotherapy, in major depressive episodes: a systematic review and meta-analysis. *Sleep Medicine Reviews*, *48*, 101213.
18. McQuaid, J. R., Buelt, A., Capaldi, V., Fuller, M., Issa, F., Lang, A. E., Hoge, C., Oslin, D. W., Sall, J., Wiechers, I. R., & Williams, S. (2022). The management of major depressive disorder: synopsis of the 2022 U.S. Department of Veterans Affairs and U.S. Department of Defense clinical practice guideline. *Annals of Internal Medicine*, *175*(10), 1440–1451. https://doi.org/10.7326/M22-1603
19. Papakostas, G. I., Trivedi, M. H., Shelton, R. C., Iosifescu, D. V., Thase, M. E., Jha, M. K., Mathew, S. J., DeBattista, C., Dokucu, M. E., Brawman-Mintzer, O., Currier, G. W., McCall, W. V., Modirrousta, M., Macaluso, M., Bystritsky, A., Vila-Rodríguez, F., Nelson, E. B., Yeung, A. S., Feeney, A., MacGregor, L. C., Carmody, T., & Fava, M. (2024). Comparative effectiveness research trial for antidepressant incomplete and non-responders with treatment resistant depression (ASCERTAIN-TRD): a randomized clinical trial. *Molecular Psychiatry*, *29*(8), 2287–2295. https://doi.org/10.1038/s41380-024-02468-x
20. Dalhuisen, I., van Oostrom, I., Spijker, J., Wijnen, B., van Exel, E., van Mierlo, H., de Waardt, D., Arns, M., Tendolkar, I., & van Eijndhoven, P. (2024). rTMS as a next step in antidepressant nonresponders: a randomized comparison with current antidepressant treatment approaches. *American Journal of Psychiatry*, *181*(9), 806–814. https://doi.org/10.1176/appi.ajp.20230556
21. Cole, E. J., Phillips, A. L., Bentzley, B. S., Stimpson, K. H., Nejad, R., Barmak, F., Veerapal, C., Khan, N., Cherian, K., Felber, E., Brown, R., Choi, E. E. Y., King, S., Pankow, H., Bishop, J. H., Azeez, A., Coetzee, J., Rapier, R., Odenwald, N., Carreon, D., Hawkins, J., Chang, M., Keller, J., Raj, K., DeBattista, C., Jo, B., Espil, F. M., Schatzberg, A. F., Sudheimer, K. D., & Williams, N. R. (2022). Stanford Neuromodulation Therapy (SNT): a double-blind randomized controlled trial. *American Journal of Psychiatry*, *179*(2), 132–141. https://doi.org/10.1176/appi.ajp.2021.20101429
22. Chang, Z., Quinn, P. D., O'Reilly, L., Sjölander, A., Hur, K., Gibbons, R., Larsson, H., & D'Onofrio, B. M. (2020). Medication for attention deficit/hyperactivity disorder and risk for suicide attempts. *Biological Psychiatry*, *88*(6), 452–458.
23. Zhang, L., Zhu, N., Sjölander, A., Nourredine, M., Li, L., Garcia-Argibay, M., Kuja-Halkola, R., Brikell, I., Lichtenstein, P., D'Onofrio, B. M., Larsson, H., Cortese, S., & Chang, Z. (2025). ADHD drug treatment and risk of suicidal behaviours, substance misuse, accidental injuries, transport accidents, and criminality: emulation of target trials. *BMJ*, 390, Article e083658. https://doi.org/10.1136/bmj-2024-083658
24. Todzia-Kornas, A., Szczegielniak, A., & Gondek, T. M. (2024). Suicidality and nonsuicidal self-injury in females diagnosed with attention deficit hyperactivity disorder: A narrative review. *Current Opinion in Psychiatry*, *37*, 38–42.

25. Jakubovski, E., Johnson, J. A., Nasir, M., Müller-Vahl, K., & Bloch, M. H. (2019). Systematic review and meta-analysis: dose–response curve of SSRIs and SNRIs in anxiety disorders. *Depression and Anxiety, 36*(3), 198–212.
26. Abejuela, H. R., & Osser, D. N. (2016). The Psychopharmacology Algorithm Project at the Harvard South Shore Program: an algorithm for generalized anxiety disorder. *Harvard Review of Psychiatry, 24*(4), 243–256.
27. Bandelow, B., Allgulander, C., Baldwin, D. S., Costa, D. L. D. C., Denys, D., Dilbaz, N., Domschke, K., Eriksson, E., Fineberg, N. A., Hättenschwiler, J., Hollander, E., Kaiya, H., Karavaeva, T., Kasper, S., Katzman, M., Kim, Y. K., Inoue, T., Lim, L., Masdrakis, V., Menchón, J. M., Nutt, D., Pallanti, S., Pini, S., Shioe, K., Stahl, S., Starcevic, V., Varughese, S., Watanabe, N., Zdanys, K., & Zohar, J. (2023). World Federation of Societies of Biological Psychiatry (WFSBP) guidelines for treatment of anxiety, obsessive-compulsive and posttraumatic stress disorders—Version 3. Part I: anxiety disorders. *The World Journal of Biological Psychiatry, 24*(2), 79–117. https://doi.org/10.1080/15622975.2022.2086295
28. Cardoner, N., Gutiérrez-Rojas, L., Saiz, P., Lahera, G., Álvarez-Mon, M. Á., Alonso Ortega, P., & Pérez-Páramo, M. (2025). Does pregabalin offer potential as a first-line therapy for generalized anxiety disorder? A meta-analysis of efficacy, safety, and cost-effectiveness. *Frontiers in Pharmacology, 16*, 1483770.
29. Kasper, S., Gastpar, M., Müller, W. E., Volz, H. P., Möller, H. J., Schläfke, S., & Dienel, A. (2014). Lavender oil preparation Silexan is effective in generalized anxiety disorder—a randomized, double-blind comparison to placebo and paroxetine. *International Journal of Neuropsychopharmacology, 17*(6), 859–869.
30. Volz, H. P., Rosemann, T., Burkart, M., Reineke, T., & Kostev, K. (2025). Silexan is well-tolerated for long-term use in adults and for treatment of adolescents: a real-world data analysis. *European Archives of Psychiatry and Clinical Neuroscience*. Advance online publication.
31. Morin, C. M., & Buysse, D. J. (2024). Management of insomnia. *New England Journal of Medicine, 391*(3), 247–258.
32. Juraschek, S. P., Cortez, M. M., Flack, J. M., Ghazi, L., Kenny, R. A., Rahman, M., Spikes, T., Shibao, C. A., & Biaggioni, I. (2024). Orthostatic hypotension in adults with hypertension: a scientific statement from the American Heart Association. *Hypertension, 81*(3), e16–e30. https://doi.org/10.1161/HYP.0000000000000236
33. Williams, T., Phillips, N. J., Stein, D. J., & Ipser, J. C. (2022). Pharmacotherapy for post-traumatic stress disorder (PTSD). *Cochrane Database of Systematic Reviews, 2022*(3), CD002795.
34. Elliott, J., Johnston, A., Husereau, D., Kelly, S. E., Eagles, C., Charach, A., Hsieh, S.-C., Bai, Z., Hossain, A., Skidmore, B., Tsakonas, E., Chojecki, D., Mamdani, M., & Wells, G. A. (2020). Pharmacologic treatment of attention deficit hyperactivity disorder in adults: A systematic review and network meta-analysis. *PLOS ONE, 15*(10), e0240584. https://doi.org/10.1371/journal.pone.0240584
35. Thom, R. P., Pereira, J. A., Sipsock, D., & McDougle, C. J. (2021). Recent updates in psychopharmacology for the core and associated symptoms of autism spectrum disorder. *Current Psychiatry Reports, 23*(12), 79.
36. Muit, J. J., Bothof, N., & Kan, C. C. (2020). Pharmacotherapy of ADHD in adults with autism spectrum disorder: Effectiveness and side effects. *Journal of Attention Disorders, 24*(2), 215–225.
37. Barbaresi, W. J., Campbell, L., Diekroger, E. A., Froehlich, T. E., Liu, Y. H., O'Malley, E., Pelham, W. E., Power, T. J., Zinner, S. H., & Chan, E. (2020). Society for Developmental and Behavioral Pediatrics clinical practice guideline for

the assessment and treatment of children and adolescents with complex attention-deficit/hyperactivity disorder. *Journal of Developmental and Behavioral Pediatrics, 41*(Suppl 2S), S35–S57.

38. Strauss, P., Cook, A., Watson, V., Winter, S., Whitehouse, A., Albrecht, N., Wright Toussaint, D., & Lin, A. (2021). Mental health difficulties among trans and gender diverse young people with an autism spectrum disorder (ASD): findings from Trans Pathways. *Journal of Psychiatric Research, 137*, 360–367.
39. Soto, E. F., Orantes, D., Russo, N., & Antshel, K. M. (2024). Autism and sexual and gender minority identity in college students: examination of self-reported rates, functional outcomes, and treatment engagement. *Autism, 28*(6), 1519–1539.
40. Strang, J. F., Anthony, L. G., Song, A., Lai, M. C., Knauss, M., Sadikova, E., Graham, E., Zaks, Z., Wimms, H., Willing, L., Call, D., Mancilla, M., Shakin, S., Vilain, E., Kim, D. Y., Maisashvili, T., Khawaja, A., & Kenworthy, L. (2023). In addition to stigma: cognitive and autism-related predictors of mental health in transgender adolescents. *Journal of Clinical Child & Adolescent Psychology, 52*(2), 212–229. https://doi.org/10.1080/15374416.2021.1916940
41. Nierenberg, A. A., Agustini, B., Köhler-Forsberg, O., Cusin, C., Katz, D., Sylvia, L. G., Peters, A., & Berk, M. (2023). Diagnosis and treatment of bipolar disorder: a review. *JAMA, 330*(14), 1370–1380. https://doi.org/10.1001/jama.2023.18588
42. Carvalho, A. F., Firth, J., & Vieta, E. (2020). Bipolar disorder. *New England Journal of Medicine, 383*(1), 58–66.
43. McIntyre, R. S., Berk, M., Brietzke, E., Goldstein, B. I., López-Jaramillo, C., Vedel Kessing, L., Malhi, G. S., Nierenberg, A. A., Rosenblat, J. D., Majeed, A., Vieta, E., Vinberg, M., Young, A. H., & Mansur, R. B. (2020). Bipolar disorders. *The Lancet, 396*(10265), 1841–1856. https://doi.org/10.1016/S0140-6736(20)31544-0
44. Goes, F. S. (2023). Diagnosis and management of bipolar disorders. *BMJ, 381*, e073591.
45. Miklowitz, D. J., Efthimiou, O., Furukawa, T. A., Scott, J., McLaren, R., Geddes, J. R., Cipriani, A. (2021). Adjunctive psychotherapy for bipolar disorder: a systematic review and component network meta-analysis. *JAMA Psychiatry, 78*(2), 141–150. https://doi.org/10.1001/jamapsychiatry.2020.2993
46. Miskowiak, K. W., Obel, Z. K., Gugliemo, R., del Mar Bonnin, C., Bowie, C. R., Balanzá-Martínez, V., Burdick, K. E., Carvalho, A. F., Dols, A., Douglas, K., Gallagher, P., Kessing, L. V., Lafer, B., Lewandowski, K. E., López-Jaramillo, C., Martinez-Aran, A., McIntyre, R. S., Porter, R. J., Purdon, S. E., Schaffer, A., Stokes, P. R. A., Sumiyoshi, T., Torres, I. J., Van Rheenen, T. E., Yatham, L. N., Young, A. H., Vieta, E., & Hasler, G. (2024). Efficacy and safety of established and off-label ADHD drug therapies for cognitive impairment or attention-deficit hyperactivity disorder symptoms in bipolar disorder: a systematic review by the ISBD Targeting Cognition Task Force. *Bipolar Disorders, 26*(3), 216–239. https://doi.org/10.1111/bdi.13414
47. Viktorin, A., Rydén, E., Thase, M. E., Chang, Z., Lundholm, C., D'Onofrio, B. M., Almqvist, C., Magnusson, P. K. E., Lichtenstein, P., Larsson, H., & Landén, M. (2017). The risk of treatment-emergent mania with methylphenidate in bipolar disorder. *American Journal of Psychiatry, 174*(4), 341–348. https://doi.org/10.1176/appi.ajp.2016.16040467
48. Viktorin, A., Rydén, E., Thase, M. E., Chang, Z., Lundholm, C., D'Onofrio, B. M., Almqvist, C., Magnusson, P. K. E., Lichtenstein, P., Larsson, H., & Landén, M. (2017). The risk of treatment-emergent mania with methylphenidate in bipolar disorder. *American Journal of Psychiatry, 174*(4), 341–348. https://doi.org/10.1176/appi.ajp.2016.16040467

49. Miskowiak, K. W., Obel, Z. K., Gugliemo, R., del Mar Bonnin, C., Bowie, C. R., Balanzá-Martínez, V., Burdick, K. E., Carvalho, A. F., Dols, A., Douglas, K., Gallagher, P., Kessing, L. V., Lafer, B., Lewandowski, K. E., López-Jaramillo, C., Martinez-Aran, A., McIntyre, R. S., Porter, R. J., Purdon, S. E., Schaffer, A., Stokes, P. R. A., Sumiyoshi, T., Torres, I. J., Van Rheenen, T. E., Yatham, L. N., Young, A. H., Vieta, E., & Hasler, G. (2024). Efficacy and safety of established and off-label ADHD drug therapies for cognitive impairment or attention-deficit hyperactivity disorder symptoms in bipolar disorder: a systematic review by the ISBD Targeting Cognition Task Force. *Bipolar Disorders, 26*(3), 216–239. https://doi.org/10.1111/bdi.13414
50. Viktorin, A., Rydén, E., Thase, M. E., Chang, Z., Lundholm, C., D'Onofrio, B. M., Almqvist, C., Magnusson, P. K. E., Lichtenstein, P., Larsson, H., & Landén, M. (2017). The risk of treatment-emergent mania with methylphenidate in bipolar disorder. *American Journal of Psychiatry, 174*(4), 341–348. https://doi.org/10.1176/appi.ajp.2016.16040467
51. Mucci, F., Avella, M. T., & Marazziti, D. (2019). ADHD with comorbid bipolar disorders: a systematic review of neurobiological, clinical and pharmacological aspects across the lifespan. *Current Medicinal Chemistry, 26*(38), 6942–6969.
52. Miskowiak, K. W., Obel, Z. K., Gugliemo, R., del Mar Bonnin, C., Bowie, C. R., Balanzá-Martínez, V., Burdick, K. E., Carvalho, A. F., Dols, A., Douglas, K., Gallagher, P., Kessing, L. V., Lafer, B., Lewandowski, K. E., López-Jaramillo, C., Martinez-Aran, A., McIntyre, R. S., Porter, R. J., Purdon, S. E., Schaffer, A., Stokes, P. R. A., Sumiyoshi, T., Torres, I. J., Van Rheenen, T. E., Yatham, L. N., Young, A. H., Vieta, E., & Hasler, G. (2024). Efficacy and safety of established and off-label ADHD drug therapies for cognitive impairment or attention-deficit hyperactivity disorder symptoms in bipolar disorder: a systematic review by the ISBD Targeting Cognition Task Force. *Bipolar Disorders, 26*(3), 216–239. https://doi.org/10.1111/bdi.13414
53. Viktorin, A., Rydén, E., Thase, M. E., Chang, Z., Lundholm, C., D'Onofrio, B. M., Almqvist, C., Magnusson, P. K. E., Lichtenstein, P., Larsson, H., & Landén, M. (2017). The risk of treatment-emergent mania with methylphenidate in bipolar disorder. *American Journal of Psychiatry, 174*(4), 341–348. https://doi.org/10.1176/appi.ajp.2016.16040467
54. Stoffers, J. M., Völlm, B. A., Rücker, G., Timmer, A., Huband, N., & Lieb, K. (2010). Pharmacological interventions for borderline personality disorder. *Cochrane Database of Systematic Reviews, 2010*(6), CD005653.
55. Prada, P., Hasler, R., Baud, P., Bednarz, G., Ardu, S., Krejci, I., Nicastro, R., Aubry, J.-M., & Perroud, N. (2014). Distinguishing borderline personality disorder from adult attention-deficit/hyperactivity disorder: a clinical and dimensional perspective. *Psychiatry Research, 217*(1–2), 107–114. https://doi.org/10.1016/j.psychres.2014.03.006
56. Lieslehto, J., Tiihonen, J., Lähteenvuo, M., Mittendorfer-Rutz, E., Tanskanen, A., & Taipale, H. (2023). Association of pharmacological treatments and real-world outcomes in borderline personality disorder. *Acta Psychiatrica Scandinavica, 147*(6), 603–613.
57. Chang, Z., Lichtenstein, P., Halldner, L., D'Onofrio, B., Serlachius, E., Fazel, S., Långström, N., & Larsson, H. (2014). Stimulant ADHD medication and risk for substance abuse. *Journal of Child Psychology and Psychiatry, 55*(8), 878–885.
58. Zhang, L., Zhu, N., Sjölander, A., Nourredine, M., Li, L., Garcia-Argibay, M., Kuja-Halkola, R., Brikell, I., Lichtenstein, P., D'Onofrio, B. M., Larsson, H., Cortese, S., & Chang, Z. (2025). ADHD drug treatment and risk of suicidal behaviours, substance misuse, accidental injuries, transport accidents,

and criminality: emulation of target trials. *BMJ*, 390, Article e083658. https://doi.org/10.1136/bmj-2024-083658

59. Barbuti, M., Maiello, M., Spera, V., Pallucchini, A., Brancati, G. E., Maremmani, A. G. I., Perugi, G., & Maremmani, I. (2023). Challenges of treating ADHD with comorbid substance use disorder: considerations for the clinician. *Journal of Clinical Medicine, 12*(9), 3096. https://doi.org/10.3390/jcm12093096
60. Kranzler, H. R., & Soyka, M. (2018). Diagnosis and pharmacotherapy of alcohol use disorder: a review. *JAMA, 320*(8), 815–824.
61. Kranzler, H. R., & Soyka, M. (2018). Diagnosis and pharmacotherapy of alcohol use disorder: a review. *JAMA, 320*(8), 815–824.
62. Reus, V. I., Fochtmann, L. J., Bukstein, O., Eyler, A. E., Hilty, D. M., Horvitz-Lennon, M., Mahoney, J., Pasic, J., Weaver, M., Wills, C. D., McIntyre, J., Kidd, J., Yager, J., & Hong, S. H. (2018). The American Psychiatric Association practice guideline for the pharmacological treatment of patients with alcohol use disorder. *American Journal of Psychiatry, 175*(1), 86–90. https://doi.org/10.1176/appi.ajp.2017.1750101
63. Gray, K. M., & Upadhyaya, H. P. (2009). Tobacco smoking in individuals with attention-deficit hyperactivity disorder: epidemiology and pharmacological approaches to cessation. *CNS Drugs, 23*(8), 661–668.
64. Selby, P., & Zawertailo, L. (2022). Tobacco addiction. *New England Journal of Medicine, 387*(4), 345–354.
65. Elkins, I. J., Saunders, G. R. B., Malone, S. M., Keyes, M. A., Samek, D. R., McGue, M., & Iacono, W. G. (2018). Increased risk of smoking in female adolescents who had childhood ADHD. *The American Journal of Psychiatry, 175*(1), 63–70. https://doi.org/10.1176/appi.ajp.2017.17010009

CHAPTER 7

Common medical conditions associated with ADHD

INTRODUCTION

For women living with ADHD, many physical and mental health conditions may exist simultaneously. Having a patient who has ADHD in addition to other medical conditions may significantly complicate both the diagnostic and treatment picture. For example, you may need to ask yourself:

- *Is her frequent migraine or fibromyalgia pain not responding to current treatment due to undiagnosed or untreated ADHD that creates stress and makes her functioning and pain symptoms worse?*
- *Are her disordered eating behaviors a coping mechanism she relies on to manage overwhelming anxiety exacerbated by undiagnosed ADHD?*
- *Are her chronic sleep problems due to poor time awareness, difficulty stopping an enjoyable activity and turning out the light, or a brain that is always "on" which she can't "turn off" at bedtime?*

When treating a woman with diagnosed or undiagnosed ADHD, your treatment recommendations for other medical conditions may be undermined by symptoms that impair her ability to consistently follow them.

As a result of many conditions related to lifestyle factors (poor nutrition, inadequate sleep and little exercise, smoking, substance abuse), women with ADHD, on average, have a lifespan nearly 9 years shorter than those without ADHD.[1] The mortality risk is higher when diagnosis is delayed until adulthood. Only after their ADHD is diagnosed and treated can these patients fully benefit from treatment for their other conditions. In fact, treating their ADHD is critical, as it enables them to follow your recommendations more consistently.

DOI: 10.4324/9781003542124-7

Once the risk of ADHD has been identified, you will need to make some decisions. Will you be diagnosing and treating her yourself, or will you refer her to someone in the community? If you are diagnosing her yourself, choose one screening scale and become familiar with scoring and interpreting it. This will make it easier to determine whether ADHD is part of your patient's medical picture.

CLUES TO UNCOVERING ADHD IN YOUR PRACTICE

Right now, you may be asking, "But how do I go about screening for ADHD in a busy practice?" Easy! Follow the clues!

First step

Suspecting that something is wrong and that it might be ADHD is the first step.

(Tip: Learn the symptoms of ADHD in women—see Chapter 2 on diagnosis.)

Second step

It's time to look for clues. They are everywhere!

- Which women are usually late?
- Or frequently forget their appointment? (Tip: Search your "No Shows.")
- Which women call for refills *after* they have run out of medication? (Tip: Discuss automatic refills with the patient and prescribe a three-month supply when you can.)
- Which women report forgetting to take their medications on time? (Tip: Talk to the patient about setting a timer on a watch, computer, or other device or link taking medications to another daily activity, e.g. toothbrushing, meals, etc.)

In your appointments, do you notice:

- That they forget your explanations and repeat the same questions? (Tip: Have handouts pertaining to commonly diagnosed conditions ready and available in your office or write out names and instructions for them.)

- That their disorganization prevents them from following treatment recommendations?
  (Tip: Refer them to an ADHD or life coach.)
- Your prescribed treatment doesn't seem to be working?
  (Tip: Consider ADHD before changing your approach or medications.)

Third step: Diagnosis

If the above sounds familiar, and you suspect a patient/client may have ADHD, administer one of the short **rating scales for screening for ADHD** in adults. (See Chapter 2 for a list of some of the most common scales for this purpose.) The scale you choose will depend on your specific needs, the availability of resources in your practice, and your clinical expertise.

> **A note of interest**: One internist keeps a tear-off pad of the WHO (ASRS-v1.1) scale in her examining rooms. She has found that several patients have completed the scale while waiting for her and then brought their results to her attention. This led to discussions about the possibility that they might have ADHD in addition to their original complaints. After scheduled follow-up visits and more in-depth assessment, this internist has diagnosed several cases of ADHD, significantly improving the lives and outcomes of these patients.

Fourth step: ADHD treatment

If you don't feel comfortable managing ADHD, make a referral to a local professional with expertise in this area for diagnosis and/or treatment. Explain to your patient that addressing her ADHD is imperative for your treatment of her medical condition to be optimally effective.

TREATMENT ADHERENCE ISSUES CAUSED BY UNDERLYING ADHD

Let's discuss the elephant in the room—**treatment adherence**. You may have frequently asked yourself, "Why is it so difficult for my patient to follow the treatment plan we worked on together in session?" The answer is that women with ADHD often have poor executive functioning. As a result, they have difficulty managing time, organizing their lives, and being consistent. These women live in a constant state of **OVERWHELM!** Treating their ADHD will decrease these behaviors and improve treatment outcomes. Now, let's look at some of the medical conditions that have a higher percentage of women who might also have ADHD.

OBESITY, DIABETES, AND EATING DISORDERS AND ADHD

Obesity is an extremely common condition in the United States today and one that may be accompanied by serious health consequences. What is more, the prevalence of ADHD among individuals seeking treatment for obesity can range from 27 to 50%.[2,3,4] Gender adds another dimension to this already complex picture; women with ADHD may experience unique challenges related to body image and societal pressures, which can influence their eating behaviors and weight management. Women with ADHD are more likely to report disordered eating behaviors compared with men with ADHD.[5] Obesity can be associated with other chronic conditions including high blood pressure, heart disease, and diabetes.[6]

Interventions targeting both ADHD symptoms and obesity may be beneficial because addressing one condition will positively impact the other.[7] Therefore, it's important that you develop a tailored treatment program that considers the unique challenges faced by women with both conditions.

Diabetes and ADHD

The prevalence of ADHD in individuals with diabetes is much higher than has been previously reported; this is due to the underdiagnosis of ADHD in adults, especially women. One study of type 2 diabetes (T2D) carefully screened for ADHD and found that although approximately 46% of the participants met diagnostic criteria for ADHD based on the Adult ADHD Self-Report Scale (ASRS), only 14% had a prior diagnosis or prescription for ADHD medications, highlighting the need for ADHD screening among adults with T2D.[8] While few studies of the link between ADHD and diabetes explore sex differences in the rate of this comorbidity, the documented relationship between female sex and higher rates of metabolic syndrome in ADHD suggests that ADHD may predispose women to a greater risk of type 2 diabetes.[9]

Studies looking at adults with type 1 diabetes (T1D) point to the potential impact of ADHD, with ADHD symptoms creating a feedback loop which exacerbates diabetes risk. The studies found that many adults with T1D exhibit undiagnosed ADHD symptoms as measured by the ASRS, which correlate with challenges managing the illness and depression. Women had higher ASRS scores than men.[10]

Because adults with either T1 or T2 diabetes tend to have symptoms that might indicate a risk of ADHD, both primary care physicians and endocrinologists should be aware of the need to screen adults with diabetes for ADHD.

> Primary care providers and endocrinologists should be aware of the need to screen adults with diabetes for ADHD.

Disordered eating and ADHD

Women with ADHD may overeat for many reasons—ADHD-related stress, need for stimulation, boredom, anxiety, depression, impulsivity, not being able to stop once they start eating, or eating without awareness (mindless eating). Additionally, many women with ADHD report that they often forget to eat. This can be due to hyperfocus on a particular task, being too busy trying to get everything done, or difficulty noticing how much time has passed (time blindness). This pattern of skipping meals can trigger significant overeating once hunger forces its way into a woman's awareness. In addition, executive dysfunction may cause difficulties with meal planning and monitoring eating habits, contributing to excessive intake and weight gain.

Drs. Quinn and Nadeau became interested in this relationship between ADHD and disordered eating early on in their practices, which have focused mainly on girls and women with ADHD for the last 30 years. In January 1998 they sent an informal survey to subscribers of *ADDvance*, a magazine for women with ADHD that they co-published and co-edited, asking about problems with overeating and eating disorders.[11] The majority of women who responded reported binge eating or compulsive overeating, with a significant portion also reporting purging behaviors and a smaller number reporting anorexia. Younger women (under 40) reported higher rates of these behaviors compared to women aged 40 and older.

Many women described a pattern of eating carbohydrates (sweets and starchy snacks) in the evening as a means not only of reward but also of self-calming or self-medication. Women's responses to the survey seemed to indicate that treating their ADHD with stimulants was helpful. Most respondents reported taking a stimulant for their ADHD, with a higher percentage among younger women. Both age groups reported an improvement in controlling their impulsive eating behaviors when taking stimulants.[12]

BINGE-EATING DISORDER

Women with ADHD have been found to have higher rates of **binge-eating disorder (BED)** than women without ADHD. Studies suggest that up to 30% of women with ADHD may experience binge-eating behaviors.[13] This association highlights the need for careful screening for eating disorders in women diagnosed with ADHD.

Impulsivity, a core symptom of ADHD, is often linked to disordered eating behaviors, including binge eating. Women with ADHD may engage in binge eating as a means of coping with **emotional dysregulation** or as a response to impulsive urges.[14] Research has shown that higher levels of impulsivity are associated with increased binge-eating episodes, suggesting that impulsivity may serve as a risk factor for the development of BED in these women.[15]

In addition, the presence of psychiatric conditions such as anxiety and depression is commonly reported in women with both ADHD and BED. These coexisting conditions can exacerbate the severity of binge-eating behaviors and further complicate your treatment efforts.[16] For instance, women with ADHD who also experience anxiety may use food as a coping mechanism to manage their emotional distress, leading to increased episodes of binge eating, increased caloric intake, and weight gain.[17]

CASE ILLUSTRATION: SALMA

Salma, a 46-year-old elementary school teacher, presented to her physician for her annual physical. At intake, it was noted that she had gained 35 pounds since her last visit and although she had been a little overweight in the past, she shared that she felt distressed over having recently gained a significant amount of weight fairly quickly. Her weight was now at the upper end of the overweight range, bordering on obesity, with a BMI of 29. Salma, who had always been anxious, reported that over the last year she had become more depressed and sought help from a local therapist. She had begun taking antidepressants for her depression and had seen an immediate improvement in mood, but also found that she was bingeing more and had difficulty controlling her eating. She also felt she was in perimenopause, as she had noticed that her menses had become heavier and more irregular and she was having difficulty sleeping.

There are clearly several reasons for Salma's weight gain—anxiety, depression, perimenopause, lack of sleep, and the use of antidepressants. Salma shared that in the evening she ate dinner but still felt hungry, and often snacked on chips and ice cream until she fell asleep, sometimes as late as 2:00 a.m. She confessed to visiting the teachers' lounge at school at least once a day and eating whatever was there. She mentioned that she often forgot to pack a lunch or found that she didn't have time to pack one as she got up late and was rushing most mornings.

Salma was referred to the nutritionist affiliated with the office practice and asked to schedule a follow-up visit for 6 weeks. Blood tests were drawn at this visit. Results indicated an elevated lipid profile and prediabetes.

At her follow-up visit, Salma was noted to have gained another 4 pounds. She was desperate and expressed that she felt like a failure. She had seen the nutritionist but was unable to follow any of her suggestions. Salma expressed difficulty with planning, buying, and preparing meals. She felt out of control, and it was simpler for her to order a pizza or open a bag of cookies and "dig in." She impulsively bought and ate food without thinking. She couldn't seem to generate a Plan B when Plan A failed.

At this point, her care provider had Salma complete the Wender Utah Rating Scale for ADHD. After an in-depth interview and consultation with her therapist, Salma was diagnosed with ADHD and started on a long-acting stimulant trial. Results were excellent while on her medication, but Salma reported that she began compulsively eating when her medication wore off in the late afternoon. An additional short-acting dose was added in the afternoon. Salma finally gained control of her eating through working first with her nutritionist and then with a coach to address her organizational and time-management difficulties.

In addition to many of these other causes, women with ADHD may also be more susceptible to developing eating disorders due to societal pressures related to body image and weight.[18] These women are more likely to report emotional eating and binge-eating behaviors compared to men with ADHD, which may be influenced by the interplay of ADHD symptoms and oppressive societal expectations.[19]

What can you recommend in a woman's treatment plan to address these interrelated conditions? Recently, medication commonly used for the treatment of ADHD has also been approved by the FDA to treat binge-eating disorder (BED). Oral lisdexamfetamine dimesylate (Vyvanse®; lisdexamfetamine), a prodrug of dextroamfetamine, is currently the only drug that has been approved in the United States for the treatment of moderate to severe BED in adult patients.[20]

Integrated treatment approaches that address both ADHD symptoms and binge-eating behaviors may be beneficial for these women.[21] In addition to medication, cognitive behavioral therapy (CBT) has been shown to be effective in treating both ADHD and BED, and may help women develop healthier coping strategies.

BULIMIA

The prevalence of ADHD among individuals with bulimia nervosa can range from 3 to 12%.[22,23] Women with a past history or more recent episodes of bulimia (within the last 12 months) have been found to have a significantly higher prevalence of ADHD compared to women without these episodes.[24] Women with ADHD may engage in bulimic behaviors as a means of coping with emotional dysregulation or impulsivity. As we have seen, impulsivity, a core symptom of ADHD, is often linked to disordered eating behaviors, including the binge eating and purging seen in bulimia nervosa.[25,26] As in other disordered eating patterns, the presence of comorbid psychiatric conditions, such as anxiety and depression, is common in women with both ADHD and bulimia. These coexisting conditions can further complicate the clinical picture and influence the severity of bulimic symptoms.[27] Integrated treatment approaches addressing both ADHD and bulimia may be beneficial, as effective management of ADHD symptoms can potentially improve outcomes for individuals with eating disorders.

In summary, ADHD is seen in a significant proportion of women with bulimia, with impulsivity and coexisting psychiatric conditions playing a role in the development and maintenance of bulimic behaviors. Given the association between ADHD and bulimia, we would encourage you to assess for ADHD symptoms as part of the evaluation and treatment of women with eating disorders that suggest a pattern of bingeing and purging.

ANOREXIA NERVOSA

As with other eating disorders, studies indicate that women with anorexia nervosa (AN) exhibit higher rates of ADHD symptoms than the general population, with prevalence of ADHD among individuals with AN reported to be as high as 30%.[28] This suggests that ADHD may also be a risk factor for the development of anorexia nervosa, particularly in women. Impulsivity, poor self-esteem, and societal pressures are often linked to disordered eating behaviors. Women with ADHD may engage in restrictive eating patterns as a means of coping with the emotional dysregulation associated with the disorder.[29] This relationship highlights the potential for ADHD symptoms to contribute to the onset and maintenance of anorexia nervosa.

For many women with ADHD, the presence of extreme **anxiety** exacerbated by ADHD symptoms has been associated with the development of anorexia nervosa. Research indicates that anxiety disorders, in particular, are frequently observed in individuals with AN, with estimates suggesting that over 40% of patients with AN have a lifetime history of anxiety disorders.[30] The coexistence of AN, ADHD, and anxiety can complicate the clinical picture and may influence the severity and presentation of both ADHD and anorexia nervosa symptoms.

Women with ADHD may be more susceptible than men to developing eating disorders, due to societal pressures related to body image and weight. Additionally, the manifestation of ADHD symptoms may differ between genders, with women often experiencing more internalizing symptoms, which can contribute to the development of anorexia nervosa. Integrated treatment approaches that address both ADHD and anxiety may be beneficial in the effective management of AN.

In addition, longitudinal studies have shown that childhood ADHD symptoms increase the likelihood of the development of eating disorders in adolescence and adulthood. This emphasizes the importance of early identification and intervention for ADHD to potentially mitigate the risk of developing anorexia nervosa later in life.[31]

CASE ILLUSTRATION: ALISON

Alison was a 21-year-old college junior admitted to an inpatient psychiatric facility because of lifelong struggles with disordered eating; she had been diagnosed with anorexia nervosa while in high school. Anxiety and selective eating behaviors were first noted at age 8. At that age, Alison rejected new foods, had trouble with textures, and subsequently ate a very limited diet. She was bright and did well in school academically but was often described as shy and withdrawn by teachers. She spent hours on her homework each night, copying and recopying her homework and notes. Everything had to be perfect, and she kept her room immaculate. When she was in high school, her therapist diagnosed her as having obsessive compulsive personality disorder (which often co-occurs with ADHD) as well as AN. This pattern continued, and by her junior year in college Alison was consuming only saltines and sweetened tea. She was hospitalized, medically evaluated. and treated for nutritional deficiencies. Her case was presented to a visiting expert with experience with ADHD in women. The expert suggested referring Alison for an ADHD assessment, and the diagnosis was confirmed. Alison was treated with medications for anxiety and ADHD, and received CBT. Dramatic improvements were noted; Alison even became more outgoing. She exhibited fewer compulsive behaviors, and expanded her food repertoire. She rapidly gained weight and was discharged to continue outpatient therapy. After taking a gap year, she returned to and graduated from college.

Alison's case illustrates the importance of health care providers in familiarizing themselves with the complex and varied presentations of ADHD in women to adequately address the needs of their patients. A multipronged treatment approach, which includes a range of support as well as medication, is often critical for success in these complex cases.

CHRONIC PAIN DISORDERS AND ADHD

Chronic pain occurs in approximately 8% of the general population, and research over the last few decades has significantly changed our understanding of the several disorders that cause it. While initially thought to be the result of chronic inflammation in muscles and joints, chronic pain disorders are now recognized as having a neurochemical basis, resulting from decreased dopamine in frontal and prefrontal areas of the brain, which affects pain perception.

Chronic pain and ADHD are increasingly being recognized as coexisting conditions, with evidence suggesting that individuals with ADHD may experience chronic pain conditions more frequently than those without the disorder. In addition, adults with ADHD are more sensitive to pain, with a documented **lower pain threshold**. In such cases, methylphenidate (MPH) has been seen to partly reverse this shorter pain response.[32] As another example, high ADHD scale scores have been seen among patients with chronic lower back pain (CNLBP), with 31.7% of patients with this condition scoring positive for adult ADHD.[33] Higher ADHD scores (ADHD symptom score >/= 14) were associated with higher levels of pain.[34] Conversely, chronic pain exacerbates ADHD symptoms, as it worsens attention and increases functional impairment. ADHD, however, frequently goes undiagnosed in patients with chronic pain. This is an important issue for us to address in your practices, as the co-occurrence of these two conditions leads to poorer functional outcomes in patients.

Adding to this already complex picture, the incidence of chronic pain in women with ADHD is higher than women without ADHD. Furthermore, prospective research indicates three-quarters of women with neurodevelopmental disorders (i.e., ADHD and autism) develop a **chronic pain disorder** and women with these conditions are five times more likely to experience widespread pain than women without them.[35]

Although ADHD frequently co-occurs with various chronic pain conditions, such as nonspecific lower back pain, fibromyalgia, migraine, and dysmenorrhea, these conditions are rarely recognized and treated simultaneously. In several cases, ADHD medications (both stimulants and nonstimulants) have been shown to result in significant improvement in chronic pain symptoms, indicating that treating ADHD may also relieve the coexisting pain. Accordingly, identifying and treating ADHD in patients with these conditions is critical not only to reduce their ADHD symptoms, but also to address their pain symptoms.

You will need to consider the interaction of pain and ADHD to maximize treatment outcomes for both disorders. ADHD screening is warranted in all patients with chronic pain, whether seen in their primary healthcare setting or in a pain management clinic, especially when the pain is severe and/or unresponsive to traditional therapies and accompanied by cognitive/behavioral symptoms indicative of coexisting ADHD.

Fibromyalgia and ADHD

Fibromyalgia (FMS) is a potentially disabling condition characterized by chronic widespread pain and tenderness, fatigue, cognitive impairments, such as poor memory, brain fog, and significant functional impairment. FMS is found in about 2–8% of the population in the United States, with 80–90% of these patients being women. Anywhere from one third to one quarter of those women may also have a coexisting diagnosis of ADHD, which can increase their symptom severity and severely impair functioning; but first, let's hear from a woman about her journey to obtain her fibromyalgia (FMS) and ADHD diagnoses.

CASE ILLUSTRATION: BETSY

After suffering with chronic pain, sleep problems, and low energy, Betsy was first diagnosed with fibromyalgia (FMS) in 1995 at the age of 38. Her diagnosis was confirmed at the Mayo Clinic, where she was described as "attention deficient" (a term used before ADHD in women was recognized). She received the standard treatment for fibromyalgia at the time—antidepressants and anti-anxiety medications. No medical follow-up occurred regarding her attentional issues. This previously high-energy high-school teacher struggled with brain fog and low energy. Unable to perform her duties at work due to her memory problems, she retired on disability. She had gotten to the point where she could hardly cross the room. She had no energy, and her life was filled with "pain and misery" most of the time. Two years later, Betsy was diagnosed with ADHD after a very long and careful work up. She was prescribed stimulants and saw immediate improvements, as well as improvement in her pain, although it wasn't smooth. Finally, she was placed on methylphenidate and Buspar and this combination worked well, as she benefited from increased serotonin as well as dopamine. Her pain stopped as soon as her medications reached the appropriate level—7.5 mg methylphenidate proved therapeutic; any higher and the pain control didn't work for her fibromyalgia. It seems for Betsy there was a small therapeutic window at which the stimulant worked best. She continued to take methylphenidate at 7.5 mg, three times daily. Betsy remained on stimulants for many years until perimenopause, when she began to have significant problems with brain fog, sleep, and energy. We will continue Betsy's story below when we discuss the effects of aging, hormones, and ADHD.

Research has confirmed that 25–35% of women with FMS fulfill the criteria for an ADHD diagnosis.[36,37] There is also a high frequency of diagnosis of childhood ADHD in women with fibromyalgia.[38] What is more, a coexisting ADHD diagnosis is often associated with increased FMS severity and greater functional impairment.[39] ADHD is also associated with an increased use of opiate and sedative drugs in patients with FMS. And patients with both disorders have an almost tenfold risk of substance use disorder (SUD) compared to those with FMS alone (38.5% vs. 3.8%).[40]

How can these women be helped? Certainly, treating their fibromyalgia is the first response. But given what we now know about FMS and ADHD, it is critically important to address their ADHD as well. As we have seen, in studies that found adults with ADHD were more sensitive to pain and had a significantly lower pain threshold, MPH was found to partly alleviate this response.[41]

FMS creates an attentional burden on its own, but when combined with ADHD, the cognitive issues and impaired pain sensitivity associated with it severely impair functioning. Women with this combination of conditions are some of the most severely affected patients we see, with many needing to go on disability. This raises the financial burden to them and to society. This connection *must* be explored and treated to help these patients regain their health and well-being. As Patricia Stephens, author of *Reversing Chronic Disease: A Journey Back to Health*,[42] puts it, "The RIGHT medication, in the RIGHT amount, taken at the RIGHT time of day can turn a lot of lights on in a very dark room" (personal communication).

Migraines and ADHD

Migraine headaches are extremely common and are reported in approximately 25% of the general population. So it may come as no surprise to you that various studies have found that individuals with ADHD are at a higher risk of experiencing migraines, and those with migraines often exhibit symptoms consistent with ADHD.[43,44] Migraines associated with visual disturbance are generally associated with a marginally higher risk of ADHD, independent of ADHD subtype. The association between migraine and ADHD symptoms was statistically significant irrespective of the severity of ADHD symptoms (as measured by ASRS score), with a tendency for migraines to be more frequent in those with more severe ADHD.

This association between ADHD and migraines may occur for several reasons. These include shared neurotransmitter dysregulation, sleep disturbances, behavioral dysregulation, and **stress**. In one study, results indicated not only that migraine was strongly associated with ADHD, but that co-occurrence increased with age and was higher in women.[45]

In your practice, it is important to keep these findings in mind when managing patients with migraine, and to consider that the stress associated with managing ADHD symptoms may contribute to the frequency and severity of migraine attacks. The relationship between these conditions necessitates a comprehensive approach to diagnosis and treatment to ensure that both migraine and ADHD symptoms are adequately addressed.

Toni's story is a perfect example of the complex interactions of these various factors when migraines and ADHD co-occur.

CASE ILLUSTRATION: TONI

Toni is a bright, friendly, 32-year-old accountant who works for a small, private accounting firm. She has always loved math and did well in that academic area in school. However, she reports that she has had lifelong problems with **distractibility**, often losing or forgetting things, and with **time management**, which has impacted her ability to complete assignments on time. She also has difficulties with **organizing** her work. She confesses that since she was in middle school, she has had the habit of **staying up late at night** to get everything done. She then has **trouble falling asleep** (her mind is always going) and difficulty getting up in the morning. This routine had continued since then, and she reported that she **felt that she never got enough sleep**.

She presented to her general practitioner complaining of increasingly frequent **headaches that have the characteristics of migraines**. It was tax season, and she stated that she was under a great deal of **stress** trying to get all her work done. She was afraid that she might lose her job, as the frequent headaches were forcing her to take time off and causing her to fall further behind.

After hearing her story, her primary care physician had her complete the **Adult ADHD Self-Report Scale (ASRS-v1.1)**, on which she scored positive for possible ADHD. He explained ADHD to her and how this might be affecting her functioning and adding to her distress and headaches. He also referred her to a life coach in the same building as the medical practice, in order to address her sleep hygiene and disorganization issues. He switched her medication regime from extra-strength analgesics to sumatriptan nasal spray and scheduled her for a longer appointment in a week's time to conduct a comprehensive diagnostic interview to confirm her possible ADHD. She agreed to have her mother and her best friend complete rating scales in the interim as well. At this next appointment, Toni's ADHD was confirmed as she met all the diagnostic criteria, such as having symptoms that began before the age of 12 and has a positive family history (her brother was diagnosed with ADHD as a hyperactive 7-year-old). Toni was placed on long-acting methylphenidate to address her ADHD symptoms and will continue with her life coach as her dose is adjusted over the next few months. Her headaches are responding to the sumatriptan, and it is hoped that they will decrease in frequency with better sleep and less stress.

COGNITIVE DECLINE WITH AGE AND ADHD

The prevalence of ADHD in people over 50 has been reported to be approximately 3–4%. Individuals with ADHD are at risk for an **accelerated rate of cognitive decline** as they age, and this effect has been found to be more pronounced in women.[46] Treatment of ADHD with stimulants in this age demographic has not been well studied; however, safe pharmacotherapy of ADHD in older adults is supported by the body of evidence that is currently available.[47,48,49] When considering the medical risks of prescribing stimulant medication, collaboration with the patient and her cardiologist is advised when there are cardiac concerns, but the woman's overall quality of life should also be considered. Many older women have told us that physicians routinely decline to prescribe stimulant medications, failing to carefully consider their potential benefits.

Cognitive deficits, memory, and ADHD

Decreases in estrogen levels during perimenopause and menopause may worsen ADHD symptoms and cognitive deficits. (Chapter 8 discusses menopause, estrogen, and the brain in depth.) Women with ADHD often report a worsening of their ADHD symptoms and executive dysfunction that starts in perimenopause and worsening through menopause. The cognitive difficulties caused by low estrogen have led many women to consider the possibility that they have ADHD, some for the first time. For other women, these cognitive changes represent a worsening of symptoms that they have lived with for many years.

A comprehensive assessment is called for when an older woman considers the possibility of ADHD for the first time. The criteria stipulate that symptoms must be present **before the age of 12 years** for an ADHD diagnosis. However, keep in mind that because girls' ADHD symptoms are internalized and girls work hard to mask them, they may have been present but gone unnoticed in childhood. For a separate group of women, cognitive difficulties appear only in their later years; they most likely do not have ADHD.

Also keep in mind that memory clinics are unlikely to consider the possibility of ADHD in an older woman. Goodman et al. reported that only 1 in 5 memory clinics actively screen for ADHD, resulting in many older adults with the disorder being misdiagnosed and receiving ineffective treatment.[50]

Women with ADHD often experience significant cognitive deficits, particularly in executive functions such as working memory, attention, and impulse control. These deficits may be exacerbated by aging, with research indicating that women with ADHD may show faster cognitive decline than their peers without ADHD, particularly in executive functioning.[51,52]

Given the high prevalence of cognitive deficits in women with ADHD, particularly as they age, it is crucial for you to assess **cognitive functioning** as part of the overall evaluation of ADHD. Treatment strategies may include pharmacological interventions, cognitive behavioral therapy, and lifestyle modifications aimed at enhancing cognitive functioning and managing ADHD symptoms.[53,54] Older adults treated with medication for their ADHD report better attention and improved ability to manage daily tasks. As discussed in greater detail in Chapter 8, recent studies have shown that the **medications used to treat symptoms associated with ADHD also improve these symptoms in women in perimenopause who do not have ADHD**.

Parkinson's, dementia, and degenerative brain disorders

ADHD and its relationship to **dementia and degenerative brain disorders** is not well studied and has only recently become an area of focus. A study published in 2023 found that patients with ADHD had a nearly three times **greater risk of dementia**.[55]

An earlier study, in 2018, found that the **risk of early-onset disorders of the basal ganglia and cerebellum** is 2.4 times greater among individuals with ADHD than those without ADHD.[56] In 2023, a meta-analysis of all-cause dementia, Alzheimer's disease, Parkinson's disease (PD), Lewy body dementia (LBD), vascular dementia (VaD), and mild cognitive impairment, showed that ADHD is differentially associated with all-cause and subtypes of dementia, with the highest risk found for VaD.[57]

CARDIOVASCULAR DISEASE AND ADHD

Recently, several studies have suggested a significant association between ADHD and various **cardiovascular risk factors and events**. It is reasonable to hypothesize that rates are high because this population faces myriad heart disease risk factors including chronic stress, anxiety, depression, substance use disorders, sleep disorders, obesity, and diabetes. One study found that 35% of women seeking treatment for cardiac complaints met criteria for lifetime ADHD symptoms, a rate that is nearly 10 times that found among women in general. Significantly, to date **no studies have indicated that CV events are more common in women with ADHD, even women treated with stimulant medication**, although individuals diagnosed during childhood with ADHD exhibited increased risk factors for CVD as they aged.[58,59] Moreover, a nationwide study found that adults with ADHD had a higher risk of developing cardiovascular diseases compared to those without ADHD, with no differences in risk for CVD between females and males.[60]

Cardiovascular disease and medication to treat ADHD

The implications of various **ADHD medications for cardiovascular health** have been scrutinized extensively. Although stimulant medications remain a primary treatment option for ADHD, some studies have suggested that they may elicit cardiovascular changes that could pose risks, particularly in susceptible individuals.[61,62,63] The effects of stimulant medications on **heart rate and blood pressure** have been well documented in numerous studies, which show a statistically significant increase in systolic and diastolic blood pressure as well as in heart rate.[64] Therefore, careful monitoring of blood pressure is required, especially in populations with pre-existing cardiovascular conditions.

ACCIDENTAL INJURY IN WOMEN WITH ADHD

Although accidental injury is not technically a medical diagnosis, it is important to understand this risk in relation to ADHD in women and be prepared to recognize and address it in your patient population. As mentioned earlier, the **mortality risk is significantly increased in those individuals who are diagnosed in adulthood with ADHD**. In the most recent population study, conducted in the UK and published in the

British Journal of Psychiatry (2025), the **reduction in life expectancy for women diagnosed with ADHD compared to the general population was 8.64 years.**[65]

Accidents are a common cause of death for people with ADHD. The risk of accidents and unintentional injuries in women with ADHD is high and has been found to persist across their lifespan. This higher risk can certainly be attributed to the core symptoms of ADHD, namely, impulsivity and inattention. In general, women without ADHD are at a lower risk for accidents in young adulthood than men, but at higher risk in older adulthood. However, this is not seen in women with ADHD. For them, only the risk for severe accidents requiring hospitalization follows this pattern, but for lesser accidents the risk remains higher than for those without ADHD throughout their lifespan.[66] It may also be possible that because women with ADHD often engage in compensatory behaviors to mask their symptoms, this increased stress can lead to a potentially higher risk of accidental injury.

Co-occurring conditions that are commonly seen in women with ADHD, such as anxiety, depression, substance abuse, and bipolar disorder, can further increase their vulnerability to accidents and injuries.[67,68] For example, the impulsivity associated with ADHD is often compounded by these conditions, leading to a greater likelihood that they will engage in behaviors that could result in injury. Pharmacological treatment for ADHD has been shown to mitigate some of these risks. Medications that improve attention and reduce impulsivity can lead to a decrease in accidental injuries. Treating coexisting anxiety with anxiolytics, combined with ADHD medication, has been shown to further decrease the risk of accidents and injuries.[69,70]

CONCLUSION

In this chapter, we have presented a myriad of examples of how ADHD can impact women's minds, behavior, and bodies. No matter what your specialty, you are sure to find women with ADHD within your patient population. Identification and treatment of ADHD in these women is critical both to overall outcome and to the success of your targeted treatment. For many years, it was felt that ADHD in women was a "lesser" disorder. As you can see, that is certainly **not** the case—given the risk of not only increased morbidity, but also mortality, with an almost decade-long decrease in life expectancy associated with ADHD in women. Treatment with medications for ADHD can reduce the mortality rates associated with the disorder—**an 18.75% reduction in the overall risk of death in the two years following diagnosis for those taking medication.**[71] Please keep this finding in mind when diagnosing and treating women with ADHD.

REFERENCES

1. O'Nions, E., El Baou, C., John, A., Lewer, D., Mandy, W., McKechnie, D. G. J., Petersen, I., & Stott, J. (2025). Life expectancy and years of life lost for adults with diagnosed ADHD in the UK: matched cohort study. *The British Journal of Psychiatry: The Journal of Mental Science*, *226*(5), 261–268. https://doi.org/10.1192/bjp.2024.199
2. Pagoto, S. L., Curtin, C., Bandini, L. G., Anderson, S. E., Schneider, K. L., Bodenlos, J. S., & Ma, Y. (2010). Weight loss following a clinic-based weight loss program among adults with attention deficit/hyperactivity disorder symptoms. *Eating and Weight Disorders—Studies on Anorexia Bulimia and Obesity*, *15*(3), e166–e172. https://doi.org/10.1007/bf03325296
3. Gruß, B., Mueller, A., Horbach, T., Martin, A., & Zwaan, M. (2011). Attention-deficit/hyperactivity disorder in a pre-bariatric surgery sample. *European Eating Disorders Review*, *20*(1). https://doi.org/10.1002/erv.1128
4. Cortese, S., Maia, C., Fleur, D., Morcillo-Peñalver, C., Rohde, L., & Faraone, S. (2016). Association between ADHD and obesity: a systematic review and meta-analysis. *American Journal of Psychiatry*, *173*(1), 34–43. https://doi.org/10.1176/appi.ajp.2015.15020266
5. Davis, C. (2010). Attention-deficit/hyperactivity disorder: associations with over-eating and obesity. *Current Psychiatry Reports*, *12*(5), 389–395. https://doi.org/10.1007/s11920-010-0133-7
6. Cortese, S., & Peñalver, C. (2010). Comorbidity between ADHD and obesity: exploring shared mechanisms and clinical implications. *Postgraduate Medicine*, *122*(5), 88–96. https://doi.org/10.3810/pgm.2010.09.2205
7. Pagoto, S., Curtin, C., Appelhans, B., & Alonso-Alonso, M. (2012). Attention deficit/hyperactivity disorder and the clinical management of obesity. *Current Obesity Reports*, *1*(2), 80–86. https://doi.org/10.1007/s13679-012-0012-0
8. Xu, G., Liu, B., Yang, W., Snetselaar, L., & Jin, J. (2020). Association of attention-deficit/hyperactivity disorder with diabetes mellitus in US adults. *Journal of Diabetes*, *13*(4), 299–306. https://doi.org/10.1111/1753-0407.13107
9. Di Girolamo, G., Bracco, I. F., Portigliatti Pomeri, A., Puglisi, S., & Oliva, F. (2022). Prevalence of metabolic syndrome and insulin resistance in a sample of adult ADHD outpatients. *Frontiers in Psychiatry*, *13*, 891479. https://doi.org/10.3389/fpsyt.2022.891479
10. Zhang-James, Y., Draytsel, D., Carguello, B., Faraone, S. V., & Weinstock, R. S. (2025). Attention-deficit/hyperactivity disorder symptoms are common and associated with worse glycemic control in adults with type 1 diabetes. *Journal of Clinical Medicine*, *14*(10), 3606.
11. ADDitude. (n.d.). Home page. https://www.additudemag.com/?srsltid=AfmBOoox1gOycvNrNjdiEE7NTji9k2eUNZSFWGf1DQST0MhguRX_2YXN
12. ADDitude. (n.d.). Home page. https://www.additudemag.com/?srsltid=AfmBOoox1gOycvNrNjdiEE7NTji9k2eUNZSFWGf1DQST0MhguRX_2YXN

13. Şahan, E., Zengin Eroğlu, M., & Sertçelik, S. (2021). Eating behaviors, depression, and anxiety levels of pre-bariatric surgery patients with obesity comorbid with or without attention-deficit/hyperactivity disorder: ADHD or major depression? Which is more related with eating behaviors? *Brain and Behavior, 11*(1), e01915. https://doi.org/10.1002/brb3.1915
14. Cortese, S., Comencini, E., Vincenzi, B., Speranza, M., & Angriman, M. (2013). Attention-deficit/hyperactivity disorder and impairment in executive functions: a barrier to weight loss in individuals with obesity. *BMC Psychiatry, 13*(1).
15. Kaisari, P., Dourish, C., Rotshtein, P., & Higgs, S. (2018). Associations between core symptoms of attention deficit hyperactivity disorder and both binge and restrictive eating. *Frontiers in Psychiatry, 9*. https://doi.org/10.3389/fpsyt.2018.00103
16. Fernández-Aranda, F., Agüera, Z., Castro, R., Jiménez-Murcia, S., Ramos-Quiroga, J. A., Bosch, R., Fagundo, A. B., Granero, R., Penelo, E., Claes, L., Sánchez, I., Riesco, N., Casas, M., & Menchón, J. M. (2013). ADHD symptomatology in eating disorders: a secondary psychopathological measure of severity? *BMC Psychiatry, 13*(1), 166. https://doi.org/10.1186/1471-244X-13-166
17. Sonneville, K. R., Calzo, J. P., Horton, N. J., Field, A. E., Crosby, R. D., Solmi, F., & Micali, N. (2015). Childhood hyperactivity/inattention and eating disturbances predict binge eating in adolescence. *Psychological Medicine, 45*(12), 2511–2520. https://doi.org/10.1017/S0033291715000148
18. Bray, B., Bray, C., Bradley, R., & Zwickey, H. (2022). Mental health aspects of binge eating disorder: a cross-sectional mixed-methods study of binge eating disorder experts' perspectives. *Frontiers in Psychiatry, 13*. https://doi.org/10.3389/fpsyt.2022.953203
19. Seitz, J., Kahraman-Lanzerath, B., Legenbauer, T., Sarrar, L., Herpertz, S., Salbach-Andrae, H., Konrad, K., & Herpertz-Dahlmann, B. (2013). The role of impulsivity, inattention and comorbid ADHD in patients with bulimia nervosa. *PLOS One, 8*(5), e63891. https://doi.org/10.1371/journal.pone.0063891
20. Heo, Y. A., & Duggan, S. T. (2017). Lisdexamfetamine: a review in binge eating disorder. *CNS Drugs, 31*, 1015–1022.
21. Nickel, K., Maier, S., Endres, D., Joos, A., Maier, V., Elst, L., & Zeeck, A. (2019). Systematic review: overlap between eating, autism spectrum, and attention-deficit/hyperactivity disorder. *Frontiers in Psychiatry, 10*. https://doi.org/10.3389/fpsyt.2019.00708
22. Yates, W., Lund, B., Johnson, C., Mitchell, J., & McKee, P. (2008). Attention-deficit hyperactivity symptoms and disorder in eating disorder inpatients. *International Journal of Eating Disorders, 42*(4), 375–378. https://doi.org/10.1002/eat.20627
23. Brewerton, T., & Duncan, A. (2016). Associations between attention deficit hyperactivity disorder and eating disorders by gender: results from the national comorbidity survey replication. *European Eating Disorders Review, 24*(6), 536–540. https://doi.org/10.1002/erv.2468
24. Brewerton, T., & Duncan, A. (2016). Associations between attention deficit hyperactivity disorder and eating disorders by gender: results from the national comorbidity survey replication. *European Eating Disorders Review, 24*(6), 536–540. https://doi.org/10.1002/erv.2468
25. Steadman, K., & Knouse, L. (2016). Is the relationship between ADHD symptoms and binge eating mediated by impulsivity? *Journal of Attention Disorders, 20*(11), 907–912. https://doi.org/10.1177/1087054714530779

26. Ptáček, R., Stefano, G. B., Weissenberger, S., Akotia, D., Raboch, J., Papežová, H., Domkarová, L., Stepánková, T., & Goetz, M. (2016). Attention-deficit hyperactivity disorder and disordered eating behaviors: links, risks, and challenges faced. *Neuropsychiatric Disease and Treatment, 12*, 571–579. https://doi.org/10.2147/NDT.S68763
27. Patel, R., Olten, B., Patel, P., Shah, K., & Mansuri, Z. (2018). Hospitalization outcomes and comorbidities of bulimia nervosa: a nationwide inpatient study. *Cureus.* https://doi.org/10.7759/cureus.2583
28. Brewerton, T., & Duncan, A. (2016). Associations between attention deficit hyperactivity disorder and eating disorders by gender: results from the national comorbidity survey replication. *European Eating Disorders Review, 24*(6), 536–540. https://doi.org/10.1002/erv.2468
29. Ptáček, R., Stefano, G. B., Weissenberger, S., Akotia, D., Raboch, J., Papežová, H., Domkarová, L., Stepánková, T., & Goetz, M. (2016). Attention-deficit hyperactivity disorder and disordered eating behaviors: links, risks, and challenges faced. *Neuropsychiatric Disease and Treatment, 12*, 571–579. https://doi.org/10.2147/NDT.S68763
30. Thornton, L., Dellava, J., Root, T., Lichtenstein, P., & Bulik, C. (2011). Anorexia nervosa and generalized anxiety disorder: further explorations of the relation between anxiety and body mass index. *Journal of Anxiety Disorders, 25*(5), 727–730.
31. Alsten, S., & Duncan, A. (2020). Lifetime patterns of comorbidity in eating disorders: an approach using sequence analysis. *European Eating Disorders Review, 28*(6), 709–723. https://doi.org/10.1002/erv.2767
32. Treister, R., Eisenberg, E., Demeter, N., & Pud, D. (2013). Alterations in pain response are partially reversed by methylphenidate (Ritalin) in adults with attention deficit hyperactivity disorder (ADHD). *Pain Practice, 15*(1), 4–11. https://doi.org/10.1111/papr.12129
33. Kasahara, S., Niwa, S. I., Matsudaira, K., Sato, N., Oka, H., Fujii, T., Konno, S-I., Kikuchi, S-I., & Yamada, Y. (2021). High attention-deficit/hyperactivity disorder scale scores among patients with persistent chronic nonspecific low back pain. *Pain Physician, 24*(3), E299.
34. Stickley, A., Koyanagi, A., Takahashi, H., & Kamio, Y. (2016). ADHD symptoms and pain among adults in England. *Psychiatry Research, 246*, 326–331.
35. Kasahara, S., Takahashi, M., Morita, T., Matsudaira, K., Sato, N., Momose, T., Niwa, S.I., & Uchida, K. (2023). Case report: atomoxetine improves chronic pain with comorbid post-traumatic stress disorder and attention deficit hyperactivity disorder. *Frontiers in Psychiatry, 14*, Article 1221694. https://doi.org/10.3389/fpsyt.2023.1221694
36. Pallanti, S., Porta, F., & Salerno, L. (2021). Adult attention deficit hyperactivity disorder in patients with fibromyalgia syndrome: assessment and disabilities. *Journal of Psychiatric Research, 136*, 537–542. https://doi.org/10.1016/j.jpsychires.2020.10.027
37. Yılmaz, E., & Tamam, L. (2018). Attention-deficit hyperactivity disorder and impulsivity in female patients with fibromyalgia. *Neuropsychiatric Disease and Treatment, 14*,1883–1889. https://doi.org/10.2147/ndt.s159312
38. Reyero, F., Ponce, G., Rodriguez-Jimenez, R., Fernandez-Dapica, P., Taboada, D., Martin, V., Navio, M., Jimenez-Arriero, M. A., Hoenicka, J., & Palomo, T. (2011). High frequency of childhood ADHD history in women with fibromyalgia. *European Psychiatry, 26*(8), 482–483. https://doi.org/10.1016/j.eurpsy.2010.03.012

39. Pallanti, S., Porta, F., & Salerno, L. (2021). Adult attention deficit hyperactivity disorder in patients with fibromyalgia syndrome: assessment and disabilities. *Journal of Psychiatric Research, 136*, 537–542. https://doi.org/10.1016/j.jpsychires.2020.10.027
40. Pallanti, S., Porta, F., & Salerno, L. (2021). Adult attention deficit hyperactivity disorder in patients with fibromyalgia syndrome: assessment and disabilities. *Journal of Psychiatric Research, 136*, 537–542. https://doi.org/10.1016/j.jpsychires.2020.10.027
41. Treister, R., Eisenberg, E., Demeter, N., & Pud, D. (2015). Alterations in pain response are partially reversed by methylphenidate (Ritalin) in adults with attention deficit hyperactivity disorder (ADHD). *Pain Practice, 15*, 4–11. https://doi.org/10.1111/papr.12129
42. Stephens, P. (2010). *Reversing chronic disease: a journey back to health* (p. 135). Tate Publishing.
43. Gonzalez-Hernandez, A. (2023). Attention deficit hyperactivity disorder in adults with migraine. *Journal of Attention Disorders, 28*(1), 117–122. https://doi.org/10.1177/10870547231199256
44. Fasmer, O., Halmøy, A., Oedegaard, K., & Haavik, J. (2011). Adult attention deficit hyperactivity disorder is associated with migraine headaches. *European Archives of Psychiatry and Clinical Neuroscience, 261*(8), 595–602. https://doi.org/10.1007/s00406-011-0203-9
45. Hansen, T. F., Hoeffding, L. K., Kogelman, L., Haspang, T. M., Ullum, H., Sørensen, E., Erikstrup, C., Pedersen, O. B., Nielsen, K. R., Hjalgrim, H., Paarup, H. M., Werge, T., & Burgdorf, K. (2018). Comorbidity of migraine with ADHD in adults. *BMC Neurology, 18*(1), Article 147. https://doi.org/10.1186/s12883-018-1149-6
46. Ivanchak, N., Abner, E. L., Carr, S. A., Freeman, S. J., Seybert, A., Ranseen, J., Ponto, L. L., & Jicha, G. A. (2011). Attention-deficit/hyperactivity disorder in childhood is associated with cognitive test profiles in the geriatric population but not with mild cognitive impairment or Alzheimer's disease. *Journal of Aging Research, 2011*, Article 729801. https://doi.org/10.4061/2011/729801
47. Levine, D. A., Gross, A. L., Briceño, E. M., Tilton, N., Giordani, B. J., Sussman, J. B., Hayward, R. A., Burke, J. F., Hingtgen, S., Elkind, M. S. V., Manly, J. J., Gottesman, R. F., Gaskin, D. J., Sidney, S., Sacco, R. L., Tom, S. E., Wright, C. B., Yaffe, K., & Galecki, A. T. (2021). Sex differences in cognitive decline among US adults. *JAMA Network Open, 4*(2), e210169. https://doi.org/10.1001/jamanetworkopen.2021.0169
48. Callahan, B., Plamondon, A., Gill, S., & Ismail, Z. (2021). Contribution of vascular risk factors to the relationship between ADD symptoms and cognition in adults and seniors. *Scientific Reports, 11*(1). https://doi.org/10.1038/s41598-021-03782-y
49. Tcheremissine, O. V., & Salazar, J. O. (2008). Pharmacotherapy of adult attention-deficit/hyperactivity disorder: review of evidence-based practices and future directions. *Expert Opinion on Pharmacotherapy, 9*(8), 1299–1310. https://doi.org/10.1517/14656566.9.8.1299
50. Goodman, D. W., Mitchell, S., Rhodewalt, L., & Surman, C. B. H. (2016). Clinical presentation, diagnosis and treatment of attention-deficit hyperactivity disorder (ADHD) in older adults: a review of the evidence and its implications for clinical care. *Drugs & Aging, 33*(1), 27–36. https://doi.org/10.1007/s40266-015-0327-0
51. Shanmugan, S., & Epperson, C. (2012). Estrogen and the prefrontal cortex: towards a new understanding of estrogen's effects on executive functions in the

menopause transition. *Human Brain Mapping*, *35*(3), 847–865. https://doi.org/10.1002/hbm.22218

52. Mendonça, F., Sudo, F. K., Santiago-Bravo, G., Oliveira, N., Assunção, N., Rodrigues, F., Soares, R., Calil, V., Bernardes, G., Erthal, P., Drummond, C., Tovar-Moll, F., & Mattos, P. (2021). Mild cognitive impairment or attention-deficit/hyperactivity disorder in older adults? A cross-sectional study. *Frontiers in Psychiatry*, *12*, Article 737357. https://doi.org/10.3389/fpsyt.2021.737357
53. Das, D., Anstey, K., & Easteal, S. (2012). ADHD symptoms and cognitive abilities in the midlife cohort of the path through life study. *Journal of Attention Disorders*, *19*(5), 414–424. https://doi.org/10.1177/1087054712460887
54. Goodman, D. W., Mitchell, S., Rhodewalt, L., & Surman, C. B. H. (2016). Clinical presentation, diagnosis and treatment of attention-deficit hyperactivity disorder (ADHD) in older adults: a review of the evidence and its implications for clinical care. *Drugs & Aging*, *33*, 27–36. https://doi.org/10.1007/s40266-015-0327-0
55. Levine, S. Z., Rotstein, A., Kodesh, A., Sandin, S., Lee, B. K., Weinstein, G., Schnaider Beeri, M., & Reichenberg, A. (2023). Adult attention-deficit/hyperactivity disorder and the risk of dementia. *JAMA Network Open*, *6*(10), e2338088. https://doi.org/10.1001/jamanetworkopen.2023.38088
56. Curtin, K., Fleckenstein, A. E., Keeshin, B. R., Yurgelun-Todd, D. A., Renshaw, P. F., Smith, K. R., & Hanson, G. R. (2018). Increased risk of diseases of the basal ganglia and cerebellum in patients with a history of attention-deficit/hyperactivity disorder. *Neuropsychopharmacology*, *43*(13), 2548–2555. https://doi.org/10.1038/s41386-018-0207-5
57. Levine, S. Z., Rotstein, A., Kodesh, A., Sandin, S., Lee, B. K., Weinstein, G., Schnaider Beeri, M., & Reichenberg, A. (2023). Adult attention-deficit/hyperactivity disorder and the risk of dementia. *JAMA Network Open*, *6*(10), e2338088. https://doi.org/10.1001/jamanetworkopen.2023.38088
58. Ter Beek, L. S., Böhmer, M. N., Wittekoek, M. E., & Kooij, J. J. S. (2023). Lifetime ADHD symptoms highly prevalent in women with cardiovascular complaints: a cross-sectional study. *Archives of Women's Mental Health*, *26*(6), 851–855. https://doi.org/10.1007/s00737-023-01356-7
59. Garcia-Argibay, M., Du Rietz, E., Hartman, C. A., Lichtenstein, P., Chang, Z., Fava, C., Cortese, S., & Larsson, H. (2022). Cardiovascular risk factors in attention-deficit/hyperactivity disorder: a family design study of Swedish conscripts. *International Journal of Methods in Psychiatric Research*, *31*(4), e1930. https://doi.org/10.1002/mpr.1930
60. Thapar, A., Riglin, L., Blakey, R., Collishaw, S., Davey Smith, G., Stergiakouli, E., Tilling, K. M., & Thapar, A. (2023). Childhood attention-deficit hyperactivity disorder problems and mid-life cardiovascular risk: prospective population cohort study. *The British Journal of Psychiatry*, *223*(4), 472–477. https://doi.org/10.1192/bjp.2023.90
61. Li, L., Yao, H., Zhang, L., Garcia-Argibay, M., Du Rietz, E., Brikell, I., Solmi, M., Cortese, S., Ramos-Quiroga, J. A., Ribasés, M., Chang, Z., & Larsson, H. (2023). Attention-deficit/hyperactivity disorder is associated with increased risk of cardiovascular diseases: a systematic review and meta-analysis. *JCPP Advances*, *3*(3), e12158. https://doi.org/10.1002/jcv2.12158
62. Sinha, A., Lewis, O., Kumar, R., Yeruva, S. L., & Curry, B. H. (2016). Adult ADHD medications and their cardiovascular implications. *Case Reports in Cardiology*, *2016*, 2343691. https://doi.org/10.1155/2016/2343691

63. Schelleman, H., Bilker, W. B., Kimmel, S. E., Daniel, G. W., Newcomb, C., Guevara, J. P., Cziraky, M. J., Strom, B. L., & Hennessy, S. (2012). Methylphenidate and risk of serious cardiovascular events in adults. *American Journal of Psychiatry, 169*(2), 178–185. https://doi.org/10.1176/appi.ajp.2011.11010125
64. Mick, E., McManus, D. D., & Goldberg, R. J. (2013). Meta-analysis of increased heart rate and blood pressure associated with CNS stimulant treatment of ADHD in adults. *European Neuropsychopharmacology, 23*(6), 534–541. https://doi.org/10.1016/j.euroneuro.2012.06.011
65. O'Nions, E., El Baou, C., John, A., Lewer, D., Mandy, W., McKechnie, D. G. J., Petersen, I., & Stott, J. (2025). Life expectancy and years of life lost for adults with diagnosed ADHD in the UK: matched cohort study. *British Journal of Psychiatry, 226*(5), 261–268. https://doi.org/10.1192/bjp.2024.199
66. Libutzki, B., Neukirch, B., Kittel-Schneider, S., Reif, A., & Hartman, C. A. (2023). Risk of accidents and unintentional injuries in men and women with attention-deficit/hyperactivity disorder across the adult lifespan. *Acta Psychiatrica Scandinavica, 147*(2), 145–154. https://doi.org/10.1111/acps.13524
67. Antoniou, E., Rigas, N., Orovou, E., Papatrechas, A., & Sarella, A. (2021). ADHD symptoms in females of childhood, adolescent, reproductive and menopause period. *Materia Socio Medica, 33*(2), 114. https://doi.org/10.5455/msm.2021.33.114-118
68. Sun, S., Kuja-Halkola, R., Faraone, S. V., D'Onofrio, B. M., Dalsgaard, S., Chang, Z., & Larsson, H. (2019). Association of psychiatric comorbidity with the risk of premature death among children and adults with attention-deficit/hyperactivity disorder. *JAMA Psychiatry, 76*(11), 1141–1149. https://doi.org/10.1001/jamapsychiatry.2019.1944
69. Li, L., Coghill, D., Sjölander, A., Yao, H., Zhang, L., Kuja-Halkola, R., Brikell, I., Lichtenstein, P., D'Onofrio, B. M., Larsson, H., & Chang, Z. (2025). Increased prescribing of attention-deficit/hyperactivity disorder medication and real-world outcomes over time. *JAMA Psychiatry, 82*(8), 830–837. https://doi.org/10.1001/jamapsychiatry.2025.1281
70. Libutzki, B., Neukirch, B., Kittel-Schneider, S., Reif, A., & Hartman, C. A. (2023). Risk of accidents and unintentional injuries in men and women with attention-deficit/hyperactivity disorder across the adult lifespan. *Acta Psychiatrica Scandinavica, 147*(2), 145–154. https://doi.org/10.1111/acps.13524
71. Li, L., Coghill, D., Sjölander, A., Yao, H., Zhang, L., Kuja-Halkola, R., Brikell, I., Lichtenstein, P., D'Onofrio, B. M., Larsson, H., & Chang, Z. (2025). Increased prescribing of attention-deficit/hyperactivity disorder medication and real-world outcomes over time. *JAMA Psychiatry, 82*(8), 830–837. https://doi.org/10.1001/jamapsychiatry.2025.1281

CHAPTER 8

ADHD and the hormone connection

INTRODUCTION

In our work with, writing about, and advocating for the diagnosis and treatment of women with ADHD, a piece was always missing in truly **understanding ADHD** in these women. First, we looked at **symptoms** and how they presented differently in girls and women. Next, we looked at **coexisting conditions** and **differing risk patterns**. We looked at women with ADHD and compared them to women without ADHD, rather than men with ADHD. But it was not until we looked at hormones and their fluctuations over the life cycle of girls and women with ADHD that we truly understood the disorder. **The hormone connection**—that was the final piece!

To understand ADHD in women as they are impacted by hormonal shifts, envision the changing images of a **kaleidoscope**. With each turn, the ***colors*** remain the same, but the ***image*** changes. Each turn represents a critical hormonal transition in a woman's life—puberty, monthly menstruation, pregnancy, postpartum, perimenopause, menopause, and postmenopause. Let's look at the kaleidoscope of hormonal impacts on ADHD in women.

In prepubescent girls with ADHD, the image may appear deceptively calm because, for many girls, symptoms are kept at bay by masking—trying hard to fit in with their peers and meet the expectations of parents and teachers. Then comes the first major turn of the kaleidoscope as they approach puberty.

Puberty *(Turn)*—With the onset of puberty and the significant increase in estrogen levels and hormonal fluctuations that it brings, girls with ADHD and their caregivers often report a worsening of ADHD

DOI: 10.4324/9781003542124-8

symptoms, increased mood swings (emotional dysregulation,) and, for some, more impulsivity.

Monthly menstrual cycles *(Turn)*—Now, females must contend with fluctuations of estrogen and progesterone as they cycle through each month with the accompanying increase in inattention, distractibility, impulsivity, irritability, depression, fatigue, and brain "fog" in the luteal phase.

Pregnancy *(Turn)*—If they become pregnant, women's estrogen and progesterone levels will increase. Some women with ADHD report that they feel at their best during these months, while others continue to suffer. However, this state lasts less than 10 months, and estrogen levels fall precipitously after delivery of the placenta. *(Turn)* As a result the picture becomes darker. During this time of significant change, many women experience depression, a worsening of ADHD symptoms, and an increase in anxiety.

Perimenopause *(Turn)*—In perimenopause, which can begin anywhere from 10 years to just a few years before menopause, estrogen levels begin to decline, and ADHD symptoms may be exacerbated. Women report increasing problems with short-term memory and executive dysfunction, and they may also be affected by worsening mood disorders.

In addition to these hormone-driven complications, many women report that the **medications** used to treat their ADHD symptoms **seem less effective** in the week(s) before their period or with the onset of perimenopause. To improve the quality of life for women with ADHD, you need to understand this estrogen connection, and address it appropriately by increasing their medication dose during the luteal phase of the cycle *(Turn)*. This will enable them to function optimally and lead successful and fulfilling lives.

Menopause *(Turn)*—The same holds true for postmenopausal women, who experience very low levels of estrogen and testosterone accompanied by physical symptoms, increasing cognitive dysfunction, and a worsening of ADHD symptoms that were previously under control. Some women report a leveling out of their ADHD symptoms after menopause, but the increase in cognitive symptoms (poor short-term memory, word retrieval, etc.) and physical symptoms (hot flashes, insomnia, etc.) can make life extremely difficult in other ways for them.

Hormone replacement therapy (HRT) or **hormone maintenance therapy (HMT)** during perimenopause or after menopause can change this picture and improve menopausal symptoms *(Turn)*. Some women with ADHD who use this treatment even report a leveling-off of their ADHD symptoms and a feeling of increased energy and well-being.

Why do women with ADHD experience these difficulties? And why did we overlook them for so long?

Historically, most research on ADHD has been carried out on men; although women have been included in some studies, these have usually failed to take their estrogen levels into account. Additionally, the greater propensity for women with ADHD to experience anxiety and depression has led clinicians to tend to diagnose these disorders first, seeing executive function and memory difficulties as secondary issues resulting from them rather than recognizing the patient's ADHD. Women in treatment for anxiety or depression have complained to their clinicians that though they are no longer depressed or anxious, they are still overwhelmed, disorganized, and can't seem to get anything done! What frustration!

> Dealing with undiagnosed ADHD for years can lead to demoralization or depression.

Second, even if a woman is fortunate enough to be correctly diagnosed, ADHD treatment protocols usually consist of recommendations established years ago to treat school-aged boys who were hyperactive. Hormonal fluctuations and the influence of estrogen on the brain were not even considered, much less addressed. No wonder many adolescent girls and adult women with ADHD experience only partial remission of symptoms. Many women report that although they have told their doctors that their medication doesn't work as well or symptoms seem to worsen at certain times, they are not listened to. In addition, treatment approaches that work for boys with ADHD may not work for girls or women. For example, when boys' symptoms worsen, it often helps to increase the dose of stimulant medication, but this approach frequently fails when applied to women in perimenopause, or girls as they enter puberty. Jennie is a case in point:

CASE ILLUSTRATION: JENNIE

Jennie was diagnosed with ADHD at the age of 10. In her history, the severity of her symptoms has at times been mild and at others rendered her, in her words, feeling "useless." Looking back, she reported that it seemed as though the severity of her ADHD increased during times when her hormones were going through a major change—during puberty and after giving birth, for example. She often wondered if there could be a link. She is now 37 years old, and suspects that she is perimenopausal. She has gone from being a fun-loving, outgoing person to being very antisocial, wanting to stay home all the time, and feeling very overwhelmed. Recently, her attention and memory problems have been worsening. Sleep does not come easy, even with medication. Her doctor keeps increasing the level of her stimulant medication, but this doesn't seem to help. At present, she takes 30 mg Adderall twice a day and 75–150 mg Trazodone for sleep.

No wonder many women treated for their ADHD report only partial remission or mention that their symptoms worsen at certain times. As you will see, these women with ADHD are at risk for an increase in ADHD symptoms, mood, cognitive dysfunction, and sleep disorders related to their menstrual cycle or life stage.

TRANSGENDER WOMEN, GENDER-AFFIRMING HORMONE THERAPY, AND ADHD

Although most research on hormones and ADHD has focused on cisgender women, estrogen's neurocognitive effects are not limited to individuals assigned female at birth. Transgender women receiving gender-affirming hormone therapy may be treated with estradiol, often in combination with medications that suppress endogenous testosterone. These interventions alter the hormonal milieu in ways that may affect dopaminergic and noradrenergic pathways, as well as prefrontal executive networks implicated in attention, impulse control, and emotional regulation. Further research is needed to clarify the impacts of gender-affirming hormone therapy on transgender women with ADHD.[1]

THE ADHD/ESTROGEN CONNECTION

Research over the past two decades has clearly established the significant relationship between estrogen and the brain. Estrogen plays an important role in the development of dopamine neurons[2] and affects other neurotransmitters, including norepinephrine, GABA, and acetylcholine, that have a positive impact on mood, behavior, and cognition.[3] Estrogen can boost the release of neurotransmitters by the neurons by as much as 20%.[4] However, when estrogen declines below a certain level, mood, cognition, and executive functions are impaired.[5]

How can hormonal fluctuations affect functioning in ADHD and increase ADHD symptoms?

The relationship of estrogen to brain functioning in women with ADHD has received only minimal attention. However, new studies confirm the importance of this link. In one women's health study (30 women, 18–29 years, mean age 21.73) from UC Santa Barbara, Elizabeth Rizor and her colleagues observed cycle-driven changes in the brain.[6] Structural changes in the connecting fibers that control information transfer between neurons were found to occur during all hormonal transitional phases—puberty, taking oral contraceptives, and menopause. High levels of progesterone during the luteal phase were associated with decreased cortical and cerebellar functioning, changes that could have both behavioral and cognitive implications.[7] Research by a group at the University of Kentucky Department of Psychology also suggests substantial hormonal effects on ADHD symptoms across the menstrual cycle. In a community-recruited female sample (ages 18–25), declines in estrogen over the menstrual cycle predicted clinically significant twofold increases in ADHD symptoms of inattention, hyperactivity, and impulsivity.[8]

ADHD AT VARIOUS LIFE STAGES IN WOMEN

A hormonal storm! Increasing symptoms of ADHD at puberty

Puberty marks the first significant period of hormonal changes in girls with ADHD. At menarche, estrogen levels significantly increase and there is a change in the estrogen/testosterone ratio. After ovulation begins, progesterone levels increase as well. It's a hormonal storm descending on the brain! It is these dramatic changes that influence the emotional dysregulation, impulsivity, and inattention seen in girls with ADHD at puberty.[9,10]

This phenomenon was discussed in the first edition of our book, *Understanding Girls with ADHD*, published in 2002.[11] The issue of hormones and their relationship to ADHD was first raised in 1990 by Hans

Huessy, who wrote that increased hormonal fluctuations throughout the phases of the menstrual cycle result in increased ADHD symptomatology.[12] In addition, the earlier puberty occurs, the worse ADHD symptoms tend to be. Ostojic and Miller reported in 2016 that an early onset of puberty in childhood correlated with increased ADHD symptoms among female university students.[13] This aligns with findings suggesting that adolescent girls and young women may report increased symptoms of ADHD and emotional dysregulation, resulting in a higher rate of ADHD-related complications.[14]

ADHD is highly heritable and, in some cases, symptoms (colic, sleep challenges, hyperactivity, etc.) are present from birth. For many girls, the symptoms of ADHD do not become bothersome until adolescence, when they may worsen. Additionally, a girl with ADHD may first manifest **executive dysfunction** with accompanying memory and organizational deficits at a time when the demand for organization and independence increases in middle school. A study of adolescent girls conducted in 1993, brain dysfunction as measured by reduced glucose metabolism on brain scanning correlated with Tanner stage, supports this hypothesis, no matter the age of the adolescent girl.[15]

Mothers of girls with ADHD report that their daughters experience heightened irritability and mood swings beginning at puberty, often more intense than typical adolescent mood changes. These emotional reactions and oppositional behaviors frequently target mothers specifically. Drs. Quinn and Nadeau explored this pattern, which they term the "toxic mother/daughter dyad," in their book *Understanding Girls with ADHD*.[16]

The group from the University of Kentucky introduced earlier in this chapter have come up with a novel theoretical framework for understanding this phenomenon. They suggest that women with ADHD may experience a "double whammy" of **organizational** and **activational, or activating, hormonal effects**. Their novel theory proposes that changes in hormone levels can exacerbate ADHD symptoms, with increasing risk seen at times of rapid declines in estrogen. These declines may influence executive function and control at two points of the menstrual cycle—increases in approach/risk-taking behaviors at mid-cycle and increases in avoidance/negative affect around menses. Low estrogen and lack of inhibition mid-cycle may then interact to increase hyperactivity-impulsivity symptoms post-ovulation, and inattention symptoms around menstruation.[17]

The combination of ADHD symptoms, hormonal changes, and societal pressures during adolescence can increase the risk of developing additional mental health issues, including depression and anxiety.[18] Given the complex interplay between ADHD and hormonal changes during puberty, it is crucial for healthcare providers to monitor and assess ADHD symptoms closely in girls as they enter this life stage. A multidisciplinary approach to treatment is often recommended, including behavioral interventions, psychoeducation for patients and families, and, when appropriate, medication management tailored to the girl's individual needs. Peer group therapy is useful, as is cognitive behavioral therapy (CBT) to rewrite negative scripts these girls may have adopted as a response to undiagnosed ADHD, poor self-esteem, and shame.

The rollercoaster of monthly cycles and ADHD

Recent research has revealed that naturally cycling women experience brain changes with monthly hormonal fluctuations of follicle stimulating hormone (FSH), estradiol (E), luteinizing hormone (LH), and progesterone (P). Blood tests to measure these hormone levels were taken during menses, mid-cycle, and midpoint post-ovulation, and found that each of these stages was associated with significant changes in brain microstructure and cortical thickness.[19]

Premenstrual worsening of depression has been recognized for some time, and the same pattern has now been reported for ADHD. The group from the University of Kentucky refers to this as **estrogen withdrawal sensitivity**. In research on 18–25-year-olds, they report "**activational hormonal" effects**, with decreases in estrogen levels found to predict a clinically significant twofold increase in ADHD symptoms of inattention and hyperactive-impulsive behaviors. For women with impulsivity, the study reported an increase in hyperactivity/impulsivity (HI) driven by a decline in estrogen, regardless of the levels of progesterone. However, inattention caused by a decrease in estrogen was moderated by levels of progesterone, with social withdrawal and increased inattention at the end of the cycle when progesterone levels fall and estrogen level is low.[20]

Given these findings, it may be necessary to increase the dose of stimulants depending on the phase of the cycle a woman is in. Studies have found women without ADHD to be more sensitive to the effects of stimulants during the follicular phase of the cycle and less responsive during the luteal phase. Women with ADHD may need **hormonal stabilization** to minimize the negative effects (increase in symptoms and decrease in effectiveness of medication) seen during periods of low estrogen. Hormonal birth control, HRT, and increasing doses of stimulants prior to menstruation for women with ADHD may optimize functioning. These treatments will be discussed later in this chapter.

PMS, PMDD, and premenstrual magnification of symptoms

Premenstrual syndrome (PMS) is a common disorder of women that refers to physical symptoms (such as bloating, headache, cramping, etc.) and mild mood changes and irritability during the latter half of the menstrual cycle.[21] While up to 75% of women report these symptoms, only about 5% of all women report symptoms that are severe enough to interfere with their daily functioning at home, in the workplace, or in their relationships with others.[22] Symptoms can begin any time after puberty, but most women don't seek treatment until into their thirties. Ovulation seems to be a key factor, as PMS symptoms decline and disappear during pregnancy or menopause. Symptoms can begin at any time, but for diagnosis, there must be a symptom-free period during the follicular phase of the cycle.

Women with ADHD frequently experience PMS symptoms involving mood disturbance. As one woman noted,

> *At 36, I was just diagnosed with ADHD. I am taking Adderall, and the medication is working. However, I still have severe PMS, with irritability, increased impulsivity, and sleep problems.*

There also appears to be a small group of women (3–8%) with PMS whose **symptoms are primarily related to a mood disorder**. Women in this group experience extreme mood and behavioral symptoms, **leading to a diagnosis of premenstrual dysphoric disorder (PMDD)**. They report symptoms of irritability, tension, dysphoria, and mood lability that seriously interfere with their functioning and relationships. Women with PMDD also report higher rates of previous mood disorders and are at risk of developing other psychiatric disorders, particularly major depression. There seems to be a genetic component to PMDD, with high concordance in twin studies and a link to PMS and depression in the families of these women.

PREGNANCY AND ADHD

Research suggests that women with ADHD are at increased risk of pregnancies they characterize as unplanned and become pregnant earlier in their lives than those without ADHD. Among women with ADHD, 15.3% gave birth as teenagers, compared to 2.8% of women without ADHD.[23]

Women and girls with combined or hyperactive/impulsive type ADHD often experience symptoms of impulsivity and difficulties with emotional regulation, which may be a key factor in the link between ADHD and unplanned pregnancy. One prospective study by Owens and Hinshaw found a stark contrast in rates of unplanned pregnancies throughout adulthood between women with childhood ADHD (42.6%) and those without the diagnosis (10.6%).[24] This significant difference persists even after accounting for socioeconomic factors and other variables, highlighting the need for targeted interventions.[25]

Young women with ADHD frequently encounter difficulties in maintaining stable relationships and managing their sexual health, including contraception.[26,27] For example, one study of college-aged women found that condom use was significantly lower for women with ADHD.[28] These challenges may lead not just to unplanned pregnancy but to a variety of adverse outcomes, most notably an increased likelihood of contracting sexually transmitted infections. The following example is a case in point.

CASE ILLUSTRATION: JUSTINE

Justine was a college freshman who had been diagnosed with combined-type ADHD in early adolescence. She had been treated successfully for her symptoms with Concerta 54 mg in the early morning and 18 mg at 12 noon. She was bright and did well academically, despite her ADHD. Her impulsivity did occasionally get her into trouble socially as she would often say what was on her mind without thinking about the consequences, or go off to shop and forget that her friends were waiting for her at lunch, but otherwise, she was likeable and described as fun-loving by her friends. She was on oral contraceptives for birth control and to stabilize her estrogen levels. She came to her prescribing physician for refills and a follow-up every six months, but was occasionally late or had already run out of her prescription when she called to schedule her appointment.

Mid-second semester, she still had not come in for follow-up even though she had been called twice to remind her to schedule her six-month visit. When she finally showed up for her follow-up, Justine reported that she had run out of her medication several months before and was off medication. She had also run out of her oral contraceptive and became pregnant with the child of a man she was casually dating. After a discussion of the pros and cons of resuming her stimulant while she was pregnant, she declined to go back on medication. She did well, delivered the baby, and got a job, with her mother caring for the baby. About a year later, Justine called for an appointment. She reported that she was making barely enough to pay necessary expenses and was hoping to return to college while her mother provided childcare. She wanted to go back on medication.

Although this was not the case for Justine, psychosocial factors such as low educational attainment and poor parental monitoring have been identified as risk factors for early and unplanned pregnancies in girls with ADHD.[29] Adolescent girls with ADHD often face numerous psychosocial challenges that may hinder their capacity to engage in responsible sexual behavior, thus perpetuating cycles of unintended pregnancies or sexually transmitted infections, which can lead to negative implications for both maternal and child health.[30]

Hormones and pregnancy

During pregnancy, estrogen levels rise significantly, impacting mood, memory, and attention.[31] This can lead to structural changes in the brain and transient cognitive symptoms similar to those seen in ADHD (sometimes referred to as "pregnancy brain"). However, for women with preexisting ADHD who become pregnant, these hormonal shifts can be even more devastating, increasing their ADHD symptoms or changing the efficacy of their ADHD medication.

With increasing estrogen levels, one would expect improved functioning in women with ADHD during high-estrogen states such as pregnancy. However, this does not always hold true. One of the key factors in this is the hormonal fluctuation inherent to the gestational period. Changes in sex hormones, such as estrogen and progesterone, may have modulating effects on ADHD symptoms.[32] In Kittel-Schneider's 2021 review, inattentive and hyperactive symptoms were linked to increased physical strain and depression during pregnancy. Inattentive symptoms of ADHD were associated with poorer eating habits, and hyperactive symptoms of ADHD were linked to more smoking, higher caffeine consumption, and inconsistent vitamin usage.[33]

In the following case, a mother reports on her daughter's experience:

CASE ILLUSTRATION: MARIA'S STORY: THE IMPACT OF PREGNANCY AND BREASTFEEDING ON ADHD SYMPTOMS

Maria was a popular, always busy and athletic teen, playing two varsity sports, when diagnosed with ADHD as a 16-year-old. She was very active and had a hard time sitting still when it was required, so she channeled her exceptionally high energy level into becoming an accomplished athlete.

However, when she broke her ankle and was not able to play sports in her junior year she became restless and bored, and her impulsivity significantly increased. She began having more difficulty completing schoolwork and attending class and graduated with a GPA much lower than she had expected.

A decade later, she became pregnant with her first child, shortly after making the choice to continue her education after years of working in a grocery store. The curious thing is that all through her pregnancy, and the first six months of breastfeeding, her severe ADHD symptoms vanished! She did well during her first semester of college, and she was like a completely different person. However, during her second semester, she began to cut back drastically on breastfeeding in preparation for weaning her son, and her mother suddenly realized all her ADHD symptoms were returning. Over the next six months, Maria gradually noticed her challenges with focus and attention returning to their pre-pregnancy levels.

This case is not unique. Although research findings are mixed, as we saw above, women with ADHD frequently report that they felt their best and had the least interference from their ADHD symptoms while they were pregnant. For 20% of the 1,914 women with ADHD who responded to a survey conducted by *ADDitude* Magazine in 2023, heightened hormones during pregnancy brought "greater focus, drive, organization, and sleep." Forty-four percent noticed no difference in ADHD symptoms during pregnancy, while another 36% said their ADHD symptoms had worsened, with exhaustion, poor memory, emotional dysregulation, and sensitivity topping the list. It is important to note that 98% of women with ADHD who responded to this survey said they had stopped treatment for their ADHD during pregnancy.[34]

From the few studies available, it seems like the results are mixed on the effect of pregnancy on ADHD symptoms and this area may need further investigation. However, continued medication during pregnancy may have some positive effects. The use of medication during pregnancy is discussed in greater detail in our chapter on medication.

Postpartum

Immediately after the placenta is delivered, hormone levels fall precipitously. Many women with ADHD report that their symptoms worsen postpartum due to these hormonal changes and the demands of new motherhood. Sleep deprivation, stress, and the constant demands of caring for a newborn can exacerbate existing ADHD symptoms.

> Women with pre-existing ADHD may experience heightened susceptibility to depression following childbirth.

Postpartum depression occurs in 13–20% of women who give birth, while postpartum anxiety occurs in 10%. Women with ADHD face increased risk of both conditions. A study using the Swedish Medical Birth Registry found that anxiety was reported in 24.92% of women with ADHD and 5% of those without, while depression occurred in 16.76% versus 3.29%, respectively.[35] ADHD symptoms may be exacerbated by the emotional and psychological challenges of new motherhood, contributing to this heightened vulnerability.[36]

The following experience of a young mother clearly demonstrates the relationships between ADHD, pregnancy, and postpartum anxiety and depression.

CASE ILLUSTRATION: MADDI: A YOUNG MOTHER'S EXPERIENCE

Maddi, a 35-year-old with ADHD, had had two children in the last 5 years, and during both pregnancies she found her ADHD and anxiety were greatly reduced. However, they came crashing back in the postpartum period, when she was sleep-deprived and breastfeeding. She finally got her diagnosis of ADHD after being referred to an ADHD clinic by a psychiatrist who was treating her for postpartum depression and anxiety, and who felt her symptoms might not be entirely related to pregnancy and childbirth. Maddi is now very curious about how the interplay between female hormones and ADHD will impact her in the future, particularly given the positive effects she found that pregnancy had on her ADHD symptoms.

In the *ADDitude* survey (2023) discussed previously, more than half of those women who had given birth said they had experienced symptoms of postpartum depression (PPD), including feelings of worthlessness (76%), crying spells (76%), mood swings (66%), and irritability (62%). The survey also found that nearly half of all women with self-reported

PPD said they did not receive any treatment, and nearly 18% said their symptoms had lasted longer than two years.[37]

What about breastfeeding? Women with ADHD have anecdotally reported that breastfeeding helped with mood and emotional dysregulation. Research confirms that breastfeeding can lower the risk of depression postpartum, but only if it is exclusive—combined breast- and formula-feeding resulted in 89% higher odds of postpartum depression for women with ADHD.[38]

You will want to discuss these risks with your patients with ADHD and closely monitor for postpartum symptoms of anxiety and/or depression. You may want to include ADHD screening in your practice for the general pregnant population, as well as screening for mood and other disorders in pregnant women with ADHD in order to offer counseling, medication, support, and other services during the perinatal period.[39] Women with ADHD may benefit from enhanced social support during pregnancy and after childbirth as well as education about increased risk for postpartum mental health conditions.

PERIMENOPAUSE

Perimenopause, which usually begins in a woman's forties or fifties, is defined as the time preceding menopause when estrogen levels begin to change, often fluctuating unpredictably. During this time, periods may become irregular, last for a longer or shorter time than usual, and involve heavier or lighter bleeding, before stopping altogether. Perimenopause lasts until a woman has had no periods for 12 months, at which point, she is considered to be in **menopause** and, thereafter, **postmenopausal**. This life stage is often associated with a number of physical, mental, and cognitive changes.

Symptoms during the transition of perimenopause may include memory problems, mood changes, difficulty with word retrieval, and reduced mental clarity, as well as physical symptoms such as hot flashes and insomnia. Cognitive functions, including verbal memory and executive skills, are impaired whenever estrogen level is low, no matter what the reason is (monthly cycles, surgical menopause, PCOS, perimenopause, etc.). Studies have shown this to be the case for women with ADHD as well.[40,41]

Many women seek a diagnosis of ADHD for the first time during the perimenopausal years. While women reporting midlife onset of ADHD do not meet the current DSM-5-TR criteria of symptom presentation prior to age 12 years, they do demonstrate significant impairment in executive functions (attention, organization, and memory) and report that these functional impairments respond to treatment protocols, including stimulant medications normally prescribed for those with ADHD.

In three studies, non-ADHD perimenopausal women who were experiencing executive function issues were assessed with the BADDS and BEFARS scales, which are used for testing the effectiveness of medications developed for treatment of ADHD. Results indicated that these women scored better on both assessments after treatment with either atomoxetine (ATX), a nonstimulant, or lisdexamfetamine (LDX), for which results showed the greatest improvement. Neuroimaging was used to confirm the findings and showed increased activation in brain areas associated with executive function during a working memory task after treatment with lisdexamfetamine (LDX).[42,43]

MENOPAUSE AND BEYOND

As women transition into menopause and beyond, hormonal changes, particularly a sharp decline in estrogen levels, can exacerbate both ADHD and mood disorders. Research indicates that when estrogen levels decline in menopause, women with ADHD may experience more severe symptoms, which can include both mood and cognitive impairments, such as difficulties with memory and executive function. Cognitive deficits modulated by estrogen and more recently luteinizing hormone (LH) have been reported in postmenopausal women. Increases in LH can be as much as 3 times higher than normal during the postmenopausal period, resulting in impaired memory. Hormonal changes associated with aging, including menopause, have been associated with cognitive changes and are an area of ongoing research in relation to neurodegenerative diseases such as Alzheimer's and Parkinson's. See Chapter 7 for more information on this topic.[44]

Women with ADHD face increased emotional dysregulation and cognitive deficits during menopause. Moreover, ADHD often co-occurs with mood disorders. These mood disorders may become more pronounced during menopause, underscoring the necessity for tailored treatment strategies.[45,46]

HORMONES AND MEDICATION TREATMENT DURING THE MENSTRUAL CYCLE

Little is known about the interactions between hormones and stimulant medications. Estrogen and progesterone seem to have both direct and indirect central nervous system effects. In addition, it is becoming clearer that these hormones can also affect response to psychostimulants. These identical twins are a case in point.

CASE ILLUSTRATION: MM AND ML

MM and ML are identical twin girls diagnosed with ADHD during adolescence. The psychiatrist told their surprised parents that they were not alone: ADHD is concordant in 60–80% of identical twins, highlighting the strong genetic component. The twins were both prescribed Adderall for their symptoms and took the same dose per day for years. At age 32 years, ML needed a hysterectomy and oophorectomy for endometrial cancer. After surgery, her Adderall dose was insufficient to control her symptoms and needed to be increased, while her sister's dose stayed the same. To this day, ML continues to take double the dose of Adderall her twin sister is prescribed.

As clinicians, our awareness of ADHD symptom changes and decreased medication effectiveness prior to menstruation emerged in the late 1990s, and studies by Justice and deWit caught our attention. They found that estrogen increases stimulant response: amphetamine effects were greater with estradiol pretreatment and during the follicular phase of the menstrual cycle, and lower during the luteal phase.[47,48] These results suggest women may respond differently to stimulants depending on menstrual cycle hormone levels. At our practice, we started varying the dose of stimulants based on documented increases in ADHD symptoms or decreases in medication effectiveness.

Recently, a published community case study of nine women being treated for ADHD and co-occurring conditions (including depression and premenstrual dysphoric disorder) confirmed our observations. The study increased each woman's individually prescribed psychostimulant dosage during the premenstrual period and monitored the effects of this on ADHD symptoms, mood, and somatic symptoms for the following 6–24 months. With the premenstrual dose increase, all nine women experienced improved ADHD and mood symptoms, with minimal adverse events. Premenstrual inattention, irritability, and energy levels improved, and resembled the other nonpremenstrual weeks more closely. All women decided to continue with the elevated premenstrual pharmacotherapy.[49]

As a clinician treating ADHD in women, the best way for you to view their ADHD is in concert with their hormone levels. To address the condition in this way has far-reaching implications, not only for how you diagnose it, but potentially how you treat it as well. Stabilizing hormone levels may be just as important to treating ADHD symptoms in women as stimulants and other medications are! Evidence supports the effectiveness of adjustments in pharmacotherapy, like increasing stimulant dosages during specific hormonal phases or considering hormonal supplementation (HRT) to alleviate some menopausal symptoms.[50,51,52] Yet standard medical training leaves the treatment of women with ADHD lost in a chasm, between gynecologists (trained in the prescription of hormones) and psychiatrists (trained in the prescription of stimulants). There is a critical need to bridge this chasm!

The current literature highlights a gap in understanding and applying female-specific treatments for ADHD, particularly during menopause. This emphasizes the need for continued research to develop gender-sensitive management approaches.[53] Increased awareness among healthcare providers about the unique experiences of women with ADHD during menopause is critical. Recognizing these experiences may lead to improved diagnosis and management strategies, helping clinicians to address the specific psychological and cognitive needs of these women during a transitional life phase marked by hormonal shifts.[54]

TRANSGENDER WOMEN, GENDER-AFFIRMING HORMONE THERAPY, AND ADHD

In our clinical experience treating transgender women, many report that gender-affirming care is associated with improvement in ADHD symptoms. It remains unclear to what extent these changes reflect estradiol's direct neurobiological effects on dopamine and norepinephrine systems versus indirect benefits related to reduction of gender dysphoria. Gender dysphoria itself can involve significant cognitive and emotional burden, including difficulty sustaining attention, heightened anxiety, and preoccupation with distressing thoughts, which may mimic or exacerbate ADHD symptoms. Research is needed to clarify the mechanisms underlying our clinical observations and to optimize ADHD treatment strategies for transgender women receiving gender-affirming hormone therapy.

REFERENCES

1. Coleman, E., Radix, A. E., Bouman, W. P., Brown, G. R., De Vries, A. L., Deutsch, M. B., … & Arcelus, J. (2022). Standards of care for the health of transgender and gender diverse people, version 8. *International Journal of Transgender Health*, 23(sup1), S1–S259.

2. Küppers, E., Ivanova, T., Karolczak, M., & Beyer, C. (2000). Estrogen: a multifunctional messenger to nigrostriatal dopaminergic neurons. *Journal of Neurocytology, 29*(5–6), 375–385. https://doi.org/10.1023/A:1007165307652
3. Shepherd, J. E. (2001). Effects of estrogen on cognition, mood, and degenerative brain diseases. *Journal of the American Pharmacology Association, 41*, 221–228.
4. Archer, J. S. M. (1999). Estrogen and mood changes via CNS activity. *Menopausal Medicine*, 7, 4–8.
5. Arpels, J. C. (1996). The female brain hypoestrogenic continuum from premenstrual syndrome to menopause: a hypothesis and review. *Journal of Reproductive Medicine, 41*, 633–936.
6. Rizor, E. J., Babenko, V., Dundon, N. M., Beverly-Aylwin, R., Stump, A., Hayes, M., Herschenfeld-Catalan, L., Jacobs, E. G., & Grafton, S. T. (2024). Menstrual cycle-driven hormone concentrations co-fluctuate with white and gray matter architecture changes across the whole brain. *Human Brain Mapping, 45*(11), e26785. https://doi.org/10.1002/hbm.26785
7. Rizor, E. J., Babenko, V., Dundon, N. M., Beverly-Aylwin, R., Stump, A., Hayes, M., Herschenfeld-Catalan, L., Jacobs, E. G., & Grafton, S. T. (2024). Menstrual cycle-driven hormone concentrations co-fluctuate with white and gray matter architecture changes across the whole brain. *Human Brain Mapping, 45*(11), e26785. https://doi.org/10.1002/hbm.26785
8. Roberts, B., Eisenlohr-Moul, T., & Martel, M. (2018). Reproductive steroids and ADHD symptoms across the menstrual cycle. *Psychoneuroendocrinology, 88*, 105–114. https://doi.org/10.1016/j.psyneuen.2017.11.015
9. Ostojic, D., & Miller, C. (2016). Association between pubertal onset and symptoms of ADHD in female university students. *Journal of Attention Disorders, 20*(9), 782–791. https://doi.org/10.1177/1087054714535249
10. Gogne, A. (2021). Treatment of ADHD in perinatal women with dual diagnosis: a comprehensive pharmacological and psychosocial approach. *Global Journal of Intellectual & Developmental Disabilities*, 7(5). https://doi.org/10.19080/gjidd.2021.07.555724
11. Nadeau, K. G., Quinn, P. O., & Littman, E. B. (2002). *Understanding girls with AD/HD*. Advantage Books, LLC.
12. Huessy, H. R. (1990). The pharmacotherapy of personality disorders in women. Paper at the annual meeting of the American Psychiatric Association (symposia), New York.
13. Ostojic, D., & Miller, C. (2016). Association between pubertal onset and symptoms of ADHD in female university students. *Journal of Attention Disorders, 20*(9), 782–791. https://doi.org/10.1177/1087054714535249
14. Hinshaw, S. P., Nguyen, P. T., O'Grady, S. M., & Rosenthal, E. A. (2022). Annual research review: attention-deficit/hyperactivity disorder in girls and women: underrepresentation, longitudinal processes, and key directions. *Journal of Child Psychology and Psychiatry, and Allied Disciplines, 63*(4), 484–496. https://doi.org/10.1111/jcpp.13480
15. Zametkin, A. J., Liebenauer, L. L., Fitzgerald, G. A., King, A. C., Minkunas, D. V., Herscovitch, P., Yamada, E. M., & Cohen, R. M. (1993). Brain metabolism in teenagers with attention-deficit hyperactivity disorder. *Archives of General Psychiatry, 50*(5), 333–340. https://doi.org/10.1001/archpsyc.1993.01820170011002
16. Nadeau, K., Littman, E, & Quinn, P. (2015). *Understanding girls with ADHD: how they feel and why they do what they do* (2nd ed.). Advantage Books.
17. Eng, A. G., Nirjar, U., Elkins, A. R., Sizemore, Y. J., Monticello, K. N., Petersen, M. K., Miller, S. A., Barone, J., Eisenlohr-Moul, T. A., & Martel, M. M. (2024).

Attention-deficit/hyperactivity disorder and the menstrual cycle: theory and evidence. *Hormones and Behavior, 158,* 105466. https://doi.org/10.1016/j.yhbeh.2023.105466

18. Gross, I., Gao, Y., Lee, M., Hipwell, A., & Keenan, K. (2023). The ADHD phenotype in black and white girls from childhood to adolescence: results from the community-based Pittsburgh girls study. *Journal of Attention Disorders, 28*(5), 589–599. https://doi.org/10.1177/10870547231215281
19. Rizor, E. J., Babenko, V., Dundon, N. M., Beverly-Aylwin, R., Stump, A., Hayes, M., Herschenfeld-Catalan, L., Jacobs, E. G., & Grafton, S. T. (2024). Menstrual cycle-driven hormone concentrations co-fluctuate with white and gray matter architecture changes across the whole brain. *Human Brain Mapping, 45*(11), e26785. https://doi.org/10.1002/hbm.26785
20. Roberts, B., Eisenlohr-Moul, T., & Martel, M. (2018). Reproductive steroids and ADHD symptoms across the menstrual cycle. *Psychoneuroendocrinology, 88,* 105–114. https://doi.org/10.1016/j.psyneuen.2017.11.015
21. Johnson, S. R. (1987). The epidemiology and social impact of premenstrual symptoms. *Clinical Obstetrics and Gynecology, 30*(2), 367–376. https://doi.org/10.1097/00003081-198706000-00017
22. Rivera-Tovar, A. D., & Frank, E. (1990). Late luteal phase dysphoric disorder in young women. *The American Journal of Psychiatry, 147*(12), 1634–1636. https://doi.org/10.1176/ajp.147.12.1634
23. Skoglund, C., Kopp Kallner, H., Skalkidou, A., Wikström, A. K., Lundin, C., Hesselmark, E., Kuja-Halkola, R., Larsson, H., & Fernandez de la Cruz, L. (2019). Association of attention-deficit/hyperactivity disorder with teenage birth among women and girls in Sweden. *JAMA Network Open, 2*(10), e1912463. https://doi.org/10.1001/jamanetworkopen.2019.12463
24. Owens, E. B., & Hinshaw, S. P. (2020). Adolescent mediators of unplanned pregnancy among women with and without childhood ADHD. *Journal of Clinical Child and Adolescent Psychology, 49*(2), 229–238. https://doi.org/10.1080/15374416.2018.1547970
25. Meinzer, M. C., LeMoine, K. A., Howard, A. L., Stehli, A., Arnold, L. E., Hechtman, L., Hinshaw, S. P., Molina, B. S. G., Murray, D. W., Sibley, M. H., Swanson, J. M., Tamm, L., & Chronis-Tuscano, A. (2020). Childhood ADHD and involvement in early pregnancy: mechanisms of risk. *Journal of Attention Disorders, 24*(14), 1955–1965. https://doi.org/10.1177/1087054717730610
26. Hosain, G. M., Berenson, A. B., Tennen, H., Bauer, L. O., & Wu, Z. (2012). Attention-deficit/hyperactivity symptoms and risky sexual behavior in young adult women. *Journal of Women's Health, 21*(4), 463–468. https://doi.org/10.1089/jwh.2011.2825
27. Wallin, K., Wallin Lundell, I., Hanberger, L., & Skoglund, C. (2022). Self-experienced sexual and reproductive health in young women with attention deficit hyperactivity disorder: a qualitative interview study. *BMC Women's Health, 22,* 289. https://doi.org/10.1186/s12905-022-01867-y
28. Rohacek, A. M., Firkey, M. K., Woolf-King, S. E., & Antshel, K. M. (2022). Moderation of risks to sexual health by substance use in college students with ADHD. *The Journal of Clinical Psychiatry, 83*(4), 41607.
29. Meinzer, M. C., LeMoine, K. A., Howard, A. L., Stehli, A., Arnold, L. E., Hechtman, L., Hinshaw, S. P., Molina, B. S. G., Murray, D. W., Sibley, M. H., Swanson, J. M., Tamm, L., & Chronis-Tuscano, A. (2020). Childhood ADHD and involvement in early pregnancy: mechanisms of risk. *Journal of Attention Disorders, 24*(14), 1955–1965. https://doi.org/10.1177/1087054717730610

30. Murray, A. L., Taut, D., Baban, A., Hemady, C. L., Walker, S., Osafo, J., Sikander, S., Tomlinson, M., Toit, S. D., Marlow, M., Ward, C. L., Fernando, A., Madrid, B., Van Thang, V., Tuyen, H. D., Dunne, M., Hughes, C., Fearon, P., Valdebenito, S., & Eisner, M. (2022). Associations between ADHD symptoms and maternal and birth outcomes: an exploratory analysis in a multi-country cohort of expectant mothers. *Journal of Attention Disorders, 26*(14), 1882–1894. https://doi.org/10.1177/10870547221105064 (Original work published 2022)
31. Kittel-Schneider, S., Quednow, B. B., Leutritz, A. L., McNeill, R. V., & Reif, A. (2021). Parental ADHD in pregnancy and the postpartum period: a systematic review. *Neuroscience and Biobehavioral Reviews, 124*, 63–77. https://doi.org/10.1016/j.neubiorev.2021.01.002
32. Osianlis, E., Thomas, E., Jenkins, L. M., & Gurvich, C. (2025). ADHD and sex hormones in females: a systematic review. *Journal of Attention Disorders, 29*(9), 706–723. https://doi.org/10.1177/10870547251332319
33. Kittel-Schneider, S., Quednow, B. B., Leutritz, A. L., McNeill, R. V., & Reif, A. (2021). Parental ADHD in pregnancy and the postpartum period: a systematic review. *Neuroscience and Biobehavioral Reviews, 124*, 63–77. https://doi.org/10.1016/j.neubiorev.2021.01.002
34. Broadway, C. (2023, March 27). *Study: prenatal exposure to ADHD medication does not impact neurodevelopment.* ADDitude. https://www.additudemag.com/prenatal-development-ADHD-medication-study/
35. Andersson, A., Garcia-Argibay, M., Viktorin, A., Ghirardi, A., Butwicka, A., Skoglund, C., Bang Madsen, K., D'Onofrio, B.M., Lichtenstein, P., Tuvblad, C., & Larsson, H. (2023). Depression and anxiety disorders during the postpartum period in women diagnosed with attention deficit hyperactivity disorder. *Journal of Affective Disorders.* https://doi.org/10.1016/j.jad.2023.01.069
36. Antoniou, E., Papatrechas, A., & Orovou, E. (2022). Women with attention deficit hyperactivity disorder and perinatal distress: a literature review. *International Journal of Innovative Research in Medical Science*, 7(11), 654–659. https://doi.org/10.23958/ijirms/vol07-i11/1560
37. Broadway, C. (2023, March 27). *Study: prenatal exposure to ADHD medication does not impact neurodevelopment.* ADDitude. https://www.additudemag.com/prenatal-development-ADHD-medication-study/
38. Alimi, R., Azmoude, E., Moradi, M., & Zamani, M. (2022). The association of breastfeeding with a reduced risk of postpartum depression: a systematic review and meta-analysis. *Breastfeeding Medicine: The Official Journal of the Academy of Breastfeeding Medicine*, 17(4), 290–296. https://doi.org/10.1089/bfm.2021.0183
39. Andersson, A., Garcia-Argibay, M., Viktorin, A., Ghirardi, A., Butwicka, A., Skoglund, C., Bang Madsen, K., D'Onofrio, B.M., Lichtenstein, P., Tuvblad, C., & Larsson, H. (2023). Depression and anxiety disorders during the postpartum period in women diagnosed with attention deficit hyperactivity disorder. *Journal of Affective Disorders.* https://doi.org/10.1016/j.jad.2023.01.069
40. Shaywitz, S. E., Shaywitz, B. A., Pugh, K. R., Fulbright, R. K., Skudlarski, P., Mencl, W. E., Constable, R. T., Naftolin, F., Palter, S. F., Marchione, K. E., Katz, L., Shankweiler, D. P., Fletcher, J. M., & Gore, J. C. (1999). Effect of estrogen on brain activation patterns in postmenopausal women during working memory tasks. *Journal of the American Medical Association, 281*(13), 1197–1202. https://doi.org/10.1001/jama.281.13.1197
41. Dreher, J. C., Schmidt, P. J., Kohn, P., Furman, D., Rubinow, D., & Berman, K. F. (2007). Menstrual cycle phase modulates reward-related neural function in women. *Proceedings of the National Academy of Sciences of the United States of America, 104*(7), 2465–2470.

42. Epperson, C. N., Shanmugan, S., Kim, D. R., Mathews, S., Czarkowski, K. A., Bradley, J., Appleby, D. H., Iannelli, C., Sammel, M. D., & Brown, T. E. (2015). New onset executive function difficulties at menopause: a possible role for lisdexamfetamine. *Psychopharmacology, 232*(16), 3091–3100. https://doi.org/10.1007/s00213-015-3953-7
43. Epperson, C. N., Pittman, B., Czarkowski, K. A., Bradley, J., Quinlan, D. M., & Brown, T. E. (2011). Impact of atomoxetine on subjective attention and memory difficulties in perimenopausal and postmenopausal women. *Menopause (New York, N.Y.), 18*(5), 542–548. https://doi.org/10.1097/gme.0b013e3181fcafd6
44. Beltz, A. M., & Moser, J. S. (2020). Ovarian hormones: a long overlooked but critical contributor to cognitive brain structures and function. *Annals of the New York Academy of Sciences, 1464*(1), 156–180. https://doi.org/10.1111/nyas.14255
45. Epperson, C. N., Shanmugan, S., Kim, D. R., Mathews, S., Czarkowski, K. A., Bradley, J., Appleby, D. H., Iannelli, C., Sammel, M. D., & Brown, T. E. (2015). New onset executive function difficulties at menopause: a possible role for lisdexamfetamine. *Psychopharmacology, 232*(16), 3091–3100. https://doi.org/10.1007/s00213-015-3953-7
46. Shanmugan, S., & Epperson, C. N. (2014). Estrogen and the prefrontal cortex: towards a new understanding of estrogen's effects on executive functions in the menopause transition. *Human Brain Mapping, 35*(3), 847–865. https://doi.org/10.1002/hbm.22218
47. Justice A. J., & de Wit, H. (2000). Acute effects of estradiol pretreatment on the response to d-amphetamine in women. *Neuroendocrinology, 71*(1), 51–59. https://doi.org/10.1159/000054520
48. Justice, A. J., & de Wit, H. (1999). Acute effects of d-amphetamine during the follicular and luteal phases of the menstrual cycle in women. *Psychopharmacology, 145*(1), 67–75. https://doi.org/10.1007/s002130051003
49. De Jong, M., Wynchank, D. S. M. R., van Andel, E., Beekman, A. T. F., & Kooij, J. J. S. (2023). Female-specific pharmacotherapy in ADHD: premenstrual adjustment of psychostimulant dosage. *Frontiers in Psychiatry, 14*, 1306194. https://doi.org/10.3389/fpsyt.2023.1306194
50. De Jong, M., Wynchank, D. S. M. R., van Andel, E., Beekman, A. T. F., & Kooij, J. J. S. (2023). Female-specific pharmacotherapy in ADHD: premenstrual adjustment of psychostimulant dosage. *Frontiers in Psychiatry, 14*, 1306194. https://doi.org/10.3389/fpsyt.2023.1306194
51. De Jong, M., Wynchank, D. S. M. R., Michielsen, M., Beekman, A. T., & Kooij, J. J. S. (2024). A female-specific treatment group for ADHD—description of the programme and qualitative analysis of first experiences. *Journal of Clinical Medicine, 13*(7), 2106. https://doi.org/10.3390/jcm13072106
52. Young, S., Adamo, N., Ásgeirsdóttir, B. B., Branney, P., Beckett, M., Colley, W., Cubbin, S., Deeley, Q., Farrag, E., Gudjonsson, G., Hill, P., Hollingdale, J., Kilic, O., Lloyd, T., Mason, P., Paliokosta, E., Perecherla, S., Sedgwick, J., Skirrow, C. … Woodhouse, E. (2020). Females with ADHD: an expert consensus statement taking a lifespan approach providing guidance for the identification and treatment of attention-deficit/hyperactivity disorder in girls and women. *BMC Psychiatry, 20*(1), 404. https://doi.org/10.1186/s12888-020-02707-9
53. De Jong, M., Wynchank, D. S. M. R., Michielsen, M., Beekman, A. T., & Kooij, J. J. S. (2024). A female-specific treatment group for ADHD—description of the programme and qualitative analysis of first experiences. *Journal of Clinical Medicine, 13*(7), 2106. https://doi.org/10.3390/jcm13072106
54. Cilia Vincenti, S., Galea, M., & Briffa, V. (2023, July 31). Issues which marginalize females with ADHD: a mixed methods systematic review. *Humanities and Social Science Research, 6*(2), 30. https://doi.org/10.30560/hssr.v6n2p30

CHAPTER 9

Psychotherapy for women with ADHD

A bio-psycho-social approach

INTRODUCTION

Although ADHD is one of the most common adult psychiatric disorders, few providers have been trained to recognize signs of this condition in women and treat it effectively. Because of the high prevalence rate, it is probable that women with undiagnosed ADHD have been in your office seeking treatment, perhaps for one of the many psychiatric conditions that accompany ADHD. Like many other clinicians, you may have diagnosed anxiety, depression, PTSD, or eating disorders without considering ADHD as a co-occurring condition that might even lie at the core of their difficulties.

Many women have reported to us when seeking treatment at our ADHD specialty clinic that their previous psychotherapy, while helpful, never addressed their ADHD. Today the internet is filled with information on ADHD in women. Many are self-diagnosing and then seeking treatment only to have difficulty finding mental health professionals with expertise in treating women with ADHD. If you are a general psychotherapist, then you are on the front line. Our goal is to help you to understand how the symptoms of ADHD and co-occurring conditions are interwoven and how to treat these complexities. If you are seeing a woman with ADHD, you are almost certainly treating "complex ADHD," because in adulthood, ADHD almost never presents alone. These co-occurring conditions are often related, each impacting the other, and need to be treated simultaneously.

ADHD specialists are rare because in-depth ADHD training is rare. If you are a clinician reading this book, we congratulate you. You are in the minority, seeking to understand the basics of diagnosis and treatment for

DOI: 10.4324/9781003542124-9

women with ADHD. We appreciate that you are taking the time and making the effort to learn the basics about women with ADHD. Your clients will benefit tremendously from your efforts.

As we wrote in Chapter 2, the DSM-5 diagnostic criteria don't do an adequate job of identifying women with ADHD. Today, we are experiencing a near-tsunami of women self-diagnosing their ADHD and seeking confirmation from mental health professionals. Women are often leading the way, self-advocating, and bringing books on ADHD in women to their medical practitioner or psychotherapist.

WHAT DOES IT MEAN TO "TREAT ADHD" IN WOMEN?

If we are only identifying and treating the classic triad of symptoms listed in the DSM-5,[1] i.e., hyperactivity, impulsivity and inattention, we haven't even scratched the surface of the problems faced by women with ADHD. These include:

- A longstanding sense of not belonging with other girls, often carrying into adulthood as feelings of inadequacy and difficulty feeling accepted by other women.
- Rejection Sensitive Dysphoria experienced after a lifetime of feeling socially rejected and disconnected.
- Emotional dysregulation.
- Chronic overwhelm in response to relentless daily expectations that surpass their ability to cope.
- Social withdrawal in response to countless cuts and criticisms from early childhood onward.
- Chaotic family relationships resulting from anxiety, impulsivity, and dysregulation.

While evidence-based treatment approaches such as stimulant medication and CBT have been found to significantly reduce ADHD symptoms as defined by the DSM-5, we need to question whether these treatments are targeting the most significant issues that can improve a woman's overall quality of life.

The critical question is: how best to treat women with ADHD? As is so often the case, clinical practice leads while research follows. Measures of the effectiveness of ADHD treatment continue to narrowly focus on current DSM-5 diagnostic criteria, which better describe men and cannot adequately capture the broader experience of women with this condition.

If a woman's symptoms do not "meet criteria" for an ADHD diagnosis, they are often overlooked, minimized, or attributed to other disorders. While medication and CBT can both be helpful, especially in combination, our approach to ADHD treatment uses a wider lens to consider the many ways in which it affects women in their daily lives.

What's different about ADHD in women?

As we have seen, a focus on the official DSM-5 TR ADHD symptoms has not served women well. Were we to ask women with ADHD what they most wish to change, we would see a much broader—and in some instances more gender-specific—set of concerns.

As a clinician, and especially if you are a psychotherapist, keep the following in mind:

- **ADHD behavioral symptoms may not be as evident in women because it is more of an internalized disorder among these patients**. It's very common in women with ADHD to have few observable external manifestations of ADHD during girlhood. Therefore, they may not meet the DSM-5 criterion of symptoms being present before age 12. Because the standardized questionnaires used in diagnosing children with ADHD are completed by parents and/or teachers, a child's symptoms must be observable enough to be noted by an adult. When a girl has the predominantly inattentive ADHD type and works hard to mask her symptoms, it's very likely that she will go under the radar and not be diagnosed early enough to meet the DSM-5 TR criteria.[2,3]
- **Anxiety may be secondary to ADHD and not a separate disorder**. While anxiety is a very common comorbidity for women with ADHD, in many cases the anxiety is the *result* of ADHD and not necessarily a co-occurring condition. If ADHD has been diagnosed, don't fall into the trap of "treating the anxiety first," assuming that the patient's ADHD symptoms may be the result of that anxiety.[4] In fact, ADHD and anxiety are bi-directional[5] and for many women, when hormones are addressed and stimulant medication is effective, the anxiety may be greatly reduced.[6]
- **Feelings of stress and inability to manage the demands of daily life** are a common daily experience for women with ADHD. This is often due to the interaction between the societal expectations that burden all women and ADHD challenges, including forgetfulness,

distractibility, disorganization, and time-blindness, that can make daily life feel like a whirlwind of failures and complications. Such constant feelings of overwhelm can then lead to frequent irritability.[7]

- **Addictive/impulsive behaviors**. These might include impulsive overeating, compulsive online or real-world shopping, and addiction to digital devices, especially to social media. Addictive behaviors can also include addiction to nicotine and other substances from adolescence onward.[8]
- **Emotional dysregulation**. Research shows that men with ADHD often have problems with anger control (loud arguments, angry reactions while driving, anger at being kept waiting, low frustration tolerance). However, a woman's emotional dysregulation is more likely to occur in the context of relationships. This might take the form of explosive reactions to family members and friends when she is feeling depleted emotionally or under high stress.[9] Or she might react with anger at being asked to do "one more thing" when she feels overwhelmed by constant, relentless demands from all aspects of her life. She may also frequently experience hurt feelings in interactions with female friends or coworkers.[10]
- **Low self-esteem/emotional vulnerability**. Problems with self-doubt and low self-esteem often begin early in life. Girls with ADHD raised by non-ADHD mothers who don't understand or accept their executive functioning challenges often live under a constant shower of criticism. Girls fear embarrassment in the classroom if they have not been listening carefully and are called on in class; just as mothers with limited knowledge of ADHD can be frequently critical, the same pattern may occur in the classroom. A girl's teacher may show frustration if she forgets to turn in her homework, forgets to return permission slips from home, or has difficulty completing in-class assignments. While boys with ADHD, particularly those who identify as Black or Latinx, are frequently stigmatized due to loud and disruptive conduct in classroom environments, these behaviors may be more in line with conventional wisdom about how boys tend to behave. Girls with ADHD typically receive messages from all directions—from peers, from teachers, and from parents—that their behavior is not acceptable.[11]
- **Rejection Sensitive Dysphoria (RSD)** is a term that refers to a common and intense reaction experienced by those with ADHD, who are often highly sensitive and more vulnerable to and impacted by feelings of social rejection than more neurotypical women, whether real or imagined. This is not surprising given the well-documented

history of social rejection or social neglect experienced by so many women with ADHD, who report feeling "different" from their peers from early childhood without understanding why.[12]

- **Intensification of symptoms during the low-estrogen luteal phase of the menstrual cycle** (see Chapter 8). It's important to discuss with your female client the interactions between anxiety, mood, and reactivity and phases of the menstrual cycle. If intensity or frequency of symptoms rise and fall significantly throughout the menstrual cycle, you should discuss whether hormonal treatment might be considered as part of your client's overall care.
- **Body-focused repetitive behaviors**, including hair pulling, cuticle picking, and nail biting, are not unusual in women with ADHD. Most of us are familiar with the fidget objects that are often helpful to children with ADHD, especially in situations in which they are required to sit still and listen. But much less attention is paid to the ongoing need in adulthood to fidget and make continuous micro-movements. Many women report that they wiggle their toes inside of their shoes because this is a less obvious fidget that won't draw attention. Cigarette smoking and vaping also provide activity that calms the need to fidget, although these activities are not recommended due to the clear health problems related to them. Nail biting, cuticle picking, and hair pulling are also common because these body parts are always available when the need to fidget becomes overwhelming. In some circumstances, when anxiety levels are intense and prolonged, these picking and hair-pulling behaviors can become more problematic, with nails bitten into the quick, bleeding cuticles, and the beginnings of bald spots. Adult-appropriate fidget objects can be helpful. These might include a bracelet that allows for fidgeting, a ring that can be twirled, or a ballpoint pen that can be held and manipulated during meetings or prolonged conversations. Medications to reduce anxiety can also ease the urge to fidget.[13]
- **Self-harm**, including both suicidal and non-suicidal self-injuries. Self-harm in girls with ADHD may begin in early adolescence and continue through into adulthood. There are strong associations between childhood abuse (physical, sexual, or emotional) and subsequent self-harm. In addition, rates of psychiatric hospitalizations are significantly higher in females with ADHD compared to their male counterparts.[14,15,16]
- **Intimate partner abuse (IPA)**. Women with ADHD often face unique vulnerabilities that may increase their risk of experiencing **intimate partner violence**. A systematic review found that women

with mental disorders, including ADHD, are significantly more likely to experience domestic violence compared to those without them.[17] Though a number of internal and external factors are associated with increased risk of being victimized by a partner, research suggests that the emotional profile of women with ADHD may increase their susceptibility. Avdibegović and Sinanović observed that psychosocial characteristics often found in women with ADHD, such as a **negative self-image and insufficient social support**, are prevalent among women victims of domestic violence.[18]

It is important to consider the impact of multiple traumatic experiences throughout the life course when evaluating women with ADHD.[19] Ongoing stress and PTSD symptoms can exacerbate ADHD, creating a vicious cycle that further entrenches women in abusive relationships.

CASE ILLUSTRATION: JOY

Joy is a 32-year-old who was diagnosed with ADHD and depression as a senior in high school. At that time, she had presented with symptoms of depression and academic difficulties. Meanwhile, her younger brother had already been treated for ADHD and had had significant behavior issues for several years. Raising him demanded all the attention of his parents. Since they thought Joey's behavior was typical for kids with ADHD, Joy, who was compliant and not a problem in school, had fallen through the cracks. They even commented when Joy was diagnosed that they didn't think girls could have ADHD. Once diagnosed, Joy began seeing a therapist and was prescribed medication for her ADHD and depression. She improved with these interventions, but she continued to feel she wasn't as smart as other girls in her classes.

After college, Joy worked as a receptionist in a real estate firm. The job was a good fit, as it involved interaction with both agents and clients, but none of the detailed paperwork required of real estate agents. She was doing well and began dating one of the agents and after a time, they moved in together. However, after this everything changed. He quickly began preying on her insecurities and frequently insulted her, calling her "stupid" and "lazy." This quickly escalated to yelling and physical assaults. After these incidents, he was sorry and apologetic, but always asserted that his reactions were the result of her behaviors. A friend at work noticed that Joy was becoming increasingly depressed.

Joy was careful about using makeup and long sleeves to camouflage her bruises when her boyfriend's assaults left marks. However one day, she wore an outfit that allowed her friend to notice cut marks on her thighs when she was lifting a box off of a high shelf. They talked about cutting and her friend voiced her concerns and pleaded with Joy to go to a therapist. Reluctantly, although she had not seen him for years and was no longer on medication, Joy returned to her old therapist, and confessed to being depressed, cutting, and having suicidal ideations. He recommended an antidepressant and continued to see her in therapy. Eventually, she reported to him the physical abuse and several instances of nonconsensual sex, although she could not bring herself to call it rape. Joy's therapist then worked with her to assess her readiness for change and, once she was ready, collaborated with her on a plan to safely move out.

The intersection of ADHD and intimate partner abuse in women presents a significant concern. Women with ADHD may be particularly vulnerable to experiencing IPA because they are likely to lack sufficient emotional support and have a low sense of self-efficacy, which can hinder their ability to navigate relationships safely. Understanding these dynamics is crucial to developing targeted interventions that address both ADHD and the risk of IPA, with the ultimate aim of improving the mental health and safety of affected women.

Use a wide-angle lens during treatment planning

Our **bio-psycho-social** approach to treatment is designed to address the struggles that impact women with ADHD in terms of

- their **biology** (especially the impact of female hormones starting at puberty)
- their **psychology** (tendencies to internalize distress, leading to higher rates of anxiety and depression, and difficulties forming the social connections they seek) and
- their **social roles** (societal expectations placed on women at home and at work).

The conflict between ADHD symptoms and gender norms complicates women's experiences of living with ADHD. Addressing these issues should be a central focus of research, treatment, and public discourse.

Where to begin? Reassurance and hope

Perhaps the most essential task for a psychotherapist is to listen and empathize, creating a safe place that offers reassurance and hope. Your job as a therapist is to communicate that you understand the client's challenges and that she is not alone in her struggles. By assuring the client that you have guided many women from chaos to calm, from self-blame to self-acceptance, from isolation to connection, and from feelings of urgency to a sense of agency, you communicate that help is at hand and that her suffering can be reduced. Before you and your client can develop a treatment plan, a strong, collaborative therapeutic alliance is essential.

PSYCHOEDUCATION: HELP HER UNDERSTAND HER BRAIN

It's so important for female clients with ADHD to be armed with a full understanding of their brain differences, particularly because most of these women have spent their lifetime blaming themselves for their struggles. This self-understanding is a critical phase of the healing process. A remarkable shift often occurs when a woman comes to understand that her struggles are caused by brain differences, not by personal weakness. There is a growing awareness of neurodiversity and how conditions like autism and dyslexia can impact learning, communication, and behavior. However, it seems as if the public is often more skeptical about ADHD diagnoses, suspecting that people tend to use them as an excuse for personal shortcomings that could be easily overcome with more effort.

Research and professional discussions suggest that many clinicians simply haven't had much specialized training in adult ADHD. On top of that, assessment practices can vary widely, and because ADHD symptoms often overlap with anxiety, depression, or trauma, it's not uncommon for the diagnosis to be missed—or questioned. All of this can lead some professionals to doubt whether an adult's struggles are really ADHD, which can leave people feeling dismissed, misunderstood, or not taken seriously.

A woman with ADHD seeking treatment from a psychotherapist may harbor those same doubts about herself, which is why one of you most important tasks is to validate her experiences and to explain the science behind the diagnosis.

HELP HER TO ESCAPE FROM HER PATTERNS OF MASKING, APOLOGIZING, AND WITHDRAWING

Most women with ADHD enter therapy after years, perhaps decades, of feeling battered by the demands of their daily lives. They always feel that they fail to measure up, and although they might triumph in one area of their life, they do so only by falling short everywhere else. For example, it's not uncommon for a professional woman with ADHD to maintain the appearance of control and competence in her career while secretly struggling in her private life. These women might be described as performing a daring high-wire act on weekdays, then collapsing into exhaustion and dysfunction on evenings and weekends, focusing all the while on masking their struggles from those around them.

UNDERSTAND PERFECTIONISM IN WOMEN WITH ADHD

Perfectionist women with ADHD may look put together on the outside, but their ADHD is still very much there on the inside. These intense efforts to mask the condition can present in multiple domains—at work and home, where women with ADHD sometimes make extreme efforts to stay on top of household tasks and be a flawless parent. These women rarely relax or spend time with friends because they are always "trying to get organized." Sari Solden, a pioneer in treating women with ADHD, has written eloquently about the struggles of women who spend all their evenings and weekends trying to conquer the clutter and chaos.[20] For these women, their lives are almost entirely focused on compensating for their ADHD challenges.

Sadly, perfectionist women may succeed so well in hiding their ADHD that they may never receive the diagnosis and treatment they so urgently need.

Help her to reduce her feelings of overwhelm

The most common reality for women with ADHD is overwhelm. Their experience is that no matter how hard they try to arrive on time and get everything done, something will always happen to prevent it; it is as though something attacks them from behind when they least expect it. They may make careful meal plans for the week, only to end up ordering pizza for dinner because, once again, they have forgotten to thaw the chicken. Or they may run late to pick up their child from sports practice because they lost track of time. They are exhausted and may express frustration toward a child or partner at the end of a long day. Overwhelm is the most common word that many women with ADHD use to describe their life.

Help her to throw off the yoke of impossible gender expectations

In very recent years, women with ADHD have begun to support one another and fight back against the unrealistic expectations placed on women: that they should be able to work full time outside of the house while also smoothly managing their household, keeping track of the schedules of everyone in the family, and planning and preparing meals, all while being a loving mother of well-behaved children; that they should always take the lead in planning outings with friends and be primarily responsible for keeping in touch with everyone in their lives and maintaining close relationships. These expectations are unrealistic for a woman without ADHD and near-impossible for a woman with ADHD. The burden of shame and constant defensive apologies for arriving late to appointments, forgetting to sign the permission slip for their child's field trip, sending a friend's birthday present late, or managing a misbehaving child in the grocery store can be overwhelming. It is a very hopeful sign to see women with ADHD starting to declare their independence from these impossible expectations.

As Ellen Littman, Ph.D., an expert in treating ADHD in women, writes in *ADDitude* magazine, "Societal demands for communication and cooperation require perfect choreography of the executive functions. However, women with ADHD are thwarted by unpredictable executive functions. Overwhelmed and frantic, they accept that they are not entitled to a support system, but that, in fact, they are the support system."[21]

You can help your female client with ADHD by guiding her toward reframing her life experiences through a different lens. CBT approaches can be extremely helpful in this process. Focus not only on the challenges and frustrations experienced by a woman with ADHD, but also help her to identify her strengths, such as the creativity that so often results from nonlinear thinking, and to enjoy the spontaneity of ADHD that can lead to a vital and engaging life. The key is to shift her focus from trying to "pass" as a non-ADHD woman to celebrating her differences as a woman with ADHD.

Form a strong therapeutic bond—you are her guide on a complicated journey

Listen to her, ask about every aspect of her life, and make her feel heard, understood, and supported. The more that the therapist can communicate a sense of calm and confidence, the more effective the client's therapy will be. Your first step as a therapist is to be welcoming and reassuring, communicating to the client that you have been down this road before with other clients and that many women with ADHD have been successful in creating a calmer, more functional, and more satisfying life.

Help her to prioritize her challenges

Explore her challenges and work with her to prioritize which issues to address first. Give her the confidence that you can guide her, focusing on one thing at a time so that she doesn't feel overwhelmed by the myriad challenges that lie before her. Making meaningful life changes should not be like making New Year's resolutions—diving in with the intention to make a radical change, only to feel defeated a few days or weeks later. The therapist may need to help their client use a wide-angle lens herself. Often, a woman seeks treatment due to a crisis and is narrowly focused on one topic, whether it is losing a job, marital problems, or chronic anxiety driven by feelings of failure in her life. Women with ADHD tend to have difficulty maintaining and succeeding in employment, school, and parenting and spousal roles. Moreover, although men with ADHD often rely on spouses or other family members to provide assistance and compensation, women with ADHD tend to deal with symptoms and their impact on daily life activities in isolation.[22]

What are the most common challenges faced by women with ADHD? The list can seem endless. It's no wonder that the most common word that women with ADHD use to describe their emotional state is "overwhelmed."

- **Pervasive, impossible gender role expectations**. Many mid-life adult women with ADHD, particularly those balancing work and caretaking responsibilities, report feeling deep shame and self-blame. They conclude that they are "bad at being women," rather than understanding that the expectations placed on them by society are unreasonable and unmeetable. Younger women, with and without ADHD, are less likely to accept these gendered expectations and maybe experience less self-blame.

- **Weaker social support networks**. Women with ADHD often have difficulty forming supportive social connections and tend to report not feeling accepted and understood by other women. Social impairment in women with ADHD, compared to men with ADHD, is tied to loneliness, rejection sensitivity, and rumination. These patterns can make it harder for women with ADHD to sustain stable friendships and intimate relationships.
- **History of trauma**. Women with ADHD are more likely to report a history of trauma, particularly emotional abuse, compared to women without ADHD. This link could stem from increased likelihood of having a parent with undiagnosed, untreated ADHD who was explosive and emotionally reactive, or a non-ADHD parent who was frequently critical or invalidating. These childhood experiences augment the risk of developing an insecure attachment style that studies show is associated with heightened vulnerability to IPA.[23]

CHALLENGES RELATED TO MARRIAGE AND PARENTHOOD

Let's also look at the set of challenges related to marriage and parenthood that are experienced by many women with ADHD. In addition to the above-mentioned concerns about unintended pregnancies and IPA, the research of Fuller-Thomson et al. highlights an additional difficulty women with ADHD report having to face with greater frequency than those without the diagnosis:

- **High levels of conflict with intimate partners**. Relationships in which one or both partners having ADHD are often impacted by greater emotional escalation during conflict, difficulty resolving disagreements, and recurring arguments about organization, follow-through and responsibilities.[24]

Studies have documented that ADHD mothers of adolescent daughters with ADHD experience very high levels of parenting stress. In one study conducted in 2010, these mothers indicated that they "often could not sleep and committed their entire lives to caring for their daughters, that they were socially isolated, and were suffering from stress related diseases."[25]

- **Being judged by others as being poor parents**. Because ADHD is an "invisible disability," it is often met by judgment, prejudice, stigma, and social insensitivity, with many adults attributing a child's behavior to overly indulgent parenting.[26,27]

- **Raising children with ADHD places a greater burden on parents compared to raising neurotypical children.** In a series of studies conducted over the past 30 years, parents of children with ADHD have reported facing significant challenges in parenting including frustration, exhaustion, depression, constant worry, conflicts with the other parent, feelings of guilt and self-blame, and even lack of support from the professionals they seek help from.[28,29]

Next, let's consider **financial stress and employment stress** for women with ADHD. These stress factors include:

- **Executive functioning challenges**, making work life a constant source of stress due to their poor time awareness, forgetfulness, disorganization, and overwhelm.[30]
- **Having less education than their non-ADHD peers.** Women with ADHD frequently do not complete their education, either due to dropping out of college, never attending college, or, in some cases, not completing high school due to an accidental pregnancy.[31,32] Of course, other factors, including socioeconomic status and racial identity, also play significant roles in women having less opportunity to complete their educations.
- **Financial strain** resulting from low wages and poor financial management.[33,34]
- **Being more likely to be assigned administrative work**, which is a poor match for someone with ADHD given their executive functioning challenges. Studies show that 70–90% of individuals serving in administrative roles are women.
- **Emotional dysregulation**, which sometimes results in fractured relationships with partners, friends, coworkers, and children.[35]

HOW CAN YOU KNOW IF YOU ARE ON THE RIGHT TRACK IN THERAPY WITH YOUR CLIENT?

Feedback-Informed Psychotherapy (FIT) is a relatively recent innovation developed by psychologist Scott Miller and colleagues. A Feedback-Informed Treatment approach boils down to a few simple concepts.

Routinely ask your client:

1. Do you see improvements in response to our work together?
2. Are we addressing the problems that brought you to treatment?
3. Are there other things that you think we should focus on now?
4. Do you feel heard and understood?

At first glance, this may seem like a very basic way to evaluate therapy. However, it is surprising how rarely therapists consistently ask clients for direct feedback about their experience. The focus of FIT is that you and the client are "in it together," working toward identified goals and measuring your progress. Collaboratively, you create a treatment plan and then regularly seek feedback from your client about her satisfaction with the work you are doing together. This collaborative process will build a stronger alliance and give her a clearer sense of her progress toward her goals.

A formal FIT approach may seem overly structured or invasive because it entails structured, frequent completion of standardized questionnaires. A more informal feedback approach may feel more natural to your therapeutic process. But always keep in mind that regular client feedback has been demonstrated to be a very powerful positive force in the therapeutic process. This kind of regular, structured assessment can be especially helpful for a woman with ADHD, who may have a scattered train of thought and tend to get off track within a single session, and particularly so over an extended period of time.[36,37,38]

> To learn more about FIT, read *Feedback-Informed Treatment in Clinical Practice: Reaching for Excellence* (1st edition) by David S. Prescott, Cynthia L. Maeschalck, and Dr. Scott D. Miller Ph.D., published in 2017) by the American Psychological Association Press.[39]

TREATING COMPLEX ADHD

There are usually multiple co-occurring conditions that must also be treated if ADHD treatment is going to be successful. (See Chapter 3 for a more in-depth discussion.) Keep in mind that ADHD *without* a co-occurring psychiatric condition is quite rare.[40] ADHD in women is almost always "complex," meaning that it exists alongside one or more related psychiatric conditions. In fact, psychiatric comorbidities, including depression and anxiety, are more frequently diagnosed in women with ADHD than in men with ADHD.[41,42] Anxiety accompanies ADHD so often that, as a general practitioner, it is essential that you become knowledgeable about treating it in combination with ADHD. However, there are different degrees of complexity and risk in treating co-occurring conditions. When co-occurring conditions involve a high level of acuity or risk, such as in bipolar disorder and borderline personality disorder, you might choose to refer to a specialist if one is available in your community. Substance use disorders and eating disorders are also commonly co-occurring.

The key to successfully treating the many psychiatric conditions that accompany ADHD is to always keep your client's ADHD in mind when focusing on the co-occurring conditions. It is our experience that the treatment of co-occurring conditions is less successful if it doesn't take into account how that condition might be affected and complicated by the client's ADHD.

Develop a collaborative treatment plan

As we discussed when introducing Feedback-Informed Treatment, the best and most effective treatment is reached in a collaborative process with your client, through building a collaborative treatment plan focused on the issues they have introduced. Based on your experience, you should guide your client toward addressing any other potential issues of concern she might not associate with her ADHD.

Then, start small: Success breeds success

Start with a doable goal. If a woman presents with disordered eating patterns, she'll feel overwhelmed if the therapist presents her with a "healthy meal plan" that is comprehensive and completely different from what she puts on the table every day.

It has been our longstanding approach to help our female clients, who so often come to us feeling demoralized, overwhelmed, and self-blaming, to achieve success one bit at a time. Accomplishing one small task makes it easier to tackle the next one with more confidence and energy.

Your role as case coordinator

Treating ADHD is often complex. Your client may be in psychotherapy with you, seeing a psychiatrist who prescribes medication, or working with a professional coach or organizer; at times, she might be involved in couples therapy, family therapy, and/or parenting groups. If sleep, obesity, or other medical problems are involved, the treatment plan becomes incredibly complex.

Ideally, you, as her primary psychotherapist, will help her to prioritize her needs (few have the time or financial resources to seek all these treatments simultaneously) and also help her to coordinate these various treatments. As case coordinator, you may engage in:

1. **Collaboration with her prescriber**. In most cases, your client will also be under the care of a physician who prescribes her medication. Often, this will not only be for her ADHD, but also to treat anxiety and/or depression, bipolar disorder, etc. Ideally, you should develop a collaborative relationship with her prescriber so that, with your client's permission, you can share your impressions with them. You'll be seeing your client much more often and for longer sessions than her prescriber, and can provide helpful information to support their care, especially in cases where the provider is not an ADHD specialist.
2. **Referral to and collaboration with other care providers**. You may refer your client to a hormone specialist for hormone replacement therapy (HRT). Or you may refer your client to an ADHD coach to provide more intense executive functioning (EF) support to build more consistent daily habits into her life. You may need to communicate with an eating disorders specialist if she is in their care, or other specialists treating one of the many medical conditions that she may experience. You may also need to help your client make the appointment (see the example below).
3. **Supporting your client to follow through on recommendations made by other providers**. One example that comes to mind is that of a woman with ADHD whose psychiatrist didn't want to add a particular medication to her prescription until she had seen a cardiologist and had an EKG. Each time the client saw her psychiatrist, she was asked if she had made the appointment with the cardiologist, and each time she reported that she had forgotten. Her psychiatrist ultimately provided more structure and support to help her follow through on this critical task. "Let's call the cardiologist's office during our session. You don't have the number with you? Let's look it up online." Within five minutes, the client had called the cardiologist's office, made an appointment, and, with prompting, had entered the appointment date and time into the calendar on her phone.

SUMMARY

It is critical to carefully distinguish symptoms that are specific to women's ADHD from those that overlap with depression, anxiety, and other conditions. Helping your client to understand her brain and how all her multiple challenges are interconnected is critical. She may come to you with specific ADHD concerns, not realizing that she will need to change many other aspects of her life. Just as many psychotherapists don't understand the full range of issues related to ADHD, your female client with ADHD may not understand how her various challenges are interrelated.

As part of your assessment and treatment planning, it is essential to broaden your client's focus and teach her to understand her unique brain. You should help her appreciate the roles played by her strengths, challenges, health habits, and general living environment, and how they all interact—for better or for worse—to affect her mood, cognition, and decision-making.

You are the "guide by her side" as she explores the multiple, often complex issues that she must deal with as a woman with ADHD. It is your role to problem-solve with her, to prioritize with her, and to provide ongoing structure and support as she makes critical changes in her life and within herself.

If we have achieved nothing else in this chapter, we hope that you have come to understand the range and complexity of issues faced by your female clients with ADHD: these might include chronic stress, disordered sleep, parenting challenges, difficulties on the job, conflicts in romantic relationships, emotional reactivity, addictive tendencies, poor health habits, and neglected self-care. The more therapeutic tools you have in your toolbox, the better the outcome. In the next chapter, we will introduce a range of therapeutic tools that might be helpful for you to use, depending upon your client's particular needs.

REFERENCES

1. American Psychiatric Association. (2022). *Diagnostic and statistical manual of mental disorders* (5th ed., text rev.; DSM-5-TR). American Psychiatric Publishing. https://doi.org/10.1176/appi.books.9780890425787
2. Lynch, A., & Davison, K. (2022). Gendered expectations on the recognition of ADHD in young women and educational implications. *Irish Educational Studies, 43*(1), 61–81. https://doi.org/10.1080/03323315.2022.2032264
3. Young, S., Adamo, N., Ásgeirsdóttir, B. B., Branney, P., Beckett, M., Colley, W., Cubbin, S., Deeley, Q., Farrag, E., Gudjonsson, G., Hill, P., Hollingdale, J., Kilic, O., Lloyd, T., Mason, P., Paliokosta, E., Perecherla, S., Sedgwick, J., Skirrow, C. … Woodhouse, E. (2020). Females with ADHD: an expert consensus statement taking a lifespan approach providing guidance for the identification and treatment of attention-deficit/hyperactivity disorder in girls and women. *BMC Psychiatry, 20*(1), 404. https://doi.org/10.1186/s12888-020-02707-9
4. Golubchik, P., Golubchik, L., Sever, J., & Weizman, A. (2014). The beneficial effect of methylphenidate in ADHD with comorbid separation anxiety. *International Clinical Psychopharmacology, 29*(5), 274–278. https://doi.org/10.1097/yic.0000000000000034

5. Murray, A. L., Caye, A., McKenzie, K., Auyeung, B., Murray, G., Ribeaud, D., & Eisner, M. (2020). Reciprocal developmental relations between ADHD and anxiety in adolescence: a within-person longitudinal analysis of commonly co-occurring symptoms. *Journal of Attention Disorders, 26*(1), 109–118. https://doi.org/10.1177/1087054720908333
6. Moulana, M., & Sukumaran, A. P. (2020). Polycystic ovary syndrome and increased risk of psychiatric disorders. *Endocrinology & Metabolism International Journal, 8*(6), 133–137. https://doi.org/10.15406/emij.2020.08.00296
7. Fuller-Thomson, E., Lewis, D. A., & Agbeyaka, S. K. (2016). Attention-deficit/hyperactivity disorder casts a long shadow: findings from a population-based study of adult women with self-reported ADHD. *Child Care Health and Development, 42*(6), 918–927. https://doi.org/10.1111/cch.12380
8. Archi, S., Barrault, S., García, M., Branger, S., Maugé, D., Ballon, N., & Brunault, P. (2023). Adult ADHD diagnosis, symptoms of impulsivity, and emotional dysregulation in a clinical sample of outpatients consulting for a behavioral addiction. *Journal of Attention Disorders, 27*(7), 731–742. https://doi.org/10.1177/10870547231161336
9. Archi, S. E., Cortese, S., Ballon, N., Réveillère, C., Di Luca, A., Barrault, S., & Brunault, P. (2020). Negative affectivity and emotion dysregulation as mediators between ADHD and disordered eating: a systematic review. *Nutrients, 12*(11), 3292. https://doi.org/10.3390/nu12113292
10. Bodalski, E. A., Flory, K., & Meinzer, M. C. (2023). A scoping review of factors associated with emotional dysregulation in adults with ADHD. *Journal of Attention Disorders, 27*(13), 1540–1558. https://doi.org/10.1177/10870547231187148
11. Mazzone, L., Postorino, V., Reale, L., Guarnera, M., Mannino, V., Armando, M., & Vicari, S. (2013). Self-esteem evaluation in children and adolescents suffering from ADHD. *Clinical Practice and Epidemiology in Mental Health, 9*(1), 96–102. https://doi.org/10.2174/1745017901309010096
12. Rowney-Smith, A., Sutton, B., Quadt, L., & Eccles, J. (2024). The lived experience of rejection sensitivity in ADHD: a qualitative exploration. *medRxiv*. https://doi.org/10.1101/2024.11.16.24317418
13. Cohen, P. (2022). Nail-associated body-focused repetitive behaviors: habit-tic nail deformity, onychophagia, and onychotillomania. *Cureus*. https://doi.org/10.7759/cureus.22818
14. Blay, M., De Godoy, F., Hasler, R., Nicastro, R., Pham, E., Weibel, S., & Perroud, N. (2025). Is adult attention-deficit/hyperactivity disorder associated with non-suicidal self-injury and/or suicidal behaviors? A study on the role of borderline personality disorder comorbidity. *Journal of Affective Disorders, 376*, 313–317. https://doi.org/10.1016/j.jad.2025.02.028
15. Swanson, E. N., Owens, E. B., & Hinshaw, S. P. (2014). Pathways to self-harmful behaviors in young women with and without ADHD: a longitudinal examination of mediating factors. *Journal of Child Psychology and Psychiatry, 55*(5), 505–515. https://doi.org/10.1111/jcpp.12193
16. Skoglund, C., Sundström Poromaa, I., Leksell, D., Ekholm Selling, K., Cars, T., Giacobini, M., Young, S., & Kopp Kallner, H. (2024). Time after time: failure to identify and support females with ADHD—a Swedish population register study. *Journal of Child Psychology and Psychiatry, 65*(6), 832–844. https://doi.org/10.1111/jcpp.13920
17. Trevillion, K., Oram, S., Feder, G., & Howard, L. M. (2012). Experiences of domestic violence and mental disorders: a systematic review and meta-analysis. *PLOS ONE*, 7(12), e51740. https://doi.org/10.1371/journal.pone.0051740

18. Avdibegović, E., & Sinanović, O. (2006). Consequences of domestic violence on women's mental health in Bosnia and Herzegovina. *Croatian Medical Journal, 47*(5), 730–741. https://www.ncbi.nlm.nih.gov/pmc/articles/PMC2080462
19. Snyder, J. A. (2015). The link between ADHD and the risk of sexual victimization among college women. *Violence Against Women, 21*(11), 1364–1384. https://doi.org/10.1177/1077801215593647
20. Solden, S. (2017). *Women with attention deficit disorder* (2nd ed.). Introspect Press.
21. Littman, E.. (2024, April). Women with ADHD: no more suffering in silence. *ADDitude.* https://www.additudemag.com/gender-differences-in-adhd-women-vs-men
22. Cortese, S., Faraone, S. V., Bernardi, S., Wang, S., & Blanco, C. (2016). Gender differences in adult attention-deficit/hyperactivity disorder: results from the National Epidemiologic Survey on Alcohol and Related Conditions (NESARC). *Journal of Clinical Psychiatry*, 77, e2421–e2428. https://doi.org/10.4088/JCP.14m09630
23. Antoniou, E., Rigas, N., Orovou, E., Papatrechas, A., & Sarella, A. (2021). ADHD symptoms in females of childhood, adolescent, reproductive and menopause period. *Materia Socio Medica, 33*(2), 114. https://doi.org/10.5455/msm.2021.33.114-118
24. Fuller-Thomson, E., Lewis, D. A., & Agbeyaka, S. K. (2016). Attention-deficit/hyperactivity disorder casts a long shadow: findings from a population-based study of adult women with self-reported ADHD. *Child Care Health and Development*, Nov *42*(6), 918–927. https://doi.org/10.1111/cch.12380
25. Hallberg, U., Óskarsdóttir, S., & Klingberg, G. (2010). 22q11 deletion syndrome: the meaning of a diagnosis. A qualitative study on parental perspectives. *Child Care Health and Development, 36*(5), 719–725. https://doi.org/10.1111/j.1365-2214.2010.01108.x
26. Mueller, A. K., Fuermaier, A. B. M., Koerts, J., & Tucha, L. (2012). Stigma in attention deficit hyperactivity disorder. *ADHD Attention Deficit and Hyperactivity Disorders, 4*(3), 101–114. https://doi.org/10.1007/s12402-012-0085-3
27. Lebowitz, M. S. (2013). Stigmatization of ADHD. *Journal of Attention Disorders, 20*(3), 199–205. https://doi.org/10.1177/1087054712475211
28. Ringer, N., Wilder, J., Scheja, M., & Gustavsson, A. (2019). Managing children with challenging behaviours: parents' meaning-making processes in relation to their children's ADHD diagnosis. *International Journal of Disability, Development and Education, 67*(4), 376–392. https://doi.org/10.1080/1034912X.2019.1596228.
29. Park, J. L., Hudec, K. L., & Johnston, C. (2017). Parental ADHD symptoms and parenting behaviors: a meta-analytic review. *Clinical Psychology Review, 56*, 25–39. https://doi.org/10.1016/j.cpr.2017.05.003
30. Hayashi, W., Suzuki, H., Saga, N., Arai, G., Igarashi, R., Tokumasu, T., & Iwanami, A. (2019). Clinical characteristics of women with ADHD in Japan. *Neuropsychiatric Disease and Treatment, 15*, 3367–3374. https://doi.org/10.2147/ndt.s232565
31. Henning, C., Summerfeldt, L., & Parker, J. (2021). ADHD and academic success in university students: the important role of impaired attention. *Journal of Attention Disorders, 26*(6), 893–901. https://doi.org/10.1177/10870547211036758
32. Meinzer, M. C., LeMoine, K. A., Barbaree, H. E., Stehli, A., Arnold, L. E., Hechtman, L., & Chronis-Tuscano, A. (2017). Childhood ADHD and involvement in early pregnancy: mechanisms of risk. *Journal of Attention Disorders, 24*(14), 1955–1965. https://doi.org/10.1177/1087054717730610
33. Koerts, J., Bangma, D. F., Fuermaier, A. B. M., Mette, C., Tucha, L., & Tucha, O. (2021). Financial judgment determination in adults with ADHD. *Journal of Neural Transmission, 128*(7), 969–979. https://doi.org/10.1007/s00702-021-02323-1

34. Koerts, J., Bangma, D. F., Mette, C., Tucha, L., & Tucha, O. (2023). Strengths and weaknesses of everyday financial knowledge and judgment skills of adults with ADHD. *International Journal of Environmental Research and Public Health, 20*(5), 4656. https://doi.org/10.3390/ijerph20054656
35. Grossman, A., & Avital, A. (2023). Emotional and sensory dysregulation as a possible missing link in attention deficit hyperactivity disorder: a review. *Frontiers in Behavioral Neuroscience, 17*. https://doi.org/10.3389/fnbeh.2023.1118937
36. Maeschalck, C., & Barfknecht, L. (2017). Using client feedback to inform treatment. In *Casebook for clinical supervision: A competency-based approach* (pp. 53–77). American Psychological Association. https://doi.org/10.1037/0000039-004
37. van Oenen, F. J., Schipper, S., Van, R., Schoevers, R. A., Visch, I., Peen, J., & Dekker, J. (2016). Feedback-informed treatment in emergency psychiatry: a randomised controlled trial. *BMC Psychiatry, 16*(1), 282. https://doi.org/10.1186/s12888-016-0811-z
38. Lambert, M. J., Harmon, C., Slade, K., Whipple, J. L., & Hawkins, E. J. (2004). Providing feedback to psychotherapists on their patients' progress: clinical results and practice suggestions. *Journal of Clinical Psychology, 61*(2), 165–174. https://doi.org/10.1002/jclp.20113
39. Prescott, D. S., Maeschalck, C. L., & Miller, S. D. (Eds.). (2017). *Feedback-informed treatment in clinical practice: reaching for excellence.* American Psychological Association.
40. Jameson, N., Sheppard, B., Lateef, T., Voort, J. L. V., He, J., & Merikangas, K. R. (2016). Medical comorbidity of attention-deficit/hyperactivity disorder in US adolescents. *Journal of Child Neurology, 31*(11), 1282–1289. https://doi.org/10.1177/0883073816653782
41. Skoglund, C., Sundström Poromaa, I., Leksell, D., Ekholm Selling, K., Cars, T., Giacobini, M., Young, S., & Kopp Kallner, H. (2024). Time after time: failure to identify and support females with ADHD: a Swedish population register study. *Journal of Child Psychology and Psychiatry, 65*(6), 832–844. https://doi.org/10.1111/jcpp.13920
42. Review of the psychosocial consequences of attention deficit hyperactivity disorder (ADHD) in females. (2024). *European Journal of Medical and Health Sciences, 6*(1), 10–20. https://doi.org/10.24018/ejmed.2024.6.1.2033

CHAPTER 10

Expanding your therapeutic toolkit to help women with ADHD

INTRODUCTION

Looking at therapeutic approaches through an ADHD lens

In this chapter, we move from the broader concepts that underlie our bio-psycho-social approach to introduce a set of therapeutic tools that you can choose from and that will help you address some of the most pressing issues your clients with ADHD face. You may already be familiar with many of these tools, but now we want you to look at them from an ADHD-informed perspective.

As an example, if you are focused on treatment for trauma with a woman with ADHD, it's important to always keep ADHD in mind. In some women with ADHD, their experience is better described as C-PTSD (complex PTSD), which may be characterized by what we call "death by a thousand cuts," resulting from growing up under a shower of criticism from parents, teachers, and peers. For other women with ADHD, these experiences may coexist with a range of traumatic experiences related to racial identity, gender identity, and socioeconomic status, among others.[1,2]

Therapeutic feelings and functionality

COACHING—INTERWEAVING

What we call "therapeutic coaching" refers to using ADHD-informed therapeutic tools while also focusing on helping women to become more functional in their daily lives. Even within a single therapy session, it is

DOI: 10.4324/9781003542124-10

likely that you will need to address both feelings and functionality and become adept at shifting from one to the other. The following case illustrates this dual focus.

Imagine yourself in the following situation:

CASE ILLUSTRATION: MARGO

Margo is a woman in her mid-thirties who is seeking your help regarding her highly conflictual marriage. Her husband is not interested in couples therapy, she reports, because he believes that her ADHD is "her problem." She reports: "He thinks that I just need to go and get my ADHD treated and then everything will be OK." Margot feels relentlessly criticized and belittled by her husband.

However, after you have seen her several times, you recognize a pattern that you think will be important to the success of your therapy with her. She has called to reschedule her appointment on more than one occasion and has rushed in late for the sessions that she has attended.

So here you have it—feelings and functionality. You can't effectively treat her if she continues to miss sessions and arrive late to others.

As a therapist, you need to listen and support her and help her work out how best to resolve their latest disagreement. But you also need to help her problem-solve about the frantic always-running-late way she typically goes through her days. "You're caught in a cycle," you might comment. "The more tired and frantic you feel, the more sleep-deprived you are, the more you will arrive late to our appointments and the less time you will have to get the full benefits of the therapeutic support you are seeking to help manage these stressful situations."

The above scenario is an example of "therapeutic coaching," which focuses on a blend of feelings and functionality. Therapeutic coaching begins with a stress analysis, and then a plan of action is developed collaboratively with the patient. As a therapeutic coach, you will problem-solve with your patient, providing support and structure while she works toward each goal.

In another example of "therapeutic coaching," a patient might tell you that one of the stressors that weighs most heavily on her mind is the financial strain she is under. As a therapeutic coach, you will also address her financial concerns directly. People with ADHD often make poor financial decisions, decisions that may lead to immediate temporary pleasure, but which soon result in even higher anxiety when the credit card bill arrives.

CASE ILLUSTRATION: DIANE

"Diane," a divorced single mother with ADHD, frequently spoke of how little child support she received and mentioned that she had very little money in her savings account. Diane and her therapist talked about the impulse spending that gave her those little "dopamine bursts" that she craved. The therapist pointed out that these short-term pleasures lead to chronic anxiety as they cause her credit card bill to climb.

The therapist and Diane make a plan. Diane will keep a small notebook in her purse. In it she will record all the money that she unnecessarily spends each day. Every time she decides **not** to make a purchase, she writes down the amount she **has saved**. For example, foregoing a trip to Starbucks in the morning; bringing her lunch from home rather than buying it; **not** ordering pizza for herself and her son at the end of a tiring day, but instead heating up less expensive frozen meals they choose together from the grocery store each week.

Diane's assignment was to add up those savings at the end of each day and pay herself by transferring that amount of money into her savings account. Diane was amazed to discover that she was saving a substantial amount of money each week. She began to look forward to the new "dopamine hit" that was triggered by transferring money to her savings account each evening. In only a few months, Diane had reached her savings goal, with the significant added benefit of developing a stronger sense of control over her life. She discovered that she could decide upon a goal and reach it!

To many psychotherapists, this example sounds like coaching, not psychotherapy. However, we contend that this is neither of those: instead, it is "therapeutic coaching." This teaches problem-solving skills and how to create action plans, as well as how to follow through on those plans. These steps lead the client to greater self-esteem and a sense that she can make other meaningful changes in her life.

Treatment should focus on quality of life, not on ADHD "symptoms"

In research studies, the success of ADHD treatment is usually defined as a moderate reduction in officially recognized, narrowly construed ADHD symptoms. If a woman's ability to focus is improved and she is less impulsive, then the treatment is considered to have done its job. But what about the rest of her life? Does she have time for self-care? Does she have social connections that support her and enrich her daily life? Is she feeling stretched thin and constantly distressed at home even though her ability to focus at work is greatly improved during the hours she is on stimulant medication? Often, for women, ADHD symptoms are not their primary concern. Treatment success should be measured by improvement in a woman's quality of life.

The challenges faced by women with ADHD may vary widely. One client may be hyper-organized, perfectionist, and highly stressed. Your work with her may include relaxation techniques, self-care, and an examination of the impossible expectations she places on herself. Another may be flying by the seat of her pants; she will need your help to develop habits and systems that can reduce her daily experience of chaos and overwhelm.

Collaborate with her in treatment planning

You need to assess your client's ADHD patterns and then collaboratively establish a treatment plan. It's your role to guide her through prioritizing her challenges and then begin to address them one by one. Be aware that given the challenges and changes so common in the lives of women with ADHD, your treatment plan may need to rapidly shift when a new challenge or crisis presents itself. You may need to use multiple tools in a single therapy session.

LIFE STRESSORS

As psychotherapists treating women with ADHD, we have found that it is essential to educate them about the role that stress plays in their ADHD challenges and the importance of reducing stress as a key element of their overall treatment plan.

We outlined a long list of life stressors in Chapter 9. In treatment planning, it can be helpful to list your client's stressors with her and then rank them from highest to lowest in terms of their impact and/or severity. This stress analysis can become the backbone of her treatment plan.

Stress levels and severity of the impact of ADHD symptoms go hand in hand. Because of this link, ADHD is often diagnosed in women when the demands of their situation suddenly upsurge, surpassing their ability to meet them. For some, this might occur after the appointment of a new supervisor at work who is less tolerant of their inefficiency. For others, an upsurge may follow the birth of a child, or the onset of perimenopause, when declining estrogen levels cause their ADHD to run rampant.

CO-OCCURRING CONDITIONS

It is necessary to address any co-occurring conditions (there are often more than one) when developing your treatment plan. Treatment may need to initially focus on the co-occurring condition before you can successfully address your client's ADHD-related issues. At the same time, there is evidence that treating a woman's ADHD often contributes to success in treating her co-occurring conditions. Your careful analysis as a clinician will be required to decide how and where to begin treatment.[3,4]

THE GREATEST ADHD CHALLENGE: GETTING THINGS DONE!

Many of the challenges of living with ADHD lie on the road from intention to completion. The key challenge for women with ADHD is staying on course, following through on changes in routines and habits that they have decided on in a therapy session.

> Perhaps the greatest therapeutic challenge that you will encounter as a clinician treating ADHD is your patient's lack of follow-through.
>
> Lack of follow-through is discouraging for both you and your patient. Often, after several weeks of not "doing the work," your patient may wonder if she should continue treatment. And you might feel equally discouraged, thinking that the patient's motivation is lacking and the treatment isn't progressing.
>
> But as your patient becomes discouraged, your role is to support, encourage, and problem-solve with her. You need to become skilled in problem-solving to support follow-through so that changes can be made and habits can be built outside of the therapy session.

The Cleveland Clinic's "broken agreements" approach

For some clients, the "broken agreements" approach can be very effective. Psychologists at the Cleveland Clinic view lack of follow-through, or "broken agreements," as the central challenge for those with ADHD.

These "broken agreements" go beyond agreements made in therapy sessions. They apply when the patient does not do what they were asked to do, or what they promised to do, in any aspect of her life.

The approach is simple and empowering.[5] When looking at an incomplete task, the Clinic's psychologists advise their patients to deal with it in one of three ways.

1. Complete the task.
2. Redefine the task (to make it easier).
3. Cancel the task.

Many with ADHD, especially when they feel guilt and shame for poor task completion, develop a habit of "overpromising" and "underdelivering." In the Broken Agreements Approach, the therapist guides the patient through considering how realistic their promises are. In some cases, the promised task will need to be canceled or assigned to others because it exceeds the skills, abilities, or time availability of the adult with ADHD.

To learn more about this approach, read the box below.

Strategies, Structure, and Support

How can you help your patients with ADHD to follow tasks through to completion? As you learn to apply the approaches we introduce in this book, your mantra should become: STRATEGIES, STRUCTURE, and SUPPORT.

These "Three S's" are what will help your patient follow the path from intention through action to completion. We can give women with ADHD all the strategies in the world, but little will happen without adequate structure and support. Kathleen's book *ADD-Friendly Ways to Organize Your Life*,[6] coauthored with professional organizer Judith Kolberg, introduces the concept of strategies, structure, and support. The book provides the strategies, while *you*, as her therapist, provide the structure and support.

- Strategies are the tricks of the trade, i.e., ways to make life a bit easier to manage.
- Structure provides the scaffolding around the task. It involves deciding *when*, *how*, and *by whom* a task will be done.
- Support involves other people, and different levels of support might be needed depending upon the task.

THE IMPORTANCE OF SUPPORT

In 2000, UCLA psychologist Shelley Taylor and her colleagues coined the phrase "tend and befriend" (in contrast to "fight or flight") to describe what they assert is an inborn, transhistorical female response to worrisome or fearful situations. "Tend and befriend" patterns, they propose, are the natural female response to crisis—behaviors that women use to protect themselves and their children while also reaching out to our social networks for support.[7]

Though women are often stereotyped as intrinsically community-oriented, "tend and befriend" doesn't work well for many women with ADHD, who may never have been successful in building and maintaining a social network due to executive function challenges. No wonder their stress levels are constantly so high! The need for a supportive social network may be one of the most challenging aspects of treating women with ADHD, and should be a central focus of your treatment.

The power of connection: Group treatment for women with ADHD

Many women with ADHD struggle to make and maintain fulfilling interpersonal relationships. Feeling socially rejected, misunderstood by others, or living with a pervasive sense of not fitting in is a common experience for women with ADHD. This feeling of being outside the social circle starts at an early age. The yearning and need to feel understood and accepted by others, coupled with the sense that it is exceptionally difficult to do so, often leads to constant efforts to camouflage their differences. Recent research has linked this pattern of thought and behavior to lower life satisfaction and depression in women with ADHD.[8]

There is a very recent and rapidly growing body of research showing that one of the most therapeutic approaches for women with ADHD is group treatment. We believe that groups can be a particularly powerful experience for women with ADHD because sharing with others who can relate to their struggles can help them feel accepted and heard, facilitating healing from chronic feelings of isolation and inadequacy.

Groups for women with ADHD can provide social connection and validation and reduce their feelings of stigma. Within the safe and accepting group environment, they begin to refine and improve their social skills. The power of these group communities can lead to relief and self-acceptance.[9,10,11,12,13,14,15,16]

Group therapy can be a powerful tool to foster the sense of community and shared identity that is so important to women who have felt criticized, misunderstood, and marginalized.

Different group therapy approaches

Below, we will list and briefly discuss a range of group therapies that can be helpful to women with ADHD. Each group targets a specific set of issues that women commonly face.

1. *CBT groups*
   A CBT group may provide the client with more productive ways to think about the impact of ADHD and how it affects her ability to manage the responsibilities in her life. At the same time, it can also offer her the understanding, comfort, and support of others who are struggling with the same issues. A CBT group approach can provide her not only with different, more constructive ways to think about her ADHD challenges, but also practical approaches for making changes in her life.[17]
2. *Women's ADHD therapy groups*
   We have found that groups are more effective when group members are in similar stages of life and similar situations. For example, women with children need their own group, while those who are child-free or whose children are older tend to thrive in a group that focuses more on personal issues and professional matters. Older women with ADHD face yet another set of concerns and benefit from being in a group of similar women. Our group model offers a combination of support, psychoeducation, and ADHD self-management strategies.

   Groups consist of approximately eight group members, facilitated by a clinician, and, in some cases, a trainee. Group members develop a list of ADHD topics on which they would like more information. The group leader then develops a brief presentation each week consisting of four or five slides. This focuses on one of the topics requested by the group members, e.g., sleep problems, social isolation, conquering clutter, or daily health habits.

   Our groups tend to last for eight to ten sessions, although we also had a very successful ongoing support group for older women with ADHD who found such pleasure in a group with other older women with ADHD that they elected to continue the group without professional support.

3. *Body-doubling groups*
   Some clinical practice groups have organized online "body-double groups" that take place at a specific time each week. A "body double" is a person who is present and supportive while the woman with ADHD performs an avoided or difficult task. Because a body double does not actively participate in the task, body-doubling can be provided online.

   Participants sign into an online "room" monitored by a trained ADHD coach. Each participant states the task that they intend to tackle during the session and then gets to work, staying online all the while so that they can communicate with other participants or the coach should they desire to do so.

   Body-doubling can focus on short-term tasks that have been avoided (cleaning out closets, etc.) or longer-term goals, such as completing a book or other project that may have been repeatedly set aside in order to deal with the multiple demands of daily life.
4. *A hormone-focused therapeutic group for women with ADHD*
   This group model, developed by ADHD researcher Sandra Kooij, MD, Ph.D., and her colleagues in the Netherlands, has a strong focus on helping women to become more aware of their menstrual cycle and its effect upon ADHD symptoms. The following article contains a detailed description of a seven-session group conducted and studied by Dr. Kooij and colleagues.[18]

Specialized groups for ADHD parents and partners

1. *Parent coaching groups*
   Parent coaching groups are focused exclusively on teaching parents to better understand their child in terms of brain differences and developmental issues. These groups focus on helping the parents to:

   - See their child through the lens of informed understanding.
   - Build a strong, close relationship with their child.
   - Engage in collaborative problem-solving with their child.
   - Present the child with choices, both of which are acceptable. For example, "You may do your homework before dinner, or after dinner, but before you have any screen time."

- Consequences should be clear. For example, "There will be no screen time today until today's homework is completed. And if your project is not finished, there will be no social time this weekend until it is done."

While these groups ideally involve both parents, more often we find that our parent coaching groups consist largely or entirely of mothers, many of whom have ADHD as well.

2. *ADHD-focused group treatment for couples*
Group treatment can provide an excellent learning platform for couples who are impacted by ADHD. Rather than locking horns or going through the litany of complaints that each has heard countless times, exploring the impact of ADHD on married partners or committed couples can be eye-opening. Simply realizing that our struggles are not unique can be helpful in itself. Through these groups, couples can learn well-established approaches to help them escape the blame game and begin making positive changes in how they relate to each other. This approach can be more effective than trying to work alone in marriage counseling.

While the "Gottman"[19] technique for helping couples in troubled marriages is well established and supported by research, it doesn't directly address the classic destructive patterns that couples with ADHD so often fall into. We find that introducing the concepts outlined by Melissa Orlov in her classic book *The ADHD Effect on Marriage*[20] can be a powerful and effective experience. Online groups for couples led by Orlov-trained group therapists are available and affordable. More research is needed regarding ADHD couples dynamics in the LGBTQ+ community.

The Orlov consulting group also offers online support groups for spouses of adults with ADHD. These groups are often sought by spouses whose partner is not interested in–or willing to participate in—a couples' workshop together.

Help her avoid putting herself last on the priority list for ADHD treatment

Women responding to social pressure to prioritize the needs of others over their own may put themselves last on the list for ADHD treatment. Your client may seek diagnosis so that she can be prescribed medication, feeling as if she can't afford to dedicate the time needed to get the therapeutic support that is an essential part of effective care.

It is critical for you to help her understand that effective treatment for her own ADHD can have a very positive effect on every area of her life, including her relationships. For example, untreated ADHD may lead a mother to talk to her children in ways she regrets when frustrated and to be inconsistent in establishing and enforcing household rules and routines. Help her to understand that treating her own ADHD will help her show up more often as her best self and enable her to create a supportive, safe home environment for her child with ADHD. ADHD treatment can help her to be the calm, consistent parent she aspires to be.

ADDRESSING ADHD TENDENCIES IN THERAPY

Forgetfulness

The following approaches may help with reducing forgetfulness and improving follow-through.

- Creating visual cues. One woman learned to place her empty laundry basket at the top of the stairs leading to the basement washer and dryer. This visual cue reminded her to head to the basement to put clothes from the washer into the dryer (in the past, wet clothes might have stayed in the dryer for a day or more), and was also her cue to retrieve the clean clothes from the dryer to bring upstairs and put away. But tell your client to beware of too many reminders that can lead to confusion and therefore no longer serve their purpose!
- Setting task reminders on a smartphone.
- Building in accountability. For example, ask your client to message you to report that she has completed a certain task. Accountability provides much-needed support and structure.
- Adding support at home. Ask if there is anyone in your client's life who can serve as a helpful support in accomplishing the task. Remember, using the three S's—strategies, structure, and support—can help her accomplish great change gradually.

Task avoidance

To become effective in helping our patients make behavioral changes, we need to develop a deep understanding of what it's like to live in the world with an ADHD brain. Yes, the patient may be prone to task avoidance.

But ADHD brains can dive into a project with enthusiasm if it interests them. The ADHD brain is an "interest-driven" brain. "But everything isn't going to be interesting," you might respond. "There are some things that just need to be done. That's part of being a responsible adult." Overhearing this imagined conversation, it's clear that an intervention that takes this approach will not be helpful and will only contribute to the patient's feelings of self-blame and shame. However, if you operate with an intuitive understanding of "interest-driven brains," you might engage in an enjoyable problem-solving process with your patient.

For example, you might ask her what could make cleaning up her bedroom more fun, more motivating, or, at least, less disagreeable. Here are some suggestions that you might make to your client that have helped other women with ADHD.

- **Make daunting tasks social!** Advise your client to reach out to friends or family members to make a task more social and supportive. Women in an ADHD therapy group we conducted at our center spontaneously engaged in mutual organizing sessions. "I'll come over and help you this weekend and then you can return the favor next weekend!" These women felt safe and accepted by each other and could turn a dig-out into an enjoyable enterprise.
- **Do disagreeable tasks in brief bursts**. Advise your client to set a timer for 10 minutes instead of committing to hours of work, and challenge herself to see how much she can get done. She should try this every evening for a week and come in the next week to report on her progress. There's nothing more daunting, nothing more likely to induce avoidance, than facing what looks like an overwhelming task.
- **Approach struggles with humor and mutual support**. At one session of an adult ADHD support group led by Dr. Nadeau, participants enjoyed a fun evening in which everyone brought in a photo of their biggest mess. They all voted and the winner was awarded a prize—a t-shirt reading, "I put the fun in dysfunctional!" Humor can make the most daunting task feel less overwhelming. You can advise your client to photograph her progress daily and share the photos with supportive friends, family members, or other women with ADHD. Better yet, she could reach out to another friend with ADHD so they can mutually support one another through documenting their daily progress.
- **Listen to music while cleaning up and decluttering**. Just as music helps many people exercise more vigorously, it can also help your clients tackle a difficult clean-up task. Ask your client to identify music that feels upbeat and energizing and to regularly play this music when engaging in necessary but disagreeable tasks.

- **Use a body double**. A body double is someone—either a friend or family member— who simply sits and keeps the patient company as she completes a task she's been avoiding.
- **Join *Focus Mate***. This is a low-cost online service that brings total strangers together online at a specific time to accomplish tasks they have been avoiding. The task might be the same or completely different. The two "focus mates" join each other online through the Focus Mate app, declare their task intention, and then remain online for a specified amount of time while they each tackle their dreaded task. (See Focusmate.com)
- **Do the task in a therapy session (especially in cases when avoidance is prolonged)**. Your patient may avoid tasks due to anxiety, feel too embarrassed to make an important phone call, or resist writing an important email or letter because she's not sure what to say. When a critical task is repeatedly avoided, set a task deadline, with an agreement that if the task is not completed before the next therapy session, you'll tackle it together during that session. Doing a task during the psychotherapy session provides the client with the structure, support, and strategies she needs to get the task done. While some tasks cannot be accomplished during a psychotherapy session, many can.
- **Do prep work in advance**. Coach your client to "pre-prepare" by putting everything she will need for the activity in an obvious place, where seeing it will prompt her to begin.

Poor time management

Is the client's lack of follow-through attributable to ADHD-related time-management challenges? A number of common ADHD tendencies may be at work. Her poor time-management tendencies may include:

- **Underestimating how long tasks will take**. Get her to make time estimations prior to doing a task: then she can see how inaccurate her time estimations are.
- **Impulsively taking on a task**, not considering whether she has the time.
- **Chronically overcommitting** in an effort to people-please or to get back in the good graces of people in her life that she may have let down in the past.

Helping her to recognize and begin to change these patterns will be an important part of her therapy.

Distraction

Forgetfulness and distraction go hand in hand. When we are distracted, we tend to forget. As her psychotherapist, a significant part of your work with the client will consist of problem-solving with her to decrease her forgetfulness and distractibility. Anxiety and stress in patients with ADHD both increase the more often they forget tasks or arrive late for important events.

> Decreasing forgetfulness and distractibility is one of the best ways to treat your client's anxiety.

We all live in a hyper-distracting world. We receive countless calls and messages on our phones with the expectation that a text message should receive an almost immediate response. And emails aren't far behind—today, the standard expectation is a same-day response. This hyper-connected, hyper-distracting environment makes it even harder for women with ADHD to remain focused. Here are some principles that may be useful for your client to follow.

- **Do it now!** One means of avoiding forgetfulness and distraction is to complete a task the moment one thinks of it—even if it's not particularly convenient. In other words, keep tasks off the task list by completing them as they are thought of. The one risk of this approach is that the immediate task may be a distraction from a previously planned task or one that is currently in process. **Write it down!** Not on a scrap of paper, but in a master list of things to remember to do, which you always keep in the same place.
- **Don't try to keep it in your head**. Many with ADHD continually lie to themselves, thinking that they can "keep it in their head" and that there is no need to record a to-do despite overwhelming evidence to the contrary.
- **Help her to problem-solve** to develop a to-do system that works for her.

Escapism

People with ADHD have a strong tendency to escape and avoid when faced with what feel like relentless or overwhelming daily demands.

When faced with clutter and mess at home, or with an anxiety-producing school or work task, they may resort to what is referred to in some corners of the internet as "bed rotting," binge-watching a series online or escaping into social media. Online shopping and "doomscrolling" (a compulsive pattern of scrolling online through negative or upsetting news) are other avoidant pastimes. Unfortunately, going online is like going down the rabbit hole: they lose track of time, hooked by the "one more thing" compulsion that online platforms are so good at creating. This pattern means they are not only avoiding tasks but also depriving themselves of sleep ("Revenge Bedtime Procrastination"), making the next day even more exhausting. Some approaches that may help reduce escapist tendencies include:

- **Using a carefully selected "escape" activity as a reward for task completion**. Advise your client to enjoy a phone call with a friend after she has completed folding the laundry, or plan a walk with a neighbor that she can look forward to taking after cleaning up the kitchen.
- **Using audio escapes that don't interfere with tasks**. For example, she might consider listening to an audiobook that offers pleasant escape and distraction but doesn't interfere with completion of household tasks.
- **Morning "me-time" escapes**. Because night-time escapes can expand endlessly, interfering with much-needed sleep, encourage her to develop morning "me time" instead—going to bed earlier and waking with time for tea and time in her favorite chair, social media, a podcast, yoga, or stretching before the day's demands begin.

Anxiety leading to perfectionism

When avoidance is driven by resistance to necessary but unappealing tasks, the approaches discussed previously will help get your patient motivated and able to complete them. However, when anxiety is the primary driver of avoidance, then simply giving your patient tools to reduce avoidance won't be helpful because they don't address the core issue.

This is a differential assessment that is important for you to make as a clinician. If anxiety is the primary driver of avoidance, then therapeutic techniques to recognize and reduce anxiety are an essential part of the treatment approach. (See the discussion later in this chapter in the "Co-occurring conditions" section.)

Low motivation

Sometimes the problem is low motivation. Maybe your patient feels overwhelmed by relentless daily life management demands. She may be struggling with co-occurring depression. Or she may be one of those women whose brain is intensely "interest driven"—a common ADHD trait—and can only get going on a task if she finds it interesting (in contrast to important). Some ways to help improve low motivation include:

ADHD-INFORMED ACCEPTANCE AND COMMITMENT THERAPY (ACT)[21]

Acceptance and Commitment Therapy (ACT) can be very helpful for those of your patients who have a strongly interest-driven brain. ACT focuses on helping your patient get in touch with their core values so that she can distinguish between the "oughts" imposed on her by others and her own "oughts," which are related to her deep core values.

You can find the *Valued Living Questionnaire* online. This brief questionnaire helps your patient to identify which issues are in line with her deep core values (in contrast to the values that may be imposed upon her by family, friends, and society in general).

Your task as a psychotherapist, using ACT techniques, is to help your patient get in touch with what matters most to her so that she can align her actions with those values and become motivated to pursue them.

> To read more about ACT for ADHD:
>
> Steven Hayes and Spencer Smith, *Get Out of Your Mind and Into Your Life: The New Acceptance and Commitment Therapy* (A New Harbinger Self-Help Workbook)[22]

ADHD-INFORMED MOTIVATIONAL INTERVIEWING

While some describe ADHD in very negative terms as a sort of "maladaptive personality,"[23] Motivational Interviewing[24] takes a very different approach. It begins with deep empathy for the patient, which you express by listening closely and reflecting back what you understand her to be saying. Your reaction is entirely nonjudgmental. She has come to you seeking help to lead a life more in line with her core values and true self, and you are there to facilitate that process.

As a psychotherapist using Motivational Interviewing, you:

- Are deeply empathetic.
- Work in clear collaboration with your patient.
- Help her to get in touch with what truly matters to her.
- Support her in the belief that she has the capacity—the "self-efficacy"—to do what needs to be done to create a life synchronous with her inner values. (We will write more about this in concrete terms in Chapter 11, which focuses on creating an ADHD-friendly lifestyle.)

> It's a long, slow road from escape and avoidance to task completion, a road best traveled in the company of a psychotherapist
>
> Encourage her to take one small, positive step at a time. This is the first and necessary step toward making all the other changes that she needs to slowly and consistently make in her life.

Other therapeutic techniques from an ADHD-informed perspective

ADHD-INFORMED COGNITIVE BEHAVIORAL THERAPY (CBT)[25,26]

CBT has been studied more than any other approach as a therapeutic treatment for ADHD. It involves identifying and changing maladaptive thought patterns and practical approaches to improve daily functioning to reduce forgetfulness and improve organization and task completion.

Negative, self-defeating thought patterns resulting from years of shame and self-blame are common among women with ADHD. Frequently-reported childhood experiences for women with ADHD, such as struggling to complete assigned household chores and school assignments, may have left your client with a pervasive sense of inadequacy. Among those women with ADHD who are academically successful, that success is usually achieved through an intense, stress-filled perfectionism that is punishing to maintain. Their effort to achieve in one area is often paid for by neglecting most other areas of their lives. A professional who is a high achiever at work may report to you that her house is in chaos, or that she has little to no social life because all her efforts are focused on managing professional demands.

As a psychotherapist, you are very likely to have learned CBT treatment approaches during your training. It is the most evidence-based widely practiced treatment approach today. By incorporating your understanding of the basic challenges of ADHD, you can provide your patients with ADHD-informed CBT that addresses the typical challenges women encounter, including forgetfulness, distractibility, and time-blindness.

> To learn more about CBT for ADHD, we recommend the following two books written by highly recognized ADHD authorities:
>
> *Cognitive-Behavioral Therapy for Adult ADHD: An Integrative Psychosocial and Medical Approach, 2nd Edition, by J. Russell Ramsay and Tony Rostain (Routledge, 2014)*
>
> *Cognitive-Behavioral Therapy for Adult ADHD: Targeting Executive Dysfunction*, by Mary Solanto (Paperback Edition, Guilford Press, 2013).

ADHD-INFORMED POSITIVE PSYCHOLOGY [27,28]

Traditionally, we have defined ADHD purely in negative terms—as a disability, a dysfunctional brain that we can only try to modify, or as a "maladaptive personality." The title of one of the very early books on women with ADHD, *You Mean I'm not Lazy, Stupid, or Crazy?!*, says it all.

> Using positive psychology techniques, we can shift the focus of therapy from problems to possibilities.

It's no mystery where the negativity comes from. Most children with ADHD grow up in a school environment that is ADHD-unfriendly. The classroom is highly distracting; they are expected to sit still for hours each day listening to a teacher, when their auditory learning channel may not be strong; they are expected to learn many things that hold no interest for them. Though initially researchers primarily focused on the learning challenges of openly disruptive boys with ADHD, girls with ADHD are also at a great disadvantage compared to their peers. They can be restless, tuned out, easily bored and frustrated, or highly anxious and fearful of embarrassment. In addition, many of them have learning disorders that make learning even more difficult.

After spending years in an environment ill-suited to learners with ADHD, many young adult women develop a negative self-image. They expect to fall short, make mistakes, and receive frequent criticism. After being forced to function in an ADHD-unfriendly school environment for so many years, learned helplessness sets in. After years of defeat, many women believe that trying is futile.

As a psychotherapist, your daunting task, as the old song goes, is to "accentuate the positive" and "eliminate the negative." Your patient has most likely spent her life feeling that she doesn't fit in and doesn't meet expectations. Girls are often socialized to believe they must always look perfect and be well-organized, but girls with ADHD are more likely to have untidy hair, stains on their t-shirts, and multiple items in permanent residence in the school's lost-and-found. Therefore, they may experience a painful dissonance between who they are and who they believe they are expected to be.

Positive psychology techniques can be very effective in counteracting the years of negative feedback experienced by most women. Instead of focusing on what's "wrong," this approach focuses on what's "right," emphasizing strengths and possibilities rather than symptoms or failures in an individual's life.

As a psychotherapist, when you ask a patient to list things for which she is grateful or to focus on positive feelings of joy and hope, you are taking a positive psychology approach. Through this framework, you can teach your patient to:

- **Build resilience**: resilience, or the ability to maintain a sense of self-efficacy even in the most challenging circumstances, is a useful resource for women with ADHD, as it helps them counteract the setbacks they experience.
- **Develop a growth mindset**. This involves helping the women you work with to believe that they are capable of growing and developing throughout their lives. Instead of feeling that they have no choice but to live with a "defective brain," guide them to focus on their goals, their dreams, their abilities, and the concrete steps they need to take in order to find an environment in which they can thrive.
- **Strengthen her belief in her capacity for self-determination**. Reflecting the importance of this, the theory of the "hierarchy of needs" has recently been updated to include autonomy, competence, and close connection to others.[29]

Your female patients with ADHD have likely gone through years of feeling incompetent in one or more spheres of their lives. As a result, they may doubt their ability to rely upon themselves or to build and maintain relationships in which they feel connected and cared for. You can become their guide, helping them to reach out and build close, trusting relationships, while developing faith in their own abilities and judgment.

TREATING "ADHD +": COMORBIDITIES THAT OFTEN ACCOMPANY ADHD

In this last section of our chapter on the "therapeutic toolkit," we draw your attention to the importance of treating the complex disorder that we call "ADHD +." Effective treatment requires us to always keep in mind the near inevitability of co-occurring conditions. Because there are so many co-occurring conditions that accompany ADHD, in this section we only highlight the most common ones and encourage you to explore others as needed, depending upon the needs of your patients.

Anxiety and ADHD

Anxiety is the most prevalent coexisting condition for women with ADHD, with estimates suggesting that at least 50% of women with ADHD experience anxiety. Anxiety may be caused by the client's ADHD or may be a separate, coexisting condition. We have discussed the medications used to reduce anxiety in Chapter 6. However, there are highly effective non-medication approaches to reducing anxiety. As a psychotherapist, addressing anxiety will be an ongoing focus in your work.

ADHD-INFORMED MINDFULNESS MEDITATION FOR ANXIETY AND ADHD

Guided mindfulness meditation combined with deep breathing has been shown to be a very effective way to reduce challenges associated with ADHD. Lidia Zylowska, an ADHD expert and psychiatrist, carried out research that demonstrated the powerful impact of mindfulness meditation. ADHD-specific mindfulness meditation can be conducted very successfully in a group setting; this provides patients with the additional benefit of feeling connected and validated by the presence of other women who are struggling with similar challenges.

For more information read Lidia Zylowska, *The Mindfulness Prescription for Adult ADHD: An 8-Step Program For Strengthening Attention, Managing Emotions, and Achieving Your Goals* (Trumpeter Press).[30]

BIOFEEDBACK FOR ANXIETY REDUCTION

The HeartMath emWave[31] is a biofeedback device that psychotherapists can use in a professional office setting. It focuses on using biofeedback to help the patient reduce their heart rate variability, a measure of stress and anxiety. Portable units can be purchased by patients for regular use at home. There is a strong and rapidly growing body of evidence that these devices can reduce anxiety and feelings of stress and improve the patient's overall sense of well-being. For more information, go to heartmath.com.

ADHD-INFORMED CBT FOR ANXIETY

There are multiple ways to reduce anxiety. The methods described above involve calming the sympathetic nervous system—through deep breathing, mindfulness, progressive relaxation, biofeedback, or medication. But there is a strong body of evidence that changing our thoughts about a specific situation can in turn change our feelings about that situation. For this reason, CBT has shown great promise in reducing anxiety.[32]

CBT is founded on the belief that our thoughts about a situation precede our feelings about that same situation. In other words, if we think, "I'm stupid and didn't study enough, so I'm going to fail this exam," that thought will be followed by growing anxiety that may make our prediction come true. Conversely, if we challenge that thought—telling ourselves that we are not stupid, that we are as smart as or smarter than many other people taking the exam, and that while we may not know the answer to every item on the paper, our preparation was adequate for us to pass and possibly even do very well—then our anxiety level will be much lower. We might remind ourselves that we felt this anxious before another recent exam but actually did quite well. In other words, we break the habit of predicting and anticipating the worst possible outcome.

For more information we recommend: *The Adult ADHD and Anxiety Workbook: Cognitive Behavioral Therapy Skills to Manage Stress, Find Focus, and Reclaim Your Life*, by Russell Ramsay, Ph.D.[33]

ADHD and bipolar disorder

Bipolar disorder (BD) shares several symptoms with adult ADHD including hyperactivity, impulsivity, distractibility, and emotional dysregulation with ADHD symptoms being chronic and persistent while these symptoms in bipolar disorder are episodic in nature. Besides an overlapping clinical presentation, BD often co-occurs in adults with ADHD, with comorbidity figures as high as 20%.[34]

It is critical to stabilize BD before adding psychostimulants to treat ADHD.

Psychoeducation about BD and ADHD is essential, as is careful monitoring and supervision as your patient with ADHD learns to manage both conditions through medication, therapy, and self-care—for example prioritizing sleep and a lower stress daily routine.

However, too much caution in prescribing stimulants can backfire, leaving patients without the tools to maintain habits that support bipolar stability. Stimulant medication can improve executive functions, thereby allowing your client with BD to more carefully manage her day-to-day lifestyle, which, in turn, will help her to keep BD fluctuations at bay. (See Chapter 6 on medications used to treat BD.)[35,36]

ADHD and eating disorders

There is significant overlap between ADHD and eating disorders, with one study finding that 28% of patients at an eating disorder clinic had an ADHD diagnosis, much higher than the incidence of ADHD in the adult population.[37]

The relationship between ADHD and eating disorders is complex. On the one hand, ADHD impulsivity can contribute to the development of binge-eating disorder and bulimia. These two eating disorders are distinguished in that binge-eating disorder does not involve purging, excessive exercise, or other measures to counteract the sudden intake of calories. In binge-eating disorder, stimulant medication is a recent treatment approach that has proven helpful, and, in fact, the FDA has approved Lisdexamfetamine (Vyvanse®) for the treatment of compulsive eating when not accompanied by purging behaviors.[38] More often, SSRIs (selective serotonin reuptake inhibitors) have been used effectively in treating bulimia.

But, in an apparent contradiction, ADHD is also associated with anorexia. Anorexia, an intense hyper-focused effort to drastically restrict food intake in people who are otherwise struggling with emotional dysregulation and impulsivity, can be fueled in part by the intense social pressure many women feel to avoid weight gain at any cost.

In addition to diagnosed eating disorders such as the ones named above, women with ADHD are particularly prone to disordered eating habits that don't meet DSM-V criteria, including eating without awareness of internal hunger and satiety cues (mindless eating), eating in the middle of the night to help oneself to get back to sleep, and frequent overeating of high-calorie processed foods with low nutritional value. Eating urges among some women with ADHD can be so strong that some women who have undergone gastric bypass surgery for weight loss have returned to compulsive eating patterns, behaviors that are strongly associated with the emotional dysregulation so common in women with ADHD. Therapy focused on improving emotional regulation can be very helpful in changing eating patterns that often negatively impact clients' overall quality of life.

ADHD and substance use disorders

REDUCING DESTRUCTIVE SELF-MEDICATION

Self-medication with food, alcohol, marijuana, and nicotine are other patterns common to many women with ADHD. A woman may turn to food as an immediate reward that temporarily helps her to feel calmer.[39,40] This pattern, over time, may contribute to the development of chronic health conditions such as type 2 diabetes.

Alcohol is also a commonly used "self-medication" for women with ADHD, who are at much higher risk of alcohol use dependence compared to women without ADHD.[41] Recently, concern about alcohol use has increased as it has been determined to be carcinogenic. Marijuana and CBD are also commonly turned to as forms of self-medication.[42] In our clinical experience, women report using it at night to help them calm down and fall asleep. Some report that marijuana (or CBD) is more effective than the medications prescribed by their physician to manage anxiety. The relief from anxiety certainly needs to be balanced with evidence of long-term cognitive problems linked to chronic marijuana use.

Nicotine is often the earliest form of self-medication that a woman uses, with girls as young as 11 turning to cigarettes and, more recently, to vaping. Nicotine can help women with ADHD feel temporarily calmer and more focused, but it is highly addictive and prolonged use presents substantial health risks.[43,44]

Overall, women with ADHD are at high risk of developing strong dependence upon substances used for self-medication, which are typically efforts at self-calming.

True addiction is difficult to treat and may require a referral to an addiction treatment program, but before you refer your patient elsewhere, try some of the following approaches first:

1. **Consistent use of stimulant medication**. Studies demonstrate that stimulant medication can be very helpful in controlling impulsive behaviors. Even in addiction treatment programs, there has been a gradual shift toward realizing that stimulant medication can be part of successful treatment for binge-eating disorder and alcohol abuse.
2. **Habit substitution**. Binge eating, night eating, and overeating in general can be reduced through habit substitution—developing new, health-supporting calm-down rituals and routines. Advise your client to have measured portions of nutritious, filling treats readily available when hunger strikes.
3. **Temptation avoidance—**when cigarettes, sweets, or alcohol are not readily available at home, they are less convenient and less likely to be resorted to; advise your client not to keep any treats in the house that are too tempting to avoid.
4. **Avoid visual triggers**. For example, one woman we treated had a habit of stopping by McDonald's or Dunkin' Donuts on the way home from work. Avoidance of indulging in these habits was easier after she decided to drive home via a different route.

Treatment for ADHD and self-harm and suicidality

The most effective and evidence-based psychotherapeutic treatment for self-harm is comprehensive dialectical behavioral therapy (DBT, see Chapter 6). This is distinct from DBT-informed psychotherapy, which adopts many DBT tools. Comprehensive DBT involves intensive individual and group treatment. In DBT-informed therapy, treatment is customized based on the individual needs of the client rather than following the rigid structures of full DBT.[45]

The level of DBT approach that is needed should be determined by the level of acuity and intensity of symptoms. If you are treating a woman whose emotional dysregulation is creating enormous disruption in most aspects of her life, or involves active suicidal thinking, then an intensive DBT program is advisable.

Conversely, many women, especially those who have a more hyperactive/impulsive presentation, also manifest a dramatic level of emotional dysregulation without self-harm or suicidality. These women may benefit from a less intensive, DBT-informed treatment approach that teaches core DBT modules such as mindfulness, emotion regulation, distress tolerance, and interpersonal skills to improve their emotional awareness and coping abilities.

DBT-informed therapy is emerging as an important therapeutic tool. It is used to help women with ADHD develop better emotional regulation, learn to put interpersonal conflicts in perspective, and be generally less vulnerable to the inevitable conflicts that develop in relationships.

There is a need for more research in best treatment approaches when treating women with co-occurring ADHD and borderline personality disorder. There is a clear overlap in the symptomatology of ADHD and BPD; this includes impulsive reactions, interpersonal oversensitivity to real or imagined interpersonal slights, and high levels of anxiety. Furthermore, risk of suicidality is significant both in women with ADHD and those with BPD, another critical link that needs to be addressed.

Emotional dysregulation may exist in women with ADHD, especially those who have experienced emotional neglect in childhood. If a girl with ADHD is met with invalidation and lack of support as a child, she may later develop significant rejection sensitivity (RSD) and experience intense reactions to both real and perceived criticism or rejection. For women with ADHD-related RSD, DBT-informed treatment seems a highly appropriate approach, although more research is needed to support the face validity of this methodology.

DBT specifically operates on the basis of several core principles. These are:

- **Dialectical thinking**—learning to view situations from multiple viewpoints, and realizing that two contradictory views may both be valid.
- **Mindfulness—**which we have introduced elsewhere as a core ADHD treatment.
- **Emotion regulation**—learning to calm down and use "wise mind" to view an upsetting situation more rationally.
- **Distress tolerance**—gaining confidence that one can survive intensely unpleasant circumstances and become stronger in the process.
- **Interpersonal effectiveness**—the ability to communicate one's needs, set boundaries, and build positive connections with others.
- **Validation**—acknowledging the validity of a person's thoughts and behaviors in the context of their past experiences without necessarily condoning that behavior.

Rejection Sensitive Dysphoria (RSD) is characterized by extreme emotional distress due to real or perceived rejection. DBT is not merely about reducing symptoms; it also emphasizes validating emotional experiences and developing more adaptive coping mechanisms. This alignment with the therapeutic goals is supported by findings that therapy can help individuals redefine their emotional experiences and improve their relationships.[46]

The strategies employed in DBT can also be useful ways of confronting and processing past emotional traumas, which are often at the root of emotional dysregulation.

DBT-informed therapy offers a strong framework for addressing both emotional dysregulation and RSD by building emotional skills and adaptive coping strategies.[47,48,49]

Treating C-PTSD in women with ADHD

Complex Post-Traumatic Stress Disorder (C-PTSD) involves the symptoms of PTSD, as well as features related to more pervasive traumas, often beginning in childhood. In a study of immigrant women with late-diagnosed ADHD who were struggling to complete their education as middle-aged women, most reported that trauma associated with their undiagnosed ADHD, such as feeling shamed and blamed by teachers, parents and peers, had impacted them more negatively than the many other traumas they had experienced in their very difficult lives. C-PTSD involves widespread disturbances in self-concept, self-regulation, and interpersonal relationships. C-PTSD is characterized by persistent negative emotions, feelings of emptiness, and difficulty with relationships arising from prolonged exposure to traumatic events. Relational childhood trauma, such as ridicule, abuse from caregivers, shaming by adults, and teasing and bullying by peers places people at high risk of developing C-PTSD.[50]

Our thinking about trauma has changed over the years. Formerly, the term "trauma" referred only to life-threatening or life-altering events—dangerous physical assaults, witnessing a murder, or living in a war zone or earthquake zone. Twenty-five years ago, when we published our first book on women with ADHD, we wrote about the relentless accumulation of "small-t" traumas almost apologetically, since these events weren't considered to damage people in the same way. However, more recent research has documented that individuals with C-PTSD report a higher symptom burden and greater impairment in functioning compared to those with PTSD, highlighting the clinically significant differences between these disorders and supporting the need for tailored therapeutic approaches.[51]

Making the diagnostic distinction between C-PTSD and PTSD is not only helpful for understanding these conditions but also crucial to treatment planning.[52] In treating C-PTSD, the consensus is to take a phase-based treatment approach, beginning with stabilizing a woman's emotional state, focusing on emotional regulation, and providing psychoeducation to help her better understand herself and her needs, before introducing exposure- or cognitive-based therapies aimed at trauma processing.[53,54,55]

SUMMARY

Our goal in this chapter is to introduce a range of challenges typically experienced by women with ADHD, along with an introduction to a broad variety of therapeutic techniques that can be helpful. Many of the therapeutic techniques we introduce here were not initially developed specifically for ADHD, but in recent years have been modified so that they are "ADHD-informed" in their approach. We have only been able to offer brief descriptions of each therapeutic technique, and we encourage you to develop more in-depth therapeutic skills as part of your ongoing therapeutic training.

REFERENCES

1. Adelizzi, J. U. (2002). Posttraumatic stress in women with AD/HD. In P. O. Quinn & K. G. Nadeau (Eds.), *Gender issues and AD/HD* (pp. 365–393). Advantage Books.
2. Briscoe-Smith, A., & Hinshaw, S. P. (2006). Linkages between child abuse and attention-deficit/hyperactivity disorder in girls: behavioral and social correlates. *Child Abuse & Neglect*, *30*(11), 1239–1255. https://doi.org/10.1016/j.chiabu.2006.04.008
3. Janiczak, D., Perez-Reisler, M., & Ballard, R. (2020). Diagnosis and management of comorbid anxiety and ADHD in pediatric primary care. *Pediatric Annals*, *49*(10). https://doi.org/10.3928/19382359-20200922-01
4. Pehlivanidis, A., Papanikolaou, K., Mantas, V., Kalantzi, E., Korobili, K., Xenaki, L., & Papageorgiou, C. (2020). Lifetime co-occurring psychiatric disorders in newly diagnosed adults with attention deficit hyperactivity disorder (ADHD) or/and autism spectrum disorder (ASD). *BMC Psychiatry*, *20*(1), 423. https://doi.org/10.1186/s12888-020-02828-1
5. Manos, M. J., & Short, E. J. (2023). A new paradigm for adult ADHD: a focused strategy to monitor treatment. *Cleveland Clinic Journal of Medicine*, *90*(7), 413–421. https://doi.org/10.3949/ccjm.90a.22080

6. Kolberg, J., & Nadeau, K. (2016). *ADD-friendly ways to organize your life: Strategies that work from an acclaimed professional organizer and a renowned ADD clinician* (2nd ed.). Routledge.
7. Taylor, S. E., Klein, L. C., Lewis, B. P., Gruenewald, T. L., Gurung, R. A. R., & Updegraff, J. A. (2000). Biobehavioral responses to stress in females: tend-and-befriend, not fight-or-flight. *Psychological Review, 107*(3), 411–429. https://doi.org/10.1037/0033-295X.107.3.411
8. Wicherkiewicz, F., & Gambin, M. (2024). Relations between social camouflaging, life satisfaction, and depression among Polish women with ADHD. *Journal of Autism and Developmental Disorders.* Advance online publication. https://doi.org/10.1007/s10803-024-06410-6
9. Visser, M., Peters, R., & Luman, M. (2024). Understanding ADHD-related stigma: a gender analysis of young adult and key stakeholder perspectives. *Neurodiversity, 2.* https://doi.org/10.1177/27546330241274664
10. Babinski, D., & Libsack, E. (2024). Adult diagnosis of ADHD in women: a mixed methods investigation. *Journal of Attention Disorders, 29*(3), 207–219. https://doi.org/10.1177/10870547241297897
11. De Jong, M., Wynchank, D. S. M. R., Michielsen, M., Beekman, A. T. F., & Kooij, J. J. S. (2024). A female-specific treatment group for ADHD: description of the programme and qualitative analysis of first experience. *Journal of Clinical Medicine, 13*(7), 2106.
12. Wicherkiewicz, F., & Gambin, M. (2024). Relations between social camouflaging, life satisfaction, and depression among Polish women with ADHD. *Journal of Autism and Developmental Disorders.* Advance online publication. https://doi.org/10.1007/s10803-024-06410-6
13. Young, S., Adamo, N., Ásgeirsdóttir, B. B., Branney, P., Beckett, M., Colley, W., Courtenay, K., Gudjonsson, G., Oades, R. D., Petkova, E., Sacco, R., Semahegn, A., Shiel, R., Singh, I., Street, C., Trambley, J., & Woodhouse, E. (2020). Females with ADHD: an expert consensus statement taking a lifespan approach providing guidance for the identification and treatment of attention-deficit/hyperactivity disorder in girls and women. *BMC Psychiatry, 20*(1), 404. https://doi.org/10.1186/s12888-020-02707-9
14. Gutman, S. A., Balasubramanian, S., Herzog, M., Kim, E., Swirnow, H., Retig, Y., & Wolff, S. (2019). Effectiveness of a tailored intervention for women with attention deficit hyperactivity disorder (ADHD) and ADHD symptoms: a randomized controlled study. *American Journal of Occupational Therapy, 74*(1), 7401205010p1–7401205010p11. https://doi.org/10.5014/ajot.2020.033316
15. De Jong, M., Wynchank, D. S. M. R., Michielsen, M., Beekman, A. T. F., & Kooij, J. J. S. (2024). A female-specific treatment group for ADHD: description of the programme and qualitative analysis of first experience. *Journal of Clinical Medicine, 13*(7), 2106.
16. Visser, M., Peters, R., & Luman, M. (2024). Understanding ADHD-related stigma: a gender analysis of young adult and key stakeholder perspectives. *Neurodiversity, 2.* https://doi.org/10.1177/27546330241274664
17. Babinski, D. E., Sibley, M. H., Ross, J. M., & Pelham, W. E. (2013). The effects of single versus mixed gender treatment for adolescent girls with ADHD. *Journal of Clinical Child & Adolescent Psychology, 42*(2), 243–250. https://doi.org/10.1080/15374416.2012.756814
18. De Jong, M., Wynchank, D. S. M. R., Michielsen, M., Beekman, A. T. F., & Kooij, J. J. S. (2024). A female-specific treatment group for ADHD: description of the programme and qualitative analysis of first experience. *Journal of Clinical Medicine, 13*(7), 2106.

19. Cobb, R. A. (2017). [Review of the book *10 principles for doing effective couples therapy*, by J. S. Gottman & J. M. Gottman]. *Journal of Couple & Relationship Therapy, 16*(2), 165–167. https://doi.org/10.1080/15332691.2017.1302251
20. Orlov, M. (2010). *The ADHD effect on marriage: understand and rebuild your relationship in six steps*. Specialty Press/ADD Warehouse.
21. Seery, C., Leonard-Curtin, A., Naismith, L., King, N., O'Donnell, F., Byrne, B., Boyd, C., Kilbride, K., Wrigley, M., McHugh, L., & Bramham, J. (2024). Feasibility of the Understanding and Managing Adult ADHD Programme: open-access online group psychoeducation and acceptance and commitment therapy for adults with attention-deficit hyperactivity disorder. *BJPsych Open, 10*(5), e163. https://doi.org/10.1192/bjo.2024.743
22. Hayes, S. C., & Smith, S. (2025). *Get out of your mind and into your life: the new acceptance and commitment therapy (A New Harbinger self-help workbook)*. New Harbinger.
23. Jacobsson, P., Hopwood, C. J., Söderpalm, B., & Nilsson, T. (2021). Adult ADHD and emerging models of maladaptive personality: a meta-analytic review. *BMC Psychiatry, 21*(1). https://doi.org/10.1186/s12888-021-03284-1
24. Mackenzie, G. (2017). Integrating motivational interviewing and ADHD coaching: a comprehensive approach towards treatment for youth. *Critical Intersections in Education: An OISE/UT Students' Journal, 1*(1), 1–18.
25. Ramsay, J. R., & Rostain, A. L. (2015). *Cognitive-behavioral therapy for adult ADHD: an integrative psychosocial and medical approach* (2nd ed.). Routledge/Taylor & Francis Group.
26. Solanto, M. V. (2013). *Cognitive-behavioral therapy for adult ADHD: targeting executive dysfunction*. Guilford Press.
27. Champ, R. E., Adamou, M., & Tolchard, B. (2021). The impact of psychological theory on the treatment of attention deficit hyperactivity disorder (ADHD) in adults: a scoping review. *PLOS One, 16*(12), e0261247. https://doi.org/10.1371/journal.pone.0261247
28. Schrevel, S. J. C., Dedding, C., & Broerse, J. E. W. (2016). Why do adults with ADHD choose strength-based coaching over public mental health care? A qualitative case study from the Netherlands. *Sage Open, 6*(3). https://doi.org/10.1177/2158244016662498
29. Deci, E. L., & Ryan, R. M. (2014). The importance of universal psychological needs for understanding motivation in the workplace. In M. Gagné (Ed.), *The Oxford handbook of work engagement, motivation, and self-determination theory* (pp. 13–32). Oxford University Press.
30. Zylowska, L. (2012). *The mindfulness prescription for adult ADHD: an 8-step program for strengthening attention, managing emotions, and achieving your goals*. Trumpeter Press.
31. McCraty, R. (2022). Following the rhythm of the heart: Heartmath Institute's path to HRV biofeedback. *Applied Psychophysiology and Biofeedback, 47*(4), 305–316. https://doi.org/10.1007/s10484-022-09554-2
32. Liu, C., Hua, M., Lu, M., & Goh, K. K. (2023). Effectiveness of cognitive behavioural-based interventions for adults with attention-deficit/hyperactivity disorder extends beyond core symptoms: a meta-analysis of randomized controlled trials. *Psychology and Psychotherapy: Theory, Research and Practice, 96*(3), 543–559. https://doi.org/10.1111/papt.12455
33. Ramsay, R. (2024). *The adult ADHD and anxiety workbook: cognitive behavioral therapy skills to manage stress, find focus, and reclaim your life*. New Harbinger Publications.
34. Salvi, V., Ribuoli, E., Servasi, M., Orsolini, L., & Volpe, U. (2021). ADHD and bipolar disorder in adulthood: clinical and treatment implications. *Medicina, 57*(5), 466. https://doi.org/10.3390/medicina57050466

35. Miskowiak, K. W., Obel, Z. K., Gugliemo, R., del Mar Bonnin, C., Bowie, C. R., Balanza-Martinez, V., Burdick, K. E., Carvalho, A. F., Dols, A., Douglas, K. M., Gallagher, P., Kessing, L. V., Lafer, B., Lewandowski, K. E., Lopez-Jaramillo, C., Martinez-Arán, A., McIntyre, R. S., Porter, R. J., Purdon, S. E., Schaffer, A., Stokes, P., Sumiyoshi, T., Torres, I. J., Van Rheenen, T., Yatham, L. N., Young, A., Vieta, E., & Hasler, G. (2024). *Efficacy and safety of established and off-label ADHD drug therapies for cognitive impairment or attention-deficit hyperactivity disorder symptoms in bipolar disorder: a systematic review by the ISBD Targeting Cognition Task Force. Bipolar Disorders, 26*(3), 216–239. https://doi.org/10.1111/bdi.13414
36. Viktorin, A., Rydén, E., Thase, M. E., Chang, Z., Lundholm, C., D'Onofrio, B. M., Almqvist, C., Magnusson, P. K. E., Lichtenstein, P., Larsson, H., & Landén, M. (2017). The risk of treatment-emergent mania with methylphenidate in bipolar disorder. *American Journal of Psychiatry, 174*(4), 341–348.
37. Nazar, B. P., Bernardes, C., Peachey, G., Sergeant, J., Mattos, P. & Treasure, J. (2016). The risk of eating disorders comorbid with attention-deficit/hyperactivity disorder: a systematic review and meta-analysis. *International Journal of Eating Disorders*, 49, 1045–1057.
38. Fornaro, M., Solmi, M., Perna, G., De Berardis, D., Veronese, N., Orsolini, L., Ganança, L., & Stubbs, B. (2016). Lisdexamfetamine in the treatment of moderate-to-severe binge eating disorder in adults: systematic review and exploratory meta-analysis of publicly available placebo-controlled, randomized clinical trials. *Neuropsychiatric Disease and Treatment*, 2016 Jul 25;12:1827–1836. https://doi.org/10.2147/NDT.S109637. PMID: 27524900; PMCID: PMC4966690.
39. Curtin, C., Pagoto, S., & Mick, E. (2013). The association between ADHD and eating disorders/pathology in adolescents: a systematic review. *Open Journal of Epidemiology, 3*(04), 193–202. https://doi.org/10.4236/ojepi.2013.34028
40. Jerotic, S. (2026). Stress, eating, and the structure of time in ADHD: a phenomenological perspective on ecological momentary assessment. *Neuroscience Applied*, 2026 Feb 10;5:106987. https://doi.org/10.1016/j.nsa.2026.106987. PMID: 41717215; PMCID: PMC12914867.
41. Roncero, C.,, Remón-Gallo, D., García-Ullán, L., Vicente-Hernández, B., Buch-Vicente, B., Palma-Álvarez, R. F., Grau-López, L., González-Bolaños, K. R., Álvarez-Navares, A., Pérez, J., & Aguilar, L. (2025). Gender differences in ADHD and impulsivity among alcohol or alcohol- and cocaine-dependent patients. *Frontiers in Psychiatry*, 16:1446970. https://doi.org/10.3389/fpsyt.2025.1446970
42. Coetzee, D., Truter, I., & Meyer, A. (2022). Differences in alcohol and cannabis use amongst substance use disorder patients with and without comorbid attention-deficit/hyperactivity disorder. *South African Journal of Psychiatry*, 28: 1786. https://doi.org/10.4102/sajpsychiatry.v28i0.1786
43. Elkins, I. J., Saunders, G. R. B., Malone, S. M., Keyes, M. A., Samek, D. R., McGue, M., & Iacono, W. G. (2018). Increased risk of smoking in female adolescents who had childhood ADHD. *American Journal of Psychiatry, 175*(1), 63–70. https://doi.org/10.1176/appi.ajp.2017.17010009
44. Liebrenz, M., Fisher, C. E., Nellen, R., Frei, A., Biechl, A., Hiestand, N., Schneider, M., & Eich, D. (2016). Adult attention-deficit/hyperactivity disorder and nicotine withdrawal: a qualitative study of patient perceptions. *BMC Psychiatry, 16*(1), 1–9. https://doi.org/10.1186/s12888-016-0911-9
45. Basiri, N., & Hadianfard, H. (2022). Adult ADHD treatment based on combination of dialectical behavior therapy (DBT) and transcranial direct current stimulation (TDCS) as measured by subjective and objective scales. *Journal of Attention Disorders, 27*(1), 57–66. https://doi.org/10.1177/10870547221118527

46. Halmøy, A., Ring, A., Gjestad, R., Møller, M., Ubostad, B., Lien, T., Vaaler, A. E., Engen, K., Nordby, E. S., & Fredriksen, M. (2022). Dialectical behavioral therapy-based group treatment versus treatment as usual for adults with attention-deficit hyperactivity disorder: a multicenter randomized controlled trial. *BMC Psychiatry*, *22*(1), 1–12. https://doi.org/10.1186/s12888-022-04356-6
47. Tilley, J. L., Molina, L., Luo, X., Natarajan, A., Casolaro, L., Gonzalez, A., & Mahaffey, B. (2022). Dialectical behaviour therapy (DBT) for high-risk transgender and gender diverse (TGD) youth: a qualitative study of youth and mental health providers' perspectives on intervention relevance. *Psychology and Psychotherapy: Theory, Research and Practice*, *95*(4), 1056–1070. https://doi.org/10.1111/papt.12418
48. Faßbinder, E., Schweiger, U., Martius, D., Wilde, O., & Arntz, A. (2016). Emotion regulation in schema therapy and dialectical behavior therapy. *Frontiers in Psychology*, 7. https://doi.org/10.3389/fpsyg.2016.01373
49. Birt, J., Thacher, A., Steinberg, H., Weiler, R., Poplawski, R., Dobbs-Marsh, J., & Zack, S. (2023). Effectiveness of DBT skills training in outpatient men: a naturalistic study. *Psychological Services*, *20*(Suppl 2), 122–129. https://doi.org/10.1037/ser0000686
50. Nielsen, T. T., Bali, P., Grove, J., Jensen, C. M., Werge, T., Dalsgaard, S., & Polderman, T. J. C. (2025). Genetic architecture and risk of childhood maltreatment across 5 psychiatric diagnoses. *JAMA Psychiatry*. Advance online publication. https://doi.org/10.1001/jamapsychiatry.2025.0828
51. Murphy, D., Karatzias, T., Busuttil, W., Greenberg, N., & Shevlin, M. (2021). ICD-11 posttraumatic stress disorder (PTSD) and complex PTSD (CPTSD) in treatment-seeking veterans: risk factors and comorbidity. *Social Psychiatry and Psychiatric Epidemiology*, *56*(7), 1289–1298. https://doi.org/10.1007/s00127-021-02028-6
52. Brenner, L., Köllner, V., & Bachem, R. (2019). Symptom burden and work-related impairment among patients with PTSD and complex PTSD. *European Journal of Psychotraumatology*, *10*(1), 1694766. https://doi.org/10.1080/20008198.2019.1694766
53. Perkonigg, A., Höfler, M., Cloitre, M., Wittchen, H. U., Trautmann, S., & Maercker, A. (2016). Evidence for two different ICD-11 posttraumatic stress disorders in a community sample of adolescents and young adults. *European Archives of Psychiatry and Clinical Neuroscience*, *266*(4), 317–328. https://doi.org/10.1007/s00406-015-0639-4
54. Cloître, M., Garvert, D. W., Brewin, C. R., Bryant, R. A., & Maercker, A. (2013). Evidence for proposed ICD-11 PTSD and complex PTSD: a latent profile analysis. *European Journal of Psychotraumatology*, *4*(1). https://doi.org/10.3402/ejpt.v4i0.20706
55. Dorrepaal, E., Thomaes, K., Hoogendoorn, A. W., Veltman, D. J., Draijer, N., & van Balkom, A. J. (2014). Evidence-based treatment for adult women with child abuse-related complex PTSD: a quantitative review. *European Journal of Psychotraumatology*, *5*, 23613. https://doi.org/10.3402/ejpt.v5.23613

CHAPTER 11

Making external changes to build an ADHD-friendly life

INTRODUCTION

Everyone is affected by the environments in which they live and work, but this is even more true when the person in question is a woman with ADHD. That is why ADHD can emerge at times when a woman's environment changes, demanding more of her and offering fewer supports. Her relationship to that environment can also be influenced by internal processes such as hormonal shifts, when hormone levels suddenly plummet, and in perimenopause, when shifting, declining hormone levels magnify ADHD struggles. (See Chapter 8.)

A woman with ADHD may be more impacted by stressful life events than her more neurotypical peers—a marriage that becomes toxic; the birth of a child, especially when that child also has ADHD; the loss of supportive friends and family following a move; a new supervisor who makes unmeetable demands and only points out flaws, never achievements. For example, due to impulsivity and executive functioning challenges, a woman with ADHD may unrealistically take on tasks without taking account of her need for sleep and self-care—such as a decision to move to a house in need of significant renovations, without considering the constant work the project will involve, or a well-intentioned offer to support an older neighbor, leaving inadequate time for her own household management, rest, or revitalization. Difficult changes in life circumstances may be unavoidable, for example, in the case of a woman who is forced to take on a second job to support her children, or a woman who must take on additional caretaking responsibilities for an aging parent. The symptoms of untreated ADHD can add multiple layers of hardship to already demanding situations.

DOI: 10.4324/9781003542124-11

In the following clinical vignette, a young woman with ADHD found much-needed support and made decisions that allowed her to live in a new environment that led to even more positive life changes.

CASE ILLUSTRATION: SHANDA

Shanda, a young woman with undiagnosed ADHD, arrived at a disability support office at her local community college, referred by her college counselor for an ADHD assessment. She had taken basic entry exams in math and English to determine which classes to enroll in, and her low scores had led to this referral. Shanda described her academic struggles during high school, and testing confirmed an ADHD diagnosis. Shanda returned to the academic advisor, and began to explore classes she could take to work toward a certification.

To fully understand her circumstances, let's look at the previous several years of her young life. After graduating from high school, Shanda worked as a classroom aide in an elementary school aftercare program, earning a relatively low wage, but getting by. Shanda became pregnant and moved to live with her boyfriend. After several years, her boyfriend's heavy alcohol use and abusive behavior made her fear for both herself and her young daughter's safety.

One night, she and her daughter fled their home after a particularly violent episode. She called her mother and asked if she and her daughter could come to stay until she could figure out her next steps. Her mother was relieved that Shanda had finally had the courage to leave her boyfriend, telling Shanda that she could stay with her as long as she needed to. With the support of her mother, who provided childcare, housing, and emotional support, Shanda began to make other positive changes.

She had received an ADHD diagnosis, was taking ADHD medication, had left an abusive partner, was living in a more supportive environment, and was now considering a certificate course in early childhood development at the community college that could qualify her for a better-paying job at the school. One positive step led to another. Shanda was on the way to turning her life around.

In this chapter, we'll explore how changes in the environment in which a woman with ADHD lives can bring about significant improvements in her "internal environment," leading to lowered anxiety, a greater sense of calm, and a growing sense of self-efficacy—the ability to make desired changes happen. As a therapist treating women with ADHD, your role is to guide them to balance changes on the inside with changes on the outside to help them build a life that better suit their needs.

How do you achieve this as a psychotherapist? By helping your client not only build the confidence to make critical changes in her life but also, along the way, reject unreasonable societal expectations placed on women, find more emotionally supportive, affirming relationships, and to look for employment that is a good match for her strengths and interests. Your role is to support her in self care on many levels.[1,2,3]

TENDING HER "GARDEN," OR PLANTING HERSELF IN A "NEW GARDEN"

We like to use the metaphor of a woman with ADHD planting herself in the right "garden," an environment that provides the essential nourishment that she needs to thrive. A plant may blossom and grow in one place but shrivel or even die in a less suitable environment. With your help, she can make her current garden more nurturing and supportive, or she may decide to plant herself in a completely different environment.

First, help your patient to envision her ideal garden. While no woman can realistically expect a life that is perfectly suited to her needs, neither should she passively accept a bad situation and only focus on ways to accommodate to it and survive as best she can.

The next step is to think about ways to modify her current "garden" to more closely resemble her ideal. So many women grew up masking, apologizing, and usually feeling "wrong." Growing up this way doesn't often lead to a sense of self-efficacy or even a sense that finding a more supportive environment is possible, much less deserved.

Reduce external stress to improve her emotional regulation

The best way to improve emotional regulation for a woman with ADHD is to reduce the sources of stress that contribute to her reactivity. How do we do that? Identify and then problem-solve with her to reduce her stress level.

- Too many demands hitting her from all sides: help her to gradually take on less.
- Conflicts in relationships: identify conflict triggers, then problem-solve to eliminate or reduce them.
- Sleep deprivation: focus on strategies to improve and increase sleep.

- High stress levels due to forgetfulness and disorganization: sleep, self-care, and developing new, more supportive reminder systems can lower her stress.
- The list goes on …

Explore with your patient the multiple stressors that exacerbate her problematic ADHD tendencies. Ask her about particularly stressful days in the past week, looking for patterns, repeating factors that can be reduced or eliminated. Your role is to help her identify stressors and then to collaborate in problem-solving. Mindfulness, deep breathing, and checklists can only go so far when there are truly stressful chronic problems in her daily life.

Give her the confidence to take the reins in her hands

In many cases, you'll need to address a pattern of learned helplessness, a lack of sense of agency, and low self-esteem, all of which can contribute to a pattern of remaining stuck in a difficult, high-stress environments for years.

So many women with ADHD feel battered by life and defeated by circumstances.

Furthermore, a woman with ADHD is less likely to have adequate social and financial support than her more neurotypical counterpart. Studies demonstrate that women with ADHD have a higher rate of couple conflict and divorce compared to women without ADHD.[4]

Collaborative problem-solving to make changes in her environment

Women with ADHD, when they are lucky enough to find a psychotherapist who is experienced in treating ADHD as it affects women, often come to therapy with battered self-esteem and little sense that they can have a positive impact on the course of their life. As psychotherapists, we toss out a life preserver and assure them that we won't let them drown. Then the real work begins.

How do we do it? One tiny self-nurturing step at a time

Making small but meaningful changes in an evening routine can be a very healing place to begin. For example, helping a woman to carve out a sacred half-hour each evening to engage in self-care can lead to her gaining a new sense of possibility and hope. Self-care can come in many forms—a hot bath before bed, 15 minutes of mindfulness followed by slow stretching, or sinking into bed a half-hour earlier to dive into a diverting novel—anything that helps her feel more relaxed and cared for.

TEACH HER TO ASK FOR SUPPORT FROM OTHERS

Of course, life will get in her way. For example, some families may not be accustomed to a wife and mother taking time for herself and will interrupt her self-care time whenever they need something. By trying to mask her ADHD-related executive function challenges, she may have unintentionally trained her children or partner to always expect her availability and help. A shift toward self-care and sometimes prioritizing her own needs will take time. She will need your support to quietly persist until the new routines are established. For example, she could teach family members to remember the rule: "Mom is not available after 9:30 p.m. except for emergencies."

Societal pressures starting in childhood may have trained her to de-prioritize her own needs to accommodate others. This pattern of prioritizing the needs of others is especially intense when it comes to motherhood.[5] After a lifetime of these messages, your client may be very easily discouraged and ready to believe that creating time for herself is not possible. And that's where the power of talk and self-reflection can work its magic. You might suggest that she actively practice asking for support from the family members by making requests such as: "Would you mind turning on the oven for me so that I can lie down a few more minutes before cooking dinner?" "Those grapes look good. Could you bring me some?" "Would you help your brother find his sneakers so that I can finish getting dressed for work?" Or saying to her partner, "Could you be in charge of dinner tonight? I'm worn out."

START SMALL TO BUILD CONFIDENCE

When "gardening" with your patient, it may be better to help her "weed" her garden, rather than making radical changes in the landscape. This will allow her to experience success, increasing her self-confidence and sense of agency. One small step will lead to another.

You might ask her, "What small change could you make in your world this week that would bring a smile to your face?" It may be as simple as helping her to carve out "me time"—time for self-care—for 20–30 minutes each day.

CASE ILLUSTRATION: IRENE

Irene, a stay-at-home mom with five children, underwent treatment for ADHD at our clinic. We talked about her need to find some quiet time during her day. Initially, she rolled her eyes as if to suggest that this goal was impossible with five kids in the house. We spoke of different possibilities. She eventually decided to get up earlier than usual to allow her to start her day with a half-hour of healing, calming "me time." She described going to the kitchen, making herself a cup of tea, looking out the window at her bird feeder, and reveling in the moment of calm that she had found as an entry point to her very busy day.

Many other things needed to be changed in Irene's "garden," but that quiet morning cup of tea was a great start. Each day, she used that quiet time to think about other small changes that might have big results.

CULTIVATING A WOMAN'S HOUSEHOLD GARDEN

Although the false belief that all women have a "natural affinity" for household labor remains surprisingly durable, the work of managing a household is possibly the job for which many women with ADHD are least suited![6] Housework involves countless uninteresting, repetitive, and detailed tasks, and for most women undertaking it, all of this must be done in addition to full-time employment. Rising household costs have made single-income households unattainable for most, and study after study has shown that working women still end up responsible for the lion's share of the housework when they have a male partner.[7]

Household management requires attention to detail, not to mention organizational skills, most of which are more difficult and frustrating for a woman with ADHD. For many women, additional stress is added by their feelings of shame and inadequacy because they can't seem to keep up with all these responsibilities as well as their non-ADHD peers; these feelings of shame may also be mixed with resentment that other family members aren't doing their fair share.

How can you help to make the "household garden" less burdensome?

- **Give your client permission** to **reject the impossible expectations** placed on women, especially working women, and most especially working women with ADHD.
- **Help her to give equal priority to her own needs** if she tends to consistently neglect them in favor of the rest of the family.
- **Encourage her to** negotiate with her partner about roles and responsibilities.
- **Help her to set expectations with her children** that they will take on more responsibilities.
- **Encourage her to find "me time"** for friends and leisure activities, so that there is more balance in her life.

For a woman with ADHD, daily life can sometimes feel like an overwhelming struggle for survival. When she is managing countless daily tasks, maintaining her home environment may be the last thing on her list, something that can be ignored when everything else is pressing in. In fact, women with ADHD have created a humorous acronym for their struggles on the home front—the **CHAOS Syndrome**—or Can't Have Anyone Over Syndrome. Some women with ADHD will report that they haven't allowed a friend inside their home in months or even years. And if a certain family event must take place at your client's home, preparation for it becomes a **Garbage Bag Flash Clean Up**—which involves her rushing through the public rooms of the home frantically throwing items into a large trash bag, which is stashed in a bedroom where no one will see.

From chaos to comfort

Instead, you can guide your patient to begin to create safe and nurturing spaces within her home. Just as we teach parents that their daughter with ADHD needs a **calm-down space**—a corner of her bedroom or a walk-in closet that comforts her and cues her to relax and destress, furnished with soft pillows, favorite toys, cuddly blankets, etc.—a woman with ADHD also needs her home to provide safety and comfort as an antidote to the stresses in her life. Establishing daily calm-down rituals can help. This may be an early morning cup of tea or coffee before the responsibilities of the day begin, which she drinks in a special place that cues her to relax and focus on the positive. She may also need a calm-down ritual when she ends her busy, often overwhelming day. A calm-down ritual may involve a daily phone call to a friend or family member—a few minutes of "me time" before attending to the home maintenance tasks of meal preparation, tidying up, sorting mail, and attending to her children if she is a mother, etc. Guiding your patient to create a calm-down space and calm-down rituals is essential in helping her to build a nurturing "garden" at home. Women with ADHD can benefit from creating cues to calm down.

- A cup of tea.
- A special chair to sit in.
- A calming view (looking out the window).
- Calming music.
- A phone call with a friend or family member.
- A hot bath before bed.
- Putting on a cuddly robe that cues her to slow down and engage in self-care.

CASE ILLUSTRATION: GETTING HELP WITH THE CLUTTER

Dr. Nadeau conducted a lunchtime ADHD women's support group which became the highlight of the week for these busy working women. They shared, they laughed, they problem-solved together, and eventually they became each other's source of support outside of the therapy group. These women reported, with smiles and giggles, that they had been meeting outside of the group to help one another tackle long-overdue areas of clutter in the home. Because they all struggled with chaos and clutter, the fear and shame they had previously felt if a non-ADHD woman saw their home melted away. What is more, because it's always easier to organize someone else's chaos and clutter, the work went quickly. They engaged in mutual dig-outs and benefited not only from the organizing help, but also from the support and understanding they offered each other.

Most women don't have such a support group and may need to turn to others for help in clearing out. A close friend or family member might be able to help. Professional organizers can assist for a fee, although for the majority this is not affordable. Clutter often develops for the following reasons:

- **Addition without subtraction**. Many women with ADHD self-stimulate through acquiring more "stuff"—they may shop online late at night or entertain themselves by going "thrifting" or visiting yard sales on weekends. You can help your patient slow the onslaught by setting up a rule for her to follow—for every item you bring into the house, remove two by donating, giving away, or throwing away as appropriate.

- **No place to call home**. Many women report that they can't "put things away" because so many items don't have a "home" to put them in. Helping your patient acquire appropriate storage boxes, shelves, etc. can be a step toward resolving this.
- **Don't put it down, put it away**! Help your patient identify clutter patterns. Daily mail is often one of those patterns. Advise her to deal with clutter each day, throwing away junk mail, opening important mail, and creating two baskets—one for "action items" (bills, forms to complete and return) and the second for items to file. Then she needs to establish a regular time to do the paperwork.
- **You set the standards**! Some women struggle with impossible expectations of order set by their mother or by their imagined ideas about the standards of orderly women without ADHD. Encourage your patient to actively rebel against those real or imagined expectations. If she doesn't feel like folding her underwear, who cares? She just needs to be able to find clean underwear when she needs it.

Support her in setting her own standards in the home

Help your patient to set the standards within her home, giving herself permission to do things *her way*, instead of trying to meet real or imagined standards set by others. Self-doubt and anxiety often plague a woman with ADHD when it comes to her home environment. Critical comments from a neat and tidy mother may be buzzing in her ear.

You can help her bring some humor into the process. For example:

CASE ILLUSTRATION: BETTY

Betty had been under such stress at work that she had taken a medical leave of absence to recover from her interactions with her relentless, negative, nitpicking supervisor. Her mother, worried about her daughter, decided to come to visit. The only problem was that Mom was a "nitpicker" too. In fact, in her therapy, Betty came to realize that her intense reactions to her supervisor were related to having grown up with a very tidy, detail-oriented mother. (Betty's ADHD had clearly come from her father's side of the family.)

Betty understood that her mother was coming to offer support, but in fact the upcoming visit was causing Betty great stress. Instead of relaxing and recovering from work pressures, she was racing around her apartment trying to tidy up and put everything away. Her therapist suggested taking a humorous approach, telling Betty to imagine her mother as a tiny, annoying figure sitting on her left shoulder, whispering criticisms into her ear. She suggested that every time she began to "hear" her mother's critical comments she should say out loud to this tiny, critical "mother," "Shut up, Mother!" and then flick the tiny critical mother off her shoulder.

Betty tried this at home and found herself laughing each time she told her mother to shut up and flicked her away. Betty's attempts to straighten up in preparation for her mother's visit slowed down significantly. She put sheets and pillows on the convertible couch, tossed a couple of clean towels on the bed, and tidied up a bit. Betty was surprised at how much more relaxed she felt as she waited for her mother's arrival. She no longer felt ashamed that she couldn't match her mother's housekeeping standards. Her mother had been a full-time homemaker when she was growing up, while Betty worked full-time outside the home. "No wonder my home isn't picture-perfect," Betty thought to herself with a smile.

ADHD-FRIENDLY SOLUTIONS TO HOUSEHOLD MAINTENANCE

Here are some ideas that women with ADHD we have worked with have come up with in collaboration with their psychotherapist:

- Think like a restaurant server—don't make "cleaning up" an onerous job that is put off. Instead, grab a plate, cup, sweater, etc. that is in the wrong place each time you pass through a room and put it where it belongs.
- Create a launching pad by the door—this can be a chair, bench, or small table where you automatically put items that you'll need before going out—phone, keys, purse, Amazon return items, jacket, hat, etc.
- Purchase a different, non-breakable plate and glass for each family member and make an agreement that each person will only use their own designated plate or glass and wash it as needed. This avoids a mountain of dirty dishes, and easily identifies who the culprit is when plates or glasses are left around the house.

There are plenty more ideas for creating a more ADHD-friendly home environment in Kathleen Nadeau's book *ADD-Friendly Ways to Organize Your Life* (Routledge, 2016).

ADHD-friendly household management tips

1. **Simplify, simplify, simplify**: Find ways to simplify and streamline household routines to avoid the constant, repeated crises of running late and lost belongings that create a chaotic, stressful beginning to each day.
2. **Prioritize family time/fun time over chores**: When mothers operate in overdrive, radiating stress and snapping at their children, home can become a high-stress environment for everyone.
3. **To get it done, make it fun!** Create a family chore time when everyone pitches in and a fun activity follows the chores—playing a board game, eating ice cream and cookies, or taking the dog for a walk while talking about the "best thing that happened today."
4. **Make it easy**: Give each child two laundry baskets—one for "clean" and one for "dirty." No more folding and putting away. Of course, some clothing needs to be handled more carefully, but most children's clothing can be grab and go. Make your home a no-shoes-inside household. Everyone can find their shoes near the door and your floors will stay much cleaner! Always cook twice as much as you need for one meal, then freeze half. It's a huge time-saver on busy weeknights to have pre-cooked meals available.
5. **Get the kids in on the problem-solving!** Collaborative problem-solving can be fun, and can also involve other family members, including the kids. When we encourage women to think creatively and to avoid trying to solve problems the way "everyone else" does, some wonderful, offbeat solutions can be found to reduce daily hassles.

Cool, creative ideas from patients

- Showering at night: One mom avoided the daily morning hassle of getting her son up and dressed in the morning by having him take a shower at night and then go to bed wearing his school clothes.
- Creating musical cues: Another mom reminded her children that it was time to get dressed, eat breakfast, and leave for the school bus by

playing music as a cue for each activity. Instead of starting each day with yelling and tempers flaring, everyone enjoyed the musical cue.

- Simplifying the socks: One mom solved the sock problem by buying the same socks for all the kids—no need to "match" them and no more single socks without a partner!
- Making a game out of tidiness: Another fixed a basketball hoop above the laundry basket, making it more fun to put clothes in the basket that way than dropping them on the floor.
- Managing the mail: Always sort your mail next to the recycle bin—most of it's junk mail! Then set aside a few minutes each day to file important papers or pay bills. That way, the mail will never become a mountain of dreaded paperwork.
- Creating a "launching/landing pad" to facilitate leaving on time: Some families designate a surface (table or countertop) conveniently close to the main door where each family member leaves their pile of "must-haves" for the following day—shoes, jackets, backpacks, permission slips, lunch bags, sports equipment, etc. The children learn to drop these items on the "landing pad" as they return home each day; it then serves as the "launching pad" ready for departure the following morning.
- Rewarding kids for on-time departures: One mother tucked a treat into her child's lunch when they arrived at the breakfast table fully dressed and ready to leave for school.
- Reducing extracurricular activities: After a long period of unsuccessfully trying to keep up with all the other mothers on the block, one mom decided to reduce the number of after-school activities of each of her children. This meant that instead of spending time on the road picking everyone up and dropping them off, there was more time to relax and have a family dinner at the end of the day.
- Providing each child with their own color-coded plate or cup means there's no question about "whose it is," and the child only needs to wash one or two items at a time.

CULTIVATING HER FAMILY GARDEN

Raising children as a mother with ADHD can be a high-stress endeavor; when one or more children also have ADHD, that stress level rises exponentially. Your role as a psychotherapist is to help your client to problem-solve, develop more effective parenting techniques, and simplify and structure daily life in her household. Some common challenges in a woman's "family garden" include:

- The kids always resisting doing chores.
- Arguing with the kids over screen time.
- Rarely getting the kids to bed on time.
- Having to nag and remind the kids to be ready on time for school.
- Conflicts with her partner about rules and consequences for the kids' behaviors.

A helpful approach is to work with your client, their partner, and their kids to get everyone on the same team, pitching in to take care of things at home.

One technique that has worked well for many families is to have an official "chore time" when everyone does chores at the same time. That way there is no constant pleading with each child to get off their screen to do household tasks. Family chore time can make chores more fun.

ADHD is a family affair

ADHD rarely occurs just once in a family; there is strong genetic transmission. Each child born to a woman with ADHD has a 25–50% chance of having the condition as well.[8] It's well known that parenting a child with ADHD can be challenging, and studies indicate that the challenges are even greater when both mother and child have ADHD.[9] Especially when the mother's ADHD is not well managed, the interactions between mother and child can be volatile and inconsistent. Some studies show that the reactive and inconsistent parenting responses of a mother with ADHD play a crucial role in intensifying the expression of ADHD symptoms in her child, creating a volatile feedback loop. Other studies suggest that a mother with ADHD has a strong need for effective, consistent treatment of her own ADHD symptoms to help her be a more effective, supportive parent to her child.[10,11]

So many women who bring their children for ADHD assessment and treatment casually tell us: "I probably have it too." By not seeking treatment for themselves, these mothers are trying to put their child's needs first. It is the critical role of the clinician to help a mother in this situation realize that getting treatment for herself will help her to be more effective in helping her child, and that, without treatment, she is unlikely to be able to put new systems in place for them.

As a psychotherapist, we encourage you to use the apt metaphor that mothers "should put on their oxygen mask before assisting others" to encourage your client not to neglect her own needs. Even if her only priority is the well-being of her child, effective treatment of her own ADHD is essential.

Once the family environment has been positively impacted by ADHD treatment for mother and child, you can encourage them to start working as a team. A very positive, mutually supportive relationship can be developed between mother and child once they are on the same page, problem-solving to reduce conflict and find constructive solutions.

CASE ILLUSTRATION: CINDY AND SIMON

Cindy came to psychotherapy complaining of daily conflicts with her eight-year-old son, Simon. Both mother and son had been diagnosed with ADHD. They had arguments every morning, as she felt under pressure to get out the door, drop Simon off at school, and get to work on time. Morning after morning, while Cindy was in the kitchen making Simon's lunch and putting his breakfast on the table, Simon dawdled upstairs, getting distracted and losing track of time. The psychotherapist suggested that Cindy bring Simon with her to the next session. To Cindy's surprise, the therapist talked to both her and Simon, asking them to problem-solve together to come up with ways to change their morning routine—placing the focus on how to change their environment to function better, rather than on Mom's frustration and Simon's defensiveness.

Simon jumped into problem-solving with a very positive attitude, relieved that he wasn't "in trouble." He talked about how easily he became distracted upstairs in his bedroom, with all his favorite toys and books around. He wasn't dawdling on purpose. "It just happens," he said. The therapist asked him where he could get dressed that would be a less distracting environment, and Simon made a very constructive suggestion. "I can bring my clothes downstairs and get dressed in the powder room near the kitchen," he said. "That way there is nothing to distract me and Mom will be right there to keep me on track."

The next week, Cindy and Simon returned and announced with pleasure, "Problem solved!" The family environment had changed, and the atmosphere of frustration, shame, and defensiveness had evaporated. The therapist encouraged mother and son to take a similar problem-solving approach if they encountered another repetitive problem.

For more information on "collaborative problem-solving," consult Ross Green's book

Raising Human Beings: Creating a Collaborative Partnership with Your Child (Scribner, 2016).

Cultivating her relationship with her partner

Many women with ADHD choose partners who seem strong and protective, hoping to reduce their feelings of vulnerability and helplessness. Unfortunately, such partners may become controlling and critical, reducing that woman's already-low self-esteem. Other women are attracted to partners that also have ADHD, seeking an affinity and an acceptance of their ADHD traits by their partner. These relationships, however, can become mired in instability and conflict if neither partner has the executive functioning skills required for basic life management tasks.

If a woman with ADHD is partnered with a non-ADHD individual, one of your critical tasks as a therapist will be to educate her partner about the real challenges that accompany ADHD, helping them to gain a deep understanding that her ADHD foibles are not intentional, and that although they can be improved, they will never entirely disappear.

Interestingly, in Dr. Nadeau's research on older adults with ADHD, she noted a pattern of women with ADHD finding a happy marriage later in life. The critical element of the happy later marriage usually seemed to be a partner who was described as patient, easygoing, and nonjudgmental. Many of these women had sought a first spouse who was "organized and on top of things," only to have this relationship devolve into one of criticism and belittlement. Through this experience they learned an important lesson, and later found contentment with a partner who was more patient and supportive. (See Kathleen Nadeau's book *Still Distracted After All These Years: Help and Support for Older Adults with ADHD* [Balance, 2022]).

Your task as a therapist trying to improve a conflictual relationship is to help the couple get back in touch with the positive traits that attracted them to each other, nurture those positive connections, and to understand their ADHD challenges more fully, while constructively problem-solving to deal with them more effectively. Such challenges might take the form of emotional reactivity, mutual blaming, and expectations on the part of the non-ADHD partner that the partner with ADHD could become a tidy, organized, and punctual person, if only they tried harder. Yes, there are women with ADHD who have strong perfectionist tendencies and manage to pull off that magical trick of looking non-ADHD, but that comes at the significant cost of living with high stress levels and anxiety.

Common issues for women in marriages impacted by ADHD include:

- Feeling resentful toward a partner because it feels like she is the only one managing things at home—her partner doesn't do their fair share.
- Feeling constantly criticized by her partner.
- Feeling less respected by her partner due to her ADHD challenges.
- Low self-esteem resulting from comparisons to her partner, who "has it all together."
- Stress and chaos caused by the other partner's ADHD challenges where both partners have ADHD.
- Having explosive arguments with her partner because of her emotional dysregulation.
- Feelings of low self-esteem due to her rejection sensitivity.
- Feeling controlled by a non-ADHD partner who takes on a demeaning "parental" role.

Here are some resources to help couples reduce conflict and improve mutual support:

1. Melissa Orlov, *The ADHD Effect on Marriage* (*Specialty Press/ADD Warehouse*, 2010). Melissa also offers online classes for couples impacted by ADHD.
2. *Fair Play—A Couples Conversation Deck for Prioritizing What's Important* (Clarkson Potter/Ten Speed, 2010). This deck of cards lists family/parenting/household management responsibilities, which can help a couple to rebalance their to-do lists, allowing a woman, who typically is responsible for a larger share of household responsibilities, "to reclaim her time, and rediscover and nurture the skills and interests that make her uniquely herself"

CREATING AN ADHD-FRIENDLY "SOCIAL GARDEN"

One of the most long-standing, painful realities for women with ADHD is feeling like an outcast, an outsider, a woman who is "bad at being a woman" because she cannot live up to societal ideals around womanhood. So, what's a woman with ADHD to do when the world around her consistently reinforces her negative views of herself?

- **Group psychotherapy**. As a psychotherapist, you can offer your patients a powerful intervention—group psychotherapy for women with ADHD. This may be just the impetus she needs to start building a social network that consists of other women with ADHD. Group psychotherapy can be a highly effective treatment, helping a woman with ADHD to find acceptance and validation.
- **Join a local CHADD group**. CHADD (chadd.org) is an all-volunteer nonprofit group that was formed several decades ago and has become a nationally recognized organization. If your client is fortunate enough to have a local CHADD group nearby, attending monthly CHADD meetings in person is a great way to begin to meet and network with other women with ADHD. Some CHADD chapters have formed adult support groups. If not, encourage your client with ADHD to form one through her local CHADD chapter. If there are no groups for women, encourage your female clients to attend parent groups for children with ADHD, where they are bound to meet other women with ADHD.
- **Online ADHD support groups** can be a good, if second-best, option for meeting and interacting with other women who have had similar struggles and experiences. Many are sponsored by ADDA.org (the Attention Deficit Disorder Association), a national online support and advocacy group whose mission is to support adults with ADHD.

Help them to weed their social garden

Women with ADHD sometimes report that they have long-term "friends" or acquaintances who make snide or critical comments in response to lateness or forgetfulness. Help your patient with ADHD understand that it may be time to "weed" her garden, eliminating or reducing contact with people who often make her feel judged and criticized. Sometimes these people are the woman's relatives and are not so easy to "weed out."

It may be helpful to guide her in having meaningful conversations with relatives whom she doesn't want to become estranged from, so that she doesn't have to continue to receive passive-aggressive or overtly aggressive comments in response to her ADHD tendencies.

PLANTING HERSELF IN THE RIGHT WORKPLACE GARDEN

If you are like many psychotherapists, you may overlook job/career/workplace issues, believing that this is not your area of expertise. The problem is that qualified career counselors have no training in or knowledge of ADHD. Their standard techniques may be partially helpful, but will not look at a woman's workplace struggles through an ADHD lens. Kathleen Nadeau wrote one of the first books on the impact of ADHD in the workplace[12] and was a pioneer in developing career services for neurodiverse groups, including those with ADHD, autism spectrum disorder, learning disorders, and other conditions that require careful consideration when choosing a career path, or a particular job within that path.

If your patient has had a neuropsychological assessment, the summary and recommendations from the report of that assessment can be a very useful starting point for understanding what sorts of jobs and careers are going to be the "best fit."

Here are a few considerations for psychotherapists to assist them in exploring workplace issues with their patient with ADHD.

Is it a mismatch between your patient and her supervisor?

Here are some common workplace scenarios based on the kind of supervisor the client is working with.

- **The nitpicker**: A supervisor who is easily frustrated and highly detail-oriented and has little tolerance for errors. If your patient's supervisor is causing her to lose sleep at night and feel stressed all day, help your patient to problem-solve. Could she move to another department within her organization and be assigned to a different supervisor?
- **The ADHD supervisor**: Sometimes, the problem is a supervisor with undiagnosed, untreated ADHD—a supervisor who is overly

reliant upon their assistant to keep them on time and on track. When this is the case, there is little choice but to look for a different supervisor or different job.

- **The laissez-faire supervisor**: These supervisors aren't really doing their job. They offer no structure or support and expect everyone to stay on track independently. Some of our patients have found an easy solution to this by asking for a regular, weekly 15-minute meeting with their supervisor. When this occurs, we advise the client to tell her supervisor that this level of structure will help her to be more productive and stay on track. Each week, she reports to her supervisor what she has accomplished in the past week and lists what she intends to accomplish in the coming week. If she hasn't reached her weekly goal, the meeting provides an opportunity for her to engage in problem-solving with her supervisor.

Is there a mismatch between your patient and their job? What are the jobs that might be a good match for your patient with ADHD?

- **A job that interests them**. ADHD brains are interest driven. Consider having your patient take an online "interest test" to help clarify which broad categories might be a good match for them. People with ADHD can be among the top producers and creators when they have a strong interest in their job and feel mission driven. If they find their job boring, it's unlikely they will ever enjoy or be a top performer in their position.
- **A job that doesn't require them to organize others**. Those with ADHD are more likely to thrive in a well-managed, well-organized workplace that provides them with structure and support.
- **Management positions are often a poor fit for someone with ADHD**. Bright, competent individuals with ADHD may be promoted to a management position where they are expected to manage and supervise others and keep them on track. These skills are typically very difficult for someone with ADHD and may lead to failure for those who have performed well in nonmanagement positions.
- **A job that is a good match for their personality**. Some psychotherapists almost think of ADHD as a personality type. But, in fact, people with ADHD cover the full spectrum of personality types: introverts and extroverts, intellectuals and hands-on technical workers, mission-driven caretakers and financially driven businesswomen with ADHD. Each combination of personality traits suggests a different sort of job that will be the best match.

SUMMARY

In addition to helping your client to change internally (i.e., lowering anxiety, increasing self-confidence, raising self-esteem, and helping her to understand, accept, and celebrate herself), it's also critical to help her change or eliminate aspects of her external environment that cause undue stress. The ADHD brain is especially impacted by the external environment. Your role is to help her to consider and make changes to create a more ADHD-friendly life by identifying stressors and problem-solving in collaboration with your client. At times, you'll need to be directive as well as collaborative in helping her make changes in her environment that will significantly improve her quality of life.

REFERENCES

1. Morley, E., & Tyrrell, A. (2023). Exploring female students' experiences of ADHD and its impact on social, academic, and psychological functioning. *Journal of Attention Disorders*, *27*(9), 1129–1155. https://doi.org/10.1177/10870547231168432
2. Meinzer, M. C., LeMoine, K. A., Howard, A. L., Stehli, A., Arnold, L. E., Hechtman, L., Hinshaw, S. P., Molina, B. S. G., Murray, D. W., Sibley, M. H., Swanson, J. M., Tamm, L., & Chronis-Tuscano, A. (2020). Childhood ADHD and involvement in early pregnancy: mechanisms of risk. *Journal of Attention Disorders*, *24*(14), 1955–1965. https://doi.org/10.1177/1087054717730610
3. Holthe, M. E. G., & Langvik, E. (2017). The strives, struggles, and successes of women diagnosed with ADHD as adults. *Sage Open*, 7(1). https://doi.org/10.1177/2158244017701799
4. He, Y. (2024). The impact of adult attention-deficit hyperactivity disorder on couple and marriage relationships: a review of the literature. *Lecture Notes in Education Psychology and Public Media*, *46*, 238–246. https://doi.org/10.54254/2753-7048/46/20230845
5. Simpson, K. M., Semenchuk, B. N., & Strachan, S. M. (2022). Put MY mask on first: mothers' reactions to prioritizing health behaviours as a function of self-compassion and fear of self-compassion. *Journal of Health Psychology*, 2022 Apr;27(5),1259–1266. https://doi.org/10.1177/1359105321995979. Epub 2021 Feb 18. PMID: 33601968; PMCID: PMC8978476.
6. Solden, S. (2025). Overwhelmed mom syndrome – It's a real thing. *ADDitude Magazine*. https://www.additudemag.com/overwhelmed-mom-with-adhd/
7. Seedat, S., & Rondon, M. (2021). Women's wellbeing and the burden of unpaid work. *BMJ*, 374: n1972.
8. Uchida, M., Driscoll, H., DiSalvo, M., Rajalakshmim, A., Maiello, M., Spera, V., & Biederman, J. (2021). Assessing the magnitude of risk for ADHD in offspring of parents with ADHD: a systematic literature review and meta-analysis. *Journal of Attention Disorders*, 2021 Nov; 25(13), 1943–1948. https://doi.org/10.1177/1087054720950815. Epub 2020 Aug 24. PMID: 32830611; PMCID: PMC8051515.

9. Schoenfelder, E. N., Chronis-Tuscano, A., Strickland, J., Almirall, D., & Stein, M. A. (2019). Piloting a sequential, multiple assignment, randomized trial for mothers with attention-deficit/hyperactivity disorder and their at-risk young children. *Journal of Child and Adolescent Psychopharmacology*, *29*(4), 256–267. https://doi.org/10.1089/cap.2018.0136
10. Sellers, R., Harold, G. T., Smith, A., Neiderhiser, J. M., Reiss, D., Shaw, D. S., & Leve, L. D. (2019). Disentangling nature from nurture in examining the interplay between parent–child relationships, ADHD, and early academic attainment. *Psychological Medicine*, *51*(4), 645–652. https://doi.org/10.1017/S0033291719003593
11. Chronis-Tuscano, A., Wang, C. H., Woods, K. E., Strickland, J., & Stein, M. A. (2017). Parent ADHD and evidence-based treatment for their children: review and directions for future research. *Journal of Abnormal Child Psychology*, 45(3), 501–517. https://doi.org/10.1007/s10802-016-0238-5. PMID: 28025755; PMCID: PMC 5357146.
12. Nadeau, K. (2015). *The ADHD Guide to Career Success: Harness your Strengths, Manage your Challenges*. Routledge.

CHAPTER 12

Creating and maintaining a healthy lifestyle

INTRODUCTION

ADHD is killing women! We state this boldly to grab your attention. Recent research shows that women with ADHD lose nearly a decade of life on average when compared to their non-ADHD counterparts. That's a huge penalty to pay for living with ADHD.[1]

Their deaths are not directly caused by ADHD, but indirectly through poor diet, lack of exercise, inadequate sleep, weak social networks, and chronically high stress levels. Having ADHD increases the likelihood of cigarette smoking, substance abuse, anxiety, depression, psychiatric hospitalization, and suicide. Living with inadequately diagnosed and treated ADHD sometimes results in a life that is highly stressed and fraught with crises that, in turn, make it difficult to engage in the consistent maintenance of healthy daily habits.

While you can read about the importance of a healthy lifestyle in any women's magazine, our message for women with ADHD is far more urgent. As a clinician treating these women, it's critical that you understand and communicate to your patients the risks of engaging in behaviors that negatively impact their health. However, it's equally important not to demoralize your patients. Instead, encourage and support them as they make the necessary changes one tiny step at a time (more about this later).

Most likely, your professional education did not include any training in nutrition, exercise, or sleep. Even if you choose to refer your patient to a nutritionist or physical trainer to help her develop healthier habits, as a healthcare or mental health provider you need to prioritize a healthy lifestyle as one of the key elements of your treatment approach for women with ADHD.

DOI: 10.4324/9781003542124-12

In this chapter, we are going to introduce what we call the **Circle of Healthy Habits**. In this model, each healthy habit supports others, creating a positive feedback loop. Just as habits that tax the mind and body (overeating, lack of exercise, social isolation) can reinforce one another, the opposite is true as well: healthy habits support other healthy habits. And choosing to socialize with others who lead a healthy lifestyle will provide even greater support for a woman's efforts to lead a healthier lifestyle. The Circle of Healthy Habits consists of the following:

1. Social connections
2. Nutritious food
3. Reducing stress
4. Daily exercise
5. Restorative sleep
6. Spending time in nature
7. Learning new skills

All of this might sound overwhelming. Building—much less maintaining—these healthy habits may seem like an impossible goal. With that in mind, we'd like to share a story that makes a healthy lifestyle seem more attainable.

CASE ILLUSTRATION: MARIA

Maria was a middle-aged woman with two young adult sons who no longer consumed so much of her time. She works long hours as a certified nurse assistant, a physically demanding job that pays her just enough to get by. After losing her husband to a heart attack in his forties, Maria had raised Juan and Carlos alone, focusing all her time and energy on them—especially following their ADHD diagnoses, which had been prompted by a caring elementary school teacher. Now, Maria finally had time to focus on her own needs. After speaking to her primary healthcare provider about her suspicion that she also had ADHD, she received a diagnosis in her forties, during perimenopause, a time when declining estrogen levels often increase ADHD symptoms in women. Maria was overweight, always tired after work, and tended to collapse on the living-room couch in the evening.

The idea of self-care had never occurred to her until the physician who diagnosed her ADHD encouraged her to start taking better care of herself one small step at a time. The first step was to incorporate more nutritious foods into her work lunches. The physician helped Maria to make a list of easy, affordable healthy lunches—salads, unsweetened yogurt with fruit, almonds, and hard-boiled eggs.

Maria's next step, guided by her healthcare provider, was to take a 30-minute walk during her lunch break. Slowly, she began to lose weight and have more energy. A friend at work invited her to join an after-work dance exercise class, which she really enjoyed. One thing led to another: she and her friend started going out afterward with other women in the class. Maria was having fun for the first time in years, developing a new friend group, and sleeping better at night, which gave her more energy the following day.

In this scenario, Maria gradually built new habits to support her overall health: more nutritious lunches, a 30-minute daily walk at lunch, an after-work Zumba class, and regular socializing with friends, while sleeping better at night. Maria had checked off **four** healthy habits (healthier nutrition, exercise, social connections, and better sleep), by taking them one small step at a time.

In this chain reaction of healthy habits, exercise reduced stress and supported restorative sleep; restorative sleep resulted in more energy to exercise, and improved focus and follow-through; this, in turn, strengthened Maria's intentions to make better nutritional choices. The social connections she was building at work and after work improved her mood and motivated her to maintain positive changes.

STRESS AND UNHEALTHY LIFESTYLE

As multiple studies have shown, the desire to eat high-calorie foods with low nutritional value and lack of exercise are often the result of fatigue and high stress levels.[2] For example, a woman with ADHD in a low-paying job and fewer resources is likely to have particularly high stress levels, reducing her energy and weakening her intentions around eating better and exercising more. In addition, many low-income neighborhoods are food deserts with few healthy food choices on offer in the area. Meanwhile, unhealthy fast food and junk food is more affordable and available everywhere, making it less likely that a nutritious meal will be put on the table at night.

In many ways, a healthy lifestyle is a privilege that is more readily available to higher-income women. In advising your patients to improve their health habits, it's critical that you are aware of the constraints that some of them experience, and make recommendations that are feasible given their circumstances. For example, Maria was able to develop and sustain a healthier lifestyle without an expensive gym membership, a nutritionist, or a coach.

SOCIAL INFLUENCES ON LIFESTYLE

We humans are social creatures, and social networks play an especially strong role in influencing our behavior. We are all influenced by those around us when making choices about what to eat, when to go to bed, when to exercise, and other factors in a healthy lifestyle.[3]

Most studies of the influence of others on an individual's health habits have focused on children, adolescents, and young adults, but there is no reason to believe that the same social influence doesn't apply to women with ADHD.[4] The important underlying message is: if you want to develop a healthy lifestyle, be intentional about spending some of your time with people who engage in habits you are working to build! It's harder to quit smoking if you hang out with smokers, harder to lose weight if you are constantly exposed to unhealthy sweets and snacks, and harder to get yourself off the couch to go out for exercise if everyone nearby is watching TV or always on their screens.

As a clinician, you can have a powerful impact by presenting a realistic path to a healthier lifestyle.

HABIT STACKING

The seven healthy habits may seem daunting to your patients at first. To make following a healthy lifestyle feel more doable, introduce your patients to the concept of "habit stacking," i.e., building one healthy habit on top of another. For example: if your patient is working to develop a habit of daily walks, suggest that she walk with a friend in a natural setting. By "stacking" walking with a social connection and exposure to nature, in this single activity she has combined three healthy habits—exercise, social connections, and stress management through exposure to nature. Her long walk with a friend, in a natural setting, will in turn promote good sleep. When she wakes feeling more rested and focused, she'll find it easier to plan and prepare healthy meals and will have more energy to engage in brain-stimulating activities (learning a new skill or new information). In this way, she can develop her Circle of Healthy Habits, each one supporting the next.

From self-deprivation to self-care

Changing how a woman with ADHD thinks about healthy habits will change how she behaves (a basic tenet of CBT therapy). A key element of your work with your patient is to help her see that living a healthy lifestyle is the essence of self-care and self-compassion. But it's a long way from one mindset to another, with many intermediate steps along the way. ADHD brains tend to be impatient and want immediate results. If you can help your patient acknowledge and feel proud of each small step she makes, she can feel more immediately rewarded.

Make healthy habits more rewarding!

The recently available rapid weight-loss drugs may be an ADHD-friendly approach to a healthy lifestyle, as they offer your patient "rapid rewards" that encourage her and may make it easier for her to build other healthy habits. ADHD brains are particularly susceptible to the lure of immediate rewards rather than long-term benefits. As a result, an ADHD-friendly approach is to help her find ways to make her healthy habits more immediately rewarding. For example, as we have seen, she can make a walk more rewarding by making it social and walking with a friend; she could also make the destination of the walk rewarding—a stop at a local coffee shop with her friend. She can make going to bed on time more rewarding by looking forward to listening to a favorite podcast through her earbuds after she turns out the light.

Teach her how to follow through on her intentions

We're all familiar with the standard New Year's resolutions to exercise more and to lose weight. We also know what happens to these well-meant resolutions. Soon our expensive gym membership is going to waste while we sit on the couch streaming our favorite TV series and eating potato chips or dessert. Don't allow your patient to set herself up for failure.

Instead, use **Social Cognitive Theory (SCT)**,[5] which proposes that an individual needs three things to develop a healthy lifestyle:

- **Self-efficacy**: A belief in themselves and their ability to achieve their goal.
- **Social support**: Being surrounded with people who support their goals.
- **Self-regulation**: The ability to stop themselves from making undesirable choices.

Strengthening these three elements should become your focus in psychotherapy, to help your client make the positive changes needed for her to achieve a healthy lifestyle.

First help her to start to believe in herself (self-efficacy). One woman with ADHD summed up her lack of self-efficacy by saying, "If it weren't for bad habits, I wouldn't have any habits at all." Your job is to help your patient begin to believe in herself after years (or even decades) of failure. Set a small healthy goal to help her experience success, which will, in turn, build her confidence. And as we all know, success breeds success.

Introduce social support. A recent article, humorously titled, "You are what *they* eat!," focuses on how much we are influenced by the people we spend time with. Your patient will be much more likely to achieve success in developing healthier habits if she chooses to spend some of her time with those who share the same goals.

Increase self-control. Impulsivity is a central struggle for many women with ADHD. The best way to avoid giving in to unhealthy impulses is to remove the triggers that prompt them. In other words, don't go to Dunkin' Donuts for your morning coffee, which can make it hard to resist ordering a donut as well. Don't keep tempting snacks around the house.

ESCAPE THE ADHD–WESTERN DIET FOOD LOOP

It's been demonstrated that a poor diet can exacerbate ADHD symptoms, which, in turn, lead to worse dietary choices.[6] Those living in the West are caught in a negative nutritional loop, where poor nutrition (highly processed foods, high-sugar foods) leads to worse ADHD symptoms, which in turn lead to more unhealthy nutritional choices. The US food industry has invested a fortune in research on ways to make its highly processed foods addictive.[7] Given the well-known impulsivity associated with ADHD, and the pattern of women with ADHD "self-medicating" with food, they are particularly susceptible to the addictive qualities of high-fat, high-sugar foods.

The good news is that the reverse is also true. Eating more plant-based whole foods can lead to a reduction in ADHD symptoms.[8] And when ADHD symptoms are reduced, it's easier to make healthy choices.

Let's look at the ADHD factors that contribute to unhealthy eating:

- **Disorganization and overwhelm**. Meal planning is difficult for women with ADHD, leading them to resort to fast food, carry-out, and home delivery when meal planning fails, which happens frequently.
  Approach: Help her to identify options that are healthier and easy to prepare. Create a list of healthy lunch options to purchase regularly at the grocery.
- **Impulsivity**. "See it, grab it, eat it" is often the order of the day. Resisting junk food and desserts is difficult for many adults, and near-impossible for many women with ADHD if the food is available and tempting.
  Approach: Clear out her pantry and refrigerator of all tempting but unhealthy food items so that it's harder for her to give in to unhealthy eating impulses.
- **Stimulation seeking**. Many women report snacking their way through the evening because they feel "bored."
  Approach: Staying away from snacking as a form of entertainment is much easier if a woman is engaged in something stimulating, especially an activity that keeps her hands busy such as knitting, embroidery, or beading. Working on a puzzle can keep her hands busy. Making a phone call to a friend or relative can boost her mood and provide a nonfood reward.
- **Self-soothing with food in response to stress**. Many women report feeling calmer after eating a high-carb snack. It's a quick fix in response to stress.
  Approach: Create a list of healthy self-soothing activities—reading while leaning against a warm heating pad, taking a warm bath, drinking a cup of herbal tea, or developing a soothing, stretching routine.
- **Impatience**. Making a healthier choice often involves more planning and preparation than just grabbing a bag of chips or an ice-cream bar.
  Approach: Help her to fight back against the intentionally addictive junk food industry by making a list of healthier snacks and keeping them on hand.

- **Negative views of "healthy food."** Healthy food may be viewed in terms of self-deprivation and effort—"Healthy food doesn't taste as good, and it takes too long to prepare."
  Approach: Use a CBT technique to help her shift away from thinking of self-deprivation and toward an attitude of self-care.
- **Fatigue factor**. It can feel too hard to eat healthily after a long stressful day.
  Approach: Keep healthier frozen meals on hand for particularly hard days.

Help women stop "all-or-nothing" thinking about food

"I don't like to eat most vegetables!" "I don't have time to cook!" "I am not willing to give up [fill in the blank—fast food, door dash, pizza, etc]." Instead of drastic dietary changes, the way to build a healthier diet is one step at a time.

Help her identify one unhealthy habit that she would like to work on changing. It could be:

- Shifting from a sugary breakfast to a high-protein one.
- Keeping healthy convenient snacks at work for that mid-afternoon slump—portion-controlled packets of almonds or trail mix, or a banana.
- Getting rid of snack food/junk food in the house that she can't resist.
- Bringing her lunch to work—a salad and protein.

Gradual changes that become habitual can lead, over the course of a year, to a significantly healthier eating pattern.

Use Motivational Interviewing techniques[9] to help her to explore her level of motivation for change. Use your knowledge about shorter lifespan and reduced "healthspan" (years lived in good health) to influence her motivation.

- **Strengthen her motivation** by exploring her ambivalence—reasons to stay the same versus reasons to change. Then encourage her to talk about the reasons she wants to change, focusing on her strengths and building her sense of self-efficacy.
- **Strengthen her commitment** by making plans with her to create the change she is seeking, but also allow her ambivalence and never argue with her resistance to change—always explore her ambivalence in a neutral and curious way.

- **Plan for change** by eliciting her own solutions and offering support. It can also be helpful to offer examples of steps that other women with ADHD have taken to reach their goal of eating a healthier diet.

CBT-INFORMED CHANGES IN NUTRITIONAL HABITS

The essence of CBT-informed therapy involves changing your patient's thinking so that she can change her behavior.

Help her to THINK differently about healthy nutrition: not as deprivation but as self-care. Help her to understand that she may need the support of a group approach. For example, one of the most powerful effects of programs such as Weight Watchers is group support through weekly check-ins. Help her to understand that her reflex to grab something to eat may be triggered by stress or anxiety. Help her to identify this link and develop a new, healthier habit in response to stress—maybe making a cup of herbal tea and sitting in a calm-down spot to breathe deeply, sip her tea, and de-stress. In this way she'll build new connections between stress and ways to de-stress that don't involve food.

Build "tiny habits": There is a large body of research[10] that supports the concept of achieving significant life changes through a series of small incremental changes. This approach, called "tiny habits," was first introduced by B. J. Fogg, a researcher and director at the Behavior Design Lab at Stanford University. In his book *Tiny Habits*,[11] Fogg outlines a method for behavioral change by making a new behavior so small that it's easy to do, linking it to an existing routine (an "Anchor Moment"), and then celebrating immediately afterward to create positive emotions that reinforce the habit.

Here are the key principles of B. J. Fogg's tiny habits method:

- **Anchor Moment**: An existing, established routine that serves as a prompt to perform the new tiny behavior.
- **New Tiny Behavior**: The smallest possible version of the desired habit, taking less than 30 seconds to complete.
- **A Celebration of Success**: Fist-bumping others or saying "Yeah, I did it!"

This "tiny habit" concept can be applied to dietary change. If your patient has a habit of eating ice cream with chocolate or caramel sauce—or some other high-sugar, high-calorie treat—in the evening, ask her if there is a smaller, portion-controlled alternative ice cream she could substitute for this. She would still be having her evening treat, but in a way that moves her in a healthier direction. Later, you might encourage her to introduce a healthier sweet treat, for example a bowl of strawberries with a tiny bit of ice cream on top, or a few chocolate-covered almonds.

EXERCISE

There is a strong link between daily exercise and deep, restorative sleep.[12]

It's important to teach your patient about this connection, asking her to track the days she exercised and the length and quality of her sleep each night for a week. Once she's convinced of the influence of exercise on sleep, it will give her an even stronger motivation to get daily exercise.

Because women with ADHD have "interest-driven" brains, a key element in achieving healthy, regular exercise is to make it more interesting. For some women, that means engaging in exercise that is competitive and skills-based, for example tennis or training for a race; another woman might be more motivated by exercise that is social, for example a class or group activity. When exercise is done with others and has an element of accountability (your friends, your coach, or your classmates are expecting you), women with ADHD are more likely to keep it up. Whether it's competitive tennis or a walking group in the neighborhood, when elements that increase interest and accountability are present, exercise is more likely to take place regularly.

Physical activity plays an important positive role in reducing ADHD symptoms[13] and improves concentration, executive functions, and overall cognitive functioning. For these reasons, a focus on exercise should become an integral part of your overall treatment strategy for women with ADHD.

How does exercise improve cognitive functioning?

Exercise also increases the release of dopamine, a neurotransmitter that is associated with exercise. Physical activity plays an important positive role in reducing ADHD symptoms.[14,15] Exercise has been demonstrated to improve concentration and executive functions and enhance overall cognitive functioning, suggesting that it should become an integrated part of overall treatment strategies for ADHD.

A variety of factors may be involved in this improvement in mood and cognition, including increased blood flow during exercise and the production of BDNF (Brain-Derived Neurotrophic Factor), which enhances learning.[16] Exercise also increases the release of dopamine, a neurotransmitter associated with the reduction of hyperactivity and impulsivity.[17]

What's more, daily exercise enhances deep restorative sleep.[18] It's important to teach your patient about this connection, asking her to track the days she exercised and the length and quality of her sleep each night for a week. Once she's convinced of the influence of exercise on sleep, it will give her even stronger motivation to get daily exercise.

In addition to enhancing sleep, exercise has been demonstrated to have a positive effect upon mood.[19] These results indicate that exercise is especially important for women with ADHD who are prone to anxiety and depression.

Because women with ADHD have "interest-driven" brains, a key element in achieving healthy, regular exercise is to make it more interesting. Women with ADHD are not alike in terms of what motivates them. We recommend that you discuss the following factors with your female patients, helping them to better understand what will work best for them in supporting a regular exercise regimen:

- **Make it social**: a walking group or group exercise class may make engaging in regular exercise easier for many women because it's social and structured.
- **Make it competitive**: other women are motivated by competition, for example training with a group in preparation for a 10K race, or joining a competitive tennis team.
- **Make it fun**: Zumba or dancing can be highly motivating for many women because the music creates a positive mood, and the rhythm of the music promotes movement.
- **Make it structured**: women with ADHD usually benefit from a structured exercise routine that is organized by others—a class or a walking group that occurs at a specific time in a specific place.
- **Build it into her daily routine**: for example, your patient could intentionally park a certain distance from her workplace so that she automatically builds in a brisk walk as part of her commute.

SLEEP

As you will note throughout the sections on healthy lifestyle, each aspect of a healthy lifestyle supports the next. For example, individuals with sleep disorders display a higher rate of obesity than those without these conditions, supporting the connection between sleep and nutrition.[20] Other research has found that healthy diets such as the MIND or Mediterranean diets have a positive impact upon sleep.[21] The positive message to convey to your female patient with ADHD is that as she begins to change her lifestyle in one arena, making changes in other areas will become easier.

Those with ADHD often have difficulty getting adequate levels of restorative sleep from early childhood onward. Children often have great difficulty slowing down and calming down enough to allow sleep to overtake them. Sleep deprivation typically increases in adolescence because the well-known shift in circadian rhythms is intensified by ADHD.

Sleep difficulties continue in adulthood. Many adults with ADHD report that they get a "second wind" and feel more alert and awake just around the time that they should be winding down to fall asleep. This pattern is referred to as "delayed sleep-phase syndrome." Others intentionally avoid sleep, with women in particular engaging in what has been dubbed "revenge bedtime procrastination." In this pattern, they engage in favorite pastimes, often online, because they have had little or no time to themselves throughout a long and difficult day.

There are a variety of disordered sleep patterns associated with ADHD.

Delayed sleep-phase syndrome

Delayed sleep-phase syndrome is a term indicating that ADHD brains seem to be out of sync with natural sleep–wake cycles, and often only start to feel sleepy several hours after those of people without ADHD. It's a bit like having permanent jet lag: the body lives on the East Coast but the brain lives on the West Coast, which means the brain's bedtime is three hours later.

WHAT TO DO?

Your client can treat it as she would jet lag—taking 1.5 mg melatonin an hour before bedtime and setting an alarm to wake up eight hours later, perhaps using an artificial dawn alarm that gradually brings light into the room for a more natural wakening. The latter can be especially helpful in winter when it's still dark outside in northern areas. Then at breakfast, she can expose herself to 20 minutes of high-intensity full-spectrum light from a "light box" designed to treat seasonal affective disorder. She should place the light box on the kitchen table about 20 inches away and eat her breakfast, periodically looking directly into the light box. Light boxes are so effective at waking up the brain that they are found in nearly every coffee shop in Scandinavia, where people dose themselves with coffee and bright light simultaneously.[22,23]

"Busy Brain Syndrome"

"Busy Brain Syndrome" is a term we have coined to describe the naturally hyperactive brain activity experienced by many with ADHD. This is different from worry. It may be caused by the brain's Default Mode Network (DMN)—the brain network that activates when there is no specific task at hand—failing to switch off when other brain networks are activated. The DMN is typically active during rest and can interfere with sleep onset. Its sustained activity may prevent the brain's natural transition to sleep.[24,25]

Even during initial phases of light sleep, the DMN can remain active and interfere with the brain's natural tendency to fall into deeper, more restorative phases of sleep.[26]

COUNTERACTING "BUSY BRAIN SYNDROME"

It may seem counterintuitive, but when trying to fall asleep, it can help a "busy brain" caught up in active DMN mode to have something to do. But not just anything! It's a little bit like Goldilocks—something to focus on, but not something *too* interesting. The brain stuck in DMN activity needs something to focus on to get out of the active, random associations of the DMN, but if it is too stimulating, the brain will be activated and will be unable to slow down and approach sleep onset.

Cognitive shuffling

Cognitive shuffling is an example of a task with a level of engagement that is "just right." Developed by Professor Luc Beaudoin,[27] it works as follows: choose a random word—"park," for example. Then think of as many words as you can that start with the same first letter, "p," and then picture an image associated with the word. For example, you might think: pumpkin, plane, pistol, petrol, periwinkle, peach. Inhale as you think of the word, exhale as you imagine the associated image. Keep going until you run out of words. Then move to the next letter and follow the same procedure. If you go through all the letters and are still not dozing off, choose another, longer word and go through the same process. Some sleep scientists think that this cognitive shuffling imitates the brain's natural process of producing random unrelated thoughts and images as we fall asleep, and this simple, random task helps to quiet the DMN.

MUSIC SPECIFICALLY DESIGNED TO PROMOTE FALLING ASLEEP

There is increasing interest in studying the effects of "sleep ambient music" to promote falling asleep and improve sleep quality. Sleep ambient music is tranquil, with a slow and/or irregular beat. It may include natural sounds, such as rain or ocean waves, that lead listeners to imagine a natural setting or other environment. This helps them to relax and fall asleep.[28]

There is a great deal of music of this kind for sale online, which can be found through a simple search for "sleep ambient music." Research on this is recent, but there is evidence that the approach can be very effective.

RECORDINGS AND PODCASTS DEVOTED TO PROMOTING FALLING ASLEEP

Some adults with ADHD report that it helps them to listen to a podcast while trying to fall asleep, as the podcast takes their mind off any other issues that might be worrisome or take their attention. The problem, of course, is when the podcast is of such interest that it interferes with sleep onset.

One of the most popular sleep podcasts, *Sleep with Me* (launched in 2013), seeks to address this problem. Host Drew Ackerman uses deliberately meandering bedtime stories to bore people to sleep. Your patients can find *Sleep with Me* at: https://pod.link/sleep-with-me.

Revenge bedtime procrastination

Many women report experiencing revenge bedtime procrastination. The term describes the phenomenon of intentionally delaying sleep after a long, stressful day to feel some sense of control or freedom. Women with ADHD are particularly prone to this pattern due to their sense of never-ending chores and responsibilities. Late night offers the only time when no one is requesting anything of them and they can do as they please, so they make the choice to stay up, despite knowing that they will face fatigue the next day. Online escapes often occur at night. Women give themselves permission to avoid doing the dishes, folding the laundry, or tidying up the house because "it's late," so they go online instead. Unfortunately, this becomes a rabbit hole: they lose track of time, hooked on the "one more thing" compulsion that online platforms are so good at creating. The result: not only task avoidance, but also sleep deprivation, which makes the following day even more exhausting.

WHAT TO DO

There are several approaches depending upon a woman's particular situation.

- **When it's due to kids' delayed bedtimes**: If your patient has young children in the house, often a helpful approach is to help her get her kids to bed earlier so that she has time for herself. Many women with ADHD who are raising children report that they do not have established bedtime routines and often lose track of the time, and their children end up going to bed late. In turn, these mothers can only grab a few moments of peace and relaxation by staying up too late themselves. If this is your patient's pattern, focus on encouraging her to set reminders to establish an early bedtime routine for her children. This will allow her to enjoy some peace and quiet without needing to sacrifice sleep.
- **When it's due to lack of time awareness**: For other women, their own lack of time awareness is what stops them from going to bed. If this is the case, encourage your patient to set a regular bedtime reminder that allows for some relaxing "me time" before actually going to sleep. If she habitually stays up until 1 a.m. or later, bedtime should be gradually shifted to 10 p.m. in 15-minute increments. Once she is regularly getting to bed by 10, with lights out at 11, she will naturally find relaxation and "me time" and still be able to sleep for 7–8 hours. After getting into bed, encourage a half-hour of relaxing activity, but help her avoid highly stimulating content such as social media or doomscrolling, both designed to be addictive and endless. Instead, suggest calming alternatives like reading an enjoyable book or listening to a favorite podcast. Listening in the dark is ideal, as it helps prepare the body for sleep.

- **When it's due to lack of pleasurable, personal time**: There is no easy answer to finding more personal time. The demands upon all women who work full time while raising children leave little time for relaxation or personal pleasure. Your patient needs to take multiple approaches to creating more personal time, such as:
  - When possible, seek additional support from family, friends, or partners to help manage childcare and household responsibilities.
  - Streamlining household routines so that they are less time-consuming.
  - Eliminating some established activities to allow for more personal time.
  - Dual-tasking—i.e., listening to a pleasurable podcast or TV series while doing dishes, folding laundry, etc.
  - Consciously putting personal time as a "to-do" in her daily schedule and not leaving it to last.
  - Rising early before the family wakes up to have a peaceful, replenishing start to her day.

  Whatever approach(es) you take with your patient to help her get more and better sleep, it's important to repeatedly reinforce the importance of restorative sleep in supporting other aspects of a healthy lifestyle and reducing ADHD symptoms.

BUILDING SOCIAL CONNECTIONS

Women have long relied on each other for support. In fact, in 2000, UCLA psychologist Shelley Taylor and her colleagues coined the phrase "tend and befriend" (in contrast to "fight or flight") to describe the common female stress response of protecting oneself and one's offspring while also creating and maintaining social networks that can provide support during stressful times.[29] Tending and befriending is how the human race has survived through countless crises.

Now, let's consider this strong, instinctual need in the context of women with ADHD, who may never have been successful in building and maintaining social networks. Steven Hinshaw's research on girls with ADHD reported that even in elementary school, girls with ADHD are often socially "rejected" or "neglected" (ignored) by their non-ADHD peers. Given the likelihood of such a long and painful history, your patient with ADHD has a lot of healing to do in psychotherapy before she can gain the courage (and skills) to begin to weave a supportive social network for herself.

As psychotherapists, we need to help the women we treat to become more conscious of ways in which they can create and maintain those social networks. We find that such social networks develop more easily and spontaneously between women who have ADHD in common, as they can be authentic in each other's company and can expect understanding and encouragement from each other.

In the previous chapter we wrote about why group therapy can help women with ADHD find support and affirmation. Social connections are a crucial source of well-being, and yet we know that many women with ADHD have struggled throughout their lives to build a web of friendships that can comfort and support them. In addition to developing social anxiety, women with ADHD can become isolated due to their difficulties with initiating social contacts.

In this chapter, we outline ways of building and maintaining social connections outside of a therapeutic setting. Let's go back to the mantra of strategies, structure, and support. A woman with ADHD cannot rely long term on a therapy group as her primary social support network. In fact, she may not even have the opportunity to join a women's ADHD group. So what are her alternatives? Advise your client to try the following:

1. Join ADDA (the Attention Deficit Disorder Association adda.org)—a long-established source of information and support for adults with ADHD. ADDA frequently offers free online support groups for women. While no substitute for having friends in her community, this is a good place in which your client can start building her social skills, gaining self-confidence, and finding support.
2. Look for Meetup Groups in her community that focus on something of interest to her. Because Meetup Groups are organized around common interests, she will automatically have something in common with the other group members. When she becomes more confident, you might even encourage her to form a women's ADHD Meetup Group that gathers at a local coffee shop.
3. Look for organized activities in her neighborhood—like environmentally focused community cleanup groups, hiking groups, sports groups, or water aerobics at a neighborhood pool, for example. Generally, these groups are casual and accepting—not like women's social groups that may have a "cliquey" divide between insiders and outsiders. If a woman is reluctant, it may be helpful to do a search for such groups together during a therapy session (structure and support).
4. Look for a walking group in her neighborhood. These are usually casual, come-one, come-all groups that allow for friendly chat while

walking. This way of making conversation is often more comfortable for women with ADHD because there is movement, no constant need for eye contact, and no complex etiquette of return invitations or provision of beverages.

5. Look for a local community center that offers a variety of activities.
6. If your patient is retirement age, she could move to senior housing that offers a wide variety of activities. This may provide just the right amount of structure and support to allow her to comfortably make acquaintances, some of whom may become true friends.

Social networks require habits and routines that can be hard for women with ADHD to develop. These include keeping in touch between in-person encounters, remembering birthdays, sending thank-you messages after a social gathering, and remembering what a friend may have shared with them about difficulties that they are experiencing and inquiring about that later. Forgetfulness and distraction can be difficult to overcome for women with ADHD, causing hurt feelings and fraying of friendship ties. Along with encouraging your patient to adopt healthy habits such as exercise, good nutrition and sleep, etc. you should add a daily task of reaching out to someone. This can be a quick phone call, a text message, an email, or commenting on a friend's social media post. Help her to make it a habit to "reach out and touch someone" every day, and soon she will begin to weave that crucial network of support that most women need and crave.

STRESS REDUCTION

In the previous chapter, our focus was on eliminating stress factors in a woman's environment. But there is no perfect, stress-free life. So now, we turn our attention to teaching your patient ways to manage her responses to inevitable stressors.

Lidia Zylowska, MD, an ADHD specialist, has developed a structured eight-week mindfulness training approach specifically designed to reduce ADHD symptoms. This approach is supported by a significant body of research. While it is designed for group treatment, it can also be taught individually to your patient over an eight-week period.

Her method modifies mindfulness strategies to specifically address ADHD symptoms, helping individuals to focus better as well as to manage impulsivity and emotional dysregulation.[30]

To learn more about Zylowska's mindfulness approach to treating ADHD, read *The Mindfulness Prescription for Adult ADHD* by Lidia Zylowska (Shambhala Publications, 2012).

ADHD-friendly mindful moments to manage ADHD

Many adults with ADHD report that they don't have the time or the patience to engage in prolonged mindfulness meditation. The good news is that mindfulness can be integrated into actions that take place every day. In this way, developing a mindfulness practice doesn't require extra time, but can simply be engaged in while doing daily activities. You might want to consider teaching your patients to engage in these mindful moments.

MINDFULNESS AT THE TRAFFIC SIGNAL

Instead of feeling frustrated and impatient at red traffic signals, teach your patient to see these as moments to focus and de-stress. Teach her to lower her shoulders and engage in slow deep breathing, noticing how her stress level decreases with each exhale. She might even begin to look forward to these mindful moments.

BODY SCAN

Teach your patient to engage in the body scan technique when waiting for a meeting or at a doctor's office. Teach her, while sitting, to close her eyes, take deep breaths, and slowly move her attention from her toes upward, noticing sensations, without judgment, in each part of her body.

FIVE SENSES EXERCISE

A quick technique that can help to reduce boredom or impatience while waiting—teach her to focus on her surroundings using her five senses. She could identify five things she can see, four things she can feel, three she can hear, two she can smell, and one that she can taste.

MINDFUL WALKING

Mindful walking is especially appealing to women with more hyperactive symptoms of ADHD. Rather than sitting still with eyes closed, which can seem frustrating and unnatural to women who are more restless, teach her to connect with her body through walking. She can take a slow walk, paying close attention to the physical sensations of walking as well as to her environment. This can be done indoors in a quiet space. She can then gently redirect her focus back to walking if her mind drifts.

MINDFUL EATING

Your patient can focus on savoring your food by observing a small piece, and noting its characteristics, smell, and taste as she chews slowly and mindfully.

MINDFUL SHOWERING

It is also possible to focus on the sensory experience of showering, paying attention to the feeling of the water, the smell of soap, and the sensation of washing.

From chaos to comfort: Creating calm-down spaces and calm-down rituals

CALM-DOWN SPACES

As we saw in Chapter 11, a woman with ADHD needs some corner of the home environment that brings her a feeling of calm and safety. Guide her to begin to create a safe and nurturing space within her home. This could be a favorite chair, or a spot where she can look out the window at a bird feeder.

CALM-DOWN RITUALS

Guide your patient to create a calm-down space and calm-down rituals that can become an essential part of helping her to build a "garden" at home that nurtures her. See Chapter 11 for more details.

Exposure to nature

Spending time in the natural world should become an integral part of our "healthy lifestyle prescription." There is an interesting body of research that demonstrates a direct inverse relationship between ADHD symptoms and exposure to nature—the more time we spend in a natural setting, the less restless, distractible, and impulsive we become. Psychologists Steve and Rachel Kaplan developed their Attention Restoration Theory in the late 1980s. In their book, *The Experience of Nature: A Psychological Perspective,*[31] they proposed that prolonged directed attention, especially when combined with the necessity to ignore distractions, led to "directed attention fatigue" that could be effectively restored through exposure to the natural world, a setting in which attention is not directed, but drawn, sometimes referred to as "soft attention." The effects of nature are seemingly so powerful that they can be measured even when exposure to nature consists only of a view of green trees through a window. The similarities between attention fatigue and ADHD are so great that a standard ADHD measure has been used in research to measure directed attention fatigue.[32]

"Forest bathing," which is the practice of intentionally spending time outdoors in nature—strolling in a city park, finding a shady walking trail, or walking in the woods—is becoming a popular practice, with many organizations hosting meetups that are open to the public. Recent research has found that natural environments can also enhance attention through decreasing cognitive load. This is especially relevant in the context of the overstimulating screen-based lifestyles prevalent today. Furthermore, nature exposure enhances executive function, reducing inattention and impulsivity.[33]

Although the Kaplans' research has been around for a full generation, not nearly enough attention had been paid to it until the publication of their student Marc Berman's best-selling book, *Nature and the Mind.* Berman talks in the book about meeting the Kaplans as an undergraduate student at the University of Michigan. He is now one of the world's leading environmental neuroscientists, and is the director of the Environmental Neuroscience Lab at the University of Chicago.[34]

The prescription is simple. Look outside, get outside, with no smartphones or earbuds, and experience the natural world. We encourage you to actively spread the message of the power and importance of escaping from our constantly overstimulating digital world and bathing ourselves in the world of nature.

Before making recommendations, clinicians need to be mindful of income disparities. People with fewer financial resources often lack easy access to parks and walking trails. Collaborate with your client to get an understanding of what may be feasible for them.

HEALTHY LIFESTYLE SUMMARY

There is growing evidence that eating a Western diet, getting little exercise, having difficulty obtaining adequate, restorative sleep, experiencing chronically high stress levels, and feeling socially isolated contributes to a significantly higher risk of dementia. Furthermore, this kind of lifestyle can result in a lifespan shortened by nearly a decade for women with ADHD.

As a clinician treating women with ADHD, we urge you not to relegate such concerns to sleep specialists, personal trainers, and nutritionists, but to interweave support in building a healthy lifestyle into all your appointments with your patient.

Instead of asking, "How's your nutrition/weight/sleep/exercise routine?"—an approach that will likely only make your patient feel guilty, nagged, or apologetic—suggest that gradual, sustained healthy changes are easier than she might think, and that you can guide and support her in making them. It's important not to overwhelm your patient by suggesting changes in all areas at once. Just as you do in other areas of her life, prioritize which change to focus on first; then remember "strategies, structure, and support," and start with a "tiny habit." Emphasize that change is within her reach. For example, going for a daily walk with a friend or neighbor will "check" several boxes—exercise, exposure to nature, and social connection.

You can provide the support that shifts your patient toward a healthier lifestyle, extending her lifespan and reducing her chances of developing dementia.

REFERENCES

1. O'Nions, E., Baou, C., John, A., Lewer, D., Mandy, W., McKechnie, D. G. J., Petersen, I., & Stott, J. (2024). Life expectancy and years of life lost for adults with diagnosed ADHD in the UK: matched cohort study. *The British Journal of Psychiatry*, *226*(5), 261–268. https://doi.org/10.1192/bjp.2024.199
2. Hill, D., Conner, M., Bristow, M., & O'Connor, D. B. (2023). Daily stress and eating behaviors in adolescents and young adults: investigating the role of cortisol reactivity and eating styles. *Psychoneuroendocrinology*, *153*, 106105. https://doi.org/10.1016/j.psyneuen.2023.106105
3. Barnett, N., Ott, M., Rogers, M., Loxley, M., Linkletter, C., & Clark, M. (2014). Peer associations for substance use and exercise in a college student social network. *Health Psychology*, *33*(10), 1134–1142. https://doi.org/10.1037/a0034687
4. Zhang, Z., Abdullah, H., Ghazali, A., D'Silva, J., Ismail, I., & Huang, Z. (2024). The influence of health awareness on university students' healthy lifestyles: the chain mediating role of self-esteem and social support. *Plos One*, *19*(10), e0311886. https://doi.org/10.1371/journal.pone.0311886

5. Bandura, A. (1989). Human agency in social cognitive theory. *American Psychologist, 44*(9), 1175–1184. https://doi.org/10.1037/0003-066x.44.9.1175
6. Ryu, S. A., Choi, Y. J., An, H., Kwon, H. J., Ha, M., Hong, Y. C., Hong, S. J., & Hwang, H. J. (2022). Associations between dietary intake and attention deficit hyperactivity disorder (ADHD) scores by repeated measurements in school-age children. *Nutrients,14*(14), 2919. https://doi.org/10.3390/nu14142919
7. LaFata, E. M., Allison, K. C., Audrain-McGovern, J., Brown, A. J., Cao, Z., Cassiello-Robbins, C., Chen, E. Y., Coniglio, K. A., Cummings, J. R., Dagher, A., Dochat, C., Gearhardt, A. N., Mason, S. M., Mead, C., Merwin, R. M., Schiestl, E. T., Sidani, J. E., Sonneville, K. R., Stojek, M., Sun, C. ... Lowe, M. R. (2024). Ultra-processed food addiction: a research update. *Current Obesity Reports, 13*(2), 214–223. https://doi.org/10.1007/s13679-024-00569-w
8. Abd El Baaki, O. M., Abd El Hamid, E. R., Zaki, S. T., El Nashar, N. A., & El Masry, S. A. (2021). Diet modification impact on ADHD outcome. *Bulletin of the National Research Centre, 45*, 15. https://doi.org/10.1186/s42269-020-00466-x
9. Miller, W. R., & Rollnick, S. (2024). *Motivational interviewing: helping people change and grow* (4th ed.). Guilford Press.
10. Shadat, M. S. A., & Chowdhury, S. (2025). Small changes, big impact: a mini review of habit formation and behavioral change principles. *World Journal of Advanced Research and Reviews, 26*(1). https://doi.org/10.30574/wjarr.2025.26.1.1333
11. Fogg, B. J. (2021). *Tiny habits: the small changes that change everything*. Harvest Press.
12. Liu, D. C., Tian, Y., Liu, M., & Yang, S. (2025). The impact of physical exercise on sleep quality among college students: the chain mediating effects of perceived stress and ruminative thinking. *Psychology Research and Behavior Management, 18*, 361–373. https://doi.org/10.2147/prbm.s510207
13. Liang, X., Li, R., Wong, S., Sum, R., & Sit, C. (2021). The impact of exercise interventions concerning executive functions of children and adolescents with attention-deficit/hyperactive disorder: a systematic review and meta-analysis. *International Journal of Behavioral Nutrition and Physical Activity, 18*(1). https://doi.org/10.1186/s12966-021-01135-6
14. Ratey, J. J., with Hagerman, E. (2013). *Spark: the revolutionary new science of exercise and the brain*. Little, Brown.
15. Liang, X., Li, R., Wong, S., Sum, R., & Sit, C. (2021). The impact of exercise interventions concerning executive functions of children and adolescents with attention-deficit/hyperactive disorder: a systematic review and meta-analysis. *International Journal of Behavioral Nutrition and Physical Activity, 18*(1). https://doi.org/10.1186/s12966-021-01135-6
16. Ratey, J. J., with Hagerman, E. (2013). *Spark: the revolutionary new science of exercise and the brain*. Little, Brown.
17. Berger, N., Müller, A., Brähler, E., Philipsen, A., & Zwaan, M. (2014). Association of symptoms of attention-deficit/hyperactivity disorder with symptoms of excessive exercising in an adult general population sample. *BMC Psychiatry, 14*(1). https://doi.org/10.1186/s12888-014-0250-7
18. Liu, D. C., Tian, Y., Liu, M., & Yang, S. (2025). The impact of physical exercise on sleep quality among college students: the chain mediating effects of perceived stress and ruminative thinking. *Psychology Research and Behavior Management, 18*, 361–373. https://doi.org/10.2147/prbm.s510207
19. Blackman, J., Gabb, V., Carrigan, N., Wearn, A., Meky, S., Selwood, J., & Coulthard, E. (2024). Sleep quality during and after severe acute respiratory syndrome coronavirus 2 (COVID-19) lockdowns in the UK: results from the

SleepQuest study. *Journal of Sleep Research, 33*(6), e14205. https://doi.org/10.1111/jsr.14205

20. Du, Y., Wang, M., Wang, Y., He, Y., Guo, Y., Jia, X., Liu, Y., Zhang, J., & Li, M. (2024). The association between dietary quality, sleep duration, and depression symptoms in the general population: findings from cross-sectional NHANES study. *BMC Public Health, 24*, 2588. https://doi.org/10.1186/s12889-024-20093-9
21. Muscogiuri, G., Barrea, L., Aprano, S., Framondi, L., Di Matteo, R., Laudisio, D., Pugliese, G., Savastano, S., & Colao, A. (2020). Sleep quality in obesity: does adherence to the Mediterranean diet matter? *Nutrients, 12*(5), 1364. https://doi.org/10.3390/nu12051364
22. Fargason, R. E., Fobian, A. D., Hablitz, L. M., Paul, J. R., White, B. A., Cropsey, K. L., & Gamble, K. L. (2017). Correcting delayed circadian phase with bright light therapy predicts improvement in ADHD symptoms: a pilot study. *Journal of Psychiatric Research, 91*, 105–110. https://doi.org/10.1016/j.jpsychires.2017.03.004
23. Surman, C. B. H., & Walsh, D. M. (2021). Managing sleep in adults with ADHD: from science to pragmatic approaches. *Brain Sciences, 11*(10), 1361. https://doi.org/10.3390/brainsci11101361
24. Gujar, N., Yoo, S., Hu, P., & Walker, M. (2010). The unrested resting brain: sleep deprivation alters activity within the default-mode network. *Journal of Cognitive Neuroscience, 22*(8), 1637–1648. https://doi.org/10.1162/jocn.2009.21331
25. Høgestøl, E., Nygaard, G., Alnæs, D., Beyer, M., Westlye, L., & Harbo, H. (2018). Symptoms of fatigue and depression are reflected in altered default mode network connectivity in multiple sclerosis. *bioRxiv*. https://doi.org/10.1101/505974
26. Horovitz, S., Fukunaga, M., Zwart, J., van Gelderen, P., Fulton, S., Balkin, T., & Duyn, J. (2007). Low frequency BOLD fluctuations during resting wakefulness and light sleep: a simultaneous EEG-fMRI study. *Human Brain Mapping, 29*(6), 671–682. https://doi.org/10.1002/hbm.20428
27. Beaudoin, L. P. (2025). Towards a somnolent information-processing theory: understanding the human sleep-onset control system from an integrative design-oriented perspective. *PsyArXiv*. https://doi.org/10.31234/osf.io/8n6qc_v1
28. Shun-Ping, H., Ya-Meng, Y., Wen-Hao, C., & colleagues. (2023). Effect of sleep ambient music on sleep quality and mental health in college students: a self-controlled study. *Frontiers in Psychology, 14*, 2023. https://doi.org/10.3389/fpsyg.2023.1171939
29. Taylor, S. E., Klein, L. C., Lewis, B. P., Gruenewald, T. L., Gurung, R. A., & Updegraff, J. A. (2000). Biobehavioral responses to stress in females: tend-and-befriend, not fight-or-flight. *Psychological Review, 107*(3), 411–429. https://doi.org/10.1037/0033-295X.107.3.411
30. Zylowska, L. (2012). *The mindfulness prescription for adult ADHD*. Trumpeter/Penguin Random House.
31. Kaplan, R., & Kaplan, K. (1989). *The experience of nature: a psychological perspective*. Cambridge University Press.
32. Kuo, F. E., & Taylor, A. F. (2004). A potential natural treatment for attention-deficit/hyperactivity disorder: evidence from a national study. *American Journal of Public Health, 94*(9), 1580–1586. https://ajph.aphapublications.org/doi/full/10.2105/AJPH.94.9.1580
33. Wang, B., Wang, G., Wang, X., Cao, R., Xiang, J., Yan, T., & Zhao, S. (2019). Rich-club analysis in adults with ADHD connectomes reveals an abnormal structural core network. *Journal of Attention Disorders, 25*(8), 1068–1079. https://doi.org/10.1177/1087054719883031
34. Berman, M. (2025). *Nature and the mind*. Simon and Schuster.

CHAPTER 13

Looking at ADHD in a new light

It's not just for little boys anymore

INTRODUCTION

These are exciting times for women with ADHD, who have been overlooked or misdiagnosed for so long. Women with ADHD are becoming vocal self-advocates within the organizations where ADHD specialists gather. And within ADHD professional organizations, a small but growing number of specialists have turned their attention to the different symptom patterns and needs of women with ADHD.

But all too often, we continue to receive messages from women telling us that they have sought treatment from local practitioners, only to realize that they know more about ADHD in women than the professional whose help they are seeking. The fact that you have purchased and read this book sets you apart. You are among a small, but rapidly growing cohort of professionals who understand the different ways in which ADHD impacts women profoundly, and does so from an early age. We encourage you to make your awareness and interest known to your patients. You might adopt the practice of including a short screening questionnaire as part of your standard intake process, or placing a copy of this book in your waiting room to indicate your interest in women with ADHD.

Whether you are a physician or mental health practitioner, we hope you have found this book to be the informative, useful, and practical guide you've been looking for to provide better assessment and treatment for the women who come to you seeking your services. One of the challenges in providing the treatment that women need is that few

DOI: 10.4324/9781003542124-13

professionals are trained across specialties, which would help them to understand the psychiatric/mental health issues faced by women with ADHD as well as the intricate hormonal issues that play an integral role in optimal treatment for them. If you are a primary care physician, psychologist, psychotherapist, or psychiatrist, we urge you to form a collaborative partnership with a gynecologist in your area who can work with you to achieve optimal ADHD treatment for the women in your practice.

Remember, ADHD is accompanied by serious consequences for those women who live with it under the most challenging circumstances. These consequences can include chronic and intense anxiety, demoralization and full-blown depression, suicidal thinking, suicide, and psychiatric hospitalization. In many cases, women with ADHD are also raising children with ADHD. Given the at times overwhelming responsibilities of parenthood, women often ignore their own ADHD while trying to help their children, not realizing that the most impactful change would be having a mother who felt calmer and more focused, and who was well informed about how best to support her child at home and at school.

Living with ADHD is often very difficult and can have wide-ranging negative impacts on quality of life. In addition to everyday challenges stemming from symptoms like poor executive function and impulsivity, research reveals several correlations of note. Studies point to a potential link between ADHD in women and a shorter lifespan due to many factors, including suicide, fatal accidents, and chronic stress and overwhelm. Remember, your patient may not have come to you seeking an ADHD diagnosis; she might be seeking help for her depression, anxiety, obesity, cardiovascular disease, fibromyalgia, chronic pain, or diabetes. Your awareness of the patterns common among women with ADHD could lead her to a life-changing diagnosis.

We thank you and congratulate you for having read our guide to diagnosing and helping women with ADHD. You are part of a small but rapidly growing cohort of health and mental health practitioners who recognize that ADHD in women is a common, serious, and highly treatable disorder. Putting into practice the many tips and procedures outlined in this guide will allow you to help countless women in your care.

As a quick review, consider the possibility of ADHD if a woman in your care has the following symptoms or characteristics:

- Chronic feelings of stress and overwhelm.
- Explosive verbal (and sometimes physical) altercations at home in reaction to frustration.
- Chronic feelings of low self-esteem and failure.
- Frequent forgetfulness.
- Constantly misplacing personal items.
- Chronic lateness (look out for chronic lateness in her appointments with you).
- Difficulty with paperwork and bills.
- Social isolation, feelings of not fitting in with other women.
- Repeated conflicts or ruptured relationships with friends.
- Chronic marital conflict, often focused on poor household management and discipline of the children.
- Incomplete education despite obvious intellectual ability.
- Family members who have also been diagnosed with ADHD.
- Chronic difficulty falling asleep.
- Poor self-care (little exercise, does not make regular medical appointments to attend to health problems, not enough time to herself to de-stress and calm down.)
- Poor follow-through on recommendations that you make to her.
- Disordered eating patterns such as binge eating; eating from boredom/restlessness; stress eating; frequently eating junk food to self-soothe while watching TV or going on social media; relying on fast food, carry-out, and delivery food for herself and her family.
- Obesity related to overeating or binge eating.

Index

For Product Safety Concerns and Information please contact our EU representative GPSR@taylorandfrancis.com Taylor & Francis Verlag GmbH, Kaufingerstraße 24, 80331 München, Germany